Catbird seat: an advantageous situation or condition:
His appointment as acting dean put him in the catbird seat.

The Random House Dictionary of the
English Language (1967)

In the Catbird Seat

William L. Marbury

The Maryland Historical Society
Baltimore, Maryland

*To the Memory of
Robert Porter Patterson,
the Noblest Roman of them all.*

❧ Contents

❧ Foreword

This engaging memoir portrays the full and useful life and career of a distinguished Marylander. While I have known Bill Marbury over half a century, embracing most of his mature life, I am impressed anew by the breadth and variety of his activities and interests as they pass in review in these pages.

Marbury's lifetime spans the turbulent twentieth century which has radically changed our nation and its role in the world; those changes are mirrored in brief compass in this memoir. The lively depiction of his early years—family life on grandmother's farm, in Baltimore and at school—evokes a bygone era. In that period, his father was seeking to restrict black voting out of conviction that it was bound to corrupt the electoral process; fifty years later, Marbury, writing to a Southern friend, was defending the civil rights revolution. When he began to practice law, the largest firms had a handful of lawyers; during his lifetime, his firm grew to some 200 lawyers, with specialties unheard of even a few years earlier. Into the 1930s, the United States was largely isolated from world affairs and pre-occupied with domestic concerns. By mid-century, Marbury was on an extended tour to inspect far-flung U.S. installations in Europe, the Middle East, and Africa, and was wrestling with the implications of atomic fission.

Adapting our society and nation to these new conditions has been a demanding challenge. Bill Marbury had a significant role in this process by reason of his abilities and character. He began as a superb lawyer: a sagacious advisor and a persuasive advocate. The range of cases he discusses attests to that. Those abilities had already earned him high standing at the bar by the mid-1930s, when we first became acquainted as opposing counsel in several cases, working together on modernizing procedure in the courts, and arguing about the growing tensions in Europe.

Inevitably, Marbury's talents destined him to play important parts in the events of our times. During World War II, he was at the nerve-center of military procurement, as the right arm of Judge Robert Patterson, the Under Secretary of War, and General Lucius Clay, who served under him. As a member of Marbury's staff I saw how much they and others relied on him in coping with the novel problems posed by the struggle to mobilize our resources efficiently and speedily. After the war came his participation in the endeavor to develop a regime to manage the atom. When the Cold War and Korea dramatized the need for the United States to rearm, he joined in forming the Committee on the Present Danger to assist in mobilizing public support for that effort. In the McCarthy period, he was involved with the Hiss libel suit, and with the issues of faculty testimony and tenure at Harvard. His contacts with James Conant, president of Harvard, had prompted his being named as a member of the Harvard Corporation—the select board that, with the president, provides the direction for the university. As a faculty member, I was aware of how much he contributed to Harvard under both Conant and his successor, Nathan Pusey.

Besides these commitments, he devoted his energies after World War II largely to building up his law firm from modest size into the preeminent firm in Maryland. Yet he also took time for voluntary activities for nurturing the arts and music in Baltimore, for the economic progress of the city, for fostering racial justice, and for other civic purposes.

In telling of his experiences, Marbury writes in a clear and lively style and adds interest by sketching their context. And he has clearly striven for objectivity and candor.

Yet his reticence to discuss his guiding values leaves the reader with two questions. One relates to his personal traits and character. The reader must deduce an answer from the record of what Marbury did and how others called upon him for critical tasks. But reflection on that evidence is revealing. The outstanding men he worked with—Judge Patterson, General Clay, President Conant, and many others—were not only able and intelligent; more importantly, they were men of complete integrity with a profound dedication to the public weal. They valued his perceptive and balanced judgment and unusually lucid mind. He had the capacity to get at the heart of a problem, to analyze it objectively, and to develop practical ways to solve or cope with it. And his advice would not be warped by hidden motives or ambition. Those qualities underlie his standing in his profession and his service to the nation and the community.

These exemplary abilities were spiced by other very human qualities, especially during his strenuous wartime service. The Legal Division of the War Department, which he headed, was composed of a remarkable group of younger lawyers. His deputy was Colonel R. Ammi Cutter, a meticulous and able Boston lawyer and later a judge on the highest appellate court in Massachusetts. As Marbury says, the younger colleagues dubbed the two of them, "Arsenic and Old Lace." The fact was that, on occasion, Marbury, who suffered from an ulcer inflamed by the strain of long hours, would sometimes explode when not satisfied with a memo or draft. But his associates realized that the cause was not personal but insistence on high standards of performance. They described Marbury as having an "even disposition": he never raised his voice above a shout.

A second question is: what were the primary formative influences which shaped his character and values? Here any answer is bound to be speculative and selective. But the memoir indicates that family was especially important. His grandmother Slingluff and the family experience during the extended stays on her farm seem to have left a profound impression on Marbury. That shines through the vivid and charming description of those early years. His parents were also a major influence, and especially his father, who set an example and model for distinction in his profession and for concern with public affairs beyond personal ambition. Those values were surely nurtured as well by the manifest pride in the heritage of the forebears of both parents. And last, but not least, there was Natalie, his wife for over fifty years. Her strength, integrity, and quiet humor surely contributed not only to his happiness but also to his stability and balance.

This record of a life well lived in challenging times is rewarding both for what it tells us and for what it leads us to ponder on our own.

Robert R. Bowie

❧ Preface

This book was begun when I was a student at the University of Virginia. My roommate, Frederick S. Wight, was a poet of sorts who taught me the pleasure as well as something of the pain of authorship. Ever since then, I have tried to record in written form the principal ideas and experiences which have come my way, and many of the pages of this book have been adapted from, or in some cases lifted bodily from, letters, speeches, and narratives which I wrote many years ago.

While the book is in no sense intended to be a history of my family, it has borrowed freely from a privately printed booklet written by me about twenty years ago at the request of my children, entitled *The Story of a Maryland Family*. As the author of that booklet, I have felt free to take from it such pages as I think may be of interest to a wider readership. I must emphasize, however, that it has not been my purpose to bring up to date the history of my family, and there is no significance in my failure to describe the careers of my brothers and sisters or of my children and their descendants. My relationships with all of them has been affectionate and I am proud of my family and grateful to them for their encouragement and support over the years.

I wish also to stress my indebtedness to others who have been of special help to me in some of the activities which I have described in this book. To my law partners and associates, I owe deep gratitude for their tolerance and help. Any failure to mention one of them must be ascribed to the limitations of space and to editorial judgment as to which of my professional activities are most likely to be of interest to the reading public.

I am especially indebted to Bradford Jacobs, who has devoted many hours to reading drafts of this manuscript. To his thoughtful suggestions, I owe the elimination of many blemishes. However, if the reader should find any errors of fact or judgment in this book, or should come to the conclusion that there is too much tedious detail, the respondibility is mine and not his.

Finally, I wish to acknowledge my indebtedness to two other people who were of the greatest help in the preparation of this manuscript. During World War II, my secretary, Virginia Laird, was largely responsible for the fact that I appeared to know what I was doing most of the time. Everybody in the Legal Branch regarded her as a major contributor to what we were trying to do. Those portions of the book which deal with my career as a war department lawyer could never have been written without that contribution.

Similarly, Lourice Abdallah, my secretary for twenty-seven years until her untimely death in December 1986, brought me the comfort of an ideal secretarial performance.

William L. Marbury

I ❧ My Grandmother Slingluff

I was born on September 12, 1901, at my grandmother Slingluff's farm on Chestnut Ridge in Baltimore County. When sometime later I undertook to inquire into the circumstances attending that event, I was advised that my mother had gone out into the vegetable garden on that afternoon and had found me under a cabbage leaf. That explanation seems to have satisfied me until the birth of my youngest brother, by which time it had become clear to me that the cabbage leaf story would no longer wash.

In the meantime, I had come to understand that the date and place of my birth had a significance beyond that which would ordinarily attend so unremarkable an event. First as to the date: September 12 was not just my birthday, it was the date of the British attack on Baltimore during the War of 1812. My mother's great-grandfather Jesse Slingluff was one of the troops who, after an inauspicious initial contact with the British at North Point, withdrew to "prepared positions," where they held their ground until the enemy, demoralized by the death of their commanding general (who had been picked off by the marksmanship of two young Baltimoreans) and by the failure of the bombardment of Fort McHenry, abandoned the attack on the city. My grandfather Slingluff always maintained that his ancestor had been standing on a fence post near North Point when a stray cannonball from the British fleet knocked the post out from under him and pitched him headfirst into the posthole, where he remained until extricated by a passing farmer. In the meantime, the rest of his company had disappeared in the direction of the city, where he rejoined them in time to share in the glory which soon attached to those who had successfully defended the city.

The Slingluffs were not alone in remembering "Old Defenders Day" as a family event, for there was "Uncle Beanes," whose sister had married Luke Marbury. This was the Dr. William Beanes who, after the British burned the national capitol at Washington in the War of 1812, incautiously seized a straggler from the troops who were retiring to the Patuxent River to rejoin the British fleet and was himself arrested. This so shocked his friends and neighbors in Upper Marlboro that they employed Francis Scott Key to intervene on his behalf, with consequences every American must wrestle with when trying to sing our national anthem.

The special significance of the place of my birth lay in the fact that the farm belonged to my grandmother. Shortly before I was born, my maternal grandparents had left Towsontown (then and now the county seat of Baltimore County) and moved to Chestnut Ridge, where my grandmother had purchased 114 acres of land on a country ridge north of the Greenspring Valley. Here she ruled over a household such as might have been found in the rural areas of her native Austria.

My grandmother Slingluff was the daughter of Franz von Dorsner, a general in the Austrian army who had gained the gratitude of the emperor by virtue of his role in helping to suppress the Kossuth Rebellion. Franz von Dorsner had married a Baroness Marie Kotz von Dobrj, who came from a very old Bohemian family connected with the high nobility of Central Europe and who, until her marriage, was entitled to display as a crest a coronet with seven balls and thereafter was cut down to five, a demotion she never let her husband forget. One of my grandmother Slingluff's first cousins was a lady-in-waiting at the Court of the Empress Elizabeth; another was lady-in-waiting to the Archduchess Maria Annunciata, the mother of Franz Ferdinand, whose assassination at Sarajevo in the summer of 1914 precipitated World War I. My grandmother's nephew Oscar von Dorsner was an officer in the Imperial Guard at Schonbrunn Palace. Required to wear a brand-new pair of white kid gloves every day, he threw up the job and emigrated to the United States, where he ultimately became the mayor of Bismarck in North Dakota.

My grandmother had been educated to take her place in the most cultivated circles of a society which was then at the peak of European civilization. She was an accomplished linguist who was well grounded in French and English as well as in her native literature. She was trained in the arts, especially music, and was a gifted pianist who never traveled without a silent keyboard, on which she would practice exercises to keep her hands in condition. With all her aesthetic accomplishments, my grandmother was every inch the general's daughter, who could command without ever raising her voice. Without fear of contradiction, it could be said that she received respect from everyone with whom she came in contact, including a young newspaperman named Henry L. Mencken, whose column had begun to appear in the *Baltimore Sun*. My grandmother found his style amusing, was much entertained by his conversation, and pronounced that he was very good company, although somewhat lacking in sophistication.

As a result of all this, the Slingluff farm came to have a special ambience which European visitors immediately recognized, as did one of my brother Fendall's Princeton classmates, who always referred to my mother's sisters as "the Potsdam guards." Had she known it, my grandmother, who had no use for Prussians, would have been outraged.

Grandmother Slingluff regarded Baltimore social circles with an amused tolerance and, in a sense, the farm was for her a means of escape from the provincialism of Towsontown, where my grandfather had somewhat halfheartedly practiced law. True, there were some congenial families in that community, such as the Turnbulls, the Pleasants, the Ridgelys, the Poes, and the McIntoshes. But my grandmother really preferred the company of the ladies who had organized the Alliance Française and those who, like Mrs. Joseph Jenkins, would spend hours with her at the piano performing arrangements of the symphonies of Haydn, Mozart, Beethoven, and Schubert for four hands or for two pianos. The director and several members of the faculty of the newly organized Peabody Conservatory were frequent visitors, especially a voice teacher named Heimendahl who played the violin and used to bring his own compositions to my grandmother for her approval.

My grandfather Charles Bohn Slingluff added a rather Chekhovian touch to this household. He was essentially a scholar manqué, whose natural bent might well have led him to a university professorship. By the time he had graduated from Yale in 1859, he had already become an addicted bibliophile. At the same time, he had begun to show a streak of financial irresponsibility which his father found most alarming. Jesse Slingluff, a son of the veteran of the War of 1812, was a successful merchant and banker who had established a position for himself in Baltimore financial circles and who wished his son, Charles Bohn, to become a lawyer. To that end, he decided to send him to Germany to study the civil law at Heidelberg, with the idea that doing so would give Charles an entrée to the German mercantile families which had recently established themselves in Baltimore. What it actually did was to introduce my grandfather to the social life of Heidelberg and to German literature, in which he became quite learned.

Shortly after my grandfather returned from Heidelberg, the Civil War broke out and he embarrassed his family by undertaking to run medical supplies to the Confederate troops through Point of Rocks on the Potomac in Frederick County. As a result, he was threatened with arrest and had to leave the country. He returned to Heidelberg, where he took a degree in law in 1864. On this trip he brought back with him (in addition to a large library of German literature and the law books written in Latin from which he had studied the civil law) my grandmother, whom he had married in 1864. He had met her in Heidelberg, where she had gone to visit her married sister.

After his return to Baltimore, my grandfather nominally practiced law but in fact spent most of his time following rare book auctions and acquiring additions to his already extensive library. Finally it became clear that if he was ever to support his wife and growing family, a change would have to be made, and at his father's suggestion, he moved his residence to Towsontown, where the legal profession was less crowded. Here he became active in county politics and went to the state Senate.

But as the years went by, his family responsibilities grew heavier and his willingness to shoulder them grew less. While he occasionally lectured on German literature at the Peabody Institute and the newly organized Johns Hopkins University, his law practice did not prosper and he became increasingly dependent on the financial support of his father, until one day Jesse Slingluff decided to teach his son a lesson and refused to pay his bills, with the result that the family household goods were sold at public auction. Although Mrs. Jesse Slingluff bought everything in at the sale and gave it all back to my grandmother, the family felt disgraced and from that day forward, my grandfather was no longer regarded as the head of the house. Nevertheless, his scholarship was still respected by the entire family, who settled most arguments by "asking father," whose knowledge made the encyclopedia superfluous.

Soon after the move to Chestnut Ridge, my grandfather, who had become increasingly deaf, gave up all pretense of practicing law. Instead, he turned to botany and horticulture and became known throughout the county for his orchards, flower beds, and exotic shrubs. Year after year he exhibited at the County Fair at Timonium and year after year he won prizes for his dahlias, his strawberries, and the greatest variety of fruits.

Here, at last, he found a sort of happiness which he had never known before. True, he made no money, but he needed very little. He still had a little income from fees which were turned over to him by those who had succeeded to his law practice, and he occasionally sold some fruits, berries, and plants. He scarcely ever bought any new clothing, but when compelled to do so he always went to a cut-rate store on Gay Street where he could buy a straw hat for 25¢. Generally he took any hat that was lying around, and guests were warned not to leave theirs in the front hall. The responsibility of running the farm he left entirely to his son, Jesse, and to his wife and daughters.

As his grandchildren grew older, my grandfather regaled them with colorful tales of his college years at Yale and Heidelberg as well as with rather ribald accounts of his days at the legislature in Annapolis. He was full of stories about President Chester Arthur, who seems to have rivaled Jack Kennedy in his amatory exploits. Throughout his life his eyesight was superb, although in his seventies he would occasionally buy eyeglasses at the five-and-ten-cent store and use magnifying glasses to read fine print.

In 1895 Chestnut Ridge was completely rural and most of the land was covered with standing timber, although there were a number of small farms, owned mostly by families of Pennsylvania-Dutch extraction, such names as Wilhelm, Baublitz, Haar, Zink, Cronhardt, and Dearholt predominating. Some of these farms were improved by frame houses, but on many there was nothing but a primitive hut made of rough-hewn logs and plaster. On such a farm, known as the Old Friendship Tract, which bordered on Ellengowan Lane (now called Broadway) near its intersection with the Dover Road (now called Green Spring Avenue), stood the home which a local carpenter had built for the Charles Bohn Slingluffs.

The house itself was of no great architectural merit, but it was large and comfortable. The first floor was high above the ground, and across the front and right side of the house as you faced it ran a porch which must have been 15 feet deep. On the left as you faced the house was a porte-cochere where the carriages and later the automobiles could stand under cover. Inside the house, on the first floor, was a large living room with a very large fireplace. In the corner stood a Knabe grand piano. To the left as you entered the front door was a small study and behind this a dining room large enough to seat 24 people. In the hall which ran down the center of the house were two stands, each of which supported an enormous plaster bust, one of Beethoven and the other of Mozart. On one occasion the director of the Peabody Conservatory wished to borrow the bust of Beethoven for an exhibition, but the weather turned bad and it was impossible to get the bust down to the railroad station. My grandmother called the director to explain the situation and in his absence talked to his maid, who reported to him, "Mrs. Slingluff says that Beethoven is on a bust in the country and can't get here."

Behind the dining room was a very large pantry which served also as a dining room for the small children of the family, and still farther on was an enormous kitchen where the servants, usually six or seven in number, ate their meals. Even farther back was a laundry with six zinc tubs and ample room for ironing boards. There was a small back porch near which were smokehouses, a large combined tool shed and storeroom which had at one time housed incubators, and, about a hundred yards away, a stable large enough to hold six carriages and six horse stalls. Above the carriage room were two bedrooms for the coachman and stable boy, a loft for hay, and a tack room for the harness. Behind the stables was a small two-room cottage in which the butler and gardener lived.

Down over the hill about a quarter of a mile away was the barn. Here the farm machinery was kept and here was a corn crib, a large hay loft, and a cow stable. Nearby was a small frame house where Mr. and Mrs. Herbert Thomas lived with their three children. Mr. Thomas attended to the milking of the cows and took care of the vegetable garden.

The main residence stood on the edge of a grove of fine trees, mostly chestnut, which completely screened it from the public road. From the front porch there was a very pleasant view looking down over rolling ground to a little valley and then up to the ridge along which ran the

Dover Road. Around the house was a fairly extensive lawn on which stood some fine trees and shrubs and an occasional flower bed. On the other side of the driveway there was an icehouse and to the left of that a clay tennis court which had been laid out by Cousin Ben Fendall (then chief engineer for the city of Baltimore) and which Uncle Jesse and some of his friends had built with their own hands. As the number of children in the family increased, a cottage was built next to the tennis court with two rooms, a bath, and a porch large enough to hold eight cots. This was called "the playhouse," and here the young males of the family lived in bachelor quarters.

In the center of the farm, down in the valley, stood a log cabin which had been the old homestead on the property. This primitive four-room house was used to store apples and was always known as "the cider house." Here several barrels of cider were made every fall.

My grandmother was a superb and learned cook whose collection of recipes was renowned. In all of this she was a perfectionist of the first water. A family connection, Rosemary Kernan, recalled an incident when she was in the kitchen with Mrs. Slingluff and Aunt Valerie, helping to prepare a strudel. Mrs. Slingluff sat on a stool and supervised the girls as they rolled the dough and under her detailed directions spiced it with raisins, nuts, and cinnamon. Just as the oven door was being opened Mrs. Slingluff said, "Wait a minute, Valerie, I do not think that we have put in enough raisins," whereupon the pan was brought back to the table, the strudel was opened, and three raisins were added. Mrs. Slingluff was then satisfied and permitted the pan to go into the oven.

Aside from the preparation of food for the table, the kitchen was the scene of a series of canning and preserving activities. Vegetables and fruits in season were prepared for winter consumption, and all sorts of jellies, pickles, and other condiments were produced. This activity lasted all summer long, so that the kitchen was the busiest place in the household. Nearly all of the food consumed on the farm was grown and prepared right on the premises.

Charles Bohn Slingluff had planted a half-acre in wine grapes, and every September these were harvested and brought into the old incubator house. There the grapes were stripped and thrown into wooden tubs, where they were gently pounded with a fat round pole until the skins (but not the seeds) were broken. This mash was then poured into a wine press, producing juice which flowed into containers, where it was sweetened according to a formula which Mrs. Slingluff had brought from Austria. The juice was then poured into fermenting barrels, where it remained until immediately after the following spring solstice. When the wine was racked off (always on a day after the moon had appeared in a clear sky, otherwise it was sure to run cloudy), it was then sweetened once more and put into other barrels, where it remained for at least two years before being consumed.

The quality of this wine varied from year to year. Sometimes it turned out to be a rather heavy port and at other times a lighter claret, but I strongly suspect that it was always sweeter than a sophisticated taste would approve. Nevertheless, it was potable and some of the vintages were of a quality similar to the Austrian Voslauer. The preparation of the wine was a wonderful ritual and fascinating to the children, although the hundreds of bees that managed to find their way into the wine room during the process were apt to frighten all but the boldest. Actually the bees were far too sodden with drink to sting unless one trod on them with bare feet, as a child would occasionally do, with painful and resounding results.

When the weather got really cold, hog-killing time arrived. This was another ritual process. First came the bloody pig sticking (really a throat slitting) which we children watched with fascinated horror. Then the carcasses were loaded in carts and brought up to the backyard, where barrels of boiling water awaited them. The water in these barrels was always warmed with stones which had been heated red-hot in brush fires. The carcasses of the dead hogs were rubbed up and down in the steaming water against the rim of the barrel until all of the bristles had been removed and the skin glowed pink as a baby's. The entrails were then removed with a knife and placed in big vats, after which the abdominal cavity was propped open with slats. The gutted carcasses were then hung by the heels on a stout stick for several days, after which they were taken into the laundry and cut into hams, shoulders, spareribs, jowls, chine, and so on. The feet, ears, tails, and brains were carefully removed, as all of these were considered to be delectable by true pork lovers. Other parts were ground up into sausage meat or panhaus (which Philadelphians call scrapple), and even the entrails produced tripe and chitterlings, which were especially savored by the black help.

Milk products were the result of another important activity. Every day Mr. Thomas came to the house late in the afternoon with a wooden yoke on his shoulders, from which hung pails of milk freshly taken from the cows' udders. These were removed to the pantry, where the milk was put in big stone crocks and placed in a huge refrigerator which was kept supplied with ice from the icehouse. This milk produced cream so rich that it had to be spooned out of the pitcher, clabber, cottage cheese, butter, and buttermilk. It was, of course, unpasteurized, and the way it had been handled would, I am sure, give the modern-day health officer a heart attack. Yet the entire family drank vast quantities of it and no one was ever the worse for doing so—except for the excessive pounds of flesh, of which not a few were added.

Thus the farm life was genuine enough and went through the entire cycle from spring planting to hog killing. Nevertheless, its orientation was quite different from that of the normal working farm, since the farm was not designed to produce a livelihood but simply to make the family and their guests as comfortable as possible. The produce of the fields was used almost entirely to supply the livestock with food and bedding. The livestock itself was not such as would have been selected by an ordinary working farmer, since the cows were chosen primarily for the richness of their milk, and the horses were expected to serve as mounts as well as to pull carriages. The only real farmhorse on the place was used to draw Mr. Thomas' cart.

On the other hand, life on the Slingluff farm was quite unlike that on the well-groomed country estates of the wealthy which surrounded Baltimore at that time. True, there was a constant flow of weekend guests, the tennis court was in use every day, and there were horses to be ridden. My father and my brother Fendall frequently hunted with the Green Spring hounds, and my mother regularly entertained her friends at bridge and at times drove down into the Green Spring Valley for horse shows, Hunt Cup races, receptions, and other social functions.

But the whole atmosphere of the farm was unsuited to the pattern of formal social life which was followed at the other country estates. At first my mother attempted to institute afternoon tea as a regular feature, but the attempt failed miserably. To begin with, there was always a group of barefoot, scantily clad, dirty-faced children who were accustomed to having the run of the place and could be counted on to disrupt any effort at decorum. Then the chickens were ubiquitous. "Dominickers," Leghorns, and Rhode Island Reds popped up all over the premises, and at any moment an old rooster might attack a young pullet in full view of the guests. Or one of the house dogs would be found curled up in the chair intended for the visitor. And if by some miracle none of these things happened, then Charles Bohn Slingluff would appear in somebody's old hat, dressed like a country farmer, and impart in stentorian tones some information about a rare plant or mushroom he had just discovered. As he became increasingly deaf, conversation with him had to be conducted in a loud bellow, with the result that all other conversation was silenced for the time being.

Thus, the only thing for the family to do was to relax and enjoy life, and that is precisely what everybody did. From late spring to late fall the Slingluff family and their in-laws gathered together at this place and lived very much as the Russian upper classes seem to have lived in their country villas in the nineteenth century, if one may judge by the descriptions of that life in the novels of Turgenev and Tolstoy. Everyone pitched in and made a contribution to the activities, yet everyone managed to do what he liked a good part of the time. Books were read, games were played, music was made on the piano and on the violin, horses were ridden, and conversation was lively, with frequent arguments, mostly good-humored.

Visitors came in a steady stream, some for Sunday dinner or to play a game of tennis, some to spend a week, some to stay all summer. A business friend of my father's who had been invited to dinner became so enthralled that he stayed nearly all summer and was finally gotten rid of by an entirely unprecedented hint that he had worn out his welcome. The Marbury children were allowed to invite their friends to stay with them, and there were some who came very frequently.

Many of the visitors to the farm were colorful characters, but none could hold a candle to "Aunt" Isabel Sypher. Aunt Isabel had been my mother's maid of honor. She had married a man from Philadelphia who, while very handsome and of good family connections, was a complete deadbeat. He had paid for his wedding by passing off a bad check on Uncle Jesse, and there was not a doubt in anybody's mind that he had married Aunt Isabel for her money.

Aunt Isabel was certainly an extraordinary character. She was as round as a butterball but laced herself as tightly as possible and was inordinately proud of her babylike skin, which she treated with watermelon rind and buttermilk. Her emotions were more easily stirred than those of anyone I have ever seen. One moment she would be literally screaming with laughter, with the tears flowing down her cheeks, the next moment she would be sobbing. Storms of emotion of one sort or another were always sweeping around her, and life was never calm in her presence. A more absurd person or an easier butt for ridicule would be hard to imagine, and yet when she left after a visit, everyone, while sighing with relief, would feel that the chief source of entertainment and amusement had disappeared.

Aunt Isabel could make fun of herself, and I remember one occasion when she was describing how on a very hot day in Philadelphia she had stuffed her bosom with some paper. As it turned out, she had inadvertently picked up along with the paper her last ten dollar bill, all that stood between her and starvation. When a little later in the afternoon she started out to buy food, the money was lost. In despair she searched her little room on hands and knees, pulling all the bedclothes off the mattress, weeping wildly—at this point in the story tears spurted from her eyes and rolled down her cheeks—until in utter exhaustion she threw herself on the bed and loosened her stays, whereupon the bill fell out on the floor. Here she described her exultation and relief with shrieks of laughter while the tears were still wet on her cheeks. We all sat entranced while this drama unfolded before us and marveled how anyone could laugh and cry at the same time.

When the Marbury children were small they were in the charge of nursemaids, but as we got older a German tutor arrived, fresh from the

Rhineland. He had no sense of humor, was convinced that everything was done better in Germany than anywhere else, and was completely dogmatic. He did not have the slightest idea how to handle American children, and we made his life miserable. In fact, on one occasion my brother Taylor and I lured him into the chickenhouse and locked him in, and he had to escape through a window. For that we got a spanking from Aunt Val, but I am afraid that it did not make us behave much better. "The Herr," as he was called, was constantly appealing to my grandmother for help. She would try to back him up and then would take him aside privately and try to beat some sense into his head, and in the end he did improve considerably. His clinching argument always was "ich hab es gelesen!" This was intended to be a silencer and was usually advanced in support of some perfectly absurd proposition. One thing we learned from Herr Joestlein was a native German accent.

Everyone who stayed on the farm had to perform chores, including the children. In performing these duties, we looked to Miss Almeda Bailey for guidance. Miss Almeda had come to Baltimore from her native Sharptown on the Eastern Shore, where her family was well known. Instead of staying down on the farm, she had decided to look for work in Baltimore as a seamstress, and my grandmother had taken her in for the summer. She remained as a part of the household for nearly fifty years and by the time of her death had come to be regarded by all of us as a member of the family. Miss Almeda took care of the refrigerator, placing the milk in big crocks, skimming the cream, setting the sour milk aside to make clabber and the sour cream to make butter. She also mended all the clothes and looked after the linens. Aunt Ella and Aunt Valerie did all the ordering and took over the general management of the household. My grandmother supervised the kitchen. The children helped with cutting the grass, drying the dishes, churning the butter, freezing the ice cream, picking flowers (I will never forget the nasturtium beds, which seemed to me to be surely the most fertile in the world); we also swatted the flies and put around fresh flypaper, collected eggs, gathered in fruit, helped to shuck the corn, and weeded the flower beds. All these things were tiresome, but the children's tasks really took only a small part of the day. After that we were free to do pretty much as we pleased. We roamed around the place, climbing the fruit trees and stuffing ourselves with whatever fruit happened to be in season, swam in the ice pond, and rode horseback—particularly on an extremely good-natured pony called Ruth, who would frequently be seen with three children on her back at once and who permitted them to slide down her tail without protest. Sometimes we went farther afield, taking long bicycle rides. On a rainy day a child could be found in every corner curled up in a chair with a book. The tennis court, of course, was in constant use.

During the week the men of the family all went into town for work, driving down to Rogers Station on the Greenspring Valley branch, which was about three miles away. My father always rode his sorrel mare to the station. There he would take off his boots, put on a pair of ordinary shoes, put the boots in the station wagon which brought the other commuters to the train, throw the stirrups over the saddle, and give the mare a whack on the flank, whereupon she would turn and canter back the three miles to our stable. At times people tried to catch her, under the impression that she was a runaway, but nobody ever succeeded and soon the neighborhood became accustomed to the sight of the sorrel cantering along by herself on her way back from the 8:20 morning train.

The weekends were unfailingly interesting. In those days everybody worked on Saturday morning, but in the afternoon people would begin to arrive by the 2:30 train, and there would be tennis and horseback riding and, in the evening, bridge and sniff (a form of dominoes). On Sunday, breakfast was not served until 9:30, but long before that hour the children would be out on the tennis courts and some of the adults would go riding. The rest of the family would be roused by violent thumps as the beaten biscuit was hammered out in the kitchen on a big wooden block which had been the stump of a chestnut tree.

Sunday Breakfast was a tremendous meal, starting with fruit, then oatmeal or clabber with brown sugar, kidney stew, beaten biscuits, hot muffins or waffles, fried apples and bacon, grits, and, in the autumn months, panhaus, pigs' feet or sausage. With the fruit, cereal, and coffee there was served a wonderfully thick Jersey cream.

Shortly after breakfast the sporting events would begin. The tennis court and all the horses would be kept busy until about 2:30, when juleps would be handed around to the adults. Then everyone would retire to bathe and dress for dinner, which began at 3:30. On Saturday, six or seven chickens would have been killed, and on Sunday a huge platter of chicken fried in bread crumbs would be placed at the head of the tables and parceled out by my grandmother. The very young usually got drumsticks, with an occasional wing. The server was permitted to reserve for herself the Pope's nose, which, of course, was the tail end of the chicken and contained some of the sweetest meat.

At the other end of the table was a ham which had been brought in from the smokehouse two days before. Typically on a Sunday in August or September there would be consumed at dinner one hundred ears of corn, two bushels of lima beans, five dozen stuffed tomatoes, and a huge quantity of mashed potatoes. As side dishes there were cucumbers, lettuce, radishes, and rhubarb, and the meal came to an end when a dish was brought in with a two-gallon column of freshly made ice cream, strawberry or peach or vanilla with chocolate sauce, according to the season.

There was always wine on the table which had been made on the farm. The family thought that it was exceptionally good, and guests were polite enough to say the same thing. Cocktails were never served and, indeed, aside from a Sunday julep, hard liquor was never seen in that household. Except for a few occasions when some of Fendall's Princeton friends would come to spend the night and go to a debutante party, I do not remember having seen anyone under the influence of alcohol. Even those boys were careful not to come around the main house but went straight down to the playhouse when they got back from the party.

After Sunday dinner the entire family would gather on the front porch and sit in rocking chairs, digesting their meal. Soon, after chasing the dogs around the lawn and making them run after tennis balls, the younger element would start a baseball game, while their elders would go strolling through nearby woods and fields, accompanied by three or four dogs. About nine o'clock everyone would gather in the pantry and eat ham sandwiches and drink milk before going to bed. By ten o'clock everyone had turned in, and by half past ten the house was dark and silent.

Anyone who got sick was dosed with castor oil or calomel or Epsom salts and somehow within a few days seemed to get well again. It is true that there were one or two occasions when this home treatment did not work out so well. As a matter of fact, Aunt Val nearly killed Johnny Howard when, thinking that he had eaten too many grapes, she gave him a laxative. Actually he had an attack of appendicitis, but he was fortunate enough to vomit up the medicine before it took effect. Cuts and bruises were legion and were all given home treatment. Only in the rare cases which stubbornly refused to yield to the usual remedies was a doctor sent for. By modern standards of medical practice we were shockingly neglected, yet we all lived to grow up and learned to minimize those bodily discomforts which are the inescapable lot of all mankind. This was surely a valuable lesson.

It would have been impossible to run such a household without the help of a large staff of servants. Some of them were very colorful figures, particularly old Hester, who could neither read nor write; nor could she tell time by the clock. When Jim Houston (who knew her weaknesses) sent word to her that he must have his eggs boiled exactly three and one-half minutes, she sent back word to him that he would have to boil them himself as "her clock was slow." When the census man came in 1910 and asked how to spell her name, she replied, "jest according to your tastes and fancy, sir." When he asked how old she was, she said that she was "twelve years old when Richmond fell."

There was always a butler (usually a young black man), who waited on the table, washed the dishes, cleaned the first floor, and did all sorts of odd jobs, such as cleaning, trimming, and oiling the kerosene lamps. There were at least two maids; in addition to making the beds and cleaning the entire house, they took turns helping in the kitchen and waiting on the table. There were two laundresses, a coachman, a stable boy, and a gardener, who assisted Mr. Thomas in looking after the barn, milking the cows, and taking care of the vegetable garden.

There were always three and sometimes four saddle horses in the stable. All of these except my father's hunter were pressed into service from time to time as carriage horses. There was also the pony, Ruth, who belonged to the children and sometimes pulled the pony cart. There were a number of different kinds of vehicles, including a buckboard, a buggy, a rubber-tired trap, a station wagon, and a big double-teamed wagon. There was even a Victoria which my mother bought at an auction sale, but this was used only twice and then given up as entirely too much trouble and too hard on the horses. The stable was fascinating to the children. For many years it was presided over by a black coachman named Thomas (who doubled as butler in the wintertime). Thomas was anxious that the children not get hurt, and since he did not have time to watch them, he used terror tactics to keep them away from his preserves, threatening to whip them with a buggy whip. We never could understand why our parents would permit such a vicious character to stay on the place. I can still remember our amazement when Thomas finally left us and my mother bewailed his loss, especially because he had "been so good with the children."

Looking back, I think I can honestly say that few places in my experience have contributed so much to the happiness of so many. All of us are constantly meeting people who remember the farm with affection. Some were there only a few times, yet it seems to have made an indelible impression on their memories. For those of us who were privileged to live there, it was much more than just a summer home. Here we learned to get along with people of all ages and dispositions. No one who was raised in that atmosphere could feel the "alienation" between the generations which is apparently so prevalent today. Best of all, we learned a feeling of family solidarity, to be kindly disposed toward our relatives and friends, to put up with their foibles, and to help them when they were in trouble.

II ❖ My Parents:
A Cause Lost, a Cause Found

While the Slingluff farm was an important influence in my childhood, the Marbury family home was at 159 West Lanvale Street in the city of Baltimore. Just as my grandmother was the presiding genius at the farm, so our family life at 159 reflected the personalities of my parents.

My father, the second William Luke Marbury, was born in 1858 at Wyoming, a tobacco plantation located in Prince George's County, Maryland, near the village of Surattsville (now Clinton), about fifteen miles south of the District of Columbia line. His family had taken a prominent part in the life of Prince George's since the county first came into existence in the latter part of the seventeenth century. At that time Francis Marbury was appointed constable of Piscataway Hundred and later a justice of the county court.

Francis Marbury's grandson, Luke Marbury, was a delegate to the constitutional convention of 1776, which established Maryland as an independent state, and in 1777 he was named lieutenant of the county and commander in chief of the county militia, with the rank of colonel. He seems to have been regarded as something of a hero during the Revolutionary War. According to family legend, he and his brother-in-law, Dr. William Beanes, had saved General Washington's army during the battle of Long Island by "swimming across the island." However, the only military exploit of his for which there is a record appears to have taken place at the battle of Germantown, where he got lost in fog and was captured by the British. His great-grandson (my grandfather), Fendall Marbury, represented the county in the constitutional conventions of 1864 and 1867.

My grandfather Fendall Marbury's mother, Susan Fitzhugh Fendall, was a direct descendant of Provincial Governor Josias Fendall and of "Light-Horse Harry" Lee. She was also connected with George Washington through her uncle Townsend Dade Fendall. "Uncle Towny" was a well-known character whose old schoolmate President John Tyler had appointed him warden of the District of Columbia jail to console him for his failure to persuade the British to recognize him as Viscount Townsend.

He is also remembered in the family for the occasion on which his nephew, in the lean days after the end of the Civil War, apologized to him for not being able to offer the customary brandy in his mint julep, whereupon Uncle Towny pointed to the sideboard on which the family silver service was standing and suggested that his nephew "dispense with the superfluities and obtain the necessities of life."

My grandmother Marbury was Catharine Taylor Marshall of Virginia, whose father was a nephew of Chief Justice John Marshall. Two of "Kate" Marshall's brothers had been killed fighting for the Confederacy, and her brother Charles had served as General Lee's Military Secretary, performing many of the duties now assigned to a chief of staff. My father, who was three years old when the Civil War began, was taught by his mother to pray every night for her brothers and for General Lee.

My father was old enough when his mother died in 1866 to feel the blow keenly, and the effect on the boy was profound. As it turned out, his mother's death was soon to be followed by a complete change in the fortunes of the family. For a little while plantation life continued much as before. True, young slaves began to slip away one by one, but enough of the older ones remained to carry on. The education of the little boys was in the hands of a young lady named Ruth Hebb who was brought to Wyoming for that purpose and who taught them in a little schoolhouse which stood near the gate.

But the sands were running out. The old way of life was near an end, and the tobacco planters of Southern Maryland who had been so prosperous a decade before suddenly found themselves land poor, without labor to work their acres, and faced with the loss of those foreign markets to which their product had always been sold in the past. In 1869, Fendall Marbury married for a second time and moved to another part of the county.

Fendall Marbury's second wife was Sarah Clagett Berry, the daughter of William Jeremiah Berry, a man who by the standards of the day was comparatively wealthy. It was to the Berry home called Mattaponi near the Patuxent River that the young Marburys moved in 1871. Life at Mattaponi was very different indeed from life at Wyoming. To begin with, the second Mrs. Marbury was quite unlike the first, although she was a very handsome woman and not without wit. A cousin of hers told me that at the wedding breakfast the bridegroom, to the consternation of all present, toasted his lovely "Kate." Instead of ignoring this slip of the tongue, the bride arose and thanked her husband for the "most beautiful compliment in his power to pay." Nevertheless, she lacked the peculiar fascination and gaiety that Kate Marbury had possessed, and although my father was always dutiful and affectionate toward her, she could not fill the empty place in his heart left by the loss of his own mother.

Moreover, there was far less in the way of comfort in the life at Mattaponi. The absence of slave labor and the shortage of ready money were felt here as everywhere else in the country round about. Thanks to the fact that the Berrys were relatively well off, there were no severe hardships, but the refinement and elegance which had accompanied the life at Wyoming were things of the past. Nor did my grandfather's career prosper. While he continued to be active in politics and repeatedly sought public office, both elective and appointive, his efforts never again met with success, although on several occasions he narrowly missed being elected to Congress. He attributed his defeat to the chicanery of the political machine which had gained control of Democratic politics in Baltimore City, and he inculcated in his son a detestation of that organization. Law practice seems to have been equally unremunerative, and the Marbury finances drifted from bad to worse.

Thus, it was a dreary atmosphere in which my father was growing to manhood. Of course, there were distractions. He came to know his Bible, the plays and poems of Shakespeare, and the works of John Milton. At school in Fauquier County, Virginia, together with a few young Virginians, many of them relatives, he lived the Spartan life (the boys cut wood every Saturday afternoon to heat the water for their Saturday-night bath) and received instruction in those subjects considered suitable for the education of a young gentleman, including, of course, Latin and Greek. My father was not well coordinated physically, but through constant practice he learned to hold his own with other boys in the sports which were then popular. He learned to ride a horse at a very early age and became an excellent horseman, contesting in the "tournaments" which had become an institution in Southern Maryland. These contests, which were inspired by the novels of Sir Walter Scott, required the rider, while holding a lance in his right hand, to stand in the stirrups and ride under wooden arches, from the center of each of which hung a small metal ring. If the rider succeeded in placing the tip of the lance in the exact center of the ring, he could carry it away. Each contestant rode under the arches three times, and he who most often speared the ring was proclaimed the victor and was entitled to crown a lady of his choice as "Queen of Love and Beauty." These tournaments brought whole counties together and were great social occasions with much speechmaking of a flowery and exaggeratedly rhetorical nature.

As he grew older, my father became increasingly interested in political affairs. He would accompany his father to meetings held in various parts of the county and in neighboring counties as well. In this way he got to know a great many people in all walks of life. On one occasion he was called upon unexpectedly to make the charge to the knights at a local tournament. This he did with great success after strengthening himself for the ordeal by biting off a huge chew of tobacco, which he kept in his cheek all during the speech.

Unfortunately there were serious obstacles in the way of a college education. The state of the family finances was by this time such as to make it quite out of the question for him to follow his father's footsteps to Princeton and to the University of Virginia. For a year he taught school at Upper Marlboro, but it soon became apparent that he, like a great many other young Southerners of his generation, was faced with a choice. He could remain in Prince George's County, where he had been born and raised, find employment as a schoolteacher or a clerk in a store, read law in his father's office, and take part in local politics while his intellectual powers faded and withered in a society which was becoming increasingly provincial and out of touch with the trends of national development; or he could abandon the people and the land that he loved and begin a new life elsewhere.

For my father the choice was not an easy one, for his attachment to Southern Maryland was deep. But there was the sharp contrast between the decline in his father's fortunes and the rise in those of his uncle Charles Marshall. Colonel Marshall had remained with General Lee to the end and had been the only officer to accompany him to the little room in Appomattox Court House where the sword of the Confederacy was finally surrendered to General Grant. Then he had gone back to Baltimore to resume the practice of the law and was now rapidly rising to a prominent position at the bar. Colonel Marshall had been devoted to his sister Kate and was ready to help her son in any way that he could. Finally, there was the example of that great lawyer Reverdy Johnson, who, after practicing for a few years in Upper Marlboro, had moved to Baltimore and become attorney general of the United States, United States senator from Maryland, and finally minister to Great Britain. So, in the autumn of 1878, at the age of 20, my father left Prince George's County and entered the recently opened Johns Hopkins University as a special student.

Baltimore in 1878 was a city of striking contrasts. Physically it was not prepossessing. Its streets were ill lighted and ill paved, and on washdays the water ran blue in the gutters. Indeed, in many places the streets and alleys were little better than open sewers. In order to avoid soiling their shoes, pedestrians crossed the main streets of the city on large paving stones, which were hazards to vehicular traffic. Public sanitation was deplorable and malaria and typhoid fever were constant threats to the health of the community. The transit system was primitive, many different lines competing for the public patronage with horse cars of different colors. The city government was corrupt and inefficient, and the community had an ugly reputation for spawning gangs of rioters. Since the war, there had been a notable falling off in the quality of leadership in the business community, and it seemed as if the initiative and enterprise which had built the city's commercial and financial institutions, as well as the great fortunes of men like George Peabody and Johns Hopkins, Enoch Pratt, and William T. Walters, had been lost.

But while Baltimore was lagging in material progress, it was developing institutions which were to give it a leading position in the next important phase of national development, that is to say, in the growth of scientific knowledge, the appreciation and practice of the fine arts, and the development of public education. When my father arrived in Baltimore, two of these institutions were just reaching maturity. The Peabody Institute under the expert guidance of its provost Nathaniel Morison had brought together a library of scholarly reference works unrivaled in America outside of Boston. Its Conservatory of Music, established on the European model, was attracting to the community musicians and musical scholars of a quality previously unknown in a country which had thought of music largely in terms of ballads or displays of agility by a Jenny Lind or a Paganini.

The Johns Hopkins University under the leadership of Dr. Daniel Coit Gilman was developing into the first educational institution in America which could be compared with the great European centers of learning. Modeled on the universities of Germany, it brought together a group of scholars whose primary interest was in advancing the frontiers of knowledge through scholarly research. Men such as Rowland, Remsen, Pierce, H. B. Adams, Sylvester, Guildersleeve, Brooks, Welch, and Osler set an intellectual pace that challenged the community as well as the nation. My father had the extraordinary privilege of studying with some of these men during their most productive periods.

Unfortunately the news from home grew steadily more dismaying, and it soon became apparent that it was essential that he establish himself in a profession as soon as possible. By this time he had determined to practice law, and this meant years of preparation and study. So, very reluctantly, he abandoned all hope of a college degree and found a job as inspector in one of the large warehouses in Baltimore where tobacco was handled.

Through his association with his Uncle Charles, he became familiar with other aspects of city life. Colonel Marshall was one of a group of outstanding lawyers who had become identified with the so-called Reform Movement in politics. Ever since the election of 1867, when Susan Fendall Marbury's old friend Oden Bowie had been elected governor of Maryland, the Democratic party had dominated the politics of the state. For many years the leading figure in the party was Arthur Pue Gorman, who represented Maryland in the United States Senate and had attained a position of national prominence. In Baltimore the party had been effectively organized under the iron rule of a political boss named I. Freeman Rasin, who had received his training in the days before the Civil War in the old Know Nothing party. The methods of that organization had been about as crude as can be imagined, and Baltimore had become notorious throughout the nation for its "political rowdies and plug-uglies"— or, as we would now say, for its hoods. The condition of affairs was such that on one occasion, Severn Teackle Wallis, then already a leader of the bar, had made a speech in front of the court house during which he pointed to the room in which the Criminal Court of Baltimore City was sitting and referred to it as "that sink of iniquity into which no honest man enters without a shudder and from which no scoundrel emerges without a triumph."

"Free" Rasin, as he was called, did not hesitate to use the methods he had learned in this tough school. In order to maintain his control of the electoral process, he instructed his henchmen to open sealed ballot boxes and substitute fictitious ballots favoring the machine candidate for those marked for the opponent. This practice was called "stuffing the ballot boxes." Friendly voters were permitted to cast ballots repeatedly, and trainloads of such "repeaters" were imported from neighboring cities and allowed to cast their ballots even though they were not citizens of Baltimore. Hostile voters were intimidated by threats, and the use of the awl as a weapon to drive away unfriendly voters was so widespread that this tool became a symbol of the political machine.

As was to be expected, the decent people of the community reacted to these shocking conditions with anger. The more reputable members of the bar furnished the leadership for a popular movement which had as its main objectives freeing the courts from political control, passing laws which would secure honest elections, and electing impartial prosecutors. That this movement should have been led by the lawyers was almost a matter of course. In those days the lawyers held a position of great prominence in the community. Proceedings in the courts were reported in the press with as much detail as is now accorded professional sports, and the leading advocates of the day were as well known to the public as baseball players now are.

The shining example of the lawyer as civic leader was Mr. Wallis. He had been among those who had been prevented from taking their seats in the state legislature in 1861 for fear that they would lead Maryland into the Confederacy. So great was his influence that it was thought necessary to arrest him, and throughout the war he was detained at Fort Warren in Boston Harbor without proof of any act of disloyalty to the Union on his part. He returned to Baltimore with the glamour which attaches to a public man who has been the subject of an outrage, and from then on his influence was very powerful with the better element in the community.

That my father should join this band of warriors was inevitable. He had not forgotten the injuries inflicted on his father by the Baltimore City political machine, and the desire to avenge these wrongs was hot in him.

Moreover, he was of a naturally chivalrous spirit, given to knight-errantry by training and disposition, and to serve in the cause of political righteousness under those who had fought for the Confederacy was his idea of pure happiness.

After two years of work and study, my father was able to enroll as a student in the law school of the University of Maryland. Some of the teaching in that school was of a high order, and enrolled there were a number of able students, among them William Cabell Bruce, who was later to represent Maryland in the United States Senate. My father's self-preparation had been so thorough that he was able to take his degree in one year. He and Mr. Bruce shared the honors of the class, and my father was chosen to deliver the class oration at the exercises held in June 1882 at the Academy of Music in Baltimore.

Before my father had reached his twenty-sixth birthday, his name was known to every literate citizen of Baltimore and his reputation as a political orator and a leader of the Reform Movement was established. This remarkable accomplishment for so young a man came about through what is known as the "new judges" fight. The Supreme Bench of Baltimore City then included in its membership all of the judges who sat in the trial courts in Baltimore. In 1882 there were five such judges and the terms of four of them were about to expire. Three of the old judges had shown themselves to be subservient to the political machine to such an extent that the decent people of the community had become disgusted. The *Baltimore Sun* began an editorial campaign to replace these old judges, but the politicians paid no attention and renominated them at the party convention held in October 1882. Immediately, 350 of the leading citizens of the community published an advertisement calling for the nomination of new judges and the defeat of the old. At a citizens' meeting held on October 18, three independent candidates were nominated and from that time until November 7, the town rang with the speeches of the backers of the new judges.

My father was given the chance to speak at one of the meetings arranged by the backers of the "new judges" ticket and electrified his audience with a brilliant and effective attack on the political machine which dominated the Democratic party in Baltimore. His appeal to the public to protect the courts from "the polluting touch of party politics" was quoted all over town and became one of the rallying cries of the campaign. The overwhelming victory of the "new judges" ticket at the polls on November 7 was the first setback for any regular Democratic candidate since 1867. From that time on, my father's name was bracketed with the leaders in the fight against corrupt politics. It was a spectacular beginning for the young man from Southern Maryland.

The Reform Movement had tasted blood. Its first objective of an honest judiciary had been at least temporarily accomplished. However, changes in the election laws were still essential if the government of the city was to be rescued from the corrupt political gang that continued to hold it firmly in its grasp. Since the Democratic party was dominated by the machine, there was no alternative except to work with and to some extent inside the Republican party.

This was nasty medicine for men to swallow who since 1860 had regarded the Republican party with detestation, but many of the reformers took it nevertheless, largely due to the commanding influence of John K. Cowen. Mr. Cowen, who was then the general counsel of the Baltimore and Ohio Railroad Company, came to the fore in the new judges fight. It soon became apparent that in a time when able leaders were not lacking, this man towered above them all. A learned lawyer, a superb orator, and a penetrating thinker, he also understood the art of politics and knew how to beat the bosses at their own game. Before long this extraordinary man had established his position as general of the forces of reform. For fifteen years he led the battle against the Democratic machine and in the process achieved practical domination of the Republican party in the city and state.

After the new judges fight, the next big battle was the mayoralty campaign of 1885, in which the machine retained control of the city government only by perpetrating the most shameless frauds. My father was in the thick of this fight and again achieved notoriety when in addressing an audience in one of the toughest wards in the city, the old 17th, he made a direct charge of corruption against a resident of the ward who was a prominent member of the machine. There were loud cries of "He's a liar" and "Throw him out," and the audience fell to hissing and applauding. A number of fist fights were started and the police had to quell the disturbance. After the uproar had subsided, my father calmly repeated the charge he had made and then added, "Now that the sideshow is over, I want to say that the politics of the 17th ward are controlled by a dirty clique of rowdies." This created a tremendous sensation and was reported in the newspapers on the following day. The whole town began talking about the courage of the young man from Prince George's County. Among those watching his struggle for political reform in Baltimore City were two students at the Johns Hopkins University named Woodrow Wilson and Newton D. Baker.

As a result of his activities in the Reform Movement, my father became something of a hero among the fashionable element of the community and their doors were opened to him. Baltimore society was at that time a close-knit group. The community was small enough for all those of similar tastes to know one another, and this led naturally to an established pattern of behavior to which all who made any pretension to social position were expected to conform. Baltimore had its own distinctive characteristics, chief among them the influence of the large number of Southerners who had found in Baltimore a haven from the rigors of the Reconstruction era. Most of these came from families which had occupied dominant positions in their communities, and although many of them were in reduced circumstances as a result of the war, they still retained the outlook of the plantation aristocracy. While there was some grumbling on the part of old Baltimoreans over this invasion of "Southrons" (as they were called), the community on the whole received them cordially, and because many of them were men and women of exceptional talent, they soon had a very definite effect on the community's manners.

When, therefore, Colonel Marshall's young nephew, who had created such a sensation by his brilliant oratory, began to be invited out, he found himself in very congenial company. The strong emphasis on family background, the tendency to minimize the importance of wealth and display, the love of sports—particularly of riding to hounds—and the formal and by modern standards courtly relations between young people of opposite sexes were all familiar and pleasant to him. Thus, he found it easy to make friends among what was considered to be the cream of Baltimore society. He was a man of natural modesty, gentle and considerate in his manner to all sorts and conditions of men, trustful of others, generous and hospitable and apparently without a selfish thought. He was singularly unworldly, and men and women alike delighted in protecting him from his lack of concern for his own personal welfare. While far from being an eccentric, he had a touch of the quixotic in his nature, with the usual endearing results. Add to this an urbane and gracious manner, fine eyes that sparkled with intelligence and humor, a temper that could rise quickly to boiling point on provocation and as swiftly subside, and a love for a good fight in a good cause, and you have a pretty good description of a popular favorite.

In a very short time he became identified with a group of young men, many of them scions of old Baltimore families, who went around together. This group were the founders of the Baltimore Club, which for many years was the most fashionable men's club in the city. They also organized the Baltimore Athletic Club, where under the tutelage of the former heavyweight champion Jake Kilrain, they learned how to box scientifically. They rode in the hunts together, sometimes in the Green Spring Valley, sometimes in Howard County, where a number of them lived at Lawyers Hill in summer. Some of them were interested in rowing, and my father was one of the founders of the L'Hirondelle Boat Club, which made Lake Roland look like the Charles River in Cambridge on a spring afternoon. And always there were the ladies.

During August of 1887, my father was invited to spend a week at Capon Springs; there he was introduced to a stately brunette named Silvine Slingluff. This introduction ultimately led to their engagement to marry, but not until Fendall Marbury had been satisfied that his brilliant son had made a good choice. He need not have worried. As the eldest grand-daughter of Frances Cross Slingluff, who was herself of a family well respected in Southern Maryland, she was very close to her grandmother. They were completely congenial, and the little girl came to admire her grandmother and to be deeply influenced by her. Through her she acquired a thoroughly Victorian outlook on manners and morals which never left her, although in later years there was a slightly quizzical air about the way she maintained her position, which disclosed the fact to those who really knew her that she was at heart a tolerant and understanding woman. In her girlhood, however, she seemed stern, especially to her younger sisters. The truth was that she accepted the responsibility which her father had rejected and became her mother's strong right arm. This, together with her natural dignity, gave her a very special air which is not easy to describe; never domineering, she nevertheless dominated any company in which she found herself; without commanding, she seemed always to speak with authority.

Frances Cross Slingluff also passed on to her granddaughter much of the sense of the importance of family background. As a result, anyone listening to her might have supposed that she was a snob. Once while driving through Forest Park, she sighed and said, "All these lovely houses and not a soul living in them!" In Macon, Georgia, she is still remembered for the time when she noticed the absence from the Episcopal church of many of the people whom she had met socially. When my sister explained to her that all these people were either Methodists or Baptists, she said, "Don't be ridiculous, Silvine."

She herself used to tell how she made a Roman Catholic out of her brother, Jesse. Her mother, like all Austrian aristocrats, belonged to that church, and all of her children were baptized in that faith. However, as was often the case with Austrians, she was not very strict in her views. After the family had moved to Towson, the nearest Catholic church was at Notre Dame on Homeland Avenue, and the only way to get there was by a bus drawn by a pair of mules, so that it took half a day to make the journey to church and back. My mother's friends all went to Sunday School at Trinity Episcopal Church right in Towsontown, and she begged her mother to let her go with them. At that time the priest in charge of the children at Notre Dame was a rather ignorant Irishman whom Mrs. Slingluff found very obnoxious, and in the end she agreed to let my mother go to Sunday School with her friends. All the rest of the family followed suit, and in the course of time all of them became confirmed Episcopalians except for Jesse. He had become very impatient waiting for his sisters to finish talking with their friends after church and was tired of escorting them to choir practice and complained of this to a schoolmate, Tom Butler, a Roman Catholic whose father was a local carpenter and contractor. Tom suggested that he stop going to the Episcopal church altogether and go to mass instead. After trying this once or twice, Jesse was reproached by my mother, who said, "Why do you want to go to church with servants instead of with your friends?" Jesse looked at her stubbornly and said, "I don't think that's got anything to do with religion." And from that time on he became a staunch Roman Catholic.

It is also true that my mother throughout her life chose most of her intimate friends from among men and women of so-called good families. They were congenial to her; they thought as she did about most things; and she liked their society. But in spite of all this, it would have been quite inaccurate to call her a snob for the reason that she was intensely interested in and sympathetic with all kinds and conditions of people. She soon got to know the details of the family life of everyone with whom she came in contact, including the servants, and her interest went far beyond mere curiosity. All of them consulted her about their domestic problems, and she gave them the same attention she gave members of her own family. On one occasion when she had to wait in the lobby of a building for my sister Valerie, she was discovered to be prescribing remedies for the doorman's child, who was suffering from the croup. This was completely characteristic, and as a result my mother was always waited on hand and foot by everyone as if she were naturally entitled to this kind of service.

All of her life she was surrounded by waifs and strays of all kinds and descriptions. If an indigent relative needed a place to live, my mother's home was offered to her. If friends had no place to go in summer, they were invited to spend the hot months in the country with my mother. If she planned an entertainment, the first people invited were those who would benefit the most from an invitation rather than those whose presence would grace the party. All in all, taking into account the prevailing attitudes of her time, she was a generous and outgoing person, about as far removed from an icy snob as could be.

My mother was a good-looking young woman by the standards of beauty of her time. True, she was big, but this was the day when it was permissible for a girl to be tall and even by modern standards stout without forfeiting her right to be classified as handsome. There were still some women who laced tightly, and a small waist and dainty foot were by no means to be despised, but this was a dying fashion and the Gibson Girl was just around the corner, so that, in spite of her size, Silvine Slingluff was considered to be a beauty. The permanent wave was then unknown, hairdressers were seldom patronized, and make-up was considered to be indecent, so she was not as much handicapped by her family's poverty as she would have been today.

No one could have been less of a coquette, nor did she make any conscious attempt to be fascinating. She did, however, understand people and know how to discover what interested them and to talk about it. Not that she was a woman of advanced education; she had been to Miss Hall's

School in Baltimore, where young ladies were taught various accomplishments, including a respect for and some knowledge of the humanities, especially poetry and history, as well as good manners, but there her education had stopped. However, she had the advantage of having a father who had made it a practice to read aloud to his children, and whose encyclopedic knowledge made his conversation something of an education in itself. Moreover, her mother's European culture was bound to rub off on a child as intelligent and perceptive as my mother, so that from the standpoint of education she was as far ahead of most girls of her own age as a Radcliffe graduate is ahead of the average Baltimore debutante of today.

My father and mother were engaged to be married for five years. This was not unusual in those days, as young people of social position whose families had fallen upon hard times were frequently obliged to postpone matrimony until they could be self-supporting. Young lawyers then had to undergo a long period of training before they could hope to develop a practice which would enable them to support a wife. In my father's case that period was actually relatively short, since it was not long before he had established a reputation as an outstanding trial lawyer. In 1890 he had won a celebrated victory by successfully defending a man named Burgess who had been charged with perjury for testimony he had given before a grand jury which was investigating one of the political cohorts of the Gorman-Rasin machine.

Shortly thereafter he won an even more significant victory in the successful defense of Charles H. Grasty, who had recently come to Baltimore as editor of the *Baltimore News* and had promptly cast in his lot with the Reform Movement. In a series of articles and slashing editorials he had attacked the Gorman-Rasin machine, and in one of these articles he had undertaken to expose what was then known as the policy game. This form of gambling (now known as the numbers racket) had fastened its hold on the city and under the protection of the machine was robbing the poor and the ignorant exactly as it does today. The *News* undertook to show the connection between the managers of the system that ran this nefarious enterprise and the sheriff of Baltimore City, whose name was Fledderman. The machine reacted to this by causing the state's attorney to obtain the indictment of Mr. Grasty for criminal libel.

The case immediately assumed great significance. Everyone knew that what the *News* had reported was true, and if its editor could be silenced by criminal process, then the outlook for any improvement in the government of the city was dark indeed. On the other hand, proving the truth of what had been charged was certain to be extremely difficult, since those who knew the facts were themselves deeply implicated, and most of them were much too afraid of the wrath of the machine to tell the truth. Mr. Grasty employed my father and Edgar Gans to defend him, and the case came on for trial in the Criminal Court of Baltimore City in 1893. The state's attorney was assisted by Mr. Bernard Carter, then one of the leaders of the profession, so that from a lawyer's standpoint this was to be a battle of titans, and the community followed the trial with the same interest that they would nowadays give to a World Series.

As the case progressed, it became apparent that Mr. Grasty was not going to be able to prove the truth of his charges. Witness after witness called to the stand claimed his constitutional privilege not to give self-incriminating testimony. Nothing could be clearer than the fact that Sheriff Fledderman was indeed closely connected with the policy racket, but not a shred of legal proof to that effect was obtainable. Gloom prevailed throughout the community as it seemed inevitable that Mr. Grasty would be convicted. But my father was not dismayed. Day after day he argued points of law, at the same time explaining the political background of this case. Recognizing the lack of legal proof, he appealed to the members of the jury to exercise the right which the constitution of Maryland gives them to judge the law as well as the facts. This argument was successful. Judge Calvin Chesnut, who heard my father's argument in that case, told me that it was in his considered judgment more far-reaching in its beneficial effects than any argument made before or since in the courts of this state. "That argument," he said, "broke the hold of the Gorman-Rasin machine on the government of the State of Maryland and made possible the reform of the election laws which have ever since protected the people of this state from political corruption in its most naked form." From that time on, my father's position as an advocate was established. At the age of 35 he had become a recognized leader of the bar.

Another development was in a sense a recognition of this achievement. Grover Cleveland, who had just been elected for the second time president of the United States, nominated my father for the position of United States district attorney in Maryland. Senator Gorman, who was then in a commanding position, invoked the privilege known as "senatorial courtesy," which permits a United States senator to block an appointment that is personally obnoxious to him. Aside from his bitterness against the reform element of the party, he had not forgotten that on one occasion my father had publicly refused to meet him. As a result, my father's nomination never came to a vote. In the meantime, however, he served by virtue of one recess appointment after another for the full four-year term of office.

At this point his cousin Robert Smith (who was later my godfather) came forward and told my father that he had recently come into some money and pressed him to accept a loan of $5,000 so that he could get married. My father decided to accept this offer but was careful not to let my mother know about it until after the ceremony, which took place at Trinity Church in Towson on October 11, 1894.

III ❧ Life at 159 West Lanvale Street

By the time my parents had returned from their wedding trip (to Niagara Falls, as was the custom of the times), my mother had come to realize that she was never going to lack for occupation. For this brilliant lawyer that she had married was unbelievably absent-minded and would forget that he had a wife with him. Furthermore, he never seemed able to remember the time of train departures, and as a result they had managed to get into one ridiculous predicament after another. This could be exasperating at times, as when she found herself alone on a train with all the baggage and no rail ticket, my father having gone back to get a newspaper and failed to return. Her indignation when she was met at her destination by a man from the Travelers Aid Society, who said he had been instructed by telegram not to let her out of sight until her husband arrived on the next train, can easily be imagined.

Upon their return from the wedding trip, my parents took rooms at the Albion Hotel, which still stands cater-cornered from Emmanuel Church in Baltimore, and which at that time was a fashionable address. Their stay there was not long, as it soon became apparent that a suitable place would have to be found in which to raise a family. On August 4, 1895, my sister Valerie was born. Thereafter my mother produced three more children at two-year intervals and a fifth child, my brother Taylor Marshall, only eleven months after my birth. Eight years later a sixth child, Francis Cross, was to complete the family roster.

As the family grew, my parents moved from time to time until in the year 1904 they settled down at 159 West Lanvale Street in what was then known as the Mount Royal District of Baltimore City. 159 stood at the southeast corner of Park Avenue and Lanvale Street on a lot which extended south on Park Avenue for nearly a hundred yards. On the south end of the lot was a large, two-story brick building which had stalls for six horses and carriages as well as living quarters for a coachman and a stable boy. In the main house most of the rooms had 16-foot ceilings, and other dimensions in proportion, and were correspondingly light and airy. The house had been built by Joseph Hopkins (a brother of Johns Hopkins), who had decorated it with fancy woodwork, large mirrors (reaching in one case from the floor to the ceiling), and a marble mantelpiece (reputedly carved by the famous sculptor Rinehart), over which hung a huge gilt mirror. The fireplace itself was lined with cast-iron panels excellently carved with scenes from "Tam o' Shanter."

The furnishings of that period were very comfortable, although without elegance. 159 West Lanvale had some "good pieces," and the quantity of silverware, china, and brass that were in constant use, as well as on display, would be hard to match in any but the most pretentious establishments of the present day. Of course, there were none of the mechanical conveniences which now lighten the work of the homeowner— no gas oven, electric toaster, washing machine, dishwasher, or vacuum cleaner—not to speak of TV dinners. But this made little difference, since no one who owned such a home would ever have had the occasion to use any of these devices, all such work being done by trained servants.

159 was a large double house, but it was not long before my parents began to feel cramped for space. The dining room especially could not comfortably seat more than ten people, and this was felt to be quite inadequate. So a three-story back building was added to take care of all the mechanics of the household, including a pantry, kitchen, laundry, servants' dining room, three servants' bedrooms and a bath. On top of this building an enclosed sunporch and a fenced-in roof provided a relatively safe place for children to play. The old kitchen was transformed into a large and handsome dining room, designed by Lawrence Fowler, the leading residential architect of the day, and at mealtimes the household would gather in this room and spend at least an hour at the table conversing, arguing, laughing, and eating heartily. My father was a benign and urbane host and my mother a dignified, serene, and entertaining hostess. Between them they created an atmosphere that was most attractive to people of all ages, and the pleasant times spent at that table still linger in the memories of many.

At 159 open hospitality to friends and relatives was taken as a matter of course. The food supply seemed inexhaustible and there was always enough for the unexpected guest, with the result that few meals were served in that house without at least one guest at the table. Any friend or member of the family who happened to be in town would drop in for lunch, friends who came to call would stay for dinner, and children who came to play would stay to eat or to spend the night. Sunday-night suppers in particular were great occasions. My mother would devote several hours every Saturday to the preparation of terrapin according to a special family recipe, and on Sunday night supper always began with that dish, served with sherry and beaten biscuit.

My parents did little formal entertaining, but many of their friends were invited to the Sunday-night suppers, and as the children grew up their friends also fell into the habit of dropping in at that time. A frequent guest was Charlie Pigott, a young chemist, whose researches had placed him in the vanguard of the developing field of radiation. I have a vivid recollection of a little vial that he carried in his pocket, in which a flashing display was a signal of radioactive discharge. He told us that the atomic nucleus of the enclosed specimen was breaking down and emitting the flashes and that he was on his way to England to consult the famous Professor Francis William Aston, who was at that time regarded as the leading physicist in the world.

Among the friends of my sister Silvine was a group of young doctors from the Johns Hopkins Medical School, among them several who later attained distinction. Perhaps the most colorful man in this group was Perrin Long, who, together with Eleanor Bliss, introduced the so-called "sulfa" drugs to this country by performing what looked like a miraculous cure on Franklin D. Roosevelt, Jr., who had developed a life-threatening ear infection while a student at Harvard. Eleanor Bliss also was frequently among the group that gathered at 159, as were my cousin Rebecca Marshall, Elizabeth Waters (who married Lefty Flinn), and Margaret Eyre ("Peggy") Taylor. Other visitors at 159 who made a deep impression on me included Frank Beirne, the author of *The Amiable Baltimoreans;* Raphael Semmes, who wrote books on aspects of Maryland history; Mary Gertrude Fendall, an early feminist who, after graduating from Bryn Mawr College, had become secretary for Mrs. O. H. P. Belmont; and Mary Marshall Smith, a "flapper" type whose costumes scandalized my mother.

A continuous flow of relatives and friends visited 159 over the years of my boyhood. In addition to those mentioned above, I have special recollections of friends of my first cousin Kate Marbury from Upper Marlboro, who lived with us at 159 for several years. Notable among them was Dorothy Wilson, who in those days distinguished herself by going salmon fishing in the wilds of Canada during the days when that was a sport enjoyed by few men, much less women.

My mother periodically entertained the Tuesday Bridge Club, which included many of her girlhood friends as well as such formidable ladies as Mrs. Bruce Cotten and Mrs. Tunstall Smith. I remember that one winter, in order to give employment to one of her cousins, she sponsored a class in so-called modern ballroom dancing, where her contemporaries trudged around the floor to the tune of an Edison phonograph, which I operated. I will never forget the sight of Bob Crain, for whom the Crain Highway was later named, solemnly piloting Mrs. Eugene Greenway around the room.

I also have a vivid recollection of special occasions when family and friends got together at 159. On New Year's Day a bowl of eggnog and accompanying cookies were always on a table in the back parlor for the benefit of callers, and later in the afternoon a huge family dinner was served to as many as twenty-five people. Of all these special occasions the parties on Christmas night were the most spectacular. After dinner there was always a theatrical performance, directed by my cousin Kathleen Slingluff, a sculptress, ballet dancer, poet, painter, and later a college professor, who composed her own scripts. Of the plays she wrote for these occasions I especially remember one about Captain Bing, the pirate king, who "when he found that he was drowned was taken unawares." Kathleen managed to involve most of the younger members of the family in these performances, which always ended by all concerned gathering around my Aunt Ilka Proctor at the piano. The star performer was always my father, who would sing several ballads and sea chanties and end with "Drill, Ye Tarriers, Drill," the song that used to be sung by the workers on the first transcontinental railway.

At first my father's library was on the second floor of the house. Here he would work at night, and if he had no one working with him the children were allowed to sit by the open fire and study their lessons, provided that they remained quiet. The parlors downstairs were usually reserved for the entertainment of guests, the back parlor being the particular province of young ladies who were entertaining gentlemen and wished a little privacy, although, of course, the door was always kept open into the hall. The back parlor was also the place where the piano and other musical instruments were kept and frequently resounded with the efforts of some child practicing for a lesson.

After the back building was constructed, the library was moved downstairs to the right of the front door, and every afternoon and again in the morning the butler lit a fire in this room. It soon became a family habit to gather there before and after meals, so that my father found it difficult to get much use of it for working purposes.

My father's sorrel mare was kept at a neighboring livery stable and was brought to meet him at the Mt. Royal Avenue entrance of Druid Hill Park at 6:30 every morning in good weather. Here he would join some other gentlemen and ride along the bridle paths for an hour before breakfast. Sometimes one of the children was allowed to come along, and I well remember one spring when I rode regularly with this group, mounted on an enormous horse called William Jennings Bryan. The company all thought that I made quite a comical figure sitting high up on this big brute.

To maintain such an establishment a staff of servants was, of course, an absolute necessity, and in those days there were never less than six at work in the household. The cook, the laundress, and the butler usually lived nearby, but one or two of the maids always lived in the house. Thomas, the butler, came on duty at seven o'clock in the morning and remained until nine at night, except on Thursdays, when he left the house at three o'clock, and every other Sunday, when he left at five.

Thomas kept his pantry free from raids by the children by employing the same terror tactics that he used around the stables on the farm, except that instead of a buggy whip he brandished a carving knife. As a matter of fact, the pantry, and especially the silver bowl full of fruit that was always to be found there between meals, needed a stern guardian.

In addition, there were the nursemaids who took charge of the children almost from birth. There were many of these, some white and some black, but the one who left an indelible impression on the family was Nanna Fallon. Nanna was an Irish woman who first came to take care of my brother Fendall and later returned to take care of the younger boys. She was a devout Roman Catholic who spent at least an hour every day reading her prayer book. Never raising her voice or varying its timbre, she would chant, "Billy, come to bed, come to bed, Taylor," in a monotone that was more compelling than a shout.

Nanna had a lighter side. It was from her that we learned of the sad fate of those who "wear the green," of that "daring young man on the flying trapeze" and of "poor little Buttercup," not to mention "how to become the ruler of the Queen's Navee," and we were endlessly regaled with tales of the prowess of her first charge, little "Bert" Ritchie who later became the only man to serve four terms as governor of Maryland and the only politician of presidential stature Maryland has produced in the twentieth century. Nanna was city bred and did not like the country, saying, "Me for the city lights!"

In the years before World War I the neighborhood of Lanvale Street and Park Avenue was a homogeneous one. Most of the people who lived within radius of two blocks (except to the south, where the black people lived) were, if not friends, at least people with whom our family had a speaking acquaintance and whose backgrounds were not very different from our own. When the weather got cold the favorite gathering place was 159 West Lanvale Street. Here the children were allowed a freedom from supervision which could not be found in their own homes. This was in part due to the fact that the house was the largest in the neighborhood and thus had more room for maneuvering. But even more it was attributable to the disposition of my parents, who seemed able to accept an amount of noise and confusion which other adults found intolerable.

Our next-door neighbors, the John D. Howards, had a son, John Eager, who later became an internationally known physician and a professor of medicine at the Johns Hopkins Medical School. In the opinion of many of his colleagues, he should have been awarded a Nobel Prize for his contributions to medical science. Johnny was the namesake and direct descendant of one of Maryland's Revolutionary War heroes who had distinguished himself at the Battle of Cowpens, and he never forgot it. His Aunt Julia used to inquire of his sister, Priscilla, whether the morning papers carried news of any "refined deaths." Johnny was short of stature and sharp of tongue and had an uncanny ability to excel at sports in spite of being relatively diminutive; at one time he was tennis champion of the state of Maryland.

Then there was Hanson W. Baldwin, whose father, Oliver Baldwin, wrote the principal editorials for the *Baltimore Sun*. Hanson graduated from the Naval Academy and ultimately became the military expert of the *New York Times* with an international reputation. Dick Shackelford attained a national reputation as the writer of several standard textbooks on surgery. Savington Crampton became the arbiter of Greenwich Village, New York, and could make or break literary reputations; Bill Stevenson became president of Oberlin College; and Beverly Smith became one of the editors of the *Saturday Evening Post*. Others had somewhat less edifying careers, notably one who ended his days as a notorious deadbeat.

From time to time we attended meetings of units of the Boy Scouts, which brought us into contact with other boys in the neighborhood, among them Alfred Barr, who later achieved fame as the director of the Museum of Modern Art in New York. Several of my Boy Scout activities remain in my memory, but one in particular stands out. We were required to hike for twelve miles, and my cousin Woody Ober and I walked from his home on Seminary Avenue in the Greenspring Valley to the Greenspring Kennels, which were then at Garrison near the Reisterstown Road. That walk seemed to us to be endless, but my grandchildren jeer at it, since they are expected to hike for forty miles and have done so, although under adult supervision.

Fortunately, as the family grew, so did my father's law practice. Shortly after his marriage, he and Harry Bowdoin had decided to leave Colonel Marshall's office and to form a partnership for the practice of law. My father's successful defense of Mr. Grasty in the *News* libel suit had firmly established his reputation as a first-rate trial lawyer, so it was not long before the new firm began to have an active practice. In 1900 a syndicate organized the Maryland Trust Company, and Mr. Bowdoin was persuaded to accept the vice-presidency of that institution. His place in my father's firm was taken by Frank Gosnell, a very shrewd business lawyer who had been associated with Thomas Lanahan, then a powerful figure in the financial and political life of the city. Mr. Gosnell had gained an excellent reputation as a lawyer especially skilled in trust and estate matters. With the Maryland Trust Company as a client, the firm of Marbury and Gosnell rapidly rose to prominence.

During the years before the outbreak of the First World War in 1914, my father was also rising to national prominence as a trial lawyer. His practice took him all around the country—to New York; Richmond; Charleston, South Carolina; St. Louis; Texas; and even to Mexico. Much of this traveling was due to the fact that the young Maryland Trust Com-

pany had early on gotten into serious trouble. It had made a large investment in securities of a Mexican railroad company which planned to build
a line across Mexico from Vera Cruz to the Pacific coast. The company was
having difficulty obtaining a necessary franchise from the federal government of Mexico, and, at the suggestion of the officers of the Maryland
Trust Company, my father was employed to go to Mexico City and take
the matter up with the government. Porfirio Diaz was then president of
Mexico and was a dictator of the old school who permitted nothing important to be done without his personal approval. Accordingly, my father
obtained letters of introduction and journeyed to Mexico City, where he
presented himself at the office of the president and requested an appointment. He was cordially received and told that the minister of railways
would let him know when the president could see him. It was politely suggested that in the meantime he might like to become better acquainted
with Mexico, and he was given a guest card to the leading club in Mexico
City. My father accordingly moved into the club and patiently waited for a
message from the ministry.

Soon after he arrived at the club quite a few Mexican gentlemen who
were members introduced themselves to him, and he began to receive a
number of invitations to dine and to visit their haciendas. These people
turned out to be quite like the plantation aristocracy among whom he had
been raised. They too liked to ride horses, and their relation to the peons
was not unlike that of the masters of the Southern Maryland plantations
to their black servants. My father found this life very congenial and enjoyed himself thoroughly. As often as he dared, he made inquiries at the
Ministry of Railways, only to be told very politely that the president could
not see him just yet.

Finally, just as his clients' patience was giving out and he was ready to
give up and go back to the United States, my father received a message
that President Diaz would see him the following day. He presented himself at the appointed hour and was ushered into the president's office,
where he was introduced by the minister of railways. The president,
speaking through an interpreter, asked him courteously to state his business, and he began to do so. It was quite evident that president Diaz understood English perfectly, but for formality's sake all that my father said
had to be translated into Spanish. The president soon tired of this, and
holding up his hand said, "Mr. Marbury, I think that I understand. You
may return to the United States and tell your clients that it shall be as they
wish."

With that the interview was closed and my father left, hardly knowing what to make of it. The minister of railways then explained to him
that the whole matter had been discussed with the president the day of my
father's arrival, but that the president wanted to be sure of the character

of the men who were involved. All the social engagements had been designed to give the president's friends an opportunity to size up my father. Their reports had been favorable and that was all that was necessary. From that point on the negotiations proceeded smoothly, and the sale of the railroad was completed.

In addition to its Mexican difficulties, the Maryland Trust Company had become involved in East Texas as trustee of timber certificates issued by the Houston Oil Company and the Kirby Lumber Company. As a result of wholesale timber stealing by a group of Texans led by a man named Votaw, the two companies had gotten into difficulties, and my father was sent down to Texas.

Eighty years ago Texas was still very much of a frontier state, and it was quite important to be quick on the draw. In one courtroom where my father appeared a lawyer had only a few months past been shot dead in the clerk's office by an angry litigant. After my father's case was finished, the judge invited him up to the bench, opened a drawer, and showed him a revolver, saying, "I thought there might be some trouble in this case, Marbury, so I just decided to be prepared. People get pretty rough in these land cases."

My father was never allowed to walk the streets alone but was always accompanied by Harry Black, a businessman who had been a member of the Texas Rangers and who was known as a dead shot. Mr. Votaw soon discovered that the measures my father was taking would defeat his plans for stealing the timber of the Houston Oil Company and he therefore decided to try to intimidate him. One day he came up to my father on the street and called him a foul name. My father automatically drew back his fist, only to find himself in the arms of Mr. Black, who whispered in his ear, "If you strike him, he will shoot you and plead self-defense." My father was a courageous man, but he found it difficult to keep his mind on legal problems under such circumstances. So the next time he came back East he went to Washington and had an interview with Attorney General Wickersham, who listened to his story and assigned a deputy United States marshal to be his bodyguard. Ultimately the Houston Oil Company and the Kirby Lumber Company were successfully reorganized and my father was paid a fee of fifty thousand dollars which was by far the largest fee he had ever earned. Indeed, he felt so rich that he bought my mother a diamond sunburst, which she always called her Houston oil pin and never wore.

During those years my father was very successful financially. During some years his income from his profession amounted to more than forty thousand dollars, and when you remember that the purchasing power of the dollar was at least ten times what it now is and that no income tax was payable at that time, you can see what that meant. Looking back, it seems almost incredible that people without inherited wealth could live as my parents did in the years before World War I. While my father was a successful lawyer, few lawyers nowadays can earn enough to live in such a style.

All during this period my parents traveled every summer. On several occasions they went to Europe and toured England, Ireland, Germany, and Austria. Before the children were old enough to go along on these trips, my parents usually took one or more of the aunts, and on one occasion they took my grandmother Slingluff as well. When they did not go to Europe, my parents traveled in Maine, Cape Cod, and the Adirondacks, to the St. Louis Fair, to the Colorado Rockies, to the Pacific Northwest, to Vancouver, Banff, and Lake Louise, to Murray Bay, Nova Scotia, and, of course, to Mexico. The children occasionally went to summer camps and sometimes went along with my parents, so that all of us got a trip of some kind nearly every summer.

All of us were taken from time to time to concerts at the Peabody and at the Lyric and occasionally to the theater, usually to see a Shakespearean performance by Sothern and Marlowe, Forbes Robertson, or David Warfield. We all attended dancing classes, had music lessons, and took part in tennis tournaments at the L'Hirondelle Club and the Green Spring Valley Hunt Club, where we had a family membership. Thus, our life was generally an interesting one. There was much more leisure than today, and although there was no lack of activity, there was much less tension. Our parents were not problems to us, although we were all, in greater or lesser degree, problems to them. The truth of the matter is that we loved our home, liked most of our relatives most of the time, and our days were, on the whole, happy ones.

IV ✦ School Days: A Green Twig Bending

All of the Marbury children were sent to private schools. The girls went to Bryn Mawr and the boys to Boys' Latin School or Marston's. My sister Silvine went to Bryn Mawr College. My brother Fendall went to Princeton and the Harvard Law School. My sister Valerie, who was the eldest, did not go to college because at the time she graduated from school, young females were not expected to do so and only a few exceptionally head-strong types ever had the benefit of a college education. So when Valerie graduated from Bryn Mawr School in 1913, she was sent to Madame Marty's in Paris to be "finished" in the best Continental style along with a carefully selected group of young American ladies of "good" families.

Although Valerie derived some benefit from her Parisian schooling, a visit she paid to Austria the following summer turned out to be more interesting. Here she stayed with an old friend of the family, Agnes Carroll of Baltimore, who had married an Austrian nobleman, Count Toni Heusenstamm. The Heusenstamms lived in the village of Matzlainsdorf, next door to the local "schloss" where Count Toni's first cousin lived. This lady was the widow of Field Marshal Galgoczy and was consequently always referred to as "Excellenz." She was regarded as the most important person in that part of the country and every week had her "jour" on which she received formal visits from all the socially eligible people in the neighborhood. As there were only two families within visiting distance who fell into this category, her jour was not apt to be crowded, but it was always observed. Men in livery, smelling strongly of the stables, served strawberries, tea, and cakes to the guests with great formality, after which everyone sat down and played cards until it was time to go home. All of these people knew the Almanach de Gotha by heart and could gauge to a millimeter the exact social standing of everyone with whom they came in contact.

Whenever military maneuvers were held in the neighborhood, Count Toni would take the ladies out in an old farm cart to watch the fun, very much as the country turns out for a fox hunt in the hunting shires of

England. Valerie found this life very entertaining. Except for the occasional formalities, it had a relaxed quality not wholly unlike the life on the Slingluff farm, and perhaps for this reason the Villa Heusenstamm was a favorite place for the ladies of the Slingluff family to stay when they visited Austria.

The titular head of Count Toni's regiment was the Archduke Franz Ferdinand, at whose birth my grandmother's cousin Malvine von Dorsner had been in attendance as a lady-in-waiting to the Archduchess Marie Annunciata. After Franz Ferdinand was assassinated at Sarajevo, the entire Heusenstamm family was invited to the funeral, and Valerie was allowed to go with them and to witness the burial of the man whose birth had been commemorated by a silver cup which she later inherited. My brother Fendall always insisted that he had been brought up in the shadow of the imperial Austrian throne, and this was one more proof of that.

The events which followed closely on the death of Franz Ferdinand produced great excitement in the family back in the United States. Arrangements had previously been made for my Aunt Ella to meet Valerie at the Villa Heusenstamm and bring her back to Baltimore in time to make her debut in the autumn of 1914, but by the time Aunt Ella got to Munich, Austria was at war and the trains were filled with troops moving up to the front. At that time there happened to be staying at Aunt Ella's pension in Munich a young American named Taylor Starck (later professor of German at Harvard University). This young man, who spoke fluent German, offered to go to Matzlainsdorf and escort Valerie to Munich, and as he was quite evidently a perfectly harmless young man, of a rather ladylike sort, Aunt Ella decided that she had better accept his offer, since the international situation was rapidly moving from bad to worse and it looked as if any American who did not leave Europe soon would have to remain there until the war was over. Accordingly, she gave Mr. Starck all the information she could and sent him on his way with letters of introduction to the Heusenstamm family.

Unfortunately, Mr. Starck was a very cautious young man, and when he arrived in Matzlainsdorf he proceeded to make inquiries before presenting himself. This fact was promptly reported to Countess Heusenstamm, who was outraged at the presumption of the young American, so that when he presented his letters of introduction, she peremptorily refused to permit Valerie to accompany him, saying that she herself would see that Valerie got to Munich under proper chaperonage as soon as the mobilization had been completed. So Mr. Starck had to return to Munich empty-handed, and Aunt Ella had to wait a month longer before Valerie was able to join her. This so delayed them that they had difficulty in getting out of Germany to Holland and were finally able to get passage back to the United States only on the last passenger boat to leave Europe until the end of the war.

My own education was less colorful. What is probably my earliest recollection is the day I learned to read. I think that I was four years old, and
I wanted to go to school very badly. So in some fashion I managed to find
the key to unlock the door of the printed word. Shortly thereafter I was
taken to see Miss Virginia Page, who ran a kindergarten and elementary
school on Linden Avenue, about three blocks from 159. Miss Page was a
relative of Thomas Nelson Page's, whose nostalgic romances about the
Old South were obligatory reading in most of the homes in our neighborhood. I have a definite memory of that first interview because I took the
occasion to demonstrate my abilities as a pianist by producing sounds
which would be instantly recognized by any modern composer as a series
of tone clusters but which in that unsophisticated era was called simply
"banging on the piano." I recall that Miss Page suggested that my effort
might appropriately be called "The Storm," which made me very happy.

I remained in that school for five years, but what happened there has
almost completely passed from my memory. I do, however, recollect the
occasion on which Miss Page, who taught us American history, advised us
to skip the next thirty pages of our textbook, saying that she herself
would tell us about the "War between the States." It turned out, of course,
that our textbook had been written by a man from Massachusetts, so this
blatant censorship produced no protest whatsoever from any student or
parent. So far as I can remember, it was regarded as a wholesome effort to
counteract Yankee propaganda.

When I was 9 years of age, I was transferred to the Boys' Latin
School, which was then always known as Dunham's. Apparently my record at Miss Page's school was such as to cause Mr. Dunham to suppose that
I was ready to enter the first form of his upper school. It soon became
apparent, however, that I was over my head, and so I was sent back to the
intermediate grade, where I was taught by Miss Eleanor Reiley, who was
then in charge of the lower school. As it turned out, that was a very good
thing, for it brought me in contact with a remarkably fine teacher who
really did manage to inculcate a love of learning in many of her pupils.
When in the following year I moved on to the upper school, I found the
work which had previously so baffled me quite easy, and from that time
on, I led my class every year except one. When I was in the fifth form, an
interloper named Wilbur Grose entered the form and ousted me from
my accustomed position as the head boy of the class.

Mr. Dunham had gathered together a remarkable group of teachers.
Most notable among them was Edward Lucas ("Whiskers") White, who
taught Latin and Greek to the older students and somehow managed to
make Caesar's *Commentaries on the Gallic Wars* and Cicero's *Orations against
Cataline* seem as contemporary as the pages of the *Baltimore Sun*. Mr.
White's classroom was notorious for being freezing cold all through the
winter. He preferred to have the windows open at all times in order to

eliminate the body odors of his students, which he found intolerable. However, there were so many protests from parents that he finally compromised by opening the windows between every class, during which time he would put on his heaviest jacket. During the next fifty minutes, he changed his jacket as many as three or four times for a lighter weight at each change, in the meantime taking out a bottle of smelling salts, from which he took a whiff from time to time. The boys lived in awe of him, but somehow he managed to beat into their heads a remarkable amount of information about Rome and Athens in their palmy days. In the opinion of many of his students, he was the most gifted teacher under whom they ever sat. I had the benefit of Mr. White's tutelage for two and a half years, and so remarkable was the impact that I continued to study Latin and Greek until I went to law school.

In his old age Mr. White could no longer teach and became dependent upon the charity of friends. My last contact with him occurred when one of his neighbors on Mt. Royal Avenue was evicted from her home for nonpayment of rent. He asked me to look into it. I talked to the woman, who seemed to me to be quite irrational. I then called the landlord, who recited a long list of grievances and said that he thought she was crazy. I replied that I thought so too and suggested that it might be better for him to see that she got help rather than scandalize the neighborhood by putting the furniture of a crazy woman out on the street in the snow. He grumblingly agreed and actually did move the furniture back in. Mr. White called me that evening to thank me and to say that he was especially gratified that I had finished the job as it would now be possible for him to do something which he had previously planned to do that evening. That same night he took his own life in the classic Roman style.

The academic standards of Dunham's School were quite high. We read *The Vicar of Wakefield, Lorna Doone,* and *Silas Marner,* all of which, by some strange perversity, were considered appropriate reading for adolescents, and we were called upon to memorize Gray's "Elegy" and Wordsworth's "Intimations of Immortality in Early Childhood." Unto this day I remember the opening lines of "The world is too much with us," although it was many years before I could understand what the poet meant in calling our hearts "a sordid boon." In French class we read Hugo's *Ernani* and Rostand's *Cyrano de Bergerac,* and, in German, Goethe's *Hermann und Dorothea* and Schiller's *Wilhelm Tell,* all of which were an introduction to adult ideas. Here our guide was a young graduate of Yale whom I remember as being somewhat bored and cynical and, perhaps for that reason, an interesting character.

I should not overlook our gymnasium instructor—a German named Chris Beuerlein who was a member of one of the German Turnvereins which flourished in Baltimore at that time. Every day we had a "gym period" when we walked across the yard to a three-story gymnasium which was equipped with a swimming pool, basketball court, indoor track, parallel and horizontal bars, weights, wrestling mats, fencing foils, and locker room. Every student was required to practice all the different exercises that were supposed to build up his body and once a year to exhibit his prowess to his parents. I think that I was clearly the bottom rung of the ladder in every form of exercise except "push-ups," in which for some mysterious reason I excelled.

One boy who sat next to me in the study hall came from Talbot County. His name was Donnell Tilghman, and his family owned a beautiful old place on the banks of the Wye River, next to the famous Lloyd place, where his aunt was living in one of the great houses of colonial America. Donnell and I developed a warm friendship. We were both students at the Peabody Conservatory of Music, and my grandmother thought that he played the piano quite well for an American boy. We communicated with each other in German script, which each of us had been taught by German tutors. At one time we actually planned to write an opera in German. I was to be primarily responsible for the libretto and he for the music, but both of us were too indolent to get very far with that project.

My brother Fendall complained to my parents that my behavior at school humiliated him and that I was the laughing stock of the student body. He particularly objected to my habit of skating backward on one loose skate while carrying my violin, which I brought along to school when I had a music lesson that afternoon. He was outraged when I told him that I would rather be laughed at than not noticed at all. The truth is that while I was in many ways more mature than most of my classmates, I was physically and emotionally far less developed than they were. I had not even begun to grow up to my rather big feet, and my voice had not yet begun to change. I was physically clumsy and timid and tended to make up for it by being intellectually overbearing. The result was that to my elders I seemed to be an obnoxious brat.

My father was aware of this and tried several experiments to deal with the problem. In the summer of 1914 he sent me to a boys' camp which Woodruff Marston was running on a lake in the Western Adirondacks. There I was almost the only boy who was not a student at Marston's School. My tent mate was Johnny Howard, with whom at that particular time I was rather on the outs. He had developed into a far better tennis player than I and was quicker to catch on to the ways of the camp. Fortunately, Woodruff Marston ran an unstructured and relaxed camp where every boy was fairly free to follow his own line. Although I was slow to catch on, I did manage to take the lead for a while in one of the water sports, which involved swimming down some fast water and over a small falls. My first trip down was involuntary because I upset my canoe in trying to land at the head of the falls, and the next thing I knew, I was on my

way down. When I found that I had survived unharmed, I deliberately
went down again and was promptly imitated by the other boys, who
found, as I had, that this was a delightful way to go swimming. From that
time on, life at the camp became happier for me, and by the time our six
weeks were up, I had acquired a taste for the life of the North Woods
which has never left me.

There was a boy from Watertown who one evening started to behave
rather strangely. The other boys began to taunt him, whereupon he
seemed to froth at the mouth. This excited everyone and he was wrestled
to the ground and everybody began to pummel him. At this point Woodruff Marston rushed up to break up the melee. As it turned out, the boy
was having an epileptic fit and, of course, had to be sent home, and the
rest of us felt ashamed, especially as we had enjoyed ourselves thoroughly
in ganging up on this poor devil.

I also remember August 4 as a red-letter day. We had just begun a
canoe trip when the Middendorf twins paddled up to join us. They
brought with them a copy of the *New York Times* which bore huge black
headlines proclaiming that Great Britain had declared war on Germany.

Near the end of that trip, we were invited to a so-called marshmallow
roast at a camp on upper Saranac Lake. The owner of the camp was a
wealthy Bostonian who employed six guides to build a huge bonfire with
railroad ties. Of course, none of the boys could get near enough to roast
any marshmallows, but this was all taken care of by caterers, who fed us
from plates. The whole affair was on a grand scale, and the boys unanimously reacted with scorn to this display of opulence.

Two years later the war in Europe had engulfed the whole continent,
and the German submarine campaign was beginning to threaten the ability of President Wilson to hold our country on a course of neutrality.
Someone in authority had the bright idea of training schoolboys who
were too young for military service. As a result, a summer training camp
was established at Fort Terry on Plum Island in Long Island Sound under
the official sponsorship of the United States Army.

My father thought that this was just what I needed, and although I
was not quite 15 years of age, he managed to persuade the army to accept
me, violin and all. As a matter of fact, the violin turned out to be not such
a bad idea, as the commanding officer at the camp, although a West
Pointer, was himself a pretty good amateur violinist. I was promptly ordered to show up for an orchestra rehearsal on the strength of the fact
that I had been a student at the Peabody Conservatory of Music.

Unfortunately I lacked the experience which a student at the conservatory is expected to have today. I could not read a score at sight, and
while with practice I could manage to play a few standard pieces, I was
quite lost when the second violin part of a Mozart overture was put before
me. However, there seemed to be quite a large number of boys from New

York City who took all this in their stride and helped to carry me along. It was an eye-opener to me and taught me how limited my musical accomplishments really were.

As the summer wore on, I came to the conclusion that the army did not take this assignment very seriously, which no doubt explained why they had entrusted it to a violinist. One of our instructors was a rather corpulent New York lawyer who had some difficulty in managing the calisthenic exercises; another was a West Point cadet who turned out to be the son of a boyhood acquaintance of my father's. This was unfortunate, as he lost no time in making it quite clear to me that more was expected of me than I was able to do. From a strictly military standpoint I learned nothing of value, but it was my first experience in living with a group of boys of a totally different background. I shared a tent with five others, most of whom were ethnic Italians or Irish from the Greater New York area. All of them were students in the public schools, and one or two of them were what we would now call "streetwise." They groused about the food, which was really not too bad, and had no table manners and regarded me as a strange phenomenon. Fortunately for me, none of them was a bully, and I was allowed to go my own way.

I have no real recollection of the instruction that we received, but I do remember swimming on the beach and looking across Long Island Sound to the Connecticut shore on a series of lovely summer days. We were not far from Fishers Island, and I used to take binoculars and explore the shoreline with longing. I also have a dim recollection of visiting the Montauk light as well as some obsolete fortifications with which the Coast Artillery was expected to defend the harbor of New York.

When I got back home to Baltimore, I was told that I was being sent to the Episcopal High School in Alexandria, Virginia, where my cousin Billy Marbury had made a reputation as a track star. My father thought that perhaps boarding-school life would prepare me better for what was to come, which looked increasingly like military service. The school was known throughout the South as "The High School" and was modeled on an English public school. While there were a few students from the neighborhood, most of them came from all over the South, and everyone was required to live in the dormitories and to attend chapel every morning.

For more than half a century the school had been ruled by Launcelot Minor Blackford, who might have stepped out of the pages of *Tom Brown at Rugby*. He had been succeeded as headmaster by Archibald T. Hoxton, who made few innovations and likewise inspired awe in the faculty and students. I well remember one night during World War I when a substitute teacher, called in to replace a teacher who had just left for service in the army, lost control of the study hall. The boys were on a rampage, throwing chalk and books around and yelling at each other, when the door suddenly opened and "Flick" (as the headmaster was always called, but never to his face) stood there. At once the rioting stopped and everyone slunk sheepishly back to his seat. "Flick" took charge of the study hall for the rest of the evening, and the substitute teacher departed the next day.

This was my first school year away from home, and I found it a very lonesome experience. Once again I was an outsider. There were a few boys from Baltimore, but I had not known them before, although one of them, Arthur Lee Kinsolving (known as "Tui"), was the eldest brother of a girl who had been in my dancing class. All the rest of the student body were complete strangers. I was two years younger than the other boys in my class, nearly all of whom were expecting to go to college the next year. I had just turned 15 and was physically and emotionally young for my age. I could not compete with my classmates in any sport except tennis, which was not regarded by the other boys as worthy of serious attention.

At that time the school had no swimming pool. I cannot remember that any student was interested in music except for a few boys who were learning to play the banjomandolin. I did play my violin with a few faculty wives and with the organist at the Seminary. When the boys got together, they would tell each other dirty stories or boast about their girls back home. Every mail brought scores of letters to the older boys, on scented pink or green stationery. These were read aloud in the dormitories with much relish. In none of these enjoyable pursuits did I have any part.

The curriculum was rigorous and well taught, especially in the classics and mathematics. In the classroom I did well except in trigonometry, in which I barely got a passing grade. The truth is that I disliked the drudgery of handling figures. Moreover, I managed to accumulate quite a few demerits, primarily for non-observance of rules, through sheer absent-mindedness. The fact that I was not regarded as leadership material was made clear to me when I was not selected as a monitor to serve during the following year.

Nearly all the boys in my form went on to college. But as I was not yet 16, my father wanted me to stay in school for another year. So in the fall of 1917 I returned to the High School to continue my studies along with a handful of other classmates who for one reason or another were not yet ready to enter college.

Somewhat to my surprise, I found that I was glad to be back. Dick Shackelford and Charlie "Buck" Stewart from Baltimore had just entered the school, and I was again put at the headmaster's table in the dining room, along with a bright boy from Richmond named Joe Bryan. I was beginning to grow up physically and emotionally and found that I had made quite a few friends who seemed glad to see me back. I was even allowed to play football on one of the "cake" teams, which were made up of younger boys who were not yet ready for varsity sports, and to my astonishment discovered for the first time that I liked contact sports.

During the summer I had worked at Camp Meade, driving a jitney bus between headquarters and the railroad station. I had recently gotten my driver's license under rather exceptional circumstances. When I went to take my examination, I was sent to the second floor of the office of the commissioner of motor vehicles and given a written examination to make sure that I understood the rules of the road. There was an open window beside the desk at which I was sitting that looked out on what appeared to be a tin roof. Somebody threw a lighted cigarette onto the roof, and it ignited some oily rags that were lying there. In order to put out the flames, I stepped out on the roof, which turned out to be made of glass (covered by several inches of black soot), with the result that I went crashing down into the commissioner's office and landed on his desk. Fortunately he had stepped away from his office and was not hurt.

The next thing I knew, I was being restored to consciousness at Mercy Hospital, where I was declared to be unharmed except for a slight cut on one hand. I insisted on going back to the examination and passed the driving examination without difficulty. The examiner told me that if I could drive under such circumstances, he thought I was fit to drive anywhere.

However, I soon discovered that he had never dealt with Anne Arundel County sand. Camp Meade was apparently built on a sand hill, and it seemed as if most of the motor vehicles were stuck most of the time. I learned the art of deflating my tires so as to improve traction, and before the summer was over had become quite an expert in driving under circumstances which I later discovered were very similar to those created by blizzards in New England.

In addition to this somewhat esoteric driving experience, by some process which I cannot exactly explain I did a lot of growing up during that summer. Physically there was no marked change, but I came in contact with a wide variety of adults, and it was a revelation to see how their behavior under stress ranged from the petty to the masterful. I remember that one officer became so distracted by the chaos which seems to be inevitable in a rush construction job of that magnitude that he committed suicide one morning; I actually heard the pistol shot.

As a result of all this, by the time that I got back to school, I had learned a good deal about how to get on in the world. Moreover, I found that the academic work was quite interesting. In the classics I read some of the poems of Horace and several chapters of Ovid's *Metamorphoses*, as well as Plato's *Apology* and *Crito* in Greek. In English I won the Shakespeare Medal and in mathematics began the study of college algebra, which, to my surprise, I found that I could understand. I represented the Fairfax Literary Society in reading and debating contests and won the school medal as the best reader. Finally, to my genuine amazement, I was told that I had been awarded what was then regarded as the school's highest academic honor, the Randolph Fairfax Medal for character, conduct, and scholarship.

V ❧ My Father's Near-Miss as Politician

All during my school days, my father continued to be at the top of his profession and at the same time to take an active part in political affairs. Fresh from his spectacular part in the *News* libel suit, he had taken a leading role in the gubernatorial election of 1895. Under the leadership of John K. Cowen, the Republican party had nominated Lloyd Lowndes for governor and had put up a strong ticket for the legislature. My father and his associates in the battle for political reform had become convinced as a result of bitter experience that only by combining with the Republican party could the program of the Reform League ever have a chance of adoption.

The Gorman-Rasin machine fought desperately, and election day was the most turbulent and disorderly in years. Many Reform League watchers were assaulted and driven from the polls. But the tide of reform was too strong. The Republicans swept the city and the state, gaining control of the governor's office and of the state legislature for the first time since 1867. At the next session of the General Assembly bills drafted by the Reform League revising the election laws were introduced and passed by the newly elected legislators under the leadership of William Cabell Bruce. From that day on, elections in this state have been conducted with relative decency and the crude methods by which the will of the voters had on so many occasions in the past been frustrated could no longer be employed.

My father's experience in the long fight for electoral reform had made him a political realist. For the rest of his life he had no use for what he called "parlor politics." Instead, he believed in working with practical politicians who got out the vote on election day, and he became a faithful attendant at meetings of the Eleventh Ward Democratic Club. My brother Fendall and I were taught to do likewise, and we worked as precinct leaders in several elections.

A curious by-product of my father's interest in electoral reform was his leadership in the movement to disfranchise the Negroes, which developed at the turn of the century. Following the Civil War the ballot had been made available to former slaves in Maryland as in other Southern states. Unfortunately, few of them were qualified to understand what they were voting for. Many of them were illiterate, and the more unscrupulous politicians boasted of their ability to buy their vote. There were vigorous debates as to whether it was more profitable to buy the votes of the blacks or to pay someone to see that they stayed away from the polls.

This situation was thoroughly revolting to my father and to the other people who had worked so hard for electoral reform. To them it seemed idiotic that the ballot should be conferred on a group so little qualified to exercise it, and they therefore studied with deep interest the various schemes for disfranchising the Negro which were being tried out in other states where the black population was large.

The election of Austin Crothers as governor of Maryland in 1907 placed my father in a position of considerable influence. Governor Crothers had great confidence in him and was accustomed to consult him on almost every matter of importance. My father assisted in drafting the so-called Straus amendment to the state constitution, which was intended to disfranchise what was referred to as "the venal and illiterate Negro vote." With the support of Governor Crothers, this amendment was adopted by the legislature but defeated at the polls in 1909.

Finally my father took a case all the way to the Supreme Court of the United States in an effort to uphold an ordinance of the city of Annapolis which would have effectively disfranchised blacks. In this case he argued that the Fifteenth Amendment to the Federal Constitution had been invalidly adopted and that it was not binding on the state of Maryland. Of course my father's argument was unsuccessful, and to many it seemed quixotic that he should have made such an attempt. Nevertheless, Professor Benno C. Schmidt, Jr., formerly dean of the Columbia Law School and now president of Yale University, in a recent study of the case, commented favorably on the scholarly quality of my father's brief in that case. The *New York Times* in a lead editorial published on June 28, 1915, characterized the case as a well-meant but forlorn attempt to undo the harm which had been caused by the adoption of the Fifteenth Amendment. Curiously enough, the decision in that case was delayed until nearly two years after it was argued. In the meantime, Justice Lurton had died and been succeeded on the court by James C. McReynolds, a friend of my father's who had been attorney general in the cabinet of President Wilson. Justice McReynolds told my father that Justice Lurton had intended to file a dissenting opinion adopting my father's argument and that this had so outraged his colleagues that they held up deciding the case until after Lurton's death.

When Governor Woodrow Wilson of New Jersey was looking for someone to manage his presidential campaign in Maryland, he turned to my father, whose participation in the new judges fight and in the subsequent battles for political reform he had admired when he was still a graduate student at the Johns Hopkins University in the 1880s. Obviously Governor Wilson was not deterred by my father's activities in connection with Negro suffrage. Indeed, nearly all the leaders throughout the Southern states had been engaged in similar efforts, and from very much the same motives. In their eyes most of the black people were completely unfit for the ballot, and to them the idea that they could be educated for citizenship seemed absurd. Some of the leading statesmen of the world had publicly stated their conviction that blacks as a race lacked the capacity for self-government, and in this they were supported by respectable anthropologists like Professor Madison Grant of Columbia University, who was a prominent exponent of the theories of Count Gobineau, a scientist of worldwide reputation. So that eighty years ago it was a simple fact that many of the most high-minded citizens in this country felt that the disfranchisement of most blacks not only was compatible with but was in fact essential to political reform.

Woodrow Wilson was the embodiment of my father's political ideals, and by the time the Democratic Convention of 1912 was held in Baltimore in the Fifth Regiment Armory, the whole Marbury family was worked up to a high pitch of excitement. During the convention 159 West Lanvale Street was turned over to my aunts to run as a rooming house for delegates. Due to my father's connection with the Wilson campaign, the family always had good seats in the galleries, and nearly all of us took turns in watching the extraordinary spectacle of a national political convention.

In those days there were no electrical devices for magnifying the voices of the speakers, and the leading politicians of the day all possessed voices as powerful as the bellow of the bull of Bashan. The convention was a long one, with the early votes trending strongly toward Senator Champ Clark of Missouri. The tide was turned by William Jennings Bryan, who late one night made a speech in which he linked Champ Clark with the monopolists and robber barons of Wall Street. The nomination of Woodrow Wilson brought the convention to an exciting close, and during the summer that followed and up until election day very little was spoken of in the Marbury family except politics. We all went to political meetings to see the candidates, and I distinctly recollect the huge bulk of President Taft and the ludicrous contrast between the ferocious appearance of President Theodore Roosevelt and his voice, which was so hoarse that he could scarcely be heard.

The years immediately following the election of Woodrow Wilson were full of interest. My father had been so closely identified with the Wilson campaign that the entire community tended to assume that he must be on intimate terms with the White House. While this impression was undoubtedly exaggerated, it is true that my parents were invited to small and intimate dinners in honor of President and Mrs. Wilson. On one occasion they attended a birthday dinner given in honor of the secretary of state, William Jennings Bryan, who blew out the candles on a mammoth cake with one blast of his famous lungs. Twice the president took occasion to write letters to my father on matters of public importance which he handed to the press, thereby emphasizing the friendly relation in which they stood.

Altogether it was an exciting time, made no less so by the fact that my father's political stock was steadily rising. With the Wilsonians in control of the White House, those Maryland Democrats who had fought for political reform over the years felt that the time had come to break the hold of the State Democratic machine, which was then under the domination of Senator John Walter Smith. Senator Smith had backed his colleague Champ Clark for the Democratic nomination and had carried the Maryland delegation with him. In consequence he was not in favor with the Wilson administration, and my father seemed to be the logical man to oppose him. Various emissaries of the administration sounded him out and urged him to enter the senatorial primary election in 1913, assuring him that he would have the president's backing.

My father hesitated a good while before he made up his mind to tackle the Smith organization. He realized that he had no financial backing comparable to that available to the machine, nor did he have a political organization on which he could count for support. It was true that the *Baltimore Sun* under the leadership of Mr. Grasty was ready and eager to support him, as were a few political leaders here and there throughout the counties. His real support, however, would have to come from the administration in the shape of control over patronage.

My mother was not happy about this. She had bitter memories of her own father's political activities, which had always resulted in financial hardship for the family, and she had no faith in the promises of politicians, no matter how highly placed. Still, the campaign began most auspiciously. My father's recommendations for appointments were followed and those of Senator Smith were disregarded.

But Senator Smith did not surrender. On the contrary, he appealed to his Democratic colleagues in the Senate for help, pointing out that if the administration were permitted to cut his throat in this fashion, some of the others who had supported Champ Clark might well receive similar treatment. In the end the president was forced either to withdraw his support for my father's candidacy or to risk defeat of measures to which he was pledged. Reluctantly he concluded to withdraw from the Maryland scene, and my father learned of this indirectly when two of his nominees for appointments were passed over in favor of Senator Smith's candidates. Without control over the patronage, my father realized that he could no longer hope to succeed in the fight against the Smith machine, and he therefore decided to withdraw his candidacy. Since most of his friends had contributed to his campaign, he felt in honor bound to reimburse them, and in the end this venture cost him the sum of approximately fifty thousand dollars. My mother frequently said that my father had paid a handsome price for his whistle.

As an immediate consolation prize, my father received a letter from President Wilson, couched in very flattering language, expressing his great regret that my father had decided to withdraw from the contest. Naturally this letter was read with mixed feelings, but the compliment was appreciated nonetheless. Later, the president was called on to make an appointment to the Supreme Court of the United States. Among those consulted was Newton D. Baker, who recommended my father. Mr. Burleson then called my father and said that he and Mr. Gregory had endorsed Mr. Baker's recommendation, but that the president wished to know whether my father would accept the appointment if it were offered to him. At that time my father was the main support not only of his immediate family but of a large number of miscellaneous relatives who had come to look to him for assistance. My sister Valerie was then about ready to make her debut, and in a short while my brother Fendall would be ready for college. It was perfectly clear that my father could not live on the salary of a Supreme Court justice without imposing heavy sacrifices on his family. My father's whole life had been so oriented that a position on the Supreme Court of the United States would have capped his career to perfection. Yet he did not hesitate for one moment. He told Mr. Burleson that it was out of the question and requested that his name not be considered. This must have cost him a sharp pang, yet he never repined and only a very few people ever knew that he had been considered for this appointment.

Of course, I was not aware of my father's political activities during the early part of the century. However, by the time of his abortive senatorial campaign, I had become very conscious of what was going on. I have a distinct recollection of a weekend when Mr. Grasty came out to the farm with my father. I had ridden down to the station to meet them and was sitting in the front seat of the car beside the chauffeur when they began to discuss campaign strategy. I recall very distinctly that my father felt that the *Sunpapers* were perhaps overdoing their support of his candidacy and suggested that they moderate their encomiums, a suggestion with which Mr. Grasty did not agree.

I was then still a student at Boys' Latin School, and I remember that the boys were curious to know what it felt like to have a father whose name was constantly in the headlines. My recollection is that it was quite an uncomfortable feeling.

VI ❧ College Years

When I came home after graduating from the Episcopal High School, my father told me that he had entered me at the Virginia Military Institute. That I was a misfit at VMI was obvious from the first day they tried to fit me into a cadet uniform. What little I had learned at Fort Terry turned out to be worthless, and my natural clumsiness was exaggerated by the fact that I was now beginning to grow taller and thinner and had a scrawny look which the drill sergeant seemed to find quite obnoxious. The "rat system" at VMI was especially difficult for the boys who entered as sophomores, and the class bullies, of whom there were not a few in my class, concentrated their attacks on these hapless "third-class rats," of whom I was one.

Even in the classroom, the new boys had to submit to a form of harassment which made learning difficult, and when it was discovered that I was smarter than most of my classmates, I was subjected to intensive pressure, apparently designed to humiliate. I did not break down under this, but I resorted to subterfuges, the recollection of which still fill me with shame. With the single exception of the Latin class, which was optional and therefore quite small, I have no recollection of any satisfying experience in the classroom during that year. On the drill field I was a "ranker," and my prospects for advancement in rank were negligible.

Strangely, I became quite well known throughout the cadet corps as the result of a fluke. In those days each class at VMI had a large number of members who had been sent there because they were regarded as incorrigible problems by their families. The rebels in each class set as their goal the explosion of a number of smoke bombs equal to their class numeral. Thus, the rebels in my class, which was to graduate in 1921, planned to set off 21 bombs during the course of the year. Of course, the authorities tried to prevent this and made every effort to detect the perpetrators.

At that time there was a guardhouse in the middle of the Quadrangle, which was the barracks where all the cadets lived. Each of the cadet companies took turns in doing twenty-four hour duty at every entrance to the Quadrangle. One night I was assigned to guard duty at the main entrance to the Quadrangle during the hour from 3:00 to 4:00 A.M.

It had been rumored that the rebels in our class would attempt to explode the twenty-first bomb that night, and I was consequently very much on the alert. My post extended from the guardhouse all the way to the parapet in front of the main entrance of the building. Near the end of my duty I heard the noise of bottles being dropped, apparently from windows overlooking the parapet. It was plainly my duty to investigate, but the last thing I wanted was to catch any of my classmates in attempting to explode a bomb, so I deliberately walked away from the noise and toward the guardhouse when suddenly one of my classmates ran out of the guardhouse in his pajamas. As he went by me, he shouted, "Drag ass, Mister," which was a warning to run to cover. I had gotten about fifty feet from the guardhouse when it was blown up by dynamite, with a roar which roused the entire cadet corps.

Fortunately I was not injured, although debris rained all around me. Within moments the captain of my company came up in a livid rage and demanded to know what had happened. He became even more incensed when he learned that the culprit was a member of his company who sat at the same table with me in the mess hall. The following morning I was required to report to the commandant, who demanded that I name the culprit, which I did. As a result, he was expelled and I was booked for neglect of duty.

For some time thereafter, the corps was in an uproar. Those who sympathized with the rebels felt that I should have refused to identify the culprit. Some apparently felt that I should have denied all knowledge, although this would have been a false official statement and, as such, been ground for my expulsion. Others thought I should simply have declined to answer any questions. Still others could not understand why I had not gone to investigate the noises out front, which had apparently been designed to take me away from the neighborhood of the guardhouse. They claimed that my reaction to the noise could not have been predicted. I later learned, however, that the majority of the cadet corps felt that I had acted reasonably, and from that time on, my standing with the other cadets showed some improvement.

I do not remember making any special friends in the cadet corps. As a third-class rat, I was isolated from the other freshmen, who were nearly all in the fourth class. Fraternization between freshmen and upper classmen was possible but was pretty much confined to those who met together on the athletic fields. Toward the end of the year I did establish a few contacts outside of the classroom, but these never developed into real friendships. Undoubtedly one reason for this was the fact that I spent every free minute either in the library or at "Col Alto," the home of my father's friend Henry St. George Tucker. Mr. Tucker had been a professor at Washington and Lee University and for some years represented southwest Virginia in the House of Representatives in Washington. His home was within walking distance of the VMI campus. He had published a book on the limitations of the treaty-making power which expounded a constitutional philosophy identical with my father's, and I pored over a scrapbook in which he had collected the acknowledgments he had received from friends and acquaintances to whom he had sent copies of the book. I especially remember one typewritten letter from President Theodore Roosevelt which ended with the sentence, "I hope to see you in Oyster Bay soon." Before signing the letter, T.R. had stricken the word "soon" and written in "sometime." Mrs. Tucker thought that was a good example of Harvard manners.

Looking back over my year at VMI, I feel somewhat like Henry Adams, who thought that from an educational standpoint his entire academic career was a waste of time. Unlike him, however, I thought my year in that college taught me a good deal about my own shortcomings when under pressure. Since then I have never found it difficult to understand how the totalitarian states succeed in getting the extraordinary confessions which they use in their purge trials.

By the time the academic year had ended, I was glad to see the last of Lexington, although I knew that I would miss the Tucker family. When I first got home, all that I wanted to do was get enough sleep for a change. I found that my parents were planning to take me on a trip to Chester, Nova Scotia, where they had rented a cottage near the Hackmatack Inn for the month of August.

At that time Chester, a little fishing village on Mahone Bay on the Atlantic coast of Nova Scotia, was a yachtsman's paradise in the midst of some of the best sailing waters on the Atlantic coast. For many years several families from Baltimore and Philadelphia had made their summer home there, and there were also a few families from the suburbs of New York, Hartford, and Miami. My parents knew almost all of these families, which included a number of boys and girls of about my age, so that I had no difficulty in finding companionship on the tennis courts as well as on the water. For the first time in my life, I felt like one of the gang, and I soon learned to sail a boat and even took part in a few of the sailing races.

One expedition remains especially vivid in my recollection. The pulpit of the local Anglican church at Chester was occupied for the summer by a clergyman from Philadelphia named Johnson. Dr. Johnson had a boy and a girl who ran around with our crowd, and I was invited by them to go on an overnight expedition which would involve sleeping in a tent in an ocean cove near where the working fishermen unloaded their cargoes of cod for shipment to the packing houses. After an early breakfast we set out in a fishing schooner which stank of codfish. We had not gone far when I realized that I was about to find out what it meant to be seasick. Dr. Johnson, who apparently had an iron stomach, seemed to gloat over the prospect that the youngsters in the party would not be able to take the weather, and soon after we anchored in the ocean and started to fish, he began to taunt his son, saying that he was sure to be the first to lose his breakfast. Thereupon the captain of the vessel said in a broad Scottish accent, "No, sir—it's thot one theer," and pointed at me. Five minutes later I proved that he was right.

After losing my breakfast, I found that I could not raise my head without becoming nauseated again, so I lay down in the bottom of the boat for two hours while the rest of the party fished. I remember that Dr. Johnson opened a picnic basket and that everybody had a little midmorning snack, during which the Johnson boy joined me in getting sick after his father insisted that he eat a hot dog. I will never forget Dr. Johnson's sadistic glee at the weakness of the two young males of the party.

Mercifully, it began to rain and as the wind did not subside and the sea got higher, Dr. Johnson finally agreed to call off the party although, to my secret satisfaction, nobody had caught any fish. Years later, when Dr. Johnson was the rector of St. John's Episcopal Church on 16th Street in Washington, D.C., he got involved in some sort of scandal with a young woman in his congregation, and I was not surprised.

During the summer I had transferred from VMI to the University of Virginia. So, fresh from my holiday in Chester, I landed in Charlottesville, where I was to share a room on Dawson's Row with my sister Valerie's brother-in-law, Jack Barroll, from Chestertown, Maryland. I soon found out that these arrangements were not going to work out. Jack Barroll was very slow-witted and had never been away from home in his life, and while his manners were very gentlemanly, he did not have the faintest idea how to adjust to a roommate. Moreover, what he really needed was a guardian, and I was not cut out for that role. I have no doubt that I was a trial to him in many ways of which I was quite unconscious; at all events he became very unhappy and before the fall term ended he persuaded his brother to take him in, and I was left alone on what I had already learned was regarded by most undergraduates as the wrong side of the tracks.

In 1920 the undergraduate student body of the University of Virginia was sharply divided between the social set and the "unwashed." Most of the social set had been to private schools and all of them joined Greek letter fraternities, above which sat a pyramid of more exclusive organizations, peaking in a hallowed group of seven whose names were secret, to be revealed only at death. By the end of the fall term, nearly all the prep school boys had joined one of the fraternities. Later in the year some of the public school boys—mostly athletes—who had managed to become favorably known to the fraternity set were asked to join. All first-year men who had aspirations to belong to the social set were expected to conform to a well-understood code. They were to wear dark three-piece suits, white button-down shirts, and black knit ties. They were not to appear in public without a hat on, which they were expected to tip whenever they met a senior student on the street. They were expected to take rooms and meals in one of the many private boarding houses which were located near the fraternities, and they were expected to be at all times deferential and inconspicuous in their behavior.

With none of these rules had I complied. Dawson's Row was the wrong place to live, Monroe Hill was the wrong place to get your meals, and I was not about to get into uniform again. In almost all of my classes I was the only first-year man. The boys I had known at the Episcopal High School, and Donnell Tilghman, who had entered Virginia after graduating from Dunham's, were all friendly, but most of them frankly told me that they doubted whether I would find their fraternity brothers congenial. So for a time I felt that once again I was a misfit.

However, I was not long in discovering that there was an attractive social life at the University that was quite independent of the fraternity group. Charlottesville then, as now, was a place to which many families moved in order to participate in the activities the University had to offer. Some of these families had children who attended the University, and some had unmarried daughters. They soon made contacts with students at the graduate and professional schools as well as with congenial members of the faculty and their wives. All of them tended to participate in a variety of activities in which the students could and did share. There was a dramatic society, an orchestra of sorts, and a society which put on plays in French and Spanish. Moreover, theater parties, informal dances, and expeditions to favorite restaurants were frequent. All of these people went to see traveling groups of Shakespearean actors, Russian dancers, and even concert artists of the caliber of Kreisler and Novaes, who occasionally performed in Charlottesville. In the course of time I began to run around with a group who were derisively called "the Fast Younger Set of Charlottesville" by one of the female members. Actually they were a pretty tame lot, but they did have good fun together.

While I devoted a good part of my free time to the activities of this group, I did manage to spend quite a good deal of time in several different fraternity houses where friends of mine were living. As a matter of fact, I had the definite impression that I had a wider acquaintance among the fraternity set than many of its members, who tended to restrict their association to their fraternity brethren. At all events, I came to be on very friendly terms with a number of fraternity boys who were sufficiently broad-minded to wish to associate with others who did not quite fit the fraternity mold.

The first new friend I made at the University was a law student named Curtis Bok, who used to play the piano like a musician but who had a very faulty technique. It turned out that his mother was the founder of the Curtis Institute in Philadelphia and that his father was the publisher of the *Saturday Evening Post* and the *Ladies Home Journal*, whose autobiography had just been published under the title *The Americaniza-tion of Edward Bok,* sometimes flippantly called *The Bokinization of America.* Josef Hofmann, who was a frequent guest in the Bok household, had stopped in the middle of the staircase to listen to Curtis, who was attempt-ing to play a passage in one of Liszt's tone poems. According to Curtis, Mr. Hofmann shouted down the stairs, "There are 520 notes in that passage and you have played 35 of them wrong."

Just the same, Curtis was obviously genuinely musical, and I liked to hear him struggle through Chopin and Liszt, which were his favorites. He taught me to play chess and introduced me to Horsley Gantt, a medical student and long-distance runner who always carried a banana with him to eat while he ran. Horsley later became famous after going to Russia and studying with Pavlov. He came back to the United States and joined the faculty at the Johns Hopkins Medical School, where he learned that medical research had demonstrated that a banana is just what a long-dis-tance runner needs to refuel his body.

After the end of my first year, I shared a room with a boy I did not know named Frederic S. Wight. As it turned out, "Fritz" Wight probably had more influence·on my education than any other single person. To him I owe almost all that I know about poetry. While he was no great poet himself, he understood the art and liked to experiment by writing ses-tinas and other esoteric forms of verse. His mother was a painter whose murals are still well known in professional circles, and she gave him a thorough grounding in art.

Fred was always hard up, as his mother could not afford to give him much pocket money, and he tried to supplement his meager allowance by painting and sketching portraits. I sat as his model for many hours and have a portrait which he painted of me in 1921. He later published a novel and some poems and then became curator of modern art at a museum in Boston. Ultimately he became a professor of fine arts at the University of California at Los Angeles and director of the Frederic S. Wight Museum at that institution. In his eighties, his paintings are now being collected, and he wrote me that he had recently received a check for fifty thousand dollars from his dealer.

Notable among the group with whom I began to spend increasing amounts of my time was a professor named Frank Abbott. In his youth he made a living singing French, Italian and English folk songs on the vaudeville stage, and I have many times heard him sing in private homes in Charlottesville, where he was asked to perform for the benefit of the other guests. In addition to Frank Abbott, there was Betty Booker, who had sung in opera at Covent Garden in London. Frequently her accompa-nist was John Powell, probably the leading American pianist of that era, who had retired to Charlottesville after a successful career in Europe and America as a concert pianist. Powell was very eccentric and had a·mania on the subject of race. He had succeeded in getting a bill introduced in the Virginia legislature to forbid intermarriages between white and colored, defining as "colored" anyone who had an ancestor within the tenth degree who was not of the Caucasian race. As the bill classified as colored people all the descendants of Pocahontas, it did not get very far.

My stay at the University of Virginia was limited to two years, thanks to the expert advice of a friend of my school days who showed me how to get an A.B. in that period. This involved going to summer school at the end of my first year and thereafter taking two graduate courses, one in French and one in Greek. I also had to pass an examination to take advanced standing in some other courses and to persuade the mathematics department to give me credit for work I had done at VMI.

By the time that I had begun my second and final year at the University, I had come to know almost all the people in the community who had intellectual or artistic interests. I was disappointed not to be elected to the Raven Society (that came fifty years later) but gratified that a number of the members of that select group were sufficiently disturbed to start a campaign to have me elected, a campaign which was dropped when it developed that I was one of the very few undergraduates who had been elected to Phi Beta Kappa.

Perhaps most influential of all was my French professor, Richard Wilson. Professor Wilson introduced his students to the whole panorama of French literature. They could and did read the best of French poetry and fiction from the period of the Renaissance to the current winner of the Prix Goncourt. Every member of his graduate class was required to read and report on a current novel and to give a half-hour lecture in French to the class. Needless to say, the most torrid passages were stressed by the students, in whose quarters one would frequently find copies of current French magazines, including some which by the standards of that day were considered to be extremely salacious, such as *La Vie Parisienne*. It was not unusual to walk into a fraternity house and find students playing cards together in French, and I still remember how to bid a bridge hand in that language. Professor Wilson never spoke to his students, in or out of class, except in French.

As I look back on the two years that I spent at Virginia, some things stand out clearly in my memory. During my first year a group of students attempted to produce one of Eugene O'Neill's early plays. I was to have the role of a seaman. Our director was recuperating in Charlottesville from a nervous breakdown which he had suffered after directing the production of this play in New York, where it was a critical success but turned out to be financially disastrous. Why he tempted fate by turning his convalescence into a busman's holiday is more than I can explain. At any rate, it all came to nothing, but from him I learned how to project my voice, which proved to be invaluable to me in courtroom work. I also remember taking a minor part in a production of *The Man Who Married a Dumb Wife*. I also played in a pick-up orchestra which was thrown together at the time of the inauguration of the music department at the University.

A more painful memory is of my debut as a performer of chamber music. I was taking violin lessons at the newly established music school and was astonished when my instructor announced that I was to play the second violin part in a public performance of Mozart's G Minor String Quintet. There was no time for rehearsal but I was given the part to practice and was told that it was perfectly simple and that I would have no difficulty. As might have been expected, in the middle of the performance I lost my place and the quintet turned into a quartet until we reached the end of that movement. Fortunately the audience did not seem to notice my defection.

A third and equally vivid memory relates to my performance of the lead part in a French play by Labiche, in the course of which I was supposed to make a lightning change from a four-in-hand to a bow tie. For that purpose I was permitted to use a bow tie which clipped on the collar button. On the night of the performance, to the great amusement of the audience, the bow tie suddenly sprang away from the collar button and shot on the floor. I picked it up and threw it in the wings and then skipped a whole speech in my part. Fortunately, the boy who was playing the female lead kept his head and somehow we got through the crisis, but it was one of those terrible moments that are never to be forgotten.

One other recollection is of an event which turned out to be more significant than I realized at the time. The *Baltimore Sun* carried a news article reporting that my father had been taken to the hospital for emergency surgery. As I had heard nothing from the family, I assumed that he was getting along all right, but I wrote immediately to my father, thinking that he would be pleased to hear that the state of his health was considered news even in Charlottesville. My mother had been careful not to mention any publicity for fear of upsetting my father, who was concerned for the effect that it might have on his professional career, so my mother had to censor my letter. In actual fact, I have little doubt that the news of his illness had a negative influence on my father's earning power, which was vital to the family fortunes.

During the last few days of the term, I had about made up my mind to apply to Princeton for admission to the graduate school under Dean West, where I was told that I would find an excellent course in comparative literature. Professor Wilson had met me on the street and congratulated me on my final examination, saying that he thought I had "dépasser le cent," so I went to see him and asked if he would endorse my application to Princeton. To my astonishment he refused, on the ground that I was not cut out to be a college professor. He said that in his opinion it would be a waste of my time.

This left me in a quandary, and when I got home I spoke to my father about it. He said he would think it over, but I heard nothing further from him and was beginning to wonder what to do with myself during the coming year when he suddenly told me that he had entered me at the Harvard Law School. When I asked him how he had managed to do that, he said that he had talked to Dean Pound on the telephone and that it was all settled. I could take the room which my brother Fendall had occupied. Fendall had suffered something of a breakdown in health and had decided to transfer from Harvard to the Maryland Law School, so my father had determined to send me there in his place but had forgotten to tell me about it.

VII ❧ Harvard Law School

When "Whiskers" White heard that I was going to the Harvard Law School, he congratulated me, saying, "You are now mature enough to appreciate what Boston has to offer." What he meant had to be lived before it could be understood, and the living began at first quite gradually. Things had been made fairly easy for me to get a good start. I was sharing a comfortable suite of rooms in a rooming house on Brattle Street in Cambridge with my brother Fendall's former roommate, Ben Cory, who was four years my senior. Ben came from California; like two of his classmates who had the rooms next to ours at 44 Brattle Street, he had seen military service in World War I. None of them talked about that—it was definitely not done—but it became very clear to me that these were men and not boys. From them I absorbed a great deal of information about the law school. They told me where to eat, how to get the laundry done, and myriad other details which were very helpful in getting me adjusted to this new life.

Ben Cory was very easygoing and, all things considered, treated me very well in view of the fact that I had been dumped on him without any chance for him to size me up. He was no intellectual and did not share any of my special interests, but he was a serious, well-behaved student. As it turned out, I found more companionship in the next room, where lived a rather masterful character named Jim Osgood, who was also from California. One of the men in that room subscribed to the *Yale Review,* which I took to reading from cover to cover. Jim seemed to me to be much more sophisticated than most of my Virginia friends, although as a good Yale man he was scornful of Harvard students. His advice to me was practical and sensible and he did not hesitate to give it. Through him I was invited to join Lincoln's Inn, an eating club for law students dominated by Harvard, Yale, and Princeton graduates, which was conveniently located right across the street. From him I learned to sit on the side of the visiting team at football games so as to root against Harvard. I also learned how to keep myself physically fit. At first I took long walks by myself, exploring Cambridge out to Fresh Pond and across the Charles River, all the way, on one occasion, to Brookline. However, I found that most students got their exercise on the squash courts, so I followed suit and found it fairly easy to learn to play a passable game.

Meanwhile I was attending my classes faithfully but at first found them hard going. I was still not convinced that I wanted to be a lawyer, and the first-year classes at the law school did little to persuade me that I belonged there. I was particularly frustrated by Professor Manley Hudson, who taught a course in torts, which seemed to me to be almost incomprehensibly vague, and whose classroom manners were insufferably arrogant. (Before I left the school I joined nearly all the top students in my class in naming that course as the most stimulating one in the curriculum.)

As time went on, a bewildering variety of activities began to claim my attention. I found myself poring over the pages of the *Boston Transcript* and particularly the writings of the music critic H. T. Parker. For the first time I had the benefit of musical criticism of the first order by a genuine musicologist. It made me realize that here was a whole field of learning about which I knew next to nothing.

Then there was the theater. Boston saw many plays before they reached Broadway and had a repertory company known as the Copley Players which offered excellent productions of the plays of Shaw and Galsworthy as well as some of the best American playwrights. My introduction to that theater was to a delightful performance of Shaw's *Getting Married,* which I found hysterically funny—so much so that I embarrassed my companion, Kay Cowen, who had been a classmate of my sister's at Bryn Mawr College. Kay was studying the history of art in Boston and was living in Back Bay with her parents, where I visited them soon after I arrived in Cambridge. Mrs. Cowen was a member of the Abbott clan, who had all originally come from Salem, Massachusetts. Through her I was invited to the Salem Assembly where, after first dining at the home of Frank Benson, whose etchings of water fowl were then and still are regarded as museum pieces, we danced on a floor suspended on ropes where George Washington had danced in the eighteenth century. As each couple was presented to the hostesses, the men bowed from the waist and the ladies curtsied nearly to the floor, just as in General Washington's time.

Through Kay I met some of her schoolmates from the days when she was attending a fashionable girls' school, where the young ladies of the best Boston families received their secondary education. Through the Cowens I also was invited to a gathering of the Abbott clan on Thanksgiving Day, where at a huge dinner ceremonial speeches and toasts were given in traditional style. Incidentally, when we spent the night in Salem, I slept in a room with wallpaper depicting hunting scenes which had been on the walls since the eighteenth century.

Kay Cowen was only one of several Bryn Mawr classmates of my sister's who were living in Boston during my years at the Law School. Two others shared an apartment on Commonwealth Avenue with a third girl whose mother was a granddaughter of Cameron Forbes's. As a result, I was invited to spend a weekend at Naushon Island, where the Forbes clan gathered to get a taste of country life. Although I had not been on a horse for several years, I undertook to join a party on a morning ride around the island and found to my dismay that I no longer could sit comfortably on an unfamiliar saddle. As a result, I elected to join a young woman who had decided to walk home and turned her mount over to a groom who was attending the riding party. It turned out that she had planned this maneuver in the hope of attracting a young athlete in the party for whom she was making a dead set. She made no bones about her disappointment when she landed me.

What turned out to be the most enduring and satisfying association was with another classmate of my sister's named Elizabeth Cope. Elizabeth was studying architecture at MIT. She came from a family of Philadelphia Quakers who owned a property called Crowfield on the shore of Narragansett Bay near Saunderstown, Rhode Island. Owen Wister, who also came from Philadelphia, had the place next door. Along with the rest of literate Americans I thought of him as the author of *The Virginian,* but he was better known in Boston as the president of the Tavern Club, where artists and writers and amateurs of art and letters gathered weekly.

Elizabeth's mother was the widow of Walter Cope, the architect who introduced College Gothic to the campuses of America. In many ways Mrs. Cope reminded me of my Slingluff grandmother, but she was much more formidable. At Crowfield scions of old Philadelphia families mingled with Irish revolutionaries and leaders of the IWW, who were fresh out of jail, in an atmosphere that was rigorously intellectual. Plain living, high thinking, good music, and wholesome exercise were practiced in the true Quaker tradition, and time was never wasted. Two of the Cope children were musically talented, and there was usually a professional musician living as a guest in the household. Elizabeth herself was a brilliant student who had inherited her mother's intolerance for triflers. While at first I found the atmosphere of the household a little intimidating, I came to love it and spent some of my happiest hours at Crowfield sailing on the bay in Oliver Cope's boat, which was usually anchored nearby in Wickford Harbor.

My parents had urged me to call on Mr. and Mrs. William Lowell Putnam, who lived on Beacon Hill. Mr. and Mrs. Putnam had met my parents at Williamstown, Massachusetts, during one of the summer conferences which were then being held on the campus of Williams College. Mrs. Putnam was the sister of the president of Harvard, Lawrence Lowell, and of Amy Lowell, whose poems I had studied while at the University of Virginia. I was quite nervous about calling on such notable people, but I was persuaded that I should not miss a chance to come to know them, as they typified old Boston in its most authentic form. So one Sunday afternoon I put on my best outfit and presented myself at Beacon Street. Mrs. Putnam wore a black suit and shirtwaist with a high collar, and her hair was arranged just like my grandmother's; moreover, she spoke with the same note of quiet authority in her voice. I do not remember ever seeing her with a hat on, but Mr. Putnam once told me that after thirty years of marriage he had deliberately sat on her only hat in an effort to make her buy a new one—but to no avail. He himself wore an enormous gold watch with a fob which, he explained, had belonged to his grandfather.

At 4:30 tea was served in a dark room full of family portraits and sculptured busts. During the course of the conversation I was asked whether I played bridge, and when I said that I did they invited me to stay for dinner and make a fourth with their son, "Gus," afterward. Of course I stayed and we had a pleasant family evening. When I left they urged me to come back soon and I did so. This time their daughter and son-in-law, Mr. and Mrs. Harvey Bundy, were there, but again I was needed for a fourth at bridge because one of them had to leave after dinner. From that time on I stopped in at the Putnams on the average of once a month for a Sunday-night dinner and game of bridge, and during the course of that association I think I learned more about the customs and beliefs of old Boston than I could have learned in any other way. When later I came to read *The Education of Henry Adams,* I understood exactly what he was talking about.

The first floor of Beacon Street was given over to offices and to the kitchen and storerooms. The dining room and living room were on the second floor and the bedrooms on the floors above. It was the first time that I had seen an elevator in a private house. On the second floor there was a remarkable collection of paintings which Mr. Putnam had collected in his youth. As I remember, there were a Botticelli and several other paintings representing different Italian schools, but I was particularly struck by a very fine Monet—one of his London series—and a Degas dancer. There was also the first painting of Pissarro's that I had ever seen. Taken altogether, this collection was an introduction to the French Impressionists such as was not to be found in any private home that I had ever visited.

Mrs. Putnam was then Republican national committeewoman for the state of Massachusetts, and I was distinctly impressed when one of the Massachusetts senators came to call on her bringing greetings from President Coolidge. Whether she held that office during the Harding administration I do not know, but I have a distinct memory of hearing Mr. Putnam speak in a sad tone of "poor Fall." He was referring to Harding's secretary of the interior, whose corrupt conduct had brought disgrace to the Republican party which at that time had no parallel since the Grant administration.

Mr. Putnam was a successful businessman whose avocation was mathematics. He had established prizes in mathematics at Harvard College and to the best of my recollection had lectured on that subject. He was a charming old gentleman and could not have been kinder to me. He did warn me not to speak of Ireland or of Irish politicians in the presence of any of the servants, but otherwise I felt free to say anything that I wanted to.

My happy experience with the Putnams encouraged me to call at 17 Quincy Street, where President and Mrs. Lowell received students on Sunday afternoons. Mrs. Lowell was a cousin of the wife of my father's cousin and close friend Archibald Taylor of Baltimore, and this led to the most embarrassing experience in my Law School career. One day I received a telephone call from the president's office inviting me to lunch the following day to meet cousin Archie Taylor and his wife. Of course, I accepted but explained that I had a noon class at the Law School and might be a little late. I was told that this would be quite all right. As it turned out, Professor Edward Warren (the "Bull"), who was the model for the sadistic professor in the movie *The Paper Chase*, chose that day to call on me and to hold me up to ridicule before the rest of his class. This so upset me that I totally forgot my luncheon engagement, and when I got back to my room I found Ben Cory in a great state of excitement because the president's house had been calling to find out where I was. I ran at top speed down to 17 Quincy Street and arrived breathless to find them already at table. When I tried rather incoherently to explain what had happened, Mr. Lowell said that he had always found Mr. Warren to be a very mild-mannered man. Needless to say, I did not contradict him.

Sometime in February the first-year students at the Law School were given a practice examination which was optional. I took it and did quite poorly. From that point on I decided to pay more attention to my classroom work.

However, toward the end of the year, I began to have pains in my stomach and consulted a local surgeon at the Harvard infirmary, who diagnosed my trouble as appendicitis. Since the pains were not acute, he said that I could take my examinations but insisted that I go into the infirmary as soon as they were over. As it turned out, my appendix had not been inflamed and the surgery had been unnecessary. My trouble was a duodenal ulcer, but that was not discovered until the following winter, when I consulted Dr. Thomas Brown in Baltimore.

Following the operation I spent ten days recuperating at the Cowens' summer home in South Lancaster in the country not far from Clinton, Massachusetts. From there I went to Chatham, Massachusetts, where I spent nearly a month with Mrs. Wight and Fred at her cottage near Monomoy Point on Cape Cod. I have very pleasant recollections of listening to Mrs. Wight reading from her family diaries written during the nineteenth century as well as of canoe trips on the bay side of the peninsula, where we saw Justice and Mrs. Brandeis, who were out in their canoe every pleasant afternoon.

When I got home I found that I had made the *Harvard Law Review,* which in those days was considered to be a passport to any law firm in the country. A few weeks later I returned to Cambridge with the feeling that at last I had found my place—a feeling which grew stronger as the months went by. My classroom work went well; I was interested in the courses, liked the professors, and, thanks to my status as a member of the *Law Review,* soon got to know the professors personally and to take an active part in classroom discussion. The work on the *Law Review* itself was at first disappointing, since there was a good deal of routine drudgery which I did not relish, and the senior editors got justifiably annoyed at my reluctance to share the burden. However, I was given a rather tough assignment to write an extended report on a difficult question of partnership law, about which I knew nothing. After a good deal of study I came up with a product which the professor who taught the course in partnership pronounced to be worthy of publication in the *Review.* From that point on I was treated the way the director of an opera company handles one of his leading tenors.

My life outside the classroom was equally satisfying. Toward the end of the first year I had gotten on friendly terms with some Texas boys who during the second year lived together in Claverly Senior House. Each of these boys was in his own way colorful and amusing, and their quarters soon became a center for people looking for good conversation and cut-throat bridge. One of the Texans, Dick Knight, the son of a Dallas lawyer, was a master raconteur, and his tales of the newly rich oil families in Texas were side-splitting. He and his roommate, Tom Joyce, who came originally from California, conducted a constant stream of witty one-liners which reminded everyone of the group who hung around the Algonquin at the Two Hour for Lunch Club in New York. All of us read and enjoyed the columns of Don Marquis of the *Herald Tribune* and Franklin P. Adams, Heywood Broun, and Deems Taylor, who wrote for the *New York World.* In time I began to spend more and more hours in the Claverly Senior House almost every day, and I now realize that I looked upon it as my fraternity. There I increased my knowledge not only of life in Texas but also of a great many other subjects which were of interest to sophisticated youths all over this country.

I was also extending my participation in the cultural life of Boston. Toward the end of my first year I had occasionally been given by Mrs. Cowen a ticket to the Boston Symphony concerts, and I had discovered that while the Saturday-night concerts were generally sold out, if I waited until just before the concert was about to begin, the box office would sell me a ticket which had just been turned in at a nominal figure. In that fashion I got to hear many concerts by that superb orchestra and remember especially attending the first performance in America of Stravinsky's *Rite of Spring*, where I was introduced to John Dos Passos, who had been present at the first performance of that work in Paris when rioting broke out. To me it sounded like the random noise of fifty factory whistles, but Dos Passos obviously made more sense out of it.

On another occasion I went to the opera house to see a performance of *Siegfried* given by the first German opera company to perform in the United States since the war. I could only afford to pay for standing room, which was on the fourth floor, where one stood by a railing which looked directly down on the stage. In the opening scene Brünnhilde lies in a coma under her shield surrounded by magic flames, from which she is rescued by Siegfried, who lifts the shield and exclaims, "Das ist kein mann. Gott wie schön!" ("This is no man. God, how beautiful!") As what was revealed by lifting the shield was a mountain of flesh which was almost as broad as it was long, all of the standees burst out laughing, and I nearly fell over the railing.

It was during this period that I first visited the Dunster Book Shop. Connie Marcy's mother had lent me some books by Aldous Huxley, A. E. Coppard, and Arthur Machen, as well as T. S. Eliot's just published *The Waste Land*. This was my first introduction to the Bloomsbury Set, and I found that the only place in Cambridge which carried their books was the Dunster Book Shop. The proprietor of that store was also promoting a novel called *Moby Dick* by Herman Melville, a writer whose name at that time had been practically forgotten.

I returned to Cambridge looking forward to my final year at the law school with eagerness, and I was not disappointed. I studied international law under Professor Hudson, who was later a judge of the World Court. I also took a course in future interests under Professor Joseph Warren, who taught a rather abstruse aspect of property law. I found the subject fascinating, and when he discovered this, Professor Warren called on me so frequently that the course sounded almost like a dialogue between us. By the time I finished that course I could understand why the word *conveyancer* sounded so dignified when used by a British lawyer.

Probably the most colorful as well as controversial person on the faculty at that time was Professor Felix Frankfurter. I had skipped his courses in municipal corporations and labor law, but I did not want to leave the law school without the benefit of his teaching methods, which were obviously stimulating to his pupils. He also gave a course in administrative law to graduate students, nearly all of whom were teaching or planning to teach in law schools, and he allowed a few boys with *Law Review* standing to take that course for credit on their LL.B. degrees. I was able to persuade him to include me among them, although I gathered that he did so with some reluctance, because he said that I had the reputation of being one of the laziest members of the class. Naturally I made up my mind to overcome that reputation, but I never did complete my thesis, which was to have been a history of the Public Service Commission of Maryland. However, I did write enough to satisfy the requirements of the course and in the process came to know him very well. Indeed, I was one of a group of about a dozen students who met with him by invitation at his home to dine and discuss some legal topic of current interest. Each of us had to read a paper and then submit to his criticism and that of the other students.

At that time Professor Frankfurter was beginning to investigate the case of Sacco and Vanzetti, which was later to become a cause célèbre, largely because he had become convinced that they had been unfairly tried. This was only one of many controversies in which he became involved, and he was well on his way to becoming the leader in what was then the liberal faction of the law school faculty.

Aside from the academic work, I found my life very pleasant. I went to South Lancaster for Thanksgiving dinner with the Cowens and their neighbors the Parkers (it was snowing hard and we traveled through a blizzard on the Fitchburg Local). I went down to Woods Hole on Cape Cod for a weekend with the Redwood family from Baltimore. I was invited to New Haven for the Harvard-Yale game and stayed in a fraternity house as the guest of Parker Crenshaw, who had visited on the farm. There I went to a Yale "prom," where I ran into one or two girls from Baltimore as well as a notorious "prom trotter," who had come down for Easter week during my last year in Charlottesville. I also went to Princeton as the guest of Dick Shackelford, who was then a member of the Ivy Club, and I ran into the same "prom trotter" I had seen in New Haven. This was very high-level collegiate socializing, and the few debutante parties I attended at the Brookline Club in Boston and at Brattle Hall in Cambridge seemed pale by comparison.

As a matter of fact, I had begun to lose my taste for debutante parties. During my school and college years I went out almost every holiday night to one party or another, where I met mostly the same girls I had known in dancing class. When I graduated from college, I was invited to subscribe to the Bachelors Cotillon and made my first appearance at the Lyric on New Year's Eve the following year. There I discovered that the Cotillons were quite remarkable as a spectacle but that as a dance they were ordeals. There was always a list of girls with whom I had to dance or suffer serious reproof from my mother. Furthermore, I was expected to keep an eye on my sister and other female relatives, who had to be carefully watched to make sure they didn't "get stuck" with some "nerd" (a modern term for a type as ubiquitous then as it is now). Add to that a hopelessly crowded dance floor where you could never find the girl you were looking for, and it was easy to understand why my brothers and I always came home exhausted by the time the music stopped.

But perhaps best of everything I got from the law school were some lifelong friends, including Warren Ege, who came from Omaha, Nebraska, and was president of the *Harvard Law Review* during my last year; Harcourt Johnstone, who later became secretary and financial vice-president of the Bethlehem Steel Company; Robert Proctor, who later had a successful career in the air force and as a practicing lawyer in Boston; Bart Leach, who after some years of practice in Boston became a general in the air force and subsequently taught on the full-time faculty of the Harvard Law School; and Francis Plimpton, a New York lawyer who was later the United States delegate to the United Nations and the president of the Century Association in New York City as well as a senior member of the firm of Debevoise and Plimpton.

All through my final year I was much concerned as to where I wanted to practice law. Several of my classmates were headed for Wall Street law firms, and I had friends who were already working there. So during the holidays I went to New York and did the rounds of a number of law offices. I got the general impression that most of them were law factories, where the law clerks worked long hours and had very little opportunity for human contacts. It all seemed too big and bureaucratic.

Professor Frankfurter had suggested that I might be interested in a fellowship at the Law School and perhaps thereafter a clerkship for either Justice Holmes or Justice Brandeis, both of whom were in the habit of looking to him to select their law clerks. Emory Buckner convinced me that a clerkship with a judge, even of the Supreme Court, would be unwise unless I wanted to teach in a law school. In the end I decided to come back to Baltimore and work for two young lawyers who had recently left my father's law office and started in for themselves. They were Southern Marylanders who had served their apprenticeship under my father, were looking for a law clerk, and were willing to take on an associate at the going rate in Baltimore, which at that time was one hundred dollars a month.

VIII ❧ The Grand Tour

In June of 1924, immediately after our graduation from the Harvard Law School, Warren Ege, Hike Johnstone, and I sailed for England on a vessel of the United States Lines, the *President Warren G. Harding,* which had functioned as a troop ship during World War I. I had persuaded them to join me in traveling third class, which at that time was the most economical way of getting abroad. We spent very little time in our quarters, which were so small that there was no room to sit down except on our bunks. Instead, in disregard of the rules, we spent most of our time on the upper decks, where we played games and lay in the sun.

I think it took that old tub more than a week to make the trip to Plymouth, where we went ashore and managed to hire a car and driver for a day's tour of Devon and Cornwall. Most of the roads in that part of England were lined with high hedges which shut off the view and gave us the feeling of traveling through green tunnels. I have a hazy recollection of Truro Cathedral and of a ruin by the Atlantic Ocean which I was told was the remains of Tintagel Castle. We also stopped briefly at Boscastle, a seaside resort with a boardwalk of sorts. Finally we drove across the moors to an inn, which we were told was the headquarters of the Dartmoor Hunt, where we stopped for dinner. The proprietor of the inn and M.F.H. of the hunt turned out to be a former exchange student at the University of Michigan, with the result that we were promptly served "stirrup cups" (the equivalent of two martinis apiece), and given a superb meal ending with a "savory," which followed "the sweet." As I recall it, the savory was an omelet. This was truly a gourmet meal and the last of its kind that we were to see in Great Britain.

In that latitude the sky stayed light until after ten o'clock at night, so we drove on to Exeter in the twilight. There we found rooms in a very attractive nineteenth century hotel, where we sank into comfortable beds after putting our shoes outside the door like true Britishers. The following day we went on to Salisbury and walked around the Cathedral close, where the turf was so thick that it reminded me of what a British gardener told my mother when she asked how he had succeeded in developing so fine a lawn. His reply was, "Well, you seed it and roll it and seed it and roll it and do that for two hundred years and you will get a pretty good lawn."

When we arrived in London, we spent a week doing the usual round, visiting the Tower, St. Paul's Cathedral, Westminster Abbey, and the Houses of Parliament. Although it was not lilac time, I insisted on going down the river to Kew to see the gardens. All I remember about that trip is that it was fiendishly hot on the deck of the boat which took us down the Thames and back. I believe that I dragged my companions to the National Gallery, where I remember particularly some Sargent portraits of a Jewish family which seemed to me quite cruel. We also went to the theatre, first to see a Somerset Maugham play superbly acted except for a character who spoke in a nasal drawl which the British lady in the seat next to me characterized as "typically American." We also went to see a production of *The Merry Widow* which was English music hall at its cheapest.

At this point my companions and I parted company for the time being. They wanted to go to Dublin, and I wanted to visit Oxford and Cambridge and the cathedral towns, and we didn't have time for both. So I spent the week by myself, riding trains to Oxford, Ely, Lincoln, York, and finally to Chester, where I made a pilgrimage to Marbury Hall, which for six centuries had been the home of the Marbury family. It was then owned by Lord Barrymore, a beer baron, who had added to the old home an enormous structure imitating the style of one of the castles of the Loire Valley. As I drove up in my cab, I saw a bearded gentleman in knickers and a Tyrolean hat step out of a side door and wave to my driver to stop. He turned out to be Lord Barrymore's agent, and when I told him my name, he promptly suggested that I dismiss my cab and said that he would take me back to Chester himself. In the meantime he opened the great front doors, which were kept closed except when the owner was in residence, and invited me in. I recall that in one of the great rooms there were a number of portraits, including several which he said were members of the Marbury family. These had been painted in the time of Queen Elizabeth I. Thirty years later my son Luke took a snapshot of me standing in front of the big doors of Marbury Hall, on which he wrote "Mr. Toad of Toad Hall."

My trip through the Cathedral towns made me understand that there was still another whole field of learning about which I was totally ignorant. I listened to the vergers discussing the fine points of Gothic architecture with the British visitors and found myself completely out of my depth. Moreover, I got pretty tired of dining by myself at temperance houses, which were then the nearest thing to the youth hostels of today.

I got back to London to find that my parents and my sister Silvine were staying at Brown's Hotel. I also ran into my classmate Horry Frost, a South Carolinian who had lived at 44 Brattle Street during my first year at law school. He was staying with his family at another hotel, and our two families got together for dinner, where we found ourselves very congenial. My mother was very much taken with Horry, and when she learned that he was planning to come to Baltimore to practice law with the firm of Piper, Carey & Hall, she suggested to his parents that he might like to stay with us at 159 West Lanvale until he found accommodations. They were delighted with the idea.

At this point I joined up again with my traveling companions and we headed for Paris. There we stayed at a small hotel called Hotel de Londres, on the Left Bank near the Sorbonne. It had very primitive plumbing and was much patronized by students from the south of France who were studying at the university. During the next ten days the three of us explored the city, sometimes together, sometimes separately. Like all students, we went to Montmartre, the Folies Bergère, and the Casino de Paris, visited the Louvre to see the Mona Lisa and the Victory of Samothrace, Notre Dame Cathedral and the Sainte Chapelle, and the Trocadero. I fell in love with Paris and especially the Left Bank, its book stalls along the river and its open air cafés and restaurants. I had read many French novels which described the life of students in Paris and, of course, was familiar with du Maurier's *Trilby,* which romanticized that life for generations of English and American readers.

One day I called on Kay Cowen, who was then studying in Paris and living at the home of an impoverished French countess who took in carefully selected foreign students. It was a Sunday and she took me to a service at the Russian Orthodox church, where I was deeply impressed by the liturgy and especially the magnificent singing of the choir and congregation, which was largely made up of refugees from the Bolshevik regime, then triumphant in Russia. I especially enjoyed the Russian bass singers, who had a quality different from any I had ever heard.

I asked Kay to have lunch with me after the church service at a restaurant in the Bois de Boulogne, which was down the avenue about a mile away from the church. She said she would have to consult Countess Niyon, who somewhat grudgingly gave her approval. Kay explained to me that it would have been utterly impossible for her to walk and lunch in the Bois with any European, as it would have ruined her reputation, but since everyone would recognize that I was an American student, they would assume that I was her brother and not her lover. When I asked how they would know that I was an American student, she laughed and said it was unmistakable. This gave me quite a shock, as I had fancied that I was quite cosmopolitan looking.

Our next stop was in Geneva, Switzerland, where I have a vivid recollection of dining high above the city at a restaurant over the border in France. Our host was Professor Hudson, who was then working on the staff of the League of Nations. I recall that we sat on the balcony of a hotel looking out over the valley to the Jura Mountains and that we were given a drink of Dubonnet before dinner.

My companions and I decided that we must see the Matterhorn, and so we took off for Zermatt, arriving there in a downpour. We found that all the hotels were full but the doorkeeper at the largest hotel said that he had beds for rent in his chalet. So we spent the night in Swiss feather beds in a shack built over a mountain stream. When later on I saw "Falling Waters," I knew where Frank Lloyd Wright had gotten his idea. The next morning was bright and we climbed several miles up a steep path to the top of the Gornergratt, from which we had a stunning view of the Matterhorn.

Here I quote from a letter which I wrote to my mother on August 11, 1924:

I also spent a day in Chartres. Unfortunately it rained, but the Cathedral was quite charming just the same. The stained glass was superb but I still prefer the interior of the English cathedrals. Perhaps it is my training that makes me like the comparative bareness of the Anglican cathedrals inside but I do think they are more beautiful.

Churches are another matter. I saw three in Verona that were simply superb. There is nothing to compare with them in my experience. They are truly houses of God—not just establishments. An Italian parish church looks as though God were expected to live in it and so it is filled with thousands of knick-knacks—flowers, cards, cushions, paintings, sculpture, tiled floors, decorated ceilings and everything to make Him feel comfortable and homelike. In other words, it expresses an entirely different religious feeling from ours. It is a lovingly prepared villa into which it is not so absurd to imagine that God might enter from time to time. All of which goes to show that the Italian church organization, which in its priests and its manners seems to us so unattractive and commercial, has somehow built up a religion in which the masses of the people can take part with very little effort. In Milan (I was only there two hours but time enough to see the Cathedral) a christening was going on at a little side chapel. The whole affair was as businesslike as the daily bath (assuming that Italians ever do bathe their babies). It is, from my point of view, a purely worldly performance, especially as one of the priests dashed out from time to time to collect money from the bystanders, but it seems natural and easy to follow and there you are.

Anyhow from Paris I traveled down to Alsace as I told you before. It is a very lovely and most interesting countryside but the people were not too sympathetic. They all spoke three languages but had bad manners. The Strasbourg Cathedral was closed from 11:30 to 2 in order that everyone might be forced to pay to see the clock carry on. It is the first time I have been unable to see a cathedral for such a reason. The Alsatians are very discontented with the French because of certain laws having to do with the suppression of monasteries, etc. I am being gradually driven to the conclusion that no European nation except England has any notion of how to govern a people of different customs.

My stay in Venice was more or less standard. I did all the usual things, including visiting the Lido, where I rented bathing trunks which in that

time of modesty made me feel that I was guilty of indecent exposure. I
very soon saw that compared with the German tourists who were swarm-
ing all over the beach, I was dressed like a Victorian prude. I left via a
local train from Venice headed first for Cortina d'Ampezzo in the Dolomites. The train was crowded with people going up for a weekend in the
mountains. The little Italian which I had learned at Virginia proved almost totally useless when I tried to eavesdrop on the animated conversations that were going on around me. I was particularly fascinated by a
local magnate who seemed personally acquainted with virtually all the
other passengers and spent his time apparently mending political fences,
with evident success from the guffaws of laughter that accompanied his
progress through the car. At Cortina I felt very much alone and went to a
band concert in the open air in an unsuccessful search for amusement.

From Cortina I went by bus to a little Tyrolean village which the Italians called San Martino and the Austrians called Innichen. As part of the
spoils of war it had been annexed by Italy, but the inhabitants were all still
Austrians at heart. There I stayed at a little inn which had been recommended to me by Kay Cowen. The inn was owned and operated by Austrians, as was the rest of the village. At first I nearly put my foot in it when
I showed reluctance to hang the key to my room on the outside of the
door where any passerby could make use of it. This insulted the maid who
was showing me to my room, and she immediately called the manager
and said in German, "The gentleman thinks we are thieves." I summoned
up my rusty German and finally convinced them that I was only kidding.
The manager said I was not to worry as they kept a careful eye on
strangers.

Quoting again from my letter of August 11, 1924:

> Here in Innichen I am in what was always Austria but is now Italy. When
> the Italians took back *Italia Irredenta* which really belonged to them, they pro-
> ceeded with characteristic intelligence to take a lot of good sound Austrian
> country with the consequence that Austria now has a battle cry of "Austria
> Irridenta." Isn't it insane? The reasons were "military"—an excellent way of
> insuring a war sometime in the future. Now how do they govern these peo-
> ple? Just as you might expect. The place is full of Italian soldiers, mostly fine
> looking goodnatured fellows. All the signs are written in Italian. . . . The
> young men are conscripted into the Italian military service but with a gleam
> of sense they are quartered in the neighborhood. Mine host is named
> Guiseppe Baumgartner. Can you tie that?
>
> Last night I met a young Italian journalist from Rome—quite discon-
> tented with existence in Italy and wanting to get to America. I tried to steer
> him off. We conversed in French. He knows more words but my pronuncia-
> tion is better so we are about even. He took me to a pension nearby where I
> met about a dozen boys and girls, half of them Italians the rest Austrian. The
> Austrians talk German with one another and at me. The Italians talk French
> to the Austrians and to me. No one spoke English, consequently it was a great

party. Everyone spoke a little French and seemed quite fascinated with an American in Innichen.

We danced—they dance pretty badly (stiff legged) and their games— what do you suppose? As follows: "Going to Jerusalem"—"Railroad Train" —"Boston"—"Bump the Bumps" and "Winks." Every single one of those games we used to play in Chester. The Italian lady would explain to me in French and a little Viennese in German. All looked exceedingly astonished when I recognized each game as it came along. Furthermore I was called on to provide games but I knew only word games and the Viennese said that was impossible because nobody could speak the other's language well enough. The young ladies were "bien élevées." I might as well have been in Chester or Baltimore except for the absurd language difficulties.

And my heavens how they do treat you. There was a Hungarian about my age with whom I exchanged about two or three words. Today he came up to me and explained that he had to leave and he was so sorry etc. shook my hand three times, bowed—introduced me to his family and altogether treated me as though I were a dear and close friend. The Italians are the same. They really are charming people and ridiculously courteous. My journalistic friend insists on paying for everything, which is simply amazing to me.

The Austrians look like Baltimoreans—there's no getting around it. Their dress, everything is like that of a Baltimorean of good family. They look so darned American that I was completely fooled at first.

In my letter I mentioned that I attended a dance, but I did not say that I nearly put my foot in it again because I tried to "break" a couple who were dancing by me. Apparently that was simply not done. They looked at me with astonishment and I might have gotten into real trouble had not one of the boys who had seen American movies burst into a fit of laughter and explained that this was a barbarous American custom and not an insult. While I found their company very congenial, I was shocked by the bitterness with which they all spoke of the Jews who according to them were monopolizing all the professions in their home countries. This was long before Hitler had gotten out of jail, but I could not help remembering the anti-Semitism of these young people when the Nazis began to sing that same tune.

Again I quote from my letter of August 11, 1924:

I spent one more day in the company of the Italians. There were six young officers as good-looking a bunch of fellows as ever you saw; none of them looked as though he had ever had a care or a thought. They were most courteous to me and talked in the most friendly way. I never saw people so anxious to please—when I left every single one wanted to know if I would remember Italy and the Italians. They all asked me what I thought of Italy, etc. etc. It was a little pathetic.

From Innichen, all day long by train to Graz. How glad I am that I came. I intended to stay a few hours—I am staying two days. Uncle Pojtaz simply beams whenever he looks at me. He always takes my hand at least four times when I go and says, "Grüss dich Gott" over and over. I think he is a dear old gentleman and he still makes sense when he talks although his mind will not run along certain channels. . . .

The people here are not suffering but they are very poor. In the third class I was crowded in between eight Austrians including a Gräfin and a Baroness returning from a giddy period of three days on the Lido. The Gräfin was an old lady of 70 and as pert as you please. She got off at Graz and pushing two porters out of the way with a superb gesture, carried her own bag to the door and with the extravagance of those rich Austrians took a tramway. I could hardly restrain my indignation thinking of the starving poor etc. It really was ridiculous. The cut of their clothes and their general style would have fitted a private car much better.

During the two days I spent in Graz, Hilda von Dorsner showed me about that city with its lovely park, where we dined on top of a little mountain right in the center of the town. Hilda also introduced me to a young Austrian count named Ludwig Attems who invited me to dine with him at a local café. His father had been the Austrian foreign minister who had drafted the ultimatum to Serbia in 1914 which precipitated World War I. Lupke, as they called him, was in the contracting business and told me that he could speak seven languages but found English the most difficult of all because the grammar was so arbitrary. When I expressed astonishment at his versatility, he explained that with the dissolution of the Austrian Empire nobody could succeed in the contracting business unless he could negotiate in Hungarian, Roumanian, Czech, and Serbo-Croatian as well as German. He added that of course every educated European had to be fluent in French and English. During the course of the evening an obviously tipsy man at one of the nearby tables called out something to him at which he laughed and shook his head. He then explained to me that the man had invited him to come back to his apartment and made a homosexual proposition. Apparently, judging by the laughter and expression on the faces of the other people in the café who heard what he said, this was all regarded as "a source of innocent merriment," to quote W. S. Gilbert out of context.

From Graz I proceeded to Vienna by train and put up at a dingy hotel near the railroad station. Austria was nearing the end of a disastrous inflation of her currency, and a ride on the streetcar cost 7,000 crowns. I handed the conductor a note for 10,000 crowns, but he refused it, saying that I had to deposit the exact fare. A fellow passenger very accommodatingly made change for me, explaining that the conductor could not risk a change in the rate of exchange which might affect the value of my note before he could turn it in at the end of the day.

The lobby of the Hotel Adlon was nearly empty, as were most of the shops which were located down near the cathedral. All in all, I had a lonesome time in Vienna. As an illustration, I can mention a rather pathetic incident. On several evenings I had dined by myself in a somewhat down-at-the heels café, where I noticed a rather sad-looking middle-aged woman who appeared to be a regular patron, although I never saw her eat a meal. The third time I went to the café, she came over and sat by my table and told me that she was an American who had been left penniless in Vienna by a businessman with whom she had been living—I gathered without benefit of clergy—for more than a year. Even naive as I was I could recognize this as a typical come-on, but I was so grateful to have someone to talk to that we conversed for nearly an hour, after which I bought her a drink and gave her a substantial tip, which she accepted after a feeble protest.

At the Adlon I learned that I could fly to Munich. At that time travel by air was a novelty, and I had never been in a plane in my life, so it was with some trepidation that I rode out to a deserted airport and climbed into a single-engine plane which had space for only the pilot and four passengers. I was astonished to see that the pilot was dressed in the uniform of a German army officer. To the best of my recollection Germany was forbidden by the Treaty of Versailles to have an air force, and this was apparently one of the ways that it was training pilots.

The only other passenger was an elderly man with a long white beard who greeted me in a strange tongue. It turned out that he was an Englishman who had been attending an international conference at Vienna of teachers of Esperanto. He explained to me that they had been engaged in planning for world peace through propagation of that language. I remarked that I was sorry to have seen so little of Vienna, whereupon he said, "Just look out the window and you can see all that is worth seeing." He went on to say that on behalf of the Esperanto cause, he had visited almost every major city in the Western world and that he had never stopped anywhere more than forty-eight hours. The plane had no toilet facilities, but he undertook to make use of a paper receptacle which he then attempted to throw out the window of the plane, with the result that the contents blew back all over me.

In August of 1924 Munich had as much charm as Paris. I stayed at the Hotel de L'Univers et de Strasbourg, where accommodations were comfortable and cheap. The gardens by the river, the museums, and the broad avenues were full of delights. Whereas Vienna had been a tired old city in the throes of a devastating inflation, Munich was benefiting from a recent stabilization of the German currency. The shops were full of beautiful objects of art which could be purchased for very little in American dollars. For the first time I saw paintings by artists of the Expressionist School, which was hardly known outside of Germany. I have to admit that my taste was not sufficiently well trained for me to appreciate the value of all that I saw, but I was sufficiently informed to realize that there were unparalleled opportunities for collectors. Many local residents had survived the inflation by selling off old family heirlooms, with the result that the streets were a paradise for shoppers.

Musically speaking, Munich was very much alive. At the Prinz Regenten Theater I went to a performance of *Tristan,* which was my first experience in top-flight Wagner. The performance began at two-thirty in the afternoon and, with a two-hour break for dinner, went on until nine at night. Nearly everyone followed the opera with scores open in their laps and little flashlights. The orchestra and the singers were superb, especially the tenor, who disclosed a voice with a range and stamina the like of which I had never heard. I had seen performances of *Die Meistersinger* at the Metropolitan and had been to a complete *Ring Cycle* in Baltimore, but this was obviously a much more intellectual approach to Wagner than I had ever witnessed, and I was deeply impressed.

Shortly after my arrival, I went to call on Fräulein Hillermann, with whom my great-aunt Silvine von Dorsner had lived and shared a studio in Munich since they were students together at the Académie Julien in Paris. Hillermann, as I had been told to call her by my aunts, was a charming old lady who gave me a new insight into the artistic life of Munich. She insisted on taking me out to dinner and a movie, the name of which I have forgotten. I noticed in her studio a very handsome portrait of a lady with a cello. She told me that it was a copy of a Van Dyke which she had made for a wealthy businessman who wanted to decorate a newly acquired castle but had died before her work had been completed. As a result the deal had fallen through so the painting was left on her hands. However, she liked it and decided not to sell it to anyone else. I admired it and still do, as she left it to me in her will, and it is now hanging in my living room at 43 Warrenton Road.

With much regret I left Munich to return to France where, with a brief stopover in Paris, I took the United States Lines once more, but this time I traveled third class on their largest and most comfortable ship, which was known as the *United States.* That trip I remember making the acquaintance of a young assistant professor of psychology at Princeton named Leonard Carmichael, with whom I had long discussions about the psychology of lawyers. We planned to write a joint article on that subject, but I never got around to preparing the first draft, which was my responsibility. The next time I saw Leonard he was the president of Tufts University in Massachusetts. Later he became secretary of the Smithsonian Institution in Washington.

So ended my grand tour, and I began the practice of law in Baltimore right after Labor Day in the year 1924.

IX ✦ My Salad Days

Ten Dollars an Hour

The firm of Clagett and Thomas consisted of two young lawyers who were not fated to get along very well. Both were bright men but both had weaknesses which in the end were bound to lead to a rupture. The abler man was James Thomas from St. Mary's County, who had several relatives who had attained considerable prominence in Baltimore financial circles. Jim had a very good legal mind and an engaging personality, but he was a brooding type with a weakness for secret drinking, which in the end was his undoing. During the two years I worked for him, he was forging ahead professionally, but I now realize that all the tell-tale signs were there for those who knew how to read them. Charles Clagett, who came from an old Prince George's County family, was a gifted financial planner and draftsman, but he could fairly be described as a living anachronism who paraded all the prejudices of his grandparents with great pride in his loyalty to the family ideals. An instinctive understanding of finances was all that saved him from being a ridiculous figure.

Of all this I was unaware. I was much too busy preparing for my bar examinations, getting to know my way around the courthouse and the bar library and trying to fill in the gaps which I soon discovered in my legal education. I had not been equipped to be of much help around the office; I could draft memoranda on specific points of law, and that was about all. In short, I had a great deal to learn and had it not been for the clerks in the various courts, I would have felt quite lost. They were patronizing but nevertheless helpful, largely, I believe, because they all liked my father.

One of the first things I learned had to do with an elementary rule of professional ethics. Asked to handle the investigation of a small claim against a client of the office, I proceeded to try to question the claimant without previously notifying his lawyer. This was before the day of pre-trial discovery proceedings, and it seemed to me foolish to go to trial without knowing what the other side was going to produce in the way of testimony. It never occurred to me that it would be unethical for me to try to find that out by what seemed to me to be the most direct way. However, I learned the hard way that a lawyer could communicate with another lawyer's client only through that lawyer if he wanted to avoid being hauled before a grievance committee of the bar association. Fortunately the lawyer in that case was content with suggesting to me that I study up on the rules of ethics.

I remember two cases in which I acted as an assistant to Jim Thomas. The first was a rather substantial claim for breach of contract which one of his banking relatives was asserting against a group of small businessmen who were widely known in Baltimore City. At the first trial we lost that case before a jury, but fortunately for us the judge had made an error in instructing the jury and a new trial was granted. During the first trial I had been watching the members of the jury, and I noticed that several of them seemed displeased when Jim Thomas said anything disrespectful of the defendants. I suggested to Jim that before the second trial we ought to get hold of the jury list and find out whether any of them had had business dealings with any of the defendants. I thought that through our client's banking connections, he might be in a position to obtain that information. At first Jim said that he hesitated to investigate the jury, but one of the clerks had told me that the local transit company always did this and so he somewhat reluctantly agreed to see what could be done. Sure enough it turned out that the defendants were very close to several of the people on the jury list, and by the use of peremptory challenges we were able to eliminate them, and this time we got a favorable verdict for our client.

Another case from which I derived a useful lesson was an ejectment suit which we brought on behalf of an Ohio millionaire who had bought a waterfront property on the Patuxent River. We tried that case in Charles County before a jury, and Jim Thomas let me argue some evidence points.

Thus, I was beginning to learn something of the art of trial advocacy, and in the meantime I was asked by several of my father's partners to prepare memoranda on points of law, for which they compensated me at the rate of ten dollars an hour, which I turned over to my firm. Within a year after my admission to the bar, the firm of Clagett and Thomas dissolved and, at the insistence of my father's partners, I became associated with the firm of Marbury, Gosnell and Williams.

Marbury, Gosnell and Williams

When I started to work full time for the firm of Marbury, Gosnell and Williams, I was the only associate in a firm of seven lawyers, and I soon realized that I was sitting in the catbird seat. At Harvard, Professor Calvert Magruder, whose father had been a judge of the Court of Appeals of Maryland, had told me that Marbury, Gosnell and Williams was in need of new blood, but as a matter of fact the firm in 1926 still had a large and varied practice. Although my father had passed his prime, he was still frequently taken into difficult cases by other lawyers. Mr. Gosnell, even in his late seventies, was still being consulted by trust officers on problems arising in connection with the administration of estates. George Weems Williams had a varied and growing practice ranging from admiralty matters to corporate financing, and William L. Rawls, although handicapped by impaired vocal chords as a result of an attack of tuberculosis, was generally recognized as a brilliant and scholarly lawyer. These men generated more than enough assignments of work to keep me busy.

At first I prepared memoranda on points of law, but very soon I began working on cases pending in the Court of Appeals of Maryland. In those days that court allowed each side to argue for an hour and a half, and senior partners in the firm generally let the younger lawyers write the brief and make the opening argument. The first briefs I wrote read too much like law review articles, and I soon learned that the primary function of a brief was to show the court how it could write an opinion in favor of your client. By the same token, the chief function of the oral argument was not to engage in a discussion of abstract legal points but to marshal the facts in such a way as to incline the court to decide in your favor.

The Hearst Contempt Case

By all odds, the most remarkable matter in which I was involved during my early years with the firm arose in the Criminal Court of Baltimore City. By that time the citizens of Baltimore had come to realize that the social climate which had existed before World War I had undergone a radical change. Most Baltimoreans had grown up in neighborhoods which were virtually untouched by violent crime. However, in 1922 the murder in broad daylight of William B. Norris, a respected businessman who was carrying the payroll of his contracting business from the bank at the corner of Park Avenue and Madison Street, struck fear into the community. The sensational trial which followed concentrated attention on the functioning of the Criminal Court of Baltimore City, and this was enhanced when Judge Eugene O'Dunne was assigned to that court. Judge O'Dunne was a man for whom the adjective *flamboyant* might have been invented. He was a native of New Mexico who had changed his name from Dunne to O'Dunne when he moved to Baltimore and went to work as a reporter for the *Baltimore Sun*. Later he had served a term as assistant state's attorney, during which time he had thoroughly mastered the art of attracting public attention to himself. He had a brilliant legal mind and when he got into a controversy, which was fairly frequent, his opponents found that they needed to keep their wits about them.

In 1926 Judge O'Dunne was called on to preside at the trial of Reese Whittemore, charged with the murder of a guard while escaping from the Maryland State Penitentiary. Judge O'Dunne learned that a photographer for the *Baltimore News* had taken a picture of Whittemore as he was leaving the lock-up in the courthouse on the way to his courtroom. He sent for the photographer and demanded that he turn over the plate, at the same time advising him that he intended to forbid the taking of any photographs in or near the courtroom during the trial. The photographer surreptitiously switched plates and handed a blank to the judge. Judge O'Dunne then entered the courtroom, which was crowded with newspaper reporters from New York and Philadelphia as well as from the local press. The *Baltimore News* and the *Baltimore American* had recently been acquired by the Hearst Publishing Company, and Judge O'Dunne was outraged when the afternoon editions of both Hearst papers carried not only the lock-up photograph but also other photographs taken in the courtroom during the morning proceedings in defiance of the court order. He immediately signed an order to the sheriff to arrest the photographer and to bring him and the editors of both Hearst papers into his court at eight o'clock that night.

George Weems Williams had represented the Hearst Publishing Company in its recent acquisition of the *News* and the *American,* and he received a telephone call from Mr. Hearst's local representative asking him to appear on behalf of the photographer and the editors of the two newspapers. Mr. Williams was successful in persuading Judge O'Dunne to set the matter down for hearing a week later, but in the meantime the judge directed that the sheriff keep the photographer in his custody. Mr. Williams then got in touch with me and told me that he wanted me to be prepared to argue the question of the judge's legal authority to prohibit the taking of pictures in the courtroom and to punish as a criminal contempt the disobedience of such an order.

My argument turned into an extended debate with the judge in which I explored pretty thoroughly the history of the contempt power. According to a valedictory speech made by Judge O'Dunne when he retired from the bench some years later, my argument dissuaded Mr. William Randolph Hearst from employing New York counsel to represent his papers, although it did not succeed in persuading Judge O'Dunne to dismiss the contempt citations. On the contrary, he sentenced the photographer to a day in jail and fined the editors five thousand dollars.

A Variety of Tribunals

While my participation in the Hearst contempt case was by far the most spectacular feature of my early years at the bar, it was only one of many experiences which contributed to my development as a lawyer during that period. I tried cases before a variety of tribunals, ranging from an Anne Arundel County justice of the peace—who was not a lawyer and who held court in his kitchen—to the Supreme Court of the United States.

My first appearance in the clerk's office of the Supreme Court was a rather ridiculous one. My father had asked me to take charge of the printing and filing of a brief in a case which was pending in that court, and I discovered to my horror that the printer had failed to indicate on the cover the fact that this was the brief of the appellant. This was a clear violation of the rules, but fortunately I discovered it on the same day that the brief was delivered to the clerk's office of the court. I immediately rushed over to Washington, arriving completely out of breath. I apologized to the clerk for the error and spent the rest of the day making the necessary correction by hand on all the copies which the printer had delivered to him that morning.

While most of my work during this period was done under the nominal supervision of one of the senior partners in the firm, I was left pretty much to my own a large part of the time and soon began to feel confident of my ability to handle whatever problems came along. Indeed, this confidence soon led me into trouble. One day Mr. Williams handed me an order enjoining a labor union from proceeding with a threatened strike and told me to get it signed by Judge H. Arthur Stump, who had been assigned to summer duty in the Circuit Court of Baltimore City that week. I knew nothing about the case and had never had occasion to look up the applicable law. However, Judge Stump signed the order without asking any questions, and I arranged to have it served on the officers of the union.

Mr. Isaac Lobe Straus, who had been attorney general of Maryland, was retained by the union and immediately called Judge Stump's attention to a recently adopted rule of the Supreme Bench of Baltimore City which required that no such order be signed without giving prior notice to the union. Judge Stump then sent for Mr. Williams and told him that he felt that I had misled him by failing to tell him about the rule. The fact was that I had never heard of it, but, of course, that was no excuse.

The judge set the matter down for hearing the next morning, and when we arrived in court, he kept us waiting for nearly an hour. At the end of that time he took his seat on the bench and when the case was called announced that he had carefully read the order which he had signed and so far as he could see, it did not prevent the union from doing anything it had a legal right to do. Nevertheless, he felt obliged to rescind the order since it had been signed without the notice required by the rule, but now that proper notice had been given, he was prepared to sign an identical order, differing only in the date on which it was to become effective. When Mr. Straus rose to argue against the proposed new order,

Judge Stump said, "General Straus, the Court is always pleased to hear from you, but since I have made up my mind about this, it will serve no useful purpose, so please take your seat, Sir." He then dictated the new order from the bench and the case was over.

I expected Mr. Straus to explode with outrage but instead he turned to Mr. Williams and said, "Judge Stump always has such beautiful manners that it is a pleasure to appear in his Court." I thought he was being sarcastic, but looking back I now realize that he was perfectly sincere and I would have done better to learn from this bizarre case that good manners in the courtroom nearly always pay off. Judge Stump accomplished what he set out to do, for the strike was promptly settled and he was able to get back to his beloved golf course.

The Duchess of Windsor and What She Forgot

Equally instructive was a case which came to my father as the result of the death on October 27, 1927, of Mr. S. Davies Warfield, who had been one of my father's companions in arms during the days of the Reform Movement. "Sol" Warfield had in the meantime become one of the leading businessmen of the United States, and when he died he left an estate which was then estimated to be in the neighborhood of five million dollars. He was survived by a brother, Henry M. Warfield; a niece, Wallis Warfield Spencer, who was the daughter of his brother Wallis; a nephew, Douglas R. Warfield, who was the son of his brother Richard Emory; and a great-niece, Josephine Metcalf Warfield, whose deceased father was also a son of Emory's.

On the day following Mr. Warfield's death, a will drawn by Samuel Untermeyer of the New York City bar was offered for probate in the Orphans' Court of Baltimore City. Under the terms of that will, a trust fund of fifteen thousand dollars was established for Wallis Warfield Spencer, the income from which was to be paid to her, provided, however, that if she should remarry, her right to receive income from the trust estate would terminate. A small legacy was left to Douglas Warfield, and Henry M. Warfield was named as one of the three co-executors of the will. No mention whatsoever was made of Josephine Metcalf Warfield. The bulk of the estate was left to trustees for the purpose of establishing a home for aged gentlewomen to be located at Manor Glen, Mr. Warfield's country estate.

A few months after Mr. Warfield's death, Douglas Warfield came to see my father. He said that in view of the size of the estate, it was his feeling that his uncle should have made further provision for his family heirs. This was particularly true of Wallis Warfield Spencer, who had made an unfortunate marriage and had been dependent on her Uncle "Sol" for support, and of Josephine Metcalf Warfield, who was only seven years of age and had not even been mentioned in the will. Josephine's mother had consulted a New York lawyer, who had advised her that she should contest the will on Josephine's behalf.

Douglas Warfield said that all the heirs were agreed on the establishment of the home for aged women. However, he felt that this could be done with much less than five million dollars. He mentioned the sum of two million dollars as being one which all the heirs might be willing to see devoted to the establishment of the home at Manor Glen. He asked my father whether he would be willing to represent the heirs. My father replied that he would consider the matter but wished first to consult with Mr. Irvine Cross, who had also been closely associated with Mr. Warfield in the Reform Movement.

Douglas Warfield later presented my father with an agreement signed by him, Wallis Warfield Spencer, and the guardian of Josephine Metcalf Warfield which provided that if the will was set aside, they would agree to pay the trustees named in the will the amount my father and Mr. Cross should agree upon with the executors of the will for the purpose of establishing the home at Manor Glen. Settlement negotiations with the executors followed which were complicated by the filing of a claim by a Mr. Nutt which required the sale of most of the estate's holdings in securities of the Seaboard Railway. In the meantime, the value of the estate sank below two million dollars, and Douglas Warfield announced that he would no longer contest the will. However, Josephine Metcalf Warfield's mother, through her New York counsel, insisted that a caveat be filed on her daughter's behalf, challenging the validity of the will in its entirety. Mr. Douglas Warfield said that he could not speak for Wallis Warfield, who in the meantime had divorced her first husband and married an Englishman named Simpson. He said that he would get in touch with her and have her communicate with my father.

My father and Mr. Cross then filed a petition and caveat on behalf of Josephine in the Orphans' Court of Baltimore City, in which they challenged the validity of Mr. Warfield's will and requested that issues be sent to the Baltimore City Court for trial.

In the meantime, Mrs. Simpson, accompanied by her new husband, came to see my father. I was present at this interview and have a distinct recollection of a very well dressed, handsome woman who expressed forcibly her dissatisfaction with the way the estate had been handled. My father explained to her the problems which had been created by the Nutt claim and by the insistence of the guardian of Josephine Metcalf Warfield that a caveat be filed contesting the validity of the entire will. He pointed out that if Josephine's effort to set the will aside failed, it was her intention to bring a separate proceeding challenging the validity of the gift of the residuary estate to the trustees, on the ground that it was an illegal perpetuity. After a full discussion, in which Mr. Simpson participated, Mrs.

Simpson agreed to leave the whole matter in the hands of my father and Mr. Cross. She then signed the following paper:

KNOW ALL MEN BY THESE PRESENTS, THAT I, WALLIS WARFIELD SIMPSON, of the City of London, England, do hereby constitute nominate and appoint William L. Marbury, of the City of Baltimore, and State of Maryland, and W. Irvine Cross, of Baltimore County, in the State of Maryland, or either of them in the absence of the other, to be my true, sufficient and lawful attorneys in fact, for me, and in my name, place and stead to act for me in the following matters and no others:

To take any action that may be approved by my said attorneys in fact, or either of them, for the maintenance of any claim I may have against the estate of the late S. Davies Warfield, and in so doing to institute in my name and behalf any suit or suits, action or actions, at law or in equity, to prosecute them to judgment or dismiss or compromise the same, to negotiate for a settlement of my said claim, and in so doing to enter into any agreement of compromise, to receive any moneys coming to me, to give acquittance for the same, to sign my name to any legal paper, or any receipt, release, or order of satisfaction, with all the power I would have if personally present.

This agreement to expire July 25th, 1930.

WITNESS my hand and seal this 25th day of July, 1929.

Wallis Warfield Simpson(Seal)

When the stock market collapsed in November 1929, it became quite clear that the value of Mr. Warfield's estate was rapidly shrinking. Negotiations were then resumed, and in the latter part of November 1929, an agreement was reached by which the executors agreed to pay Mrs. Simpson the sum of $47,500 and Josephine Metcalf Warfield the sum of $27,500. Josephine Metcalf Warfield agreed to abandon her attack on the entire will, and she and Mrs. Simpson both agreed to execute quitclaim deeds transferring to the trustees named in Mr. Warfield's will any interest which they might have in any of the assets of the estate. On December 2, 1929, with the consent of all parties, a verdict was returned by a jury in the Baltimore City Court in favor of the executors on the issues which had been sent to that court for trial, and on January 9, 1930, an order of the Orphans' Court was filed sustaining the will.

Many years later, after World War II had ended, the Duke and Duchess of Windsor attended a ball given by the Baltimore Assembly at the Belvedere Hotel. On that occasion, I introduced myself to the Duchess and reminded her of the meeting in my father's office when she had employed him in connection with her uncle's will. She seemed very much annoyed and vigorously denied that she had done anything of the kind. For this reason I have set down in rather tedious detail an account of exactly what happened.

The Warfield will case taught me that an unjust will frequently fails to accomplish its purpose. My father and Mr. Cross were both pillars of enlightened conservatism, but they did not hesitate to try to rewrite Mr. Warfield's will so as to achieve a more just distribution of his assets. Since then I have seen other examples where the obvious intention of testators has been at least partially frustrated where fairness seems to require such a result. The wise counselor does not forget this in advising his clients what they can accomplish.

"The Sweet Singer of the South"

Another case which attracted much attention came to my father from a New York lawyer whose client had been injured in an unusual accident in Baltimore. She was a young woman who had just begun a professional careér as a singer and had appeared at a Baltimore theater. As she finished her song, an iron pipe fell from a rising curtain and knocked her unconscious. When she came to in her hotel room, she appeared to be partially paralyzed and remained so up until the time of trial. Her father, who lived in Waco, Texas, was a judge of the Court of Civil Appeals of that state, and he accompanied her to Baltimore for the trial of her case against the theater company.

The case was scheduled for a jury trial before Judge Charles F. Stein, an elderly lawyer who was an expert on real estate law. As part of the plaintiff's case, my father and I offered a photograph of the plaintiff which her father insisted was a faithful likeness. It was obviously posed for theatrical publicity and the defendant's lawyer strenuously objected, as the contrast between the sad-looking wreck of a woman who was sitting in the courtroom and the glamorous creature depicted in the glossy print was very striking. Judge Stein sustained the objection just as the court adjourned for the day.

As I was leaving the courtroom, I heard the deputy clerk say, "Any experienced personal injury lawyer would know better than to try a case like this before Judge Stein." Frankly, it had never occurred to me that I could do anything about the selection of the judge who was to preside at the trial, but I reckoned without the Texas judge. A reporter from the *Sun* had asked him for a picture of his daughter, and he handed the reporter the same photograph that Judge Stein had refused to let us show the jury. When it appeared on the front page of the paper the next morning, the lawyer for the theater company moved for a mistrial, and after a heated argument the judge granted the motion and the case was assigned for trial before a new judge a week later.

The new judge was Joseph N. Ulman, whose approach to the case was totally different from that of Judge Stein. He later wrote a book called *A Judge Takes the Stand*, which was published by Alfred A. Knopf in 1933. In that book he described in detail the case of the "Sweet Singer of the South." He particularly noted that when her father was on the stand, "there was introduced in evidence photographs of the plaintiff taken before the accident, not stage pictures of an actress but ordinary Kodak pictures of a wholesome looking girl photographed under the trees on the lawn of her southern home." The verdict of the jury was for fifty thousand dollars, which the newspapers said was the largest verdict ever entered up to that time in a personal injury case in Baltimore City. The case was later settled for forty thousand dollars, and considering that the doctors all agreed that the accident had caused no permanent physical injury and that the plaintiff's paralysis was entirely neurotic, this seemed to be a remarkable result.

Judge Ulman in his book quoted an item from a college newspaper indicating that less than a year after the verdict the plaintiff was again on the concert stage, but I checked on this and found that her stage career had never been resumed. Perhaps her successful suit made producers leery of offering her any more engagements.

"The Bones of the Czar"

My mother's first cousin Horace S. Whitman, after a tour of duty in the Civil Division of the Department of Justice, had opened an office in Washington where he handled a number of claims against the United States. Somehow he had met a New York lawyer named Charles Recht, who in the 1920s handled a number of legal matters for the Soviet government, which at that time was not recognized by the United States.

One of these matters involved a claim of the Russian Volunteer Fleet, a corporation which had been originally organized by the Imperial Russian government and which was doing business in the United States during World War I. In January 1917 the fleet became the assignee of certain contracts for the construction of two vessels by the Standard Shipbuilding Corporation of New York. In August of that year the United States Shipping Board Emergency Fleet Corporation, acting under the authority of an act of Congress and an executive order of the President of the United States, requisitioned these contracts and fixed the just compensation of the Russian Volunteer Fleet Corporation at approximately $1,412,000. The corporation claimed that the contracts had a value of $4,000,000 and in October 1924 brought suit in the Court of Claims against the United States for that amount as "just compensation" to which it was entitled. In the meantime, however, the Imperial Russian government was overthrown and was ultimately succeeded by a regime which had become the Soviet Union.

The United States moved to dismiss the suit on the ground that a citizen of an unrecognized government had no standing to sue the United States. This motion to dismiss was granted by the Court of Claims, and Horace Whitman employed me to draft a petition asking the Supreme

Court to review that judgment. With the aid of my cousin Jesse Slingluff, Jr., who had just come to the firm after graduating from law school, I prepared a petition which was filed in the latter part of 1929. The Supreme Court granted the petition, and Mr. Rawls was then employed to argue the case in that court.

During the course of his researches, Jesse had come across a fairly recent decision written by Chief Justice William H. Taft, in which Charles Evans Hughes, as counsel for a claimant against the United States, had succeeded in persuading the court to hold that the section of the Judicial Code on which the government was relying in our case was not applicable in a case very similar to ours. In my petition for certiorari and in the brief which was filed by us on the merits after the petition had been granted, we relied heavily on this case. Mr. Rawls in argument did likewise, and when Justice O. W. Holmes, Jr. asked some questions which indicated that he did not understand the relevance of the case, Charles Evans Hughes, who had in the meantime become chief justice of the United States, sent for a copy of the decision and handed it to Justice Holmes to read during the argument. The court reversed the judgment of the Court of Claims in a decision written by Hughes, and the case was sent back to the Court of Claims, where it was litigated for a number of years on the theory that the Russian Volunteer Fleet had been taken over by the Soviet Government and was now a mere arm of the Soviet regime. This led to what threatened to be an endless litigation. An examiner of the Court of Claims announced that he proposed to overrule all objections to evidence and would permit the "bones of the Czar" to be presented as an exhibit by either side which was able to produce them.

The case was abruptly terminated when the Soviet government agreed as a condition of recognition by the United States government to dismiss the claim of the Russian Volunteer Fleet. This left the counsel who had worked on the case high and dry, but Congress passed a bill awarding compensation to the lawyers whose case had been thus unceremoniously settled behind their backs. As a result, I received a modest fee for the time that I had devoted to the claim of the Russian Volunteer Fleet.

The Port Deposit Case

Another case came to me as a result of an unusual arrangement peculiar to Marbury, Gosnell and Williams which permitted former associates of the firm to share office space on an agreed basis, which included the use of the firm's library. One of those men was William Pepper Constable, who also had an office in Cecil County, where he was the local counsel for the Pennsylvania Railroad. As a result of the construction of the new dam at Conowingo, the right-of-way by which the railroad moved most of its freight to Harrisburg and the West from Baltimore, Washington, and the

South had to be elevated. The railroad had to ask the Public Service Commission of Maryland for permission to relocate its right-of-way through the town of Port Deposit. The Town Council feared that this would have a damaging effect on the community and appealed to the commission to require the railroad not to change the elevation within the town limits. The commission compromised and conditioned its approval of the relocation by limiting the elevation within the town with a corresponding increase in the gradient of the right-of-way between the town limits and the dam. The railroad calculated that this would substantially increase the cost of operation of an important portion of one of its main arteries; it asked Mr. Constable to begin court proceedings to have the limitations on the gradient stricken from the order of the commission.

I overheard Mr. Constable discussing the case in the library and called his attention to some opinions of the Maryland courts which I had studied in preparing my thesis on the Public Service Commission Laws of Maryland when I was at Harvard. As a result, Mr. Constable asked Mr. Williams' permission to have me help in preparing the brief in the trial court. In the end I wrote the brief and participated in the argument, both in the trial court and in the Court of Appeals. The opinion of the Court of Appeals upheld our contention that the Public Service Commission had exceeded its powers.

Thereafter Mr. Constable took me into several other matters until Mr. Williams called a halt, on the ground that the office-sharing agreement did not extend to associates. In the meantime, however, I had learned a great deal from Mr. Constable, whose thoroughness and attention to detail was truly extraordinary. Moreover, his understanding of what went on in the minds of the inhabitants of the Eastern Shore of Maryland was invaluable to me.

The WB&A Tax Exemption and Mayor Jackson

I am conscious of the fact that I have probably already exhausted the patience of the reader, even though I have by no means described all the matters of interest in which I participated during the first five years that I practiced with the firm. However, I think that one other case requires mention, since it had its origins in this period. In June 1931 the Maryland legislature passed a law exempting the railroad property of the WB&A Railroad from "all state taxes and charges . . . and from all county and city taxes and charges in the nature of a tax for a period of years." The WB&A had not earned its operating charges in the year 1930, and the act recited that it was "of the utmost importance for the welfare of the State and particularly the community served by said railroad, that the operation of said railroad be continued."

At the time of the passage of this act, WB&A was in the hands of

George Weems Williams as a receiver appointed in January 1931 by the federal District Court of Maryland. The bill was passed by a very close vote after strenuous lobbying against it by the city of Baltimore. Mr. Williams had tried to avoid this by talking to the mayor of Baltimore, Howard W. Jackson, before the bill was introduced. At that time Mayor Jackson had said that he would not oppose it. However, he obviously had changed his mind.

It so happened that Mayor Jackson and Mr. Williams were standing beside each other when the final approving vote was taken. The mayor then turned to Mr. Williams and said, "Congratulations, George. I kept my promise to you and kept my hands off." Mr. Williams turned on his heel and never spoke to the mayor again without having someone else present.

Thereafter the mayor and City Council of Baltimore and the mayor, councilmen, and aldermen of the city of Annapolis filed proofs of claim with the receiver for taxes on the railroad cars, terminals, and rights-of-way, as well as for franchise taxes and other charges. The claim of the city of Annapolis was for taxes on real property and for local taxes or charges owing for the franchise. The District Court upheld the validity of the ex-emptions statute and disallowed all the claims. The Court of Appeals for the Fourth Circuit reversed upon the grounds that the statute was invalid under the Federal Constitution and under several provisions of the con-stitution of the state.

At this point Mr. Williams asked me to prepare a petition for cer-tiorari to the Supreme Court of the United States. It so happened that at that time I had been corresponding with Alger Hiss, who was practicing law in New York. I sent him a draft of a petition that I had prepared in the WB&A case, and he called my attention to a decision of the Supreme Court which specifically held that a municipal corporation had no priv-ileges or immunities under the Federal Constitution which it might in-voke in opposition to the will of its creator. I accordingly amended my draft and have no doubt whatsoever that this was the major reason why the Supreme Court granted the writ and reversed the judgment of the Court of Appeals. Justice Benjamin M. Cardozo, who wrote the opinion for a unanimous court, said, "It is idle to say that a railroad, when once it has been organized, is under a duty to go on, and hence that its distress is not important for anyone except itself. Science has wrought her wonders, but the time is not yet here when trains will run under the impulsion of duty without more."

The State Law Department: My Political Education

In the latter part of the year 1930 I was asked by the attorney general of Maryland, Thomas H. Robinson of Bel Air, if I would accept appointment as one of his assistants in the state Law Department. At that time the attorney general was charged with the responsibility for giving legal advice to the governor of the state and the executive departments as well as the state legislature. Mr. Robinson devoted about half of his time to his duties as attorney general. He had four assistants, all of whom were permitted to have a private practice. The senior assistant, Robert H. Archer, was a partner of the attorney general's in a Bel Air law firm. The other two assistants were a brilliant lawyer named Herbert Levy, who, in fact, gave nearly full time to the work of the state Law Department, and a very capable lawyer named Willis Jones, who likewise devoted nearly all of his time to that work. Aside from the work of the State Roads Commission, which was the responsibility of a special assistant named John B. Gray, a Calvert County lawyer who had an office in Prince Frederick, the four assistants, including myself, were expected to handle all the work of the state Law Department.

I was told that I would be expected to act as the legal adviser to the bank commissioner, the insurance commissioner, the comptroller (who was responsible for collecting all state taxes), the state Board of Education, and the University of Maryland, and to represent the state in the Court of Appeals in all criminal cases. I was also to defend the state in any claim for workmen's compensation which might be brought against it. It was to be my responsibility to draft all official opinions of the attorney general relating to the work of the departments which had been assigned to me and to draft any legislation which the departments desired to present to the legislature.

Although the volume of legal business generated by the state agencies which I have listed did not compare with that of the present day, still I found the pace pretty frantic. To be perfectly frank about it, I frequently did not know what I was doing, and I doubtless made mistakes which today would render me liable to be sued for negligence. That I did no worse was the result of the constant supervision and advice of Herbert Levy and Willis Jones.

In the very first assignment given to me, I put my foot into it. I was told that the bank commissioner was engaged in an examination of the affairs of the Park Bank which might lead to the appointment of a receiver of that bank. My task was to prepare the necessary papers and to be ready to file them if called upon to do so. It so happened that I had been acting as counsel to an organization which was trying to assist small businesses which were in trouble. The organization had been sponsored by the Better Business Bureau of Baltimore and would be classified nowadays as a public interest client. The man in charge of that organization had told me that he was concerned that a company which he was trying to help had all of its working capital on deposit in the Park Bank and that he was planning to transfer some of it to a larger institution. I called him and suggested that he proceed with that plan without further delay. This was before the days of securities legislation, and it never occurred to me that I was acting improperly by passing on inside information.

However, it soon became apparent to me that the highest degree of confidentiality was attached to the work that I had undertaken for the bank commissioner. While rumors were circulating in the financial community that the Park Bank was in trouble, every effort was being made to keep secret the preparations in which I was engaged, not only in order to protect the bank and its depositors but also to avoid preferential treatment of some depositors in the event it was found that the bank was insolvent. When in fact the Park Bank was placed in receivership, I learned that the very day I had spoken to him my client had withdrawn the entire capital of the company for which he was working from the Park Bank and had put it in another bank. This left me in a quandary, which was made all the greater when the bank to which the deposit had been transferred was also taken over by the bank commissioner. While I was still meditating on what I ought to do about this, the whole banking system collapsed and it became apparent that the entire question of preferential withdrawals would become the subject of legislation. In the meantime I had learned my first lesson in the hazards of combining public office with private practice.

While my introduction to public life was thus a harrowing one, there were compensating experiences. One of the first criminal appeals assigned to me was from the Court of Appeals of Maryland to the Supreme Court of the United States. A lawyer named Thomas M. Wampler, who had a large criminal practice in the District of Columbia, bought some waterfront property on the Maryland side of the Potomac River and proceeded to erect a duck blind with a view to engaging in that sport of Maryland's elite. Unfortunately, his property was so small that his blind was closer than the Maryland law allowed to other blinds already constructed on neighboring property. In fact, there was no place on his property where he could build a blind from which he could shoot without violating the Maryland law. Feeling aggrieved, he determined to challenge the constitutionality of the Maryland law on the ground that it violated the Fourteenth Amendment to the Federal Constitution by denying him the equal protection of the laws. Overruled by the trial court, then by the Court of Appeals of Maryland, he took his case to the Supreme Court of the United States. I was assigned to write the brief and make the argument on behalf of the state of Maryland.

The Supreme Court was then still sitting in the old chamber in the Capitol Building. There was an intimacy about that old courtroom which made the lawyers feel that they were really a part of the judicial process. The appellant, who acted as his own counsel, proceeded to shout and bellow as though he were addressing a jury, so I became more confident and was planning to speak in the conversational style which I had so admired when I listened to Senator George Wharton Pepper argue in that court. I noticed near the end of Mr. Wampler's argument that Chief Justice Taft passed a note to his colleagues, and when Mr. Wampler's time had expired and I was about to rise from my seat, the chief justice leaned forward and said, "Mr. Marbury, the court will not require argument from the state of Maryland."

John W. Davis, who was sitting behind me, put his hands on my shoulders and said, "So you have won your case without saying a word. I think I had better hold you down or all that hot air will float you right up to the ceiling." The clerk then called the next case, and Mr. Davis moved into the seat which I had just occupied. As I was leaving the courtroom, the clerk said to me, "I told Mr. Davis to be ready to argue his case because I knew that Justice McReynolds had been shooting from one of the blinds which is right next to the Wampler property, and I felt sure that the court would not waste any time on that case." Sure enough the court soon filed an opinion written by Justice Brandeis which was a model of judicial brevity.

A year later I had a far more satisfying experience in that same court. The Susquehanna Power Company, which had constructed the Conowingo Dam in the 1920s, had unsuccessfully challenged on constitutional grounds the assessment of its property for tax purposes by Harford County. In a companion case the company also challenged the right of the state of Maryland to tax the shares of the capital stock of the company, again invoking the Fourteenth Amendment. In both cases the Court of Appeals of Maryland had upheld the assessments, and the cases were appealed to the Supreme Court.

I was assigned to argue these cases on behalf of the state and to write the briefs. I would have liked to devote my full time for several months to preparation of the briefs, but this was simply impossible in view of the other work which had been assigned to me. I concluded that the best tactic was to file in each case a motion to dismiss the appeal or affirm the decisions of the Maryland court on the ground that they did not present any substantial federal question. All I had time to do was to prepare and file the motions with supporting briefs, which seemed to me to be far less elaborate than the importance of the cases required.

The counsel for the power company was William Clarke Mason of the Philadelphia bar, who argued thirteen cases before the Supreme Court at that particular term. When the case came on for argument, I had the feeling that I was pretty badly outgunned, but I noticed that Justice Butler seemed interested in the points which I had made. I later heard from his son-in-law Edward Dunn, a Baltimore friend of mine, that Justice Butler had been impressed by my argument and had said that it was one of the best presentations made to the court during that term. In the outcome the court dismissed the appeals in opinions which followed very closely the outline of my briefs, and I learned from this the importance of confining written and oral arguments in the Supreme Court to the main point and to say no more than is needed to make that point clear.

In sharp contrast to this glamorous case was an assignment to go to Salisbury to respond to a call for help from the local state's attorney, Hooper Miles, in a case which had aroused much public feeling in Talbot County. By that time William Preston Lane of Hagerstown had succeeded Mr. Robinson as attorney general, and he sent me down to Salisbury to see what I could do to help Mr. Miles. Although it was no part of the responsibility of the attorney general to interfere in the prosecution of criminal cases, it is true that he was charged with representing the state in the Court of Appeals, and Mr. Lane felt that this was a sufficient basis for responding to Mr. Miles's call for help.

When I got to Salisbury, I found that the grand jury had insisted on indicting for arson a well-known local character who was always present at every fire in the county in response to that mysterious emotional drive that brings "firebugs" to conflagrations. Apparently some elements in the community had become suspicious of his behavior on such occasions and had influenced the grand jury to act in the case, although the state's attorney did not think that the case was strong enough to warrant a prosecution. However, the public feeling was so strong that Mr. Miles thought it would be a good idea for the attorney general's office to take the responsibility for dropping the case.

I listened to a review of the evidence and quickly came to the conclusion that the defendant would probably be acquitted. On the other hand, there were some very curious coincidences that made the public suspicion not unreasonable. I reported all of this to Mr. Lane, who was not at all enthusiastic about the idea of vetoing the prosecution. Instead he suggested that I offer to join in the prosecution, provided that someone from the state's attorney's office would participate actively. Mr. Miles readily accepted this suggestion, and the matter of my participation was put up to the judges who were to preside at the trial and to the counsel for the defendant. After considerable hesitation, the judges agreed to allow me to participate on behalf of the prosecution and, somewhat to my surprise, so did the defendant's counsel.

I soon found out why they did not complain. Here was a young whippersnapper from Baltimore coming down to the Eastern Shore to prosecute a poor old local boy that everyone knew was perfectly harmless. My participation was a godsend not only to the state's attorney, who got off the hook after all, but to the defense as well. In short, I was the sacrificial lamb and, of course, the result was a speedy acquittal. Mr. Lane and Mr. Miles must have had a quiet chuckle when they next met. I had begun to cut my eyeteeth as a public servant.

I learned a good deal more about how the state was governed during the regular session of the legislature in 1931. I had my first personal contact with Governor Ritchie, who was then serving his third term. The Conservation Department had been assigned to me, and with the director of the department, Swepson Earle, I had reviewed all the legislation which affected his department. I knew that some of the bills were controversial, but Mr. Earle pointed out many so-called snakes which were hidden in some seemingly innocuous provisions. We divided the bills into three piles: first, those which were clearly bad and should be vetoed; second, those which should be signed; and third, those which in Mr. Earle's opinion were doubtful.

I then made an appointment to see the governor and was prepared to discuss each bill with him. When he came into the room, he picked up the bills which we had recommended that he sign and started to read them. I said, "Governor, those are the bills that present no problems. Perhaps you would like to start with those that are doubtful or that we think you ought to veto." He looked at me quizzically and said, "Bill, you don't mind if I read them before I sign them, do you?" I mumbled something about Mr. Earle's having been over them, whereupon he said, "In my opinion Swepson is far from a reliable guide. If you can find me some sensible person who would be willing to take on his job, I would appoint him tomorrow." He then proceeded to read all the bills carefully and in the end added two of them to the veto pile, after pointing out to me that they contained "snakes" that Mr. Earle had missed. He put several others in the doubtful pile, saying that he wanted to look at them more closely. In spite of my chagrin, I was astonished and awestruck by his knowledge of marine biology and of the details of the seafood industry. It was an eye-opener to me to learn how complex the production of sound conservation legislation really is. All this was aside from the mechanics of enacting legislation, as to which I sat at the feet of a master of the craft, Dr. Horace Flack, a Johns Hopkins Ph.D. who had gained a nationwide reputation as an expert in his field.

One more lesson I learned at the legislative session was the importance of the contribution made by the paid lobbyists, whose principal function was to clarify the issues and to make sure that every essential step in the legislative process was accomplished in a timely fashion and strictly in accordance with the governing rules. The really able lobbyists were always good teachers, and the resourceful ones were also skilled in arranging deals.

Perhaps the most important lesson I learned from the months I spent in the state Law Department was that most government departments were really run by their permanent staffs. In nearly every department there were one or two individuals on whom the political heads relied for advice. If you could get them on your side, your job was more than half done. The skillful lobbyist always knew who these men were and spent most of his time with them rather than in wining and dining the legislators. This was also true of the more important legislative committees. Here again there were men and, in recent years, women who gave guidance to the legislators which often determined the fate of bills pending before that committee.

By the end of the legislative session in 1931, I began to feel that my education as a lawyer was about as complete as it would ever be. While, like Henry Adams, the most important thing I had learned was the depth of my own ignorance, at the same time I had come to realize that my contemporaries at the bar were in the same boat. My self-confidence was bolstered by the offer of a partnership in the law firm headed by Charles Markell, who was generally recognized at that time to be almost in a class by himself as a brilliant lawyer, especially skilled in public utility law. As a matter of professional courtesy, Mr. Markell never spoke to me but went directly to Mr. Williams, who reported the offer to me and at the same time offered me as an alternative a partnership in Marbury, Gosnell and Williams, to begin as soon as I had completed my service in the attorney general's office. I had been there nearly two years, and I decided that the time had come to go back to private practice. Mr. Lane had named Willis Jones as deputy attorney general and delegated to him full responsibility for the general management of the office. Herbert Levy had resigned, and while Bill Henderson, the new appointee, was an excellent lawyer and a most agreeable colleague, the team with which I was working had been broken up.

Moreover, I had decided to have a major surgical operation which would put me out of commission for at least six weeks. Ever since my first year at the Harvard Law School, I had suffered from digestive disorders which had first been incorrectly diagnosed as appendicitis and later found to be caused by a duodenal ulcer. At times of stress I suffered spasms which were quite disabling, and I was always on a restricted diet. It seemed to me that this was the time to see what the surgeons could do. My medical advisers were nationally known for their wisdom, and in the summer of 1931 I decided to go ahead with an operation which both Dr. Tom Brown and Dr. J. M. T. Finney had recommended.

Mr. Lane was very understanding and agreed to give me six weeks combined medical and terminal leave but asked that I schedule the operation after I had had an opportunity to turn over to Bill Henderson the work that I had been doing. He was particularly concerned about a suit which I had filed on behalf of the State Roads Commission against Lloyd's of London to recover on the bonds which they had issued to a group of employees of the State Roads Commission during the time when John N. Mackall was chairman of the commission. Mackall was an able and aggressive chairman who had shown great imagination in planning a system of state roads, but he had failed to give enough attention to administrative detail and had become the victim of a group of skillful thieves who manipulated the accounts of the commission and succeeded in concealing their defalcations for years.

In the end they were caught by a diligent auditor who detected some discrepancies in the accounts. At first Mr. Mackall reported these discrepancies in a public statement which indicated that the building program of the state would in no way be affected by these relatively trifling losses. Thereafter, as during Watergate, new revelations came almost daily and the press began having a field day, while all sorts of reckless charges were made before legislative committees which were eagerly seeking publicity. Governor Ritchie intervened and appointed a committee of outstanding businessmen to investigate the affairs of the commission. He named as counsel to the committee the leading corporate lawyer in the state— Edwin G. Baetjer, who was a prominent money-raiser for the Republican party and who had recently presided at a convention of that party. Mr. Baetjer immediately announced that he would investigate all of the charges that had been made and that he intended not only to establish guilt where there was guilt but to "disestablish perjury where false charges have been made."

In the end the bipartisan committee found that some of the charges were without foundation but that at least a dozen of the employees of the commission had been involved in stealing large sums over a long period of years. Mr. Lane then directed me to bring suit against the company which had bonded these employees. Since the adjournment of the legislature, I had devoted nearly all of my time to preparing for the trial of this case, which was the most complicated matter that I had ever been called upon to handle by myself.

Thus, in October of 1931, I returned to private practice as a partner in the firm of Marbury, Gosnell and Williams. My "salad days" were over.

X ❧ Extracurricular Activities

When my uncle Jesse Slingluff came to notify me formally that I had been elected as a partner in the firm, he informed me that he had been instructed to say that, while the partners were more than satisfied with my legal ability, they hoped that I would take steps to mend my manners in dealing with my fellow lawyers. I was a bit shocked by this. I was aware of some of my shortcomings, but I had not realized that I had generated a compensating aggressiveness in my behavior that would prove obnoxious to others. When on several occasions Uncle Jesse's mild words were underscored by unpleasant remarks made to me by other members of the bar and on one occasion by Judge Samuel K. Dennis, an old friend of the family's who used to visit on the farm, I decided that the time had come to take action.

I believed that one of the causes of my failure in deportment was the state of my health, which had already led me to submit to surgery. Stomach ulcers are perfect examples of the old conundrum about which comes first, the chicken or the egg. Does the ulcer produce bad temper or is it the other way around? Sufficient to say that my professional life probably had suffered considerable impairment from constant dyspepsia and nervous tension.

Even more important than my ill health, and perhaps contributing to it, was what it is now fashionable to call "stress." I had become increasingly concerned with the finances of my family, and this concern became acute after the stock market crash in 1929. As spectacular suicides and bankruptcies began to take place in the community, even the most self-absorbed types became conscious of the shaky economic underpinnings of their daily lives. My family had always been dependent on my father's earnings as a lawyer, and these began to shrink considerably. Moreover, his health was not good. While all of the family were out of school or college and the farm had been sold in 1925, his financial outlook was still pretty grim. The garage building behind 159 West Lanvale, which had been rented for years to an automobile repair shop, was a casualty of the Depression and was now vacant. For two years I ran it myself as a neighborhood parking facility, with the assistance of a boy who lived in the neighborhood and helped me shift cars around.

Finally it became clear to me that my father could no longer afford to maintain the family in the style to which it was accustomed and that the task of reducing living expenses was more than my mother could manage. I persuaded my parents to leave 159 West Lanvale Street and move to a residential hotel called The Altamont, which was located three blocks east on Lanvale Street. After a fairly short stay there, we rented 1307 Park Avenue, where we stayed for several years. In the meantime, 159 West Lanvale was leased until we decided to turn it into apartments according to a plan designed by my friend Francis Jencks.

All of this was very distressing to my parents, especially as my father had belatedly discovered that he was suffering from glaucoma, which had blinded his father. While my father did not go totally blind, he could no longer read print and his career as a lawyer was practically at an end. As a result, I gradually took over full responsibility for the financial management of the family's affairs. Fortunately, the renovation of 159 West Lanvale was entirely successful, and we moved back there into a large apartment which occupied approximately half of our old living quarters. While our style of living was much modified, it was enough like the old times to keep us all reasonably happy.

During this stressful time, a special source of solace to me was my increasing participation in musical activities. I was asked to join a record club which had acquired a library of carefully selected recordings. Among those who belonged to the club was Willem Wirtz, whose brother Bart had for many years been head of the cello department at the Peabody Conservatory and had given me piano lessons when I was a small boy. Another member of the club was Mrs. Clarence Keefer, known to the entire musical community as "Lubov," who taught piano at the Preparatory Department of the Peabody and also taught Russian at Johns Hopkins University. I became friendly with both of them and the three of us joined several other members of the club in organizing a chamber music society called the Bach Club, which proposed to sponsor public performances of music which was almost never being heard publicly in Baltimore at that time. I believe that our first offering was a performance at the Alcazar by Adolf Busch of all four Bach sonatas for unaccompanied violin. My recollection is that one of the members of the club had some connection with the Busch family and had succeeded in persuading Adolf Busch to come to Baltimore for a nominal fee. The concert was one of the outstanding musical events of the season and was followed by other well-attended events.

During succeeding years the Bach Club sponsored some of the best concerts available to serious musicians in the Baltimore community. Among those who performed were Artur Schnabel, Myra Hess, Harold

Samuel, Bela Bartok, and the Roth Quartet, to name only a few. In addition to performing complete cycles of the chamber music of Beethoven and Brahms, the club gave the first public performances in Baltimore of Bartok's string quartets as well as a complete performance of the Art of the Fugue and the Goldberg Variations of Bach. I was very active in promoting these concerts, and upon the untimely death of Willem Wirtz, I was elected president of the club.

It was through Lubov Keefer that I was introduced to the household of Joe Wickes, who lived on Park Avenue within a few blocks of 159 West Lanvale. He was a retired civil engineer who liked to play the cello and knew all the old guard of professional musicians and amateurs who had played together in Baltimore. His wife, a very lovely woman from Somerset County, was an accomplished pianist. Every Sunday night a small group met at the Wickes home to play chamber music, and when Mrs. Wickes heard that I could play the violin, she asked me to join them.

The first violinist was a young Hopkins graduate student named Frank Oppenheimer. The second violinist was Mr. John Greiner, the head of the construction company which had built all of the major bridges now an integral part of the highway system of Maryland. John Greiner was past 70 years of age and owned a superb Stradivarius instrument on which he played with a quavering tone. The violist was a Hopkins professor of physics named Pfundt, and the cellist was Joe Wickes himself. Occasionally Frank Bibb, who was teaching voice at the Peabody and numbered Joe Wickes's daughter Page as one of his students, would drop in and play the piano part of a quintet, quartet, or trio, but generally Mrs. Wickes was our pianist, who somehow held the ragged ensemble together.

I gradually came to be a regular member of the group, substituting from time to time for Mr. Greiner, who tired rather easily. After each performance the group would sit around the table and have something to eat while general conversation took place. Talk of politics was generally avoided on these occasions because young Oppenheimer was regarded by the rest of us as a radical. To the embarrassment of his brother Robert, the famous physicist who was a major contributor to the development of the atomic bomb, it was later revealed that his young brother had joined the Communist party while he was a student at Johns Hopkins. Even so, Mr. Greiner and Professor Pfundt could not resist an occasional jab at this callow youngster who seemed to hold such extreme views.

For me, these musical sessions were an important emotional outlet and did much to relieve the tension of an existence which seemed rather hectic at the time. The result was that I looked forward eagerly to these Sunday-night sessions, although I recognized that my technical equipment was far from adequate and that I was a far less sophisticated musician than the rest of the group.

The Depression years were also times when I was developing an altogether different group of friends. When I first returned to Baltimore in the fall of 1924, I found it quite difficult to adjust to the absence of the friends I had made in Boston. Fortunately, Horry Frost had made a great hit with the family, and it was not long before, by mutual consent, he was permitted to join us permanently at 159 West Lanvale, in the back building where my brother Fendall and I had sleeping quarters in the rooms originally intended for servants who "lived in." Horry was going through a training period at Piper, Carey and Hall, and we worked together on our bar examinations, which we both passed with no difficulty. My mother arranged to have him invited to all the social affairs to which my brother Taylor and I received invitations, and he fitted comfortably into the Baltimore social life.

Horry did not get along so well as an associate in the Piper firm. After being there for three years, he decided to go back to Charleston and practice in the city of his birth, but before he could carry out his plan, he came down with a fever which was diagnosed as tuberculosis by a young doctor named Woody who lived in our neighborhood. He was taken to the Johns Hopkins Hospital, where it developed that he had tubercular pneumonia in both lungs. In those days the accepted treatment for tuberculosis was to put the patient to bed, preferably in a mountain climate, and as soon as Horry's temperature moderated his family made arrangements to take him down to Asheville, North Carolina. Without Horry I felt that a good deal of the fun had gone out of life in Baltimore.

During this period I began to see more of some of my Slingluff cousins, whose mother, Kathleen Kernan, had married my Uncle Jesse. One summer my brother Taylor and I were invited to an old-fashioned house party at the Kernan family place, Springbank, which lies between Aldercreek and Forestport on the edge of the Adirondack forest in upper New York State. Among the party was Jesse, Jr.'s classmate Alger Hiss. They had both just graduated from the Johns Hopkins University and were about to enter the Harvard Law School. I found Alger a stimulating companion and wrote letters on his behalf to Felix Frankfurter and others at the Harvard Law School.

A year later Jesse, Jr., and I drove up to Williamstown in Massachusetts, where he invoked the reluctant hospitality of his fraternity brothers at Williams College and we spent the night in the Alpha Delta Phi House. In Williamstown we ran into Herbert Brune, Jr., and his new wife, the former Elaine Milburn, who were taking a summer course at the Williamstown Institute. They introduced us to a Dr. Mendelsohn, the grandson of the famous composer, who was lecturing at the institute. Dr. Mendelsohn was a judge of a high court in the Weimar Republic, and I was astonished to hear him say that he had been impressed by Elaine Brune's familiarity with the work of German jurists. He said that she and her mother, Mrs. Milburn, were engaged in translating an article by the legal philosopher Erlich which had just recently been published in Germany.

I had heard of Mrs. Milburn as a German woman who had married an American army officer shortly after World War I. He had brought her back with him to South Baltimore, where he lived and practiced dentistry. When Mrs. Milburn discovered that she was living on the wrong side of the tracks, she apparently made up her mind to solve that problem by using her very pretty daughter as an entering wedge into Baltimore society. Somehow she had gotten Elaine an invitation to a party where she had met Herbert, who, to the horror of his parents, fell in love with her. Mrs. Brune, who was a longtime friend of my mother's, had told her all about this terrible German woman who had refused to permit her daughter to become engaged to Herbert when the Brune family had insisted that any marriage would have to be postponed until Herbert had finished law school. Mrs. Milburn promptly forbade her daughter to see him again, saying that long engagements were "not healthy." My mother agreed with Mrs. Brune that such a remark was inexcusably vulgar. They were especially indignant because the result had been that Herbert and Elaine eloped. Many years later I learned that Mrs. Milburn's father was the retired German ambassador to France, whose home at Potsdam was next door to that of Count Luttichau, who later married a Baltimore girl.

Through the Slingluffs, I was introduced to the family of Clifford Lewis, who was living in Philadelphia down near Christ Church in a home on Fourth Street, in which the second oldest mutual fire insurance company in the United States had maintained its offices since the eighteenth century. Mr. Lewis as secretary and general manager of the company by right of inheritance (a Lewis had been secretary since the company was founded) was required to live in the same building as the company office. Through the Lewises, I was invited to several parties in Philadelphia as well as to spend a weekend at their summer home on the Mainline and came to know the younger members of quite a number of old Philadelphia families.

Through Horry Frost I had been introduced to the household of Dr. J. Hall Pleasants in Baltimore, whose son Wilmer had been a classmate of Horry's at Harvard. I also met Wilmer's classmate Francis Jencks, whose parents lived in the old Thomas house on Mt. Vernon Place. Wilmer had a sister, Betsy, who was then a senior at St. Timothy's School, who was about to make her debut in Baltimore. Through Mr. Constable I had come to know Charlie Carroll, who lived out in Howard County, where his mother owned Homewood, which at one time belonged to his ancestor Charles Carroll of Carrollton, a signer of the Declaration of Independence. In all of these homes I began to feel welcome, and, widely as they differed in their interests, I came to appreciate and admire Mrs. Pleasants, Mrs.

Jencks, and Mrs. Carroll, who showed me how the best of Virginia, New England, and California had adapted themselves happily to the Baltimore scene. Their children became my lifelong friends.

While I was a student at Harvard, I heard George W. Wickersham give an informal talk to a group of students on the topic of public service as the highest ideal of the bar. Mr. Wickersham defined the term *public service* broadly to include membership on the governing boards of educational and other similar institutions. My first opportunity to engage in such an activity came as a result of the initiative of "Jake" Waxter, a remarkable young Baltimore lawyer who had determined to devote his life to public service. He began by organizing the first Legal Aid Bureau in Baltimore and asked me to serve as a member of its board, along with a group of his friends who had all graduated from Gilman School and Princeton. Our task was largely to be window dressing to protect Jake from the criticism of some lawyers who tended to resent what seemed to them to be a form of unfair competition. We were also to help in fundraising, since the services rendered by the Legal Aid Bureau were generally gratuitous.

The next step in my education in public service came at the suggestion of Dr. Hall Pleasants. The Baltimore Museum of Art, in which he was interested, had suddenly taken a new lease on life with the completion, at the taxpayers' expense, of a handsome new building in Wyman Park adjacent to the Hopkins campus. Up until that time the museum collections had been housed in the old Garrett House on Mt. Vernon Place, and the board of trustees was made up of rather elderly patrons of the arts who had been content to sponsor occasional exhibitions on a very modest scale. With the assistance of public funds and the new building, a new era was about to be inaugurated, and new trustees were being sought for the board. Among the newly elected members of the board in addition to myself were Henry Treide and Philip Perlman. Phil Perlman had been one of Governor Ritchie's young Turks and had later become a sort of "grey eminence" to the then current mayor of Baltimore City.

Very shortly after my election to the board, the director of the museum resigned to go to St. Louis, and the board was faced with a crucial appointment. It soon became apparent that Phil Perlman had a candidate for the job in a young curator from the Albright Museum in Buffalo. Henry Treide took me aside and suggested that Perlman was acting at the behest of the mayor, who was trying to take control of the museum. Henry suggested that a committee be appointed to take over the direction of the museum temporarily and that meanwhile the appointment of a new director should be deferred until the board had an opportunity to explore plans for the future. Thinking that I was frustrating a political power play, I fell for Mr. Treide's idea and helped him get a majority of the board to vote for his proposal. As a result, a committee of three was appointed.

Mr. Perlman then told me that I had been taken in—that Treide had just lost his job and was looking for something to do and wanted to take over the direction of the museum himself.

For several years Mr. Treide tried to run the museum and made one excuse after another for not pursuing the search for a new director. In the end, he realized that he would not be named as director and found a young man named Leslie Cheek, who turned out to be innovative and competent. In the meantime, however, Perlman had transferred his interest to the Walters Gallery, where he proved to be a most valuable trustee with a cultivated taste as a collector of drawings.

At the museum, I got my first lesson in the art of fund-raising, which is now euphemistically called "development." I ran a combined membership and capital fund drive which succeeded in building up what proved to be a valuable corps of members who made annual contributions, but the capital campaign raised just enough to pay the expenses of the entire effort. In this campaign my most helpful lieutenant was Fannie Blaustein (Mrs. Alvin) Thalheimer, who organized an effective group of solicitors and saved me from a humiliating failure as a campaign manager.

In 1935 I was elected to the Board of Trustees of the Peabody Institute, which at the time was, next to the Johns Hopkins University, the most "prestigious" institution in Baltimore. At the first meeting I attended, I was informed that the Peabody board had just recently reluctantly agreed to pick up a deficit of $25,000 which had been incurred by the Conservatory of Music. The director of the conservatory, Mr. Otto Ortmann, had been informed that no further deficits would be tolerated, and I was requested to help him to solve his financial problems.

I went to see Mr. Ortmann, who seemed quite distracted. He had never had to raise money and seemed to have no idea how to start. He had a list of people who had demonstrated an interest in the school and suggested that we invite them to a dinner and see if we could raise $25,000, which would be enough to see the school through the current year. Beyond that he had no idea what to do. I suggested that he fix his goal at $125,000 and turn his dinner into the opening gun of a campaign by including a speaker such as Ernest Hutcheson, a former faculty member who was then the director of the Juilliard School in New York.

After much trepidation, he agreed to this and the dinner was held. I made a speech in which I outlined the financial predicament of the Peabody Institute. Mr. Hutcheson, with whom I had a long and confidential talk, told me very bluntly that the conservatory had lost prestige in recent years and that a careful study should be made to find out what was the trouble. The campaign netted more than $100,000 and gave the trustees a breathing space in which to decide what to do.

During the following months I talked to the dean of the conservatory, Virginia Carty, and the superintendent of the preparatory department, Virginia Blackhead. I soon came to the conclusion that the problem was in the leadership of the conservatory. Mr. Ortmann was a scholarly gentleman who had made a significant contribution to music education in his studies of acoustics, but he was almost totally lacking in administrative ability. I asked him why the string departments had suffered a sharp drop in enrollment. He said he thought it might be due to the fact that the heads of the violin and cello departments were no longer in their prime and did not attract the talented students. I asked why they had not been retired, and he said that this was impossible, as the school had no pension plan. I asked him if he had ever suggested to the trustees that a pension be provided, and he said that he had never done so. Finally he agreed to discuss the matter with the men involved and to ask the board to provide a pension for them, with the understanding that they could continue to take private pupils as they had been doing in the past.

The question then arose as to where to find new blood to take the place of the men who had retired. I found to my astonishment that Mr. Ortmann had no suggestions to make. About that time I heard from a friend of mine in New York that Oscar Shumsky might be interested in an appointment to the Peabody faculty. I reported this to Mr. Ortmann, who was incredulous, as Shumsky had a growing reputation which, according to Mr. Ortmann, made it most unlikely that he would be willing to settle in Baltimore. Shumsky promptly accepted.

I found this timidity to be typical and finally, with the permission of the trustees, I asked Mr. Hutcheson to put together a small committee to inspect the operation of the conservatory and to make recommendations to the board as to what, if any, changes should be made. Mr. Ortmann immediately assumed that he was about to be fired as director and asked some of his friends to bring pressure to bear on the trustees to retain him. Mr. Hutcheson organized his committee and tried to make an appointment to come to Baltimore to see Mr. Ortmann, who refused to see them. Mr. Hutcheson then reported that his committee was unanimously of the opinion that a change in the directorship was needed.

About this time I happened to be in Canada, where I saw a Canadian news magazine which had a feature article about a pianist named Reginald Stewart, who had organized a new symphony orchestra in Toronto. The more I read about him, the more interested I became, and later on, in Baltimore, I spoke to Fred Huber, who was then the manager of the Baltimore Symphony Orchestra, which was faced with the imminent departure of its conductor. I thought that Mr. Huber might be interested in trying to find someone who could fill both positions. Although he was not receptive to this idea, he did introduce me to Mr. Arthur Judson, who arranged for me to meet Reginald Stewart in New York. I found that he was very much interested in the idea of taking over both jobs. I told him that I could make no promises as to the orchestra and that he would have to take his chances on that. After considering the matter, he said that he would be interested in coming to Baltimore as the director of the Conservatory of Music.

I then had a long talk with Mr. Ortmann, in which I suggested that he ask to be relieved as director of the conservatory and accept appointment as head of the theory department. He flatly refused to do this. The board of trustees then decided to terminate his appointment as director and to give him a year's terminal leave at full pay. At the same time, they made it clear that they hoped that Mr. Ortmann would reconsider and stay on the faculty. When he again declined to do this, the appointment of Mr. Stewart as director was publicly announced.

At first there was quite a furor in musical circles, as Mr. Ortmann told all of his friends that he had been unceremoniously fired. The members of the board decided to make no further statement, and public attention soon shifted to the situation of the orchestra, where the musicians were engaged in a bitter fight with Mr. Huber. In the final outcome, the orchestra board was reorganized, a new manager was selected, and Reginald Stewart, who in the meantime had taken office as director of the Peabody Conservatory of Music, was named conductor of the Baltimore Symphony Orchestra as well.

XI ❖ "That Is Natalie Jewett—
Go and Speak to Her"

Just after I left the state Law Department, the Eastern Shore of Maryland underwent a convulsion. A black man named Euel Lee was indicted for an atrocious murder of a white family in Worcester County, Maryland. Since he had no counsel, the local judges appointed a leader of the local bar to represent him. As a precaution, he was taken from the local jail and transferred to a neighboring county. Shortly thereafter, a lawyer employed by the International Labor Defense—a notorious group generally engaged in radical agitation—appeared and announced that he had been asked by Lee to represent him. This lawyer moved to have the trial of the case removed to the Western Shore of the state on the ground that Lee could not get a fair trial anywhere on the Eastern Shore of Maryland. At the same time, inflammatory statements emphasizing the racial aspects of the case were issued by the International Labor Defense to the metropolitan press of Washington and Baltimore.

This so enraged the people of that area that rumors began circulating that a lynching was about to take place. Shortly thereafter, a mob broke into the jail in Worcester County looking for Lee, whereupon he was removed to Baltimore City. At this point, the local judges denied Lee's motion to remove the case to the Western Shore but ordered that it be set for trial in the city of Cambridge in Dorchester County, which was in the same judicial circuit as Worcester, where the crime had been committed. Within a few weeks another mob broke into a jail in neighboring Wicomico County, removed a black man, and lynched him.

The International Defense League then appealed to the Court of Appeals of Maryland from the order assigning the case for trial in Dorchester County. In the midst of the ensuing uproar, I volunteered my services to the attorney general. At his request I prepared a brief in which, while pointing out that the order of the lower court might not be appealable, the attorney general clearly stated that in his opinion the case should not be tried in Dorchester County. A majority of the Court of Appeals agreed. Following this opinion, the local judges removed the case to Baltimore County, where it was tried before a panel of three judges and a jury. Lee was convicted and that conviction was upheld on appeal. Thus the final outcome was satisfactory to the people of the area which Henry Mencken customarily referred to as "Transchoptankia," but their pride had been badly bruised.

The furor aroused by the Lee case had not yet died down when I was asked by the attorney general to act as counsel to the bank commissioner in taking over the Title Guarantee & Trust Company, which had been found to be insolvent. The news of this appointment came to me at lunch at the Jencks home just as I was engaged in telling Margaret Sullavan, Henry Fonda, and Robert Montgomery of the University Players, who were then acting in repertory at a Baltimore theater, all about the Lee case. The Title Company had over a long period of years insured the titles of most of the real estate which had changed hands in the Baltimore metropolitan area. My task was to represent the bank commissioner in applying for a receiver to liquidate the banking business of the company while at the same time keeping the profitable title business alive.

With the permission of the bank commissioner and the court, I asked Alex Fairbank to help me in that task. Mr. Fairbank was generally recognized as the leading authority in the state on titles and had been a vice-president and general counsel of the Title Company. He was a deeply embittered man who at our first meeting described himself as the object of my "charity." While his advice was indispensable, his emotional instability added to the difficulty of my assignment. This was especially true because he quite frankly hated the chief officer of a subsidiary mortgage company, whom he believed to be largely responsible for the collapse of the Title Company, with the result that all communication between them had to pass through me.

In the end, we did succeed in getting the affairs of the company in sufficiently reasonable order to make possible the adoption of a plan of reorganization which called for the creation of a new company limited to the title insurance business, the stock of which was issued to the depositors in the old company. This plan of reorganization was the idea of Jesse N. Bowen, a senior partner in the firm of Semmes, Bowen and Semmes, who had been employed by some of the large depositors in the bank to represent their interests.

One by-product of this complicated matter gave me further insight into the mores of the Eastern Shore of Maryland. Among the practices which were frequent in certain banking circles before 1929 was the making of loans to directors and officers of the bank. One such borrower was the president of the Title Guarantee & Trust Company, Albert G. Towers, and there was a large and growing gap between the amount of his loan and the value of the collateral which supposedly secured it. Mr. Towers had originally come from Denton, the county seat of Caroline County, where his family had for long been prominent. He had died shortly after the stock market crash in 1929 and left a will naming his brother Lawrence as his executor.

Lawrence Towers had the reputation of being a very shrewd businessman, and when I demanded payment of the loan by his brother's estate, he came to Baltimore and asked the bank commissioner to give him more time. As the stock market was then going from bad to worse, the deputy bank commissioner, John Hospelhorn, who handled all the insolvency cases in that office, agreed with me that this could not be done. Accordingly, I filed a claim against the Towers estate and asked permission of the Orphans' Court of Caroline County to sell the collateral.

My local counsel in Denton, W. Brewster Deen, was supposed to follow up on this matter, but nothing ever seemed to happen. He never answered my letters, nor could he be reached by telephone. Finally, one morning, Alex Fairbank and I drove down to Denton and went before the Orphans' Court ourselves after having accepted Mr. Deen's apologies for having been incommunicado "because it was canning season." I made a piteous appeal on behalf of the depositors, and the judges then adjourned for lunch. After adjournment, they advised me that they needed more time to reflect on the problem and would let Mr. Deen hear from them in due course.

As I was leaving the court, Lawrence Towers asked me to his house to have a drink. He included Alex Fairbank in this invitation, but Fairbank morosely declined, saying that he had other business to attend to. I found that Mr. Towers was a cheery old gentleman. He congratulated me on my eloquence and told me that I had so shaken the judges of the Orphans' Court that they had come to him for advice as to what they should do, as they were accustomed to do when he was register of wills. He had told them that it made no sense to sell stock at that time and suggested that they put the matter on the shelf for the time being, which is exactly what they did. I finally had to take the matter to the Circuit Court for Caroline County, where, after more than a year of litigation, I finally succeeded in liquidating this loan.

As the Title Company receivership wound its slow way to an end, I became involved in two other matters which were of interest. The first was a case which took me once more to the Supreme Court of the United States, where I undertook to uphold a Maryland statute which had been enacted during the depths of the Depression. This statute had the effect of eliminating the power of the courts to foreclose by summary procedure defaulted Maryland mortgages at the suit of the holders of less than a 25 percent fractional interest in the debt. The court decided in our favor.

The other matter in which I became engaged at this time arose out of the receivership of an inter-urban railway company in West Virginia.

Robert Garrett & Sons of Baltimore had sold to their customers a number of bonds of the Charleston Interurban Railway Company, and when the bonds went into default, Garrett asked Mr. Williams to represent the bondholders. Mr. Williams was then spending nearly all of his time on the WB&A receivership, and he simply dumped the file on my desk and told me to look after it. I had never handled such a problem before and felt very much like Eliza crossing the ice. Fortunately for me, Garrett had employed the firm of Price, Smith and Spilman of Charleston as their local counsel, and T. Brooke Price, a partner in that firm, turned out to be an old hand at the game. Without his guidance I would have been lost, but I proved to be an apt pupil and even thought out some improvements on the usual procedure in such cases.

Brooke Price's neighbor on the hills which overlooked Charleston was a man named Arthur Hill, who insisted that the reorganized company be given power to abandon the street railway system altogether and substitute motor transport. He foresaw that Interurban's trolleys would be supplanted by buses, and over the protests of the management of the old company, of which he had been a junior member, he succeeded in getting what he wanted. As a result, the bondholders got new securities, which turned out to be much better investments than the old bonds.

During my visits to Charleston I met Harrison Smith, Jr., who was working for one of the local Charleston banks in a rather dull job. One day he told me that Jascha Heifetz was going to give a concert in Charleston the following evening and that he was lunching with him on the day of the concert. When he found that I played the violin, he invited me to the concert as his guest and told me that he had discovered that he and Heifetz bought their violin bows from the same maker in Philadelphia. Heifetz actually borrowed Smith's most recently acquired bow and used it at the concert.

Smith and I got along so well that he insisted that I bring my violin on my next visit to Charleston and said that he would arrange a little chamber music session. Thinking that I would be among amateurs, I accepted and found to my consternation that all the other players were professional musicians. In very short order it was apparent that I could not keep up with them, and I withdrew, while they proceeded to play one of Bartok's most recent compositions.

Smith himself was the most gifted amateur violinist I have ever heard play. He was a Princeton graduate who wanted to be a professional musician, but family and peer pressure had been too much for him. At his home I met a group of charming people, including a South African lady who talked about "hedgehopping" in a private plane just as we might speak of a fox hunt. By contrast, I was introduced at the Charleston Country Club to a group whose behavior at a club dinner was an eye-opener to a staid Baltimorean, although I had heard tales of similar unbridled conduct among some of the hunting set in Baltimore County.

During this time I was beginning to feel more secure in many ways. I felt that I had won my spurs professionally, and the financial affairs of my parents' household had become stabilized. I had renewed several old friendships, notably those with Johnny Howard and Dick Shackelford, and had developed new ones. I was keeping in touch with Horry Frost and made a point of visiting him at least twice a year, first in Asheville, North Carolina, where his family had rented a house near the Grove Park Inn, and later in Summerville, South Carolina, where many Charlestonians were in the habit of retreating from the city during the summer months. Through the Frost family, I learned to understand Charleston very much as I had learned to understand Boston through the Putnams and Philadelphia through the Lewises. I found that all these cultures were very much alike.

On my first visit to South Carolina, Horry's father met me at the train. At lunch when I inquired about the absence of the wife of Horry's younger brother, Horry's mother and her sisters smiled gently and said that she had gone out of town to look at a recently discovered manuscript which mentioned some of her ancestors. When I expressed some surprise that an interest in ancestors should be the source of amusement in Charleston, they replied, "She is from North Carolina." I later learned from Laura Frost that her ancestor had owned a plantation where John Paul Jones was raised and where the first shots were fired at the beginning of the Revolutionary War.

Mrs. Frost said that she quite understood how Laura must feel, as she herself had been raised near Columbia and was, therefore, regarded by Charlestonians as being "up country," although her friends always hastened to add that the Prestons were not really like up-country people and had always been considered perfectly acceptable in society.

During this time I was spending many evenings and holidays with Betsy Pleasants and her friends or with the Carrolls at Homewood. Unlike a number of my contemporaries, I had not married and, indeed, until the financial affairs of my family had been brought under control, I could not think seriously about matrimony. However, toward the end of this period, one after another of my friends got married. I acted as an usher for Johnny Howard, Dick Shackelford, and Coke Andrus and finally was invited to be present at the quiet wedding of Betsy Pleasants and Francis Jencks.

Physically, I was entering a period when for the first time in many years I had begun to feel healthy. I played tennis frequently on the grass courts at the Baltimore Country Club and while I shared with Francis Jencks the bottom of the tennis ladder, I came away from each session on the courts feeling relaxed and rested. In the winter I was equally content to take my place near the bottom of the squash ladder at the Baltimore Club. At least twice a week I went to the Baltimore Athletic Club and swam for half to three-quarters of an hour in the pool. One summer I discovered that surf bathing at Ocean City was a form of exercise that just suited my needs, and thereafter I spent most of my holidays there, sun and surf bathing and swimming up and down the beach a mile at a time. As a direct result of all this, my muscular development improved to the point where I was no longer conspicuous on the beach.

During the winter of 1935 I decided that I could afford for the first time in my life to take a midwinter vacation. I had read somewhere that Lord Frederick Hamilton, a famous British traveler of the nineteenth century, had said that the finest swimming in the world was at Doctor's Cove near Montego Bay on the northern coast of the island of Jamaica. My brother Fendall's wife, Jane Marbury, was going to Palm Beach to visit her brother Joel Massie and his wife, and we drove down together in my new Model A Ford convertible. I left my car at Palm Beach and took the train to Miami and from there flew to Kingston on one of the earliest flights of the Pan American flying boats over the open ocean. I remember that the pilots' quarters were crowded by crates of live chickens and was told that these were being flown down to Buenos Aires to gratify the palates of American tourists who found South American chicken too gamey for their tastes.

In Jamaica I spent three weeks at Doctor's Cove in a setting which looked as if it were designed by Somerset Maugham. On the night of my arrival I wandered over to the Hotel Casa Blanca, which was across the street from my more modest lodgings. As I strolled through the hotel, I ran into a mature American lady who asked my name and where I had gone to school and college. When I said the Episcopal High School and the University of Virginia, she said, "Hallelujah! I'm chaperoning three young girls who need male companionship. You are just what I have been looking for. Come with me."

From that time on, I spent nearly all of my days on the beach at Doctor's Cove, where I enjoyed the company of three very attractive girls from New York. One of them was the daughter of Mr. William Woodward, who was the owner of the Bel Air Stables in Maryland, and another was an exceptionally lovely young girl named Adelaide Whitehouse, who had recently made her debut in Newport and whose parents were social leaders in conservative New York circles.

A group of us met almost every day at the beach or at the grass tennis courts of the Montego Bay Club. Suddenly one of our tennis partners—a Mrs. O'Malley-Keyes, whose husband owned a department store in Hartford, Connecticut—announced to us that she had promised to look after the Duke of Kent and his beautiful bride, the Princess Marina of Roumania, who were arriving on their wedding trip. Of course, we thought that she was pulling our leg, but that afternoon the bridal couple arrived and dined with Mrs. O'Malley-Keyes at the hotel! They had taken a nearby cottage and were soon joined by the Duke of Gloucester, who had flown down to Jamaica with a polo team. Mrs. O'Malley-Keyes asked me if by any chance I had ever met a Mrs. Simpson who came from Baltimore. When I said that I had met her professionally, she confided to me that Mrs. Simpson had lived at the O'Malley-Keyes villa at Cannes while the Prince of Wales (whom she called "David") was a daily visitor. All of this turned out to be true and became public knowledge at the time of the abdication of Edward VIII.

When I got back to Baltimore, life seemed pretty tame. I found that the Whitehouse family had made inquiries about me from Mrs. Gordon Wilson, a friend of our family's who had lived in Newport, and, accordingly, I was not entirely surprised when I received an invitation to a ball which was being given at Newport for Adelaide Whitehouse, with whom I had kept up a correspondence for several months.

The following summer, I spent the weekend with my parents at Blue Ridge Summit, where my mother pointed across the dining room of the hotel to a young woman and said in very audible tones, "That is Natalie Jewett—go and speak to her." I had known Natalie Jewett as a schoolgirl classmate of my cousin Silvine Slingluff's and as the sister of Hugh Jewett, who was a fraternity brother of Jesse Slingluff, Jr.'s, at Johns Hopkins. I knew that she had recently married a man named Yandes Wheeler and was living in Washington and that he had been killed in an automobile accident. After his death, she had produced a son and was now living with the Wheelers in their home on 16th Street with little Yandes, who was then a year and a half old. During the next month I managed to spend several weekends at Blue Ridge Summit, and the more I saw of the widow Wheeler, the more I was attracted.

At that point I was invited to Canada to spend a weekend at a camp on the Jacques Cartier River north of the City of Quebec, where the Kernan family and their friends fished for trout. Here for the first time in my life I was called upon to do fly fishing. Learning to cast in fast water when the wind was blowing briskly was not easy, and at first I was shunned by the guides, who obviously regarded me as a menace. And rightly so, although the only victim of my clumsiness was my scalp, in which I embedded a Montrealer so firmly that I had to be taken into Quebec City to have it removed by a surgeon. He broke off the point of the hook and yanked the rest out of my scalp while laughing uproariously. I had sat through a long dinner at the camp headquarters with the Montrealer in the side of my head. The rest of the company acted as if it weren't there.

During that week I made up my mind to marry the widow Wheeler if she would have me, and when I got back to Baltimore, I set about courting in earnest. I regretted the Whitehouse party at Newport but sent orchids, for which, through some misunderstanding, my mother got the bill and demanded to know to whom I was sending flowers at the White House. For some weeks I commuted to Washington every week and finally persuaded the lady to marry me. All during this time my father had been ill with influenza, which he had contracted at Blue Ridge Summit and which resulted in his death in the latter part of October. While my father had been inactive for quite a few years, his death produced a flood of letters from people in all walks of life who were eager to testify to their regard and affection for him. Perhaps the most remarkable tribute came in a handwritten letter addressed to me by Henry L. Mencken, in which he said:

> I need not tell you how distressed I was to hear of your father's death. He was one of the best citizens Maryland ever had, and he will be missed. I only hope he left some account of his life, and that you will publish it. If he didn't, then you must do it.

Although I kept no copy of my reply, I apparently expressed doubts as to my ability to carry out his suggestion, because on November 2, 1935, he wrote once again as follows:

> I certainly hope you try to do that memoir of your father. Once you get started it will almost write itself. And once the news gets about that you are engaged upon it, you'll receive a lot of help from unexpected sources.
> I surely hope that the chance offers for a meeting soon.

Under the circumstances, Natalie and I decided to have a very quiet wedding in the presence of our two immediate families and a few close friends. Immediately after the wedding ceremony we left for New York on the train, and the wedding guests went back to the Wheeler house for a supper. I had made arrangements to spend our honeymoon in the city of Quebec. Unfortunately, I had not confided to Natalie where we were going, and she simply assumed that in December we would be headed south. The result was that we found ourselves in Montreal one morning with the temperature at zero, and after a few hours sightseeing, she was so cold that we went back to the hotel. I remembered that one of the girls that I had met in Philadelphia was living in Montreal, where her husband was working for a newspaper. I called her on the phone and told her about Natalie's predicament, and she told me to take her to Ogilvie's department store and get her a suit of long woolen underwear, which all the women wore when they had to go out in zero weather. She also invited us to come to dinner. Natalie got on the telephone and was told that the female guests would all be taken to a dressing room where they could take off the woolen underwear and come down to dinner properly dressed. From Montreal we went on to the city of Quebec and stayed at the Chateau Frontenac. We were entertained at dinner by Aunt Rose and by

Uncle Rob Kernan and his wife, whose father, Sir Charles Fitzpatrick, had been chief justice of Canada and then lieutenant-governor of the province of Quebec. We were invited to the Winter Club for lunch and to the Country Club for a hike on snowshoes. Altogether, it turned out to be a pretty good choice of a place to spend our honeymoon.

XII ✤ 1937–1940: Tumultuous Years

The year 1936 in many ways marked a change in what it is now fashionable to call my "life style." Domestically, matrimony and the acquisition of a ready-made family in little Yandes, soon supplemented by the arrival of a son of my own begetting, was a far cry from the life which I had been living. It is true that my wife and I came from the same social set; our mothers both belonged to the Tuesday Bridge Club, and our fathers had both been raised on country estates and had come to Baltimore to practice law. Furthermore, we were both confirmed Episcopalians. Still, there were marked differences in our approach to living and we both had many adjustments to make.

For example, a Marbury family party typically numbered anywhere from twenty-five to fifty people and sometimes even more. My wife's family consisted of four people: her mother, a brother, a sister, and an aunt. True, she had other relatives living outside the state, but it was years before I met any of them, and then the contact was very brief. Again, music had played an important role in my life, and I was accustomed to spend hours at the piano or listening to phonograph records, not to speak of regular meetings of our Sunday-night group. My wife's contact with music and musicians consisted of occasional trips to the opera on the rare occasions when it came to Baltimore. She also was fond of old-fashioned musical comedies and remembered the words of every popular song going back to the 1890s, claiming that she had learned them at her mother's knee. Moreover, she went to St. Paul's Church in downtown Baltimore every Sunday morning, whereas I was accustomed to spend those mornings on the tennis courts or walking in the country.

Some of these differences were solved easily—she went to concerts with me, and I went to church with her—but there were others which were less easily adjusted. Fortunately for me, she was more than willing to devote herself to making things comfortable for me, and I did my best to reciprocate. So we got through the early months of living together with less friction than might have been expected of people of our age. But the truth is that for both of us, the change was fairly radical.

At the death of her great-uncle Kennon Jewett in 1936, Natalie had inherited a small estate which together with my professional earnings made it possible for us to maintain a style of living which by present-day standards seems almost luxurious. At first we lived in an apartment on Mulberry Street, while little Yandes and his nurse stayed at the Preston Apartments with Natalie's mother. My mother had trained a young boy named Gough Jimerson as cook, butler, and general houseman, and she graciously let him work for us on a full-time basis. After three months we moved to a rented house on Roland Court, where we were joined by Yandes. Gough and the nurse made us quite comfortable while we awaited the arrival of our first child.

Natalie's mother, Mrs. Hugh Jewett, still owned the old Jewett place in Harford County where Natalie had been raised as a girl. The Victorian mansion was unoccupied, but other buildings were rented, as were the fields, but for barely enough to take care of the taxes and other expenses. At her request, I looked into the arrangements which had been made with the tenants and, with the help of Brodnax Cameron's law partner Frank Jacobs, explored the possibility of selling or renting the entire property. At that time it appeared that real estate in that remote corner of the county was a drug on the market. Somehow I managed to get up to Harford County enough to begin to understand the woes of the absentee property owner who could see her land literally running away in gullies and streams while the old buildings creaked and groaned in every storm.

At the office also new responsibilities came my way. As a result of my father's death, I took over the legal representation of the Travelers Insurance Company, which overlooked a flagrant blunder on my part. Simon Sobeloff sued the Travelers on behalf of a client who claimed total disability benefits under a policy issued by that company. The amount involved was approximately $50,000. The case came on for trial before Judge Coleman. At the conclusion of Sobeloff's opening statement of the case, Judge Coleman announced that he felt bound to instruct the jury to bring in a verdict for the Travelers on the basis of admissions made by Sobeloff in his opening statement. At this point court was adjourned until the following day.

Sobeloff then came to my office and after some discussion we reached an agreement to settle the case for $7,500. The following morning he and I went to Judge Coleman's office to tell him that the case had been settled, when, to our astonishment, Judge Coleman demanded to know how much the Travelers had agreed to pay. When he heard the amount, he said that it was not nearly enough and then revealed that the plaintiff had come unannounced to his home late the night before and had put on a scene which convinced the judge that he was indeed totally disabled. Judge Coleman said that he would have to testify as a witness to what had taken place and would therefore disqualify himself and refer the case to Judge Chesnut.

The Travelers people were indignant and instructed me to make every effort to make the settlement stick. Sobeloff, of course, felt that he had been put in an impossible position and asked Roszel Thomsen to come into the case. A hearing was set before Judge Chesnut to determine whether or not the agreement to settle could be enforced. After hearing the testimony of Sobeloff and of Judge Coleman, Judge Chesnut declined to enforce the settlement, so we went to trial on the question of permanent total disability. At the trial I was successful in convincing the jury that the disability was not total and permanent, but they brought in a verdict for $30,000 on the theory that the plaintiff was partially disabled. The Travelers instructed me to appeal the case to the Fourth Circuit Court of Appeals.

Under a peculiar rule, since abolished, the right of appeal in cases of this character expired with the term of court. I had overlooked the rule and we were still negotiating in a final effort to settle the case when I discovered that the term had expired and that it was too late to perfect an appeal. As a result, the Travelers could have held me responsible for the difference between the amount of the aborted settlement and the jury's verdict. Much to my relief, the Travelers, after consultation with the home office, said to forget it and paid the judgment.

At about this time I learned that Mr. Williams was terminally ill with cancer, and in 1937, while at the height of his career as a lawyer, he died. His death, coming so soon after that of my father, was a hard blow. Between them they had given me most of the interesting work that had come my way.

The Deeds Option

At the time of the death of Mr. Williams, a case had been pending for several years in the federal District Court of Maryland. He and I represented a number of directors of the National Cash Register Company who had been sued, along with the company, on July 5, 1934, by the holders of approximately 120 shares of the stock of the company. Our principal client was Colonel Edward A. Deeds, who was the chief executive officer of the company at the time suit was filed and who had acquired 50,000 shares of the company's stock as a result of the exercise of an option given to him at the time of his employment as chief executive officer. Among the objectives of the suit was the cancellation of those shares.

Colonel Deeds was one of the pioneers of the automotive industry. Along with Charles F. Kettering of General Motors, he had designed and placed on the market the first modern ignition system for motor vehicles, the first automatic starter for motor vehicles, the first system for supplying electric lights to motor vehicles, the first electrical house lighting system, and the first electric refrigerator. He had organized and successfully developed the Delco Company and the Delco Electric Light and Power Company. He and Mr. Kettering had designed for Mr. Leland of the Cadillac Company the first practicable eight-cylinder automobile motor. During World War I, he was primarily responsible for what a member of the British War Mission described as "the finest feat in design and production that has been accomplished during the war so far as aircraft matters are concerned," viz., the Liberty motor. Along with those of Henry Ford and the Wright Brothers, his name was a household word in industry.

For a time Colonel Deeds had been the acting chief executive officer of the National Cash Register Company, but other business interests drew him away and he was succeeded by Frederick Patterson, the son of the founder, who with the assistance of the Depression lost no time in getting the company into deep financial trouble. At the age of 75, Deeds was called back to take charge once more, and in addition to a salary of $100,000, was given an option on a total of 50,000 shares of the company stock at a figure slightly above the market price on the day that the option contract was signed. In a few years under Colonel Deeds's management, the company was restored to profitability and the market value of the option stock went way up.

It was at this point that suit was filed by the holders of 120 shares of the company stock. The counsel for the plaintiffs in the case were Arthur and Bernard Berenson of the Massachusetts bar and Lawrence Berenson of the New York bar. As the result of the illness and subsequent death of Mr. Williams, the full responsibility for handling this case fell on me and on Dorsey Watkins, who was representing the company. He and I made a number of trips together to New York and to Dayton, Ohio, where the company's headquarters were located. After spending all day interviewing witnesses and reviewing documents, we liked to relax and see a show, but, unfortunately, our tastes differed. When I persuaded him to go to a play in New York which had been highly praised by the critics as a political satire worthy of W. S. Gilbert, Dorsey protested that he had never been so bored—that it was like being subjected to a recital in verse of one of Frank Kent's columns. In retaliation, he took me to a wrestling match where two gorilla-like brutes pretended to tear each other limb from limb while emitting grunts, groans, and howls of pain, to the apparent delight of the audience. We finally got together on a comedy called *Hellzapoppin,* which both of us found amusing. I believe it was the first Broadway production in which the actors ran up and down the aisles and involved the audience in the action.

The trial of this case was an extraordinary experience, as Mr. Lawrence Berenson was as unlike the typical New York lawyer as could be. His delivery was as florid as that of Senator William Cabell Bruce, and as one listened to him, the word *thespian* took on a new meaning. I filed a brief in which I pointed out that in an effort to support his attack on the option agreement, Mr. Berenson "substituted abuse for reasoning and adjectives for record references," and that "far from being sustained, his contention was directly disproved by the evidence." Judge Coleman in his opinion quoted this language and said that he agreed with it.

Mr. Berenson appealed, and I was busy drafting the brief in the Fourth Circuit when Edwin G. Baetjer came to see me. He had been asked by New York counsel to go into the case with me and wanted to know what it was all about. Mr. Baetjer was then recognized as the outstanding corporation lawyer in Maryland and one of the national leaders of the profession in that field. A few days later he called to tell me that he had informed the New York lawyers that Colonel Deeds's case was in good hands and that he could not at this late date add anything that would be of any help. This generous action was typical of the truly great leaders of the bar in that generation. Fortunately, Dorsey Watkins and I won the case.

The Garrett Will

John W. Garrett, the former ambassador to Italy, owned Evergreen, almost the last of the great residential estates in Baltimore City. There, since his retirement from the foreign service, he and his wife, Alice, had lived in a style which had no parallel in the Baltimore community. With a retinue of Italian servants, they entertained the social leaders of Baltimore and Washington with dinner parties which were followed by concerts of chamber music performed by the Musical Arts Quartet, whose members lived in a separate building on the Evergreen Estate. While in Italy, the Garretts had rented the Villa San Michele on the Island of Capri, where they had entertained the diplomatic and social sets of Rome with concerts performed by the same quartet, for whom Mrs. Garrett had purchased four very fine instruments which she lent to them for their general use.

Mrs. Garrett had at one time taken a great interest in the Peabody Institute, of which her husband was a trustee. At the death of Harold Randolph she had tried to persuade the trustees to appoint her friend Olga Samaroff Gabrilowitch as director of the conservatory. When they chose Mr. Ortmann instead, she was vocal in her criticism and insisted that Mr. Garrett resign from the board.

I soon came to realize what an extraordinarily vital person Alice Garrett really was. She had taken up ballet dancing when she was living in Paris and had been painted by Zuloaga in the costume of a Spanish dancer. While in Paris she had also begun to paint and to study voice, all under famous instructors. Back in Baltimore at the age of 70 she took up golf and plodded her way around the golf course before the days of electric carts. She remodeled the old carriage house at Evergreen into a theater and persuaded Leon Bakst to decorate it as well as to paint her portrait. She redecorated the residence at Evergreen and added a beautiful library designed by Lawrence Fowler. Then she took up gardening and installed one of the finest examples of landscape architecture to be found anywhere in Maryland. In truth, her life was patterned on that of an Italian Renaissance princess, and Baltimore was torn between amazement and grudging admiration.

The Garretts had no children and were well aware that none of their nephews and nieces could continue the style of life which they had established at Evergreen. Accordingly, Mr. Garrett had made up his mind to leave Evergreen to the Johns Hopkins University, but he wanted to make sure that Mrs. Garrett could remain there undisturbed as long as she wished to do so. When Mr. Rawls and I met with Mr. and Mrs. Garrett, it was my responsibility to ask a number of pertinent questions, the answers to which could have a bearing on the tax consequences of any estate plan which Mr. Garrett might decide to pursue.

Obviously, a very pertinent question was that of Mrs. Garrett's age, and I began to approach this sensitive matter indirectly. Mrs. Garrett very quickly caught my drift and said, "Bill, if you want to know how old I am, the answer is, I don't know, but if you have to know, you can write to the courthouse in Xenia, Ohio, where they have my birth certificate on record. But don't tell me! I don't want to know how old I am. I am sick and tired of hearing my friends say that they are too old to undertake this or that. That is something I never intend to do."

Glenn L. Martin

Glenn Martin was a legendary figure. Among the first of the barnstorming air pilots, he was the third man to fly an airplane under power and the first to fly a seaplane over the open ocean. In both cases he was flying in a plane of his own design and manufacture. By the time of the entry of the United States into the First World War in April 1917, he had built a factory at Cleveland, Ohio, where he had adapted to the production of aircraft the assembly-line methods pioneered in the automotive industry by Henry Ford.

By 1928 Mr. Martin's early image as a daredevil stunt pilot had been superseded, and he had become recognized as one of the giants of a growing industry. In that year he began to build a new plant at Middle River in Baltimore County, Maryland. His commitment to the Baltimore area was soon confirmed when he and his mother, Mrs. Minta Martin, established their residence in Baltimore at the Ambassador Apartments. Mrs. Martin was recognized by all who knew Mr. Martin personally as the single greatest influence in his life, and those who worked for him knew the extent of her influence and were very careful to keep in her good graces. She was a shrewd, hard-headed woman who shared her son's ambition and determination. Her faith in his genius was strikingly evidenced by the fact that she accompanied him as a passenger in some of his pioneer flights, sitting on a wing of the plane. He had been heard to say that he never made any important decision without consulting her, and all candidates for executive responsibilities in the Martin Company were required to pass inspection by Mrs. Martin before their names were submitted to the board of directors.

As the Middle River plant grew, a variety of questions presented themselves which called for the services of legal counsel, and the firm of Marbury, Gosnell and Williams became quite active on behalf of this new client. The Depression which followed the collapse of the stock market in 1929 had an effect on the company sufficiently drastic to cause the company's Cleveland counsel to recommend that relief be sought by the filing of a plan of reorganization under the newly enacted Section 77B of the Bankruptcy Act, which permitted a recapitalization of business enterprises without the cumbersome and drastic procedures which had previously been the only means of reorganizing companies which were in financial difficulties. Accordingly, our firm filed on behalf of the Martin Company what was the first proceeding under that act ever brought in the District of Maryland, if not the first such proceeding in the United States.

Soon after he moved to Baltimore, Mr. Martin, at the invitation of Howard Bruce, joined the Board of Directors of the Baltimore National Bank, where he made the acquaintance of John E. Semmes. At that time John Semmes, with the possible exception of James Piper, was the most adept lawyer in this community at speaking the language of business executives, and within a relatively short time he so impressed Mr. Martin that he was invited to accompany him and his mother on a trip to Europe. Not long thereafter, the firm of Semmes, Bowen and Semmes began to appear as counsel for the company in important matters, and it became quite clear that Glenn L. Martin had changed his Baltimore lawyers.

However, John Semmes had moved his residence to Victoria in British Columbia and was spending less and less time at his office in Baltimore, and the affairs of the Martin Company had been turned over to one of the younger partners at Semmes, Bowen and Semmes, who has since died. In 1936, Mrs. Martin called my wife and invited us to spend Sunday cruising down the Chesapeake Bay on the Martin yacht. Apparently we passed inspection, for a few days later I was asked to come down to the plant and talk to Joseph Hartson, who was at that time in charge of the company's operations. Hartson told me that the company was faced with a number of new problems as a result of changes in federal laws and regulations, particularly in the field of labor relations. He said that they would like me to act as counsel to the company in these matters but that the firm of Semmes, Bowen and Semmes would continue to handle some contested matters which were then pending in the federal courts, in which the appearance of that firm had previously been entered. He assured me that this could be done without embarrassment to their relations with Semmes, Bowen and Semmes.

I gathered that up to that point the company's attitude had always been one of complete noncooperation and resistance to all efforts of the National Labor Relations Board to inject itself into the labor relations of the company. I spent several weeks at the plant, and it seemed to me that with very minor adjustments, all the complaints which were then pending (except those already in litigation) could be settled without serious interference with the company's labor objectives. With the willing cooperation of the personnel director, I proceeded to explore that possibility. In the meantime, Semmes, Bowen and Semmes had abruptly notified Hartson that they were withdrawing as counsel in all matters which they were handling for the company. In the end, we worked out a settlement with the NLRB, to the great satisfaction of the company, and during the next several years, I became the principal legal adviser on labor relations to the company.

At the same time Mr. Martin began consulting me about various problems arising in connection with some personal interests which he had acquired on the Eastern Shore of Maryland. From that time on, I acted as his personal counsel until his death on October 4, 1955, when I was named as one of his executors. Then I learned for the first time that he had an older sister, who was 73 years of age and was living in a nursing home in California. Under his will, which had been prepared for him by my partner Van Wolf, a trust fund in the amount of fifty thousand dollars had been created, the income from which was to be paid to his sister. Because of Mr. Martin's failure to complete his instructions to Van, a question had arisen as to the disposition of a large portion of his sixteen-million-dollar estate. As it appeared that his sister would have a strong claim to as much as four million dollars, I sent Van out to California to discuss the situation with her. What he found was a gaunt, shriveled old lady "who looked rather like a wild animal." She was living as a ward of the state of California, which was paying her expenses at the Monterey Sanitarium as a destitute person. As such she had been required to live in a room with three other patients and had been deprived of adequate mental and dental care. She was in need of eyeglasses and for lack of dentures had been limited to a soft diet, which she ate with a spoon from a bowl.

Her only clothing were regulation gowns supplied to her by the sanitarium. Her only recreation was watching television and attending classes in occupational therapy.

It developed that she had been living under these conditions since 1950, when she was removed from Patton State Mental Hospital at the insistence of the superintendent. Apparently she had been confined to that hospital since 1911, when she suffered a temporary mental disorder. Mr. James Sheppard, a Los Angeles lawyer who at my request had agreed to act as guardian of her property, reported to me as follows:

> I think you ought to know, in passing, that no real reason has been found as to why her mother and her brother insisted on keeping her in such an environment. Even the superintendent at the State Hospital at Patton has advised us that he went over her situation thoroughly with her brother and that her brother, nevertheless, refused to remove her from the State Hospital even though the superintendent advised Mr. Martin that there was no reason whatever for her to remain there.

A home was purchased for Miss Martin in San Marino, where she lived with a companion until her ninety-first birthday. In the meantime she traveled all around the country, as well as to Australia, and finally died on February 28, 1974, after nearly twenty years of happy existence as a normal person. All of this was made possible by the fact that she received from the estate of her brother a total of approximately three million dollars, which she never would have gotten had he not procrastinated in giving Van Wolf instructions as to what disposition he wished to make of the residue of his estate.

WFBR

Hope H. Barroll, Jr., a younger brother of my brother-in-law Wethered Barroll's, had been an employee of Baltimore Radio Show, Inc., which operated WFBR, the first radio station in the city of Baltimore. His father-in-law, Robert S. Maslin, was the largest stockholder in that company, and through this connection Hope had been employed at the station. The manager of the station was named Jack Stewart, and he and Hope did not get along. Stewart arranged to have the company issue a large block of additional shares of stock which at his instigation were purchased by Dr. Alfred R. L. Dohme, a retired Baltimore businessman who was a well-known patron of the arts. The obvious purpose and the effect of this transaction was to vest the control of the corporation in Jack Stewart, who then proceeded to fire Hope Barroll. I then brought suit on Mr. Maslin's behalf to set aside the issuance of the Dohme stock. The case was tried before Judge Eugene O'Dunne, who found that the issuance of the stock was unlawful and directed that it be canceled. Following that decision a new board of directors was elected. Stewart was fired as manager and Hope Barroll became the executive vice-president of the company, which he ran very successfully until his death.

In 1938 Hope decided on a major investment in a new transmitter for the station, which was then operating on a frequency of 1270 kilocycles, with the power of five kilowatts by day and one kilowatt by night. The new transmitter was to operate at five kilowatts day and night and was designed to give protection to other stations operating on frequencies which were similar to or adjacent to 1270. After the new transmitter had been completed at an expense in excess of $137,000, it was discovered that the government of the United States had entered into an unpublished Executive Agreement pursuant to the North American Regional Broadcasting Agreement signed at Havana, Cuba, on December 13, 1937. This Executive Agreement between the governments of the United States and Canada was dated October 28, 1938, and assigned the frequency of 1300 kc to a Canadian station operating out of Rimouski in the Province of Quebec with a power of 1,000 watts at night. When WFBR applied to the Federal Communications Commission for permission to raise its nighttime power to 5 kw, objections were filed on the ground that because of interference with the station at Rimouski, granting the application would violate the Havana Agreement as modified by the Executive Agreement.

After discussion with WFBR's engineering and communications consultants in Washington, it became apparent that the only way to salvage WFBR's investment in the new transmitter was to enter into negotiations with the owner of the Rimouski station. I found out that the owner was a French-Canadian named J. A. Brilliant who was a close political friend of the Canadian minister of transport, who was in charge of the regulation of Canadian radio stations.

At this point I decided that I needed the help of Canadian counsel. Charlie Cannon, the brother of Douglas Cannon, with whom I had gone fishing in 1935, was then practicing law in Quebec City in partnership with his uncle, who had been a premier of the province of Quebec. Three of Charlie's ancestors had been chief justices of the Supreme Court of Canada. One was named Cannon, another Taschereau, and the third was Sir Charles Fitzpatrick, who was at that time lieutenant-governor of the province of Quebec. Sir Charles's daughter Alice was the wife of Robert Kernan, the brother-in-law of my Uncle Jesse Slingluff. The Kernans, Cannons, Taschereaus, and Fitzpatricks were all members of a group who spent their summers at Murray Bay and were all related by blood or marriage.

Accordingly, I got in touch with Charlie and with his assistance opened negotiations with Brilliant. I well remember sitting in Charlie's office in Quebec City while he was talking on the telephone to Brilliant in

French. It was the first time I had ever watched a real bilinguist operate. He could shift languages as easily as I could shift gears on my car. We later went down to Rimouski and ultimately reached a meeting of the minds on a plan which required modification of the Executive Agreement. After traveling to Ottawa and meeting with the minister of transport, Mr. Howe, we were successful in having the Rimouski station moved from 1030 kc to 900 kc and WFBR to 1300 kc with the approval of both governments, and thereupon both the Rimouski station and WFBR were granted permission to operate with 5 kw at night.

I thoroughly enjoyed this experience. We had exactly the right connections, and the courteous manner in which we were received by the Canadians made the whole task a very pleasant one. There was a good deal of sitting around and waiting, as the pace of negotiations was quite stately, just as it would have been in doing business in Southern Maryland at that time. Fortunately, because of the amenities of the Chateau Frontenac in Quebec City and the Chateau Laurier in Ottawa, I relished the time that I had to spend in Canada.

Moreover, the representation of WFBR brought me into one of the most interesting cases of my entire career as a lawyer. The Supreme Bench of Baltimore City had adopted a rule of court forbidding the publication of any matter obtained in violation of a standing prohibition against the issuance by police authorities, the state's attorney, counsel for the defense, or any other person having official connection with the case, of any statement relative to the conduct of an accused person, any statements or admissions made by the accused, or any other matter bearing upon the issues to be tried, and specifically characterizing any such publications as a punishable contempt. The rule had been framed for the express purpose of protecting a person accused of crime by prohibiting the publication of facts which would be likely to prevent him from obtaining a fair trial.

WFBR and other radio stations were cited for contempt because they broadcast a United Press dispatch which clearly violated this rule. In the Court of Appeals of Maryland I argued successfully that the Supreme Bench rule was a violation of the First Amendment to the Federal Constitution which by virtue of the Fourteenth Amendment was binding on the state of Maryland. Needless to say, this ruling was hailed enthusiastically by the press, and when the judges of the Supreme Court refused to hear the case, their action was given nationwide publicity, especially as Justice Frankfurter had departed from the usual practice of the court by filing an opinion expressing his own views on this important subject.

I am sorry to say that the decision in WFBR's case opened the door to what has since become a scandalous practice of the news media of analyzing and discussing the evidence before and during the trial of cases they deem newsworthy. This has given counsel for the accused ammunition with which to delay trials and set aside verdicts of guilt and has in some cases led to the sequestration of jurors in prolonged trials where the news media have undertaken to discuss and analyze evidence even before the jury has brought in a verdict. I take little satisfaction in having taken a leading part in bringing about so unhappy a condition of affairs.

Two other developments which began during this period had a profound influence on my future. The first was an outgrowth of my support of Franklin Roosevelt for president in 1932 and again in 1936. In 1932 I had made a few speeches on his behalf and thereafter had kept in touch with some of my Harvard Law School friends who came to Washington in the early days of the New Deal. On one occasion I acted as local counsel for the Agricultural Adjustment Administration in a suit brought in the federal court in Baltimore, in which I was instructed to challenge the jurisdiction of the court on the ground that the secretary of agriculture, Henry Wallace, had not been served with process in Maryland. That issue was quickly complicated when Charlie Page, a Baltimore lawyer who represented the plaintiffs in the case, jumped on a night train in the Pennsylvania Station in Baltimore and served the papers on Mr. Wallace, who was in his pajamas and about to climb into his berth for a night's rest. Needless to say, Mr. Wallace was highly indignant, and I was instructed to challenge the validity of this service, but found Judge Chesnut unresponsive.

In 1936, I made some campaign speeches on behalf of Mr. Roosevelt, one of which was broadcast over the radio. When shortly after his reelection the president introduced what became known as the "court packing" bill, I was deeply shocked. Like most of my generation I had deplored some of the decisions of the Supreme Court invalidating acts of Congress which had been enacted in Roosevelt's first administration, but I was strongly opposed to coercing the court to change its rulings.

Accordingly, I responded with some eagerness to an invitation from Grenville Clark to join him and a number of other lawyers who had supported Mr. Roosevelt in 1936 in organizing a committee to fight the president's bill. I attended a meeting of that committee and took part in the discussion which was led by Mr. Clark. After the meeting he asked me to act as secretary of the committee, and I agreed to do so. He had made it clear that he preferred not to hold any office in the committee, and at my suggestion he offered the chairmanship to Douglas Arant of Birmingham, Alabama, whom I had known when he was a law student at Virginia. For the next year I helped in the preparation of literature designed to rally the support of influential lawyers all over the country. I became deeply impressed by Mr. Clark's knowledge of the national bar and of the members of Congress. He was a superb lobbyist and had a dogged determination which did not shrink from what at first looked to be an uphill fight. I believe that he was responsible for securing several votes against the president's bill which, together with other breaks, proved to be enough to defeat it.

Another development that was even more important to my future began in 1938. As a part of my general effort to improve my "image" among my fellow lawyers, I had become more active in bar association affairs. In that year the American Bar Association, under the leadership of Judge John J. Parker of the federal Court of Appeals for the Fourth Circuit, had adopted an ambitious program for improving the administration of justice. As a first step, the ABA recommended that each local bar association press the highest court of the state to adopt rules governing procedure in all civil cases.

Recognizing that this was a statewide issue, I asked the president of the Maryland State Bar Association to appoint a committee of lawyers from all over the state, and I was named as chairman of that committee. A statute which we drafted was presented to the legislature by the attorney general of the state as an administration measure, with the full approval of Governor O'Conor. After hearings, the bill was unanimously adopted.

At this point a group of lawyers led by Arthur W. Machen and Walter H. Buck denounced the bill as unconstitutional and unnecessary. At the next meeting of the state bar association, a heated debate took place as to whether the association should reject the report of our committee. Mr. Buck and Mr. Machen both charged that the whole idea of controlling court proceedings by rules of court was a part of the New Deal and expressed their preference for the "horse and buggy days." They were followed by Mr. Charles Markell, who came to my rescue in a fiery speech in which he said that he yielded to no man in his nostalgia for "horse and buggy days," but he drew the line at going back to "bow and arrow days." This brought down the house and the report of our committee was endorsed by an overwhelming vote.

However, the fight was not over. The Court of Appeals then asked both the city and the state bar association for written statements as to their views on the constitutionality of the exercise by the Court of Appeals of rule-making power by delegation from the legislature. I prepared a memorandum on behalf of the committee on civil procedure of the Bar Association of Baltimore City, and this memorandum was also signed by all the members of the previous committee on civil procedure of the Maryland State Bar Association.

At this point, Mr. Machen, who was the incoming president of the state bar association, appointed a brand-new committee on civil procedure and named five lawyers who had already voted against the report of my committee, leaving me in a minority of one. On November 10, 1939, the majority of the new committee filed a report urging that the Court of Appeals adopt no rules in civil cases. I filed a minority report, and the issue came before the association once more. Again, by an overwhelming vote, the association voted in favor of the exercise of the rule-making power. The legislature agreed.

While this long fight was going on in Maryland, the American Bar Association and the American Judicature Society were kept informed and, to my surprise, I found that I had been elected to the board of directors of the latter, which in those days was thought to be the first step toward important office in the American Bar Association. The association and the society were meeting in Philadelphia in the summer of 1940, and I went up there to find out exactly what my duties were going to be as a member of the board of the society. There I ran into Jim Landis, who at that time was the dean of the Harvard Law School. He told me that two of our classmates, Robert Proctor and Warren Ege, had gone down to Washington to help Judge Robert P. Patterson, who had just been appointed as assistant secretary of war. I indicated to him that I felt rather envious. By this time the "phony war" in Europe had ended and Hitler's army had overrun most of Western Europe. The president had announced an enormous program calling for the production of twenty-five thousand military aircraft. The secretary of war and his assistant had resigned and been replaced by Henry L. Stimson and Judge Patterson, and most people felt that our country would eventually become involved in the fighting. When I got back to my office, I found that I had a letter from Judge Patterson.

XIII ❧ Preparing for War at Wright Field

In the preceding chapters I have all but ignored the events which were darkening the skies over Europe during the 1930s. Like most Americans, I had not read *Mein Kampf* and did not take very seriously the early rise of Hitler and his band of revolutionaries. In Italy we had seen what had first appeared to be a relatively benign attempt to create some sort of order out of political and economic chaos, and Mussolini's bullying of Ethiopia, while distasteful, did not really alarm us. No doubt because of my Austrian connections, I was more sensitive to the political developments in that country, and for me the assassination of Engelbert Dollfuss, followed by the virtual annexation of Austria by the Nazis, set the warning signals going full tilt. Moreover, as reports began to come in from our friends who had been living in Munich and Vienna, I became aware that the Nazis were in many ways the mirror image of the Bolsheviks who had triumphed in Russia. Hitler's treatment of the Jews in particular seemed a throwback to barbarism. Nevertheless, like most of my countrymen, I at first saw no role for the United States to play except to keep our powder dry and try to avoid commitments which would involve us in what began to look like another Thirty Years War.

During the spring of 1940, Natalie and I visited the Frost family in Charleston. We were taken by Mrs. Frost to see the last of the Ravenel sisters, who lived at the old family home on the Battery in an upstairs room where she had been confined for many years by illness. She spoke to us of her childhood in Baltimore before the Civil War and seemed extraordinarily alert for one of her great age. As we were leaving, she said to Mrs. Frost, " 'Stine, you must show Mr. and Mrs. Marbury the drawing room." Then we went down the stairs, through the front hall, and out the front door. I asked Mrs. Frost about the drawing room, and she replied, "All the furniture in the room was taken away years ago, but no one has told her. She was very proud of the family antiques and they don't want her to know that they have been sold."

In that same week, Hitler's invasion of Norway and Denmark marked the end of the "phony war" in Europe and the beginning of full-scale war-fare, which was to last for another five years. The Chamberlain govern-ment fell in England, and the United States, which like old Miss Ravenel had been living in a fantasy world, came down to harsh realities and be-gan to prepare to defend itself. President Roosevelt called on Congress to finance the production of twenty-five thousand combat planes for the armed services, and Congress responded by appropriating funds to get the program under way. At the same time a group under the leadership of Grenville Clark successfully agitated for the reopening of officer train-ing camps on the Plattsburg model and the passage of a Selective Service bill which would authorize the drafting of young men into military ser-vice. As a necessary preliminary to the enactment of the draft bill, the president, at the suggestion of Mr. Clark (acting through Justice Felix Frankfurter, who had the ear of the president), had removed the secre-tary of war and appointed in his place Mr. Henry L. Stimson, who had held that office under President Taft. At Mr. Clark's suggestion, Mr. Stim-son made his acceptance conditional on the appointment of Robert P. Pat-terson as the assistant secretary of war.

This brings me back to my letter from Judge Patterson. I had long ago heard of him as a partner in a relatively small but rising law firm in New York, then as a federal district judge in the Southern District of New York, and later as a member of the Court of Appeals for the Second Cir-cuit, where he sat along with the two Hands, "Learned" and "Gus."

When I called Judge Patterson, I spoke to his secretary, Miss Mundy, who told me that the judge would like to see me and hoped that I could come to Washington. I said I would come whenever it was convenient for him to see me, but that since he was a very busy person, she would have to name the date and time. She replied that perhaps I would drop in some-time the next afternoon. So I went to his office the next afternoon without an appointment. This I later found was completely characteristic. Anyone who wanted to see the Judge could drop by his office, and unless the Judge was in a meeting, Miss Mundy would in very short order fit the visitor in. In this way people did not feel that he was trying to impress them with how busy he was, and no one wasted Judge Patterson's time.

Judge Patterson told me that a number of vitally important contracts were being held up at Wright Field, where the central procurement agency of the air force was located. He said that there was need for the services of some first-rate lawyers who could analyze the problems which were causing the hold-ups and do the necessary negotiating with the con-tractors' lawyers and accountants to get things moving again. The judge advocate general's office could not supply this need, and so Judge Patter-son had turned to the Harvard Law School for help. Dean Landis had suggested Warren Ege and Bob Proctor, both of whom had agreed to go to Wright Field for a few weeks and try to break the logjam. They found themselves badly in need of more assistance, and Landis had suggested that I might be able to join them, also on a temporary basis. Could I do so? Like them, I would be designated as an expert consultant at a very modest per diem. I told the Judge that I knew nothing about the subject, but he said that Proctor and Ege could teach me all that I needed to know.

I found Wright Field to be a beehive of activity. As in a beehive, there was an all-pervading hum, day and night, of engines and propellers being tested, and airplanes of all sizes and models were continuously taking off and landing on the adjacent runways. At one point a little single-engine training plane shot right across the path of a huge bomber which was about to land, and I later heard the bomber pilot say that for a few seconds he thought he might have to use his windshield wiper. I was told that the co-pilot of the bomber was President Roosevelt's son Elliott, who was in training there.

The man in charge of the procurement program was Colonel Aaron Jones, who was neither a lawyer nor an accountant. He had the assistance of a Major Shaw in the Judge Advocate General's Corps, who had practiced law in a small town in Kentucky. He also had the assistance of an accountant in uniform who seemed to know his business. On those three men rested the primary responsibility for negotiating the contracts for which Judge Patterson was waiting, and they were simply overwhelmed.

Our immediate task was to get these contracts signed up. The obstacles were twofold: First, the contractors did not have the necessary facilities to perform the contracts in the time required, and second, many concerns refused to participate in the program because of the imposition by the Walsh-Healey Act of a limitation of 8 percent on the profits of all contractors and subcontractors engaged in the manufacture of aircraft for the government. The second obstacle could readily be eliminated by the repeal of the profit limitation and the substitution of an excess profits tax, and such a program was recommended by the National Defense Advisory Commission with the approval of the Treasury Department.

However, it was obvious that this would not solve the problem of providing more production facilities. Normally, facilities needed for the performance of a contract are financed by including the cost in the contract price, but this method would not work in the face of a high excess-profits tax. For tax purposes the cost of new facilities is frequently not deductible over the life of a single contract, so what the government gives the contractor in the contract price to cover the cost of facilities is taken away by high tax rates.

Another objection to the traditional method of financing plant expansions was first voiced by John L. Lewis, namely, that the contractor would get a windfall in the shape of new plant facilities for which the government had in effect paid. This argument was persuasive with the administration, and the National Defense Advisory Commission after thorough consideration announced this policy: whenever a contract price included more than normal depreciation on plant facilities, steps should be taken to protect the interest of the government in those facilities. This declaration of policy, added to uncertainties as to tax deductions, had effectively closed the door to plant facilities expansion and brought the aircraft procurement program to a standstill.

In order to get it going again, two steps were taken: first, Congress authorized a special amortization deduction of 20 percent on those plant facilities expansions which had been certified as necessary in the interests of national defense, upon condition that where more than normal depreciation was included in a contract price, the interest of the government be adequately protected. Provision was made for issuance of certificates that the government's interest had been adequately protected. By this means the contractor who desired to finance his facilities expansion out of his own resources was permitted to retain additional profits to the extent of 20 percent a year for the cost of the facilities. On the other hand, the contractor who looked to the government to finance the facilities expansion, by way of inclusion in the contract price or otherwise, was required to protect the interest of the government in the facilities. The second step was to establish a method of government financing of plant facilities. By the time that I came on the scene, a so-called emergency plant facilities contract had been worked out. This provided for construction by the contractor at his own expense of new plant facilities and subsequent reimbursement to him over a sixty-month period with ultimate passage of title to the government subject to the contractor's option.

I began by making a list of all of the contracts that were under negotiation, indicating what was holding each one of them up. In this connection I found that the contracting officers were faced with directives which came down from a variety of Washington offices. Sometimes it appeared to take weeks for Wright Field to learn of decisions which bore directly on their day-to-day negotiations, and sometimes their first knowledge of important rulings came from the contractor's lawyers. I reported all this directly to Judge Patterson and got a note from him saying that it was just what he needed to know.

While I was thus engaged, Proctor and Ege had been working back in Washington with some bright young men from the office of Jesse Jones, the famous Texas businessman who had been called to Washington as head of the Reconstruction Finance Corporation. John Snyder, a Missouri banker who was later secretary of the treasury under President Truman; Clifford Durr, an Alabama lawyer who was Justice Hugo Black's brother-in-law and later a member of the Federal Communications Commission; and Hans Klagsbrunn, a thoughtful lawyer whose background remains something of a mystery to me, had worked out a plan for government financing of new facilities through a newly organized Defense Plant

Corporation, which would pay for the facilities with funds made available by the procuring agencies. Under this plan the Defense Plant Corporation would own the facilities subject to certain option rights in the contractor. This plan was much less complex in administration than the emergency plant facilities contract and became more widely used than any other where government financing of the new facilities was needed.

Before I got to Wright Field, Ford Motor Company had entered into a contract for the production of aircraft engines which called for the execution of a companion facilities contract, which I was charged with the duty of expediting. One morning Aaron Jones showed me a copy of a directive which he had just received from Washington instructing him to insert in all new contracts certain standard clauses under which the contractors undertook to comply with the National Labor Relations Act and with other applicable labor laws and regulations. Within a day or two the directive was followed by receipt of Procurement Circular no. 43, which had the force of an army regulation. By its terms this circular incorporated in all procurement contracts awarded by competitive bid after advertisement the standard provisions which had been described in the directive. The Ford Motor Company had placed a low bid on some trucks but had attached a condition expressly rejecting the labor clauses. They also announced that they would not accept any such clauses in the facilities contract. This, of course, threatened the production of aircraft engines which were vital to the defense program.

I reported at once to Judge Patterson, who directed me to go to Detroit and see Edsel Ford, president of the Ford Motor Company. I was asked to explain to him how badly these engines were needed and to urge him to instruct his counsel to go ahead with the negotiations of the facilities contract as well as the contract for the trucks. Accordingly, I flew out to Detroit, where I met the general counsel of the company and was taken to Mr. Ford's office.

Mr. Ford's office looked like it had been designed for the president of the Maryland Historical Society. It was furnished mostly with American antiques which had been chosen with fastidious taste. Mr. Ford himself was entirely unlike my concept of what the president of Ford Motor Company would be like. Indeed, I got the impression that he was as uneasy in that office as I was in mine. He very politely said that in view of the advice of counsel, the Ford Motor Company could not possibly sign a contract which contained the clauses upon which the air force was now insisting, as it would jeopardize the position which the company was taking in bitterly fought litigation with the NLRB. The company must therefore regretfully insist that these clauses be dropped; otherwise, it would have to suspend preparations for the production of the aircraft engines. Like every good citizen, Mr. Ford wanted very much to participate in the defense program, and he thought that it was most unfair for the government to try to take advantage of that fact in order to further the interests of the labor unions.

I reported this by telephone to Judge Patterson, who asked me to come back to Washington immediately. When I got back there, I was told that the issuance of the directive had been based on a misunderstanding and that the Judge proposed to withdraw Procurement Circular no. 43. However, one member of the National Defense Advisory Commission, Sidney Hillman, was objecting and threatening to take the matter to the White House. Judge Patterson asked that I try to get Mr. Hillman's consent to the withdrawal of Procurement Circular 43.

The National Defense Advisory Commission was a body of six men and one woman who had been selected by the president to advise the administration on the policies which should be followed in connection with the defense program. The membership included William Knudsen, the former president of General Motors, and Edward Stettinius, the former president of the United States Steel Corporation, as well as Sidney Hillman, who was head of the Amalgamated Clothing Workers Union. I found that each commissioner had a separate staff and each had his own legal adviser. It appeared that Hillman had tried to get his fellow commissioners to agree on requiring the inclusion by all procurement agencies in all of their contracts of the standard clauses which were later described in the War Department Procurement Circular, but that he had been unable to persuade a majority of the commissioners to do this. Instead, they had issued a statement of labor policy which embodied the substance of the contract clauses and had it approved by President Roosevelt.

Hillman had then brought a copy of the statement to the War Department and delivered it personally to Judge Patterson, who got the impression that the commission and the president were instructing him to incorporate these policies in contractual provisions. Accordingly, he had issued the original directive to that effect, and somebody on the General Staff, having seen a copy of the directive, incorporated it in Procurement Circular no. 43. The contractors thereupon appealed to Knudsen and Stettinius, who protested to Patterson against his action, but in the meantime the circular had gone out to the field. Hillman's legal adviser, Max Brandwyn, told me that Hillman would strongly object to any backtracking on the part of the War Department and would take the matter to the White House if necessary. I then talked to the legal advisers for Knudsen and Stettinius, who were both equally emphatic in saying that the War Department had blundered and should abandon any effort to force contractors to accept these provisions. From the way the lawyers talked, it sounded as if a public clash was inevitable.

At this point Judge Patterson called Justice Felix Frankfurter and asked for an appointment. I went with him down to the justice's chambers in the Supreme Court Building and we explained to him what had happened. Patterson said that he needed help in getting Sidney Hillman in line. Justice Frankfurter suggested that I talk to Ben Cohen, who was then counsel for Secretary Ickes in the Department of Interior. Before going on the bench, Justice Frankfurter had frequently given legal advice to Sidney Hillman in his capacity as president of the Amalgamated Clothing Workers Union. In sending me to see Ben Cohen, he was confirming the generally held opinion that Cohen had succeeded Justice Frankfurter as the "gray eminence" of the labor movement. In the early days of the Roosevelt administration, Cohen had teamed up with Tommy Corcoran in drafting and steering through Congress the two securities acts as well as the Public Utilities Holding Company Act. While he was nominally the chief lawyer for the Interior Department under Harold Ickes, his activities were in actuality far wider in scope, and no one could have had greater influence with Sidney Hillman and Max Brandwyn.

I found Cohen to be a rabbinical type who immediately inspired confidence in his judgment. I poured out the story of the War Department's inadvertent entry into the boiling cauldron of industrial labor relations and of Judge Patterson's ensuing frustration in his effort to get the aircraft program moving, and found him thoroughly understanding. He said that he would talk to Max Brandwyn and see whether a plan could be worked out which would get the wheels turning once more. Sure enough, after several meetings with a much more accommodating Brandwyn, we came to an arrangement under which the National Defense Advisory Commission unanimously agreed that controversial labor clauses be omitted from negotiated contracts, including emergency plant facilities contracts, and Procurement Circular no. 43 was withdrawn. The Ford Motor Company was given its facilities contract, which took care of the aircraft engines, and its bid for the trucks was thrown out and new bids invited, with the result that this contract was awarded elsewhere. Those of us at the War Department wrote this down as an object lesson on the difficulty of carrying out any program where supervisory authority was vested in a committee, the members of which had been selected in order to assure the representation of differing interests.

It was not long before it began to appear that we had swapped the devil for a witch. Under the provisions of the Internal Revenue Code, contractors seeking special tax amortization on new facilities were required to obtain certificates that no part of the cost of the facility (other than normal depreciation) had been included in the contract price or, in the alternative, that the government's interest in the property had been adequately protected. These so-called tax amortization certificates were to be issued by the procuring agency with the approval of the Office of Production Management, and John Lord O'Brian, who was the respected counsel to the OPM, had ruled that the burden was on the contractor to demonstrate that it was entitled to the certificates. Some zealous underlings at the OPM were busily dragging their feet and second-guessing the contracting officers at Wright Field and elsewhere; they demanded elaborate proof of exactly how much profit the contractors were going to realize on the contracts. This profit was in many instances a matter of estimate, so that prolonged delays were again holding up the issuance of the certificates. A notable instance was a contract with the General Electric Company, where I had personally assured the company that the certificate would be forthcoming from the contracting officer.

By chance, I rode over from Washington to Baltimore on the train with Mark Watson, an old friend whose wife had taught my children in kindergarten. Mark asked me what I was doing in Washington, and in an unguarded moment I told him that I was struggling with a bunch of ideologues at the OPM who were holding up the air force program by insisting on strict proof on what was necessarily to a large extent a matter of guesswork. While I knew that Mark was covering some aspects of the defense program for the *Baltimore Sun,* it honestly did not occur to me that he would be professionally interested in my woes. To my surprise, he apparently went to work on this lead, and a week later a column appeared in the *Sun* which described with complete accuracy the difficulties which had arisen over the General Electric contract. Fortunately for me, my name was not mentioned.

The following week Arthur Krock picked up the same subject and wrote a rather scathing column in the *New York Times* which enraged the boys at OPM, who accused the War Department of planting stories in the press in order to bring pressure to bear on them. The result of all this was that the top brass at OPM and Judge Patterson agreed to the creation of a special board to review the issuance of tax amortization certificates. Among the members of this board were Edward S. Greenbaum, a New York lawyer who was a partner of Morris Ernst's, nationally known as a leader of liberal causes; Jim Landis, dean of the Harvard Law School; and James P. Baxter III, the president of Williams College. I was also named to this board, along with a Harvard Law School classmate, Charlie Murchison.

It seemed to me that this removed the last obstacle to the facilities program, and I began to feel that the task which I had undertaken in September of the previous year had finally been accomplished. I was considering whether I could now return to my full-time law practice once more when I discovered that Eddie Greenbaum, chairman of the special board, intended to suggest that I be excluded from the panel which was about to consider an application of the Glenn L. Martin Company for a tax amortization certificate for a housing project for workers at its Middle River plant. I realized that I was in an embarrassing position, and I decided to resign forthwith from the special board. Eddie Greenbaum protested that it was not necessary for me to do this, but I stood my ground.

Bob Proctor had already gone back to Boston, and I decided that I could follow his example and return to Baltimore.

As a matter of fact, I had begun to feel that my frequent absences from my law office were jeopardizing the future of the firm. The country was not at war, and the work that I was doing in Washington seemed to me now to be more or less routine. To my surprise, I got a note from Justice Frankfurter urging me to enlist "for the duration," and I replied saying nothing about my feeling that I was no longer doing anything at the War Department of great significance. Nor did I mention a fact which had been equally important in my decision, that my wife had just been told that she was again pregnant. She was already caring for three rather high-strung little ones, and although she still had the assistance of a competent nurse, no reliable successor had been found for Gough, who had left us to enter the postal service. While I was far from being a handyman around the house, my virtual absence from home for days at a time had been trying for her, and I felt that it was important for her to have me around as a sympathetic listener and to share her troubles.

So for the next year I tried to find satisfaction in work at my law office. The attempt was not very successful, although there was one job which did have at least an indirect bearing on the defense program. Professor Abel Wolman of the Johns Hopkins University, then and at this writing still the outstanding sanitary engineer in the world, had been asked to advise the Bethlehem Steel Company how to develop new sources of water for its expanding plant at Sparrows Point. He had devised a method for the use of effluent from the sewage-disposal plant which the city of Baltimore had built at Back River. The time had come for the Steel Company to work out a satisfactory agreement with the city, and I was employed to secure that agreement.

This brought me into contact with the city solicitor, Charles C. G. Evans, a graduate of the Harvard Law School, of whom I had heard good things from Walter Graham, whose son Boyd was working at Marbury, Gosnell and Williams as an associate. As Mr. Graham was a very astute businessman who in his capacity as comptroller of the city had been in close contact with the city solicitor's office, I was not surprised to find that Charlie Evans appeared to be a very able negotiator as well as a skilled draftsman. Between us, and with the expert guidance of Dr. Wolman and several very helpful officials from the Sparrows Point plant, Charlie and I were able to work out a mutually beneficial agreement which has met Bethlehem's water requirements ever since and at the same time solved a nasty problem for the city. Dr. Wolman tells me that the facility is the largest such source of industrial water in the world and has been the model for industries elsewhere.

One other public service which I was able to render during this period has also proved to be of lasting significance. The Court of Appeals of Maryland finally got around to appointing a committee to frame the rules of civil procedure. Judge Samuel K. Dennis was named as chairman of the committee and the task of drafting the proposed rules was assigned to a young Baltimore lawyer named Robert R. Bowie, who submitted a set of rules which after thorough consideration the committee adopted substantially without change. As a member of the committee my only contribution was to appear along with Bowie at local bar association committee meetings, and meetings of the committee of the legislature where we were successful in persuading the committee to permit the rules to take effect as drafted.

Otherwise, I found very little to salve my conscience, which continued to trouble me as grim news came pouring in from all over the world. Judge Patterson wrote that he had just returned from Seattle, where he had attended the opening of a new bomber plant. He said that he had been accompanied by Eddie Greenbaum and Warren Ege and "you would have been there too if you had still been with us." I took this as a mild rebuke for my inconstancy.

XIV ❧ War Department Lawyer

Our youngest child arrived in this world on September 21, 1941, and we had barely settled down again at 43 Warrenton Road when the Japanese struck at Pearl Harbor. For the next six weeks I was very restless and began to fear that I was fated to sit out the war in Baltimore. Then, toward the end of January, I got a call from Jim Landis, who said that he and Mrs. Roosevelt had been directed by the president to organize a civil defense program designed to direct home-front activities during the war and would like me to act as their general counsel. He asked me to come to meet Mrs. Roosevelt the next day. Of course I went, and listened to what seemed to me to be rather vague plans. Before returning to Baltimore, I decided to stop by Judge Patterson's office and see what he thought about it. He said, "Pay no attention to that. Come here to the War Department and I will make you general counsel in charge of the legal aspects of the entire procurement program." I asked when he would want me to start, and he said that the department was being reorganized and would probably be ready for me shortly after the first of March.

This seemed to me to be a stroke of almost unbelievable luck, and I immediately consulted my wife and then my law partners. Natalie was a good soldier and said at once that I ought to accept the Judge's offer. My partners, on the other hand, were somewhat dismayed but finally agreed after I had ascertained that Charlie Evans was willing to resign as city solicitor and join our firm to take over the work that I had been doing.

On March 2, 1942, I reported for duty and was met by Eddie Greenbaum, who by this time was in uniform as Judge Patterson's executive officer. He said, "Well, now, I am sorry to have to tell you, but this general counsel business won't work."

I asked, "Why won't it?"

He said, "It just won't. The way that the department is organized we just can't work it out, but we have found something for which we think you would be just the man."

And then the Judge called me into his office. He looked rather sheepish and said, "What I want you to do is to take charge of these contracts. I have to sign them. They come in here and I have no time to review them myself. I have to take the whole thing on faith. I just would like to have you take charge of this business and be my delegate and when they come in with your approval, why I won't need to bother about it."

I had burnt my bridges, so I said, "All right."

Robert Porter Patterson

While I did not know it at the time, I now realize that from that moment on I was admitted to Judge Patterson's friendship, and as Judge Learned Hand has pointed out, those who were privileged to join that select company were in his eyes endowed with his own virtues and were expected to live up to his standards. At the same time they were completely trusted and the whole world soon came to know that this was so. That I should be among the elect still remains a source of amazement to me. True, our values were much the same, as I soon found out, but he possessed qualities which I sadly lacked.

For the next three and a half years I saw a great deal of him, and for two summers I lived as a guest in his home in Georgetown while Mrs. Patterson and the children were up on the farm at Garrison-on-the-Hudson. We had dinner together several times a week and talked over many things. As a result, I came to the conclusion that, aside from my father, he was the only person I had ever known well who in my opinion deserved to be called great.

The Judge, as we all called him, was first and foremost a soldier. His heart was with the combat infantrymen, who were bearing the brunt of the actual fighting. His widow, Margaret Patterson, liked to tell how during World War I, when he had risked his life in order to relieve a party of his men who were under fire, they had, in turn, risked theirs to save him when he lay wounded. This was the exploit for which he and his rescuers all received the Distinguished Service Cross.

Moreover, he had, to an extraordinary degree, the ability which General Marshall attributed to General Pershing, of inspiring others to a level of effort and achievement far beyond that of which they thought themselves capable. Physically and nervously, he was himself capable of sustained effort which seemed almost superhuman. During the years of my service under him, I felt under pressure to live up to a standard which at times seemed beyond my physical capacity. Periodically I had to rest up and try to recover my equilibrium, but he never seemed to notice my weakness.

I was no worse off in this respect than others, notably Bill Brennan, now a justice of the Supreme Court of the United States, who in 1943 accompanied Patterson on one of his whirlwind tours of industrial plants

which were designed to stimulate both labor and management to greater
heights of productivity. In an interview recorded in 1961 as a contribution
to a Columbia University oral history project, I described a conversation
which I had with Mr. Brennan immediately after his return from that
trip:

> When Brennan got back, he said to me, "That man is possessed of a
> demon."
> I said, "What do you mean?"
> "Why! I'm nearly dead. He's nearly killed me, the schedule we've had, and
> he's just driving himself every minute. He's possessed of a demon. This busi-
> ness of building up this war effort—it's almost reached the stage of a mania
> with him."
> "Well," I said, "there's nothing new about that. He's been like that all
> along."
> "Gosh," he said, "I'll tell you, I'm glad to get home and get a little rest. This
> constant driving force is just something that—I've never seen anybody like
> it."
> Well, that was true. He was driven. I remember once I'd been worried
> about something and had been plagued, and I came in and sat down. "What's
> the matter?" "Well, I'm really worried."
> He looked at me and laughed and said, "Look. What are your worries com-
> pared with those of the fellows who are over there doing the fighting. Think
> about that a little, and you won't worry. Your worries won't seem of any im-
> portance to you."
> I did, and then I realized—he thought about them all the time. His mind,
> his heart was always with the fighters.
> That's where his heart was, all that time, and that explains to some extent
> this terrific drive. . . .

In the course of the oral interview I made the following statements, which
I believe cast a light on the character of this extraordinary man:

> It did, however, take its toll of him. He got more and more impatient. The
> sort of serenity that I noted in him at the beginning began to leave him. Miss
> Mundy used to tell me a little about him. "He's getting pretty strung up,
> strung pretty tight." Then he began to get into fights with people. Of course,
> he was a tremendous driver. He had a single-minded idea, and that was that
> every sacrifice should be made for the benefit of the fighters who were giving
> their lives. He was utterly impatient of any consideration of civilian comforts,
> and the result was that he and Donald Nelson were fighting all the time, fero-
> ciously, really.
> The fact is that the man's nerves began to get worn down. I remember it
> got to the point where people were talking about it. I rode over with Jack
> McCloy to Baltimore one afternoon to a dinner, and we got to talking about
> it. I suggested to him, "The one man in the world he's afraid of is Mr. Stimson
> and if you get Mr. Stimson to order him to go up to the farm for ten days,
> he'll go. He won't go otherwise."

He said, "Well, I'll try it." Sure enough, a couple of days later the Judge said, "That'll have to wait ten days. Stimson's got the idea that I need a rest." I said, "Well, I think that's a pretty good idea." "It's ridiculous," he said, "but I have to go up on the farm." So he went up on the farm for ten days and incidentally got himself a beautiful bursitis driving a tractor. . . .

Patterson was more extreme than either Somervell or Clay when it came to pressing for the military needs as against civilian needs. You see, Clay was his representative on that committee of the War Production Board. When it came to pressing for military needs as against civilian needs, Patterson took a position. Somervell was much more of a negotiator and compromiser; he would give, he would trade, do things of that sort. Patterson hadn't any of that in him. He didn't want to trade anything. This was the position and this was the position he wanted to hold. He'd try to persuade, and if he couldn't persuade, he'd try to overbear—on what he thought was right. Somervell was a much more agile man than that.

And Clay, although his disposition was towards Patterson rather than Somervell, nevertheless Clay had a very acute sense of the possible, too. The Judge didn't have much sense of the possible. He was, to some degree, an absolutist, when it came to these things.

The Army had needs. There was no question about it, they had needs. Now, he would listen to the military people to tell him what their needs were, and then he'd fight for those needs. In other words, if he got these needs, all right. He was perfectly willing to let somebody have rubber for tires for civilians, if the Army needs were met. But when people in whom he had confidence said, "These are our needs," then his feeling was that that took priority over everything else. Whereas the other people didn't feel that way about it. They'd say, "Well, but there are other needs here that have got to be considered, that have got to be weighed." He didn't think they weighed anything, in comparison to military needs. He thought the military need was it. Now, he was perfectly willing to hold people down on the need end of it, to see that they didn't overstate the need, but once he was convinced that they had a figure here which represented the actual military needs, then he didn't see any excuse for not putting that first.

This, then, was the man I knew, and it is no exaggeration to say that I came to idolize him. When in July 1947 he resigned as secretary of war to return to private practice in New York City, I wrote to him as follows:

> I find it impossible to put in writing what I have long wanted to say to you. Nevertheless, I cannot let this opportunity go without giving you some idea of how much the association of the last seven years has meant to me.
>
> Ever since I was a boy in school studying Latin I have been powerfully influenced by the Roman concept of virtue. You seem to me to be its embodiment, and I firmly believe that you are such a man as Cato would have been glad to honor. You have set all your friends an example to emulate, and they will always be proud to have known you.

Twenty years later I wrote the following letter:

April 7, 1967

Protocol Division
United States Army Infantry Center
Fort Benning, Georgia 31905

Gentlemen:

At the request of Major General Robert H. York, I am writing a brief description of the relationship which I shared with Judge Patterson and his family, as well as an assessment of his character as I came to know it. . . .

[Between September 1940 and March 1941] I had a number of conferences with him on problems arising in connection with the facilities program. I was deeply impressed by his lack of pretension and his grasp of every facet of a very complex situation. The facilities program was the first step in an immense military procurement program which was just getting under way and which had attracted the attention of the White House and the Treasury, not to mention the Congress. Furthermore, the President had set up an Advisory Commission with rather vaguely defined powers, headed by co-equal representatives of industry, labor, agriculture, etc. Judge Patterson seemed to thread his way through this confusion with remarkable skill, considering that his previous experience had been largely confined to the courtroom.

In March of 1942, at Judge Patterson's request, I returned to the War Department and was charged by him with responsibility for the legal review of all procurement contracts requiring his signature. In addition to that, he and General Somervell, who had just been placed in charge of the Services of Supply (later the Army Services Forces), requested me to organize and supervise a law office which would give legal service to the Army Service Forces in all matters relating to procurement and to see that similar law offices were organized in the Air Force and at appropriate places in the other arms and services. From that time on until I left the War Department in September of 1945, I was in frequent and, indeed, almost daily contact with Judge Patterson. At his request I shared living quarters with him at his home during two summers, and during this period I got to know him very well. We usually had breakfast together and frequently got together in the evening. I believe that he discussed with me most of the questions that were uppermost in his mind during that period.

I came to know him as a man of brilliant mind combined with great moral power, singleness of purpose, and physical and nervous strength which made him able to bear an enormously heavy burden of work. During the three and one-half years from March, 1942, to September of 1945, I never saw him really relax except during a week which he spent on his farm at Garrison under orders from Secretary Stimson not to leave it. He drove himself hard and expected those whom he trusted with responsibilities to do the same. As a result, he got more out of his staff than we knew that we could do, although at times all of us had to drop out for occasional recuperation.

While Judge Patterson was intensely serious he did not lack humor and had a sharp sense of the ridiculous. He was broadly interested in all kinds of people and was truly democratic in his intolerance of pretension and snobbery. He was amused by colorful characters and seemed to take much enjoyment from their behavior. On the other hand, he was contemptuous of those who in his view were guilty of timidity, evasion or falsehood. He was quick to denounce opinions which he regarded as mischievous and did not hesitate to express his views forcefully and occasionally with sarcasm. As a result he made enemies who tended to exaggerate his characteristic bluntness.

Judge Patterson seemed to me to be a man of the utmost rectitude with an almost unique sense of duty and obligation. If I were obliged to use a single adjective to describe him, I think that I would say that he is the noblest man that I have ever known.

After September, 1945, I saw him on a number of occasions. If there was any change in him, I did not notice it. He seemed to me to be the same driving, forceful, dedicated man that I had previously known.

I came to know Mrs. Patterson very well and occasionally met other members of the family. During the period that I was closest to him, he had almost no time for family life, but it seemed to me that his family admired and loved him. Mrs. Patterson certainly understood the Judge very well and gave him support where he needed it. She never made any effort whatsoever to involve him in social activities, for which he had no taste and less time.

As usual, Judge Learned Hand made the definitive remarks about Judge Patterson at the memorial exercises held in 1952 at the Association of the Bar of the city of New York after the Judge's death. He said:

> Perhaps at times he was uncompromising though never more so than with himself; but it was because he always kept in sight the overall purpose: "First things first." You may suggest that it is not possible so to deal with human beings, when you must have their cooperation. Maybe; yet I suggest that one of the most effective ways of securing that cooperation is by your own inflexible example. That example he gave, it was largely by it that he succeeded, and the depth and breadth of the feelings revealed when he died, attest the measure of that success. Not only those who knew him by direct acquaintance, but those who had only read or heard of him came spontaneously to realize that here was one who was incorruptible in a sense that few men are."

Wright Field Again

During our interview on March 2, 1942, Judge Patterson had told me that Bob Lovett, who had recently been appointed assistant to the secretary for air, wanted me to go out to Wright Field and look over the handling of its procurement legal work, so once more I took the night train to Dayton and conferred with Aaron Jones, who was still in charge of the procurement program there. It did not take me long to conclude that what was needed there was a law office staffed by experienced lawyers who could give the contracting officers the kind of legal services they needed. I so reported to Bob Lovett and was happy to find that General Henry H. Arnold agreed. In short order, Don Swatland of the Cravath office in New York was persuaded to take on the job and built up exactly the kind of outfit that I had described.

The Legal Branch

On March ninth I reported for duty at the headquarters of the Services of Supply. I had left in 1941 with the impression that the office of the assistant secretary of war was a law firm superimposed on an antiquated military sideshow. Judge Patterson had drawn on his experience as one of the founders of a successful Wall Street law firm and had called to his aid such men as Eddie Greenbaum, Julius Amberg, Warren Ege, and Howard Petersen in the belief that they would stir up a creaking organization which for many years had been left undisturbed in its preoccupation with petty routines. To be blunt about it, the office had been treated as a sort of graveyard for misfits.

By the time I returned, there had been a sweeping reorganization. Judge Patterson had been promoted to under secretary, and Bob Lovett had been named assistant secretary for air. A Services of Supply had been created under the command of General Brehon Somervell, to which had been transferred nearly all of the functions previously performed in the office of the assistant secretary except those which were related to the air force, which had been transferred to a separate command under General Oliver Echols. In the Services of Supply, responsibility for procurement procedures had been centralized in an Office of Procurement and Distribution under Colonel Charles Young, who, I was informed, had recently retired as first vice-president of the Pennsylvania Railroad Company. His deputy was D. C. McKeachie, a former vice-president of Sears-Roebuck. In the Office of Procurement and Distribution was a Purchases Division under the direction of Albert J. Browning, who had been president of a Chicago wallpaper company.

Also in the Office of Procurement and Distribution was a Legal Branch, which was charged with responsibility for seeing that all contracts originating in the Supply Services which came to the under secretary for signature complied with applicable laws and regulations. Eddie Greenbaum told me that I was to be chief of that branch, and that in addition to reviewing all contracts for the Purchases Division of the SOS, I was to review all air force contracts requiring the signature of the under secretary. I was also told that Judge Patterson had made it clear to General Somervell that I was to have direct access to the under secretary's office at all times. Apparently General Somervell had accepted this military anomaly as inevitable in view of the air force situation.

When I was introduced to General Somervell, he made it perfectly clear to me that he had very little use for lawyers. Colonel Young, on the other hand, told me that it was obvious to him that somebody had to act as general counsel to the Services of Supply in business matters and that it was his intention to make use of me in that capacity. However, he said that this was a private matter between the two of us and warned me to stay out of uniform, so when General Somervell's chief of staff suggested that I accept a commission, I declined, explaining to him that it would make it too difficult for me to deal with the air force generals. I cited to him my most recent report on the Wright Field situation in which I had dealt directly with General Arnold and Mr. Lovett. He said that he got my point.

Renegotiation

I had not had a chance to get my seat warm when I was asked to sit in on a conference at which representatives of the supply services had been called together to listen to proposed regulations which had been prepared in the Fiscal Division of the SOS. As I listened to the presentation, it seemed to me that the Fiscal Division was assuming a level of sophistication in the matter of cost accounting which simply did not exist in the field. Since no one else spoke up, I said that based on my very limited experience at Wright Field, it seemed to me to be simply absurd to expect contracting officers to perform all the various tasks which compliance with the new regulations would require. Thereupon a representative of the chief of ordnance chimed in to the same effect, and it was finally agreed that the services would be asked to report on the feasibility of complying with the proposed regulations.

However, as the representatives of the Fiscal Division had pointed out, there was indeed a necessity for action of some sort on the part of the War Department, in view of a gathering storm which was the result of revelations in the press of shocking profits which had been realized by some defense contractors. The urgency of this matter became perfectly clear when, on March 28, 1942, the House of Representatives adopted the so-called Case amendment to a pending appropriation bill which forbade the use of appropriated funds to pay contractors who failed to file with the procurement agency a certificate of costs and an agreement to renegotiate the price of goods and services wherever the contract had resulted or was likely to result in profits of more than 6 percent.

This revival of the old Walsh-Healey nightmare produced consternation among all procurement agencies. I was called into consultation by McKeachie, who had been charged with the duty of preparing a statement for General Somervell to make to a subcommittee of the Senate Appropriations Committee which was considering the bill. Along with McKeachie, I accompanied General Somervell to the committee hearing. The chairman of the subcommittee was a wily old fox from Tennessee named Kenneth McKellar. After listening to General Somervell, McKeachie, and Donald Nelson, he slyly suggested that the War Department come up with a draft of legislation which would not be subject to the objections which they had raised to the Case amendment but which could accomplish the same objective. This was Saturday afternoon, and he said that the subcommittee would meet again Monday afternoon and he hoped that General Somervell would have a draft ready for consideration at that time.

General Somervell and McKeachie then left the hearing room and said that they would see me Monday morning, and I took the train back to Baltimore, hoping to spend what was left of the weekend with my family. That night two feet of snow fell on Baltimore and all traffic came to a standstill. The following morning I was beginning to wonder how I was going to get back to Washington when the telephone rang and it was General Styer telling me that General Somervell had just come from Judge Patterson's office and wanted to see me right away. I told him that no traffic was moving in Baltimore and I did not know whether the trains were still running, but that I would do the best I could. Since no cab service was available, I walked through two feet of snow for two miles to the railroad station and finally arrived in General Somervell's office at six o'clock Sunday evening.

I found that he had gone home but left instructions that I was to prepare a draft of legislation for discussion the following morning. As there was no stenographic service available, I wrote out in longhand a proposed joint resolution which authorized voluntary renegotiations of contract prices where the head of the procurement agency had determined that excessive profits had been or would be realized. The following morning McKeachie and I revised the resolution and presented it to General Somervell, who that afternoon submitted it to Senator McKellar at a hearing before the subcommittee. McKellar complimented General Somervell on his cooperation and said that the subcommittee would give the joint resolution careful consideration.

On the floor Senator McKellar offered an amendment of his own which in some instances went far beyond the War Department's proposal. This was adopted on the understanding that the whole matter would be submitted to the Conference Committee. That committee reported out a bill which prescribed mandatory renegotiation of all war contracts in excess of $100,000 and gave the head of the procuring agency power to fix unilaterally a new price. The bill as passed by Congress was full of ambiguities, but Judge Patterson directed that immediate steps be taken to develop a procedure which would carry out the overriding purpose of the legislation. Such was the beginning of compulsory renegotiation of munitions contracts, which turned out to be the means by which the armed services avoided the procurement scandals which had accompanied every previous war, going all the way back to the War of Independence.

Building an Office

Charged with the additional responsibility of preparing the papers needed to set up a War Department Price Adjustment Board under the direct supervision of the under secretary, I went back to my office and began to consider how best to develop an office which could accomplish what the under secretary expected. Fortunately a Boston lawyer named R. Ammi Cutter had already been assigned to duty at the Legal Branch. He and I immediately formed a tacit partnership which lasted for nearly three years and which was characterized by one of the office wits as "Arsenic and Old Lace." Since Cutter had a very precise Salem accent and generally employed the purest Harvard diction, no one had any difficulty in identifying which of us was "Arsenic" and which "Old Lace."

This was a time when able lawyers were getting into uniform and when capable corporation lawyers were available in a civilian capacity, and Cutter had made it his business to learn how to locate those who were already in service and how to obtain commissions for those civilians who were willing to get into uniform. By these means and by calling on civilians whose names had been suggested to us from various sources, we were able eventually to put together a first-rate law office. Perhaps the best indication of the strength of that group is the fact that from it came in later years two justices of the Supreme Judicial Court of Massachusetts, a judge of the United States Court of Appeals for the Fifth Circuit, a judge of the Court of Claims, a governor of Indiana, an under secretary of the treasury, an assistant secretary of state, a member of the National Labor Relations Board, the dean of a law school and several law school professors, a general counsel of the Internal Revenue Service, an insurance commissioner of the state of New York, a managing partner of J. H. Whitney & Company, and several heads of nationally known law firms.

I believe that our first recruit was Charles Pengra of Boston. Charlie was an experienced corporate lawyer and was asked to take over the job of counsel to the newly created War Department Price Adjustment Board. Working with Maurice Karker, the newly appointed chairman of the board, Charlie came to the conclusion that the best thing to do was to develop a workable procedure for compulsory renegotiation of a contractor's total war business and then to ask for such statutory changes as might be necessary to make the procedure stand up in court. Accordingly, Pengra drafted a bill amending the existing statute, and in August 1942, after a hearing in which I testified on behalf of all procurement agencies, the

bill was passed substantially as drafted. As I recall, Pengra was rather critical of my selection as a spokesman for the War Department, but since
Judge Patterson had done the selecting, there was nothing I could do
about it, although I was sorry to ruffle Charlie's feathers.

Another early recruit was a young Baltimore lawyer named Robert
Bowie. Bob had been the draftsman of the rules which the Maryland
Court of Appeals had adopted in 1941 and had joined me in successfully
defending them before the Maryland legislature, and I had been deeply
impressed by his ability as a draftsman. I succeeded in getting him into
uniform and assigned to the Legal Branch just as I became involved in
trying to help the under secretary fend off an attempt by Leon Henderson, the newly appointed price administrator, to regulate the prices of all
military items, including tanks, airplanes, and naval vessels. This effort
had created consternation among the procurement agencies, and Judge
Patterson asked me to prepare a memorandum giving the reasons why
the Office of Price Administration should not enter the military field.

Fortunately, Bowie turned out to be well schooled in economics and
knew just how to handle this situation. He prepared a memorandum for
Judge Patterson which stated the War Department's position with clarity
and force. Judge Patterson expressed great satisfaction with it, as did
General Somervell. For several months we engaged in a battle in which
Henderson was represented by an able young lawyer named David
Ginsburg. After many meetings, including one general round-up in
Judge Patterson's office in which General Somervell and Leon Henderson
took leading parts, a settlement was arrived at in which Henderson offered voluntarily to refrain from further extensions of his authority over
arms procurement. It was my judgment at the time that this settlement
was reached as a result of the work which Bowie did in persuading David
Ginsburg that the War Department could and would make every effort to
hold the line against inflation and could do a better job than the OPA.

Procurement Regulations

At the same time that Bowie and I were engaged in the OPA battle, Cutter
and I developed the outline of a program for improving the contractual
procedures of the War Department. This involved the organization in
every supply service of a legal department similar to that which I had recommended to Secretary Lovett for the air force and the centralization in
one publication, to be known as *Procurement Regulations,* of all regulations
and directives which were to guide contracting officers. Changes in War
Department policies and procedures could be available to them in hours
rather than weeks.

Perhaps most important of all, these regulations were in most instances to be submitted to and discussed by a weekly gathering of the

heads of all the legal branches which was also often attended by representatives of the judge advocate general's office, the Fiscal Division of the Services of Supply, and any other interested groups. Thus, the lawyers of the Supply Services and the air force would have a hand in developing the procurement regulations and would be in a position to understand the reasons for them.

Cutter and I agreed that since contractors were now to be required to refund unanticipated profits, fairness would require that they be protected from unforeseeable losses at least to the extent necessary to avoid hardship. Cutter believed that the First War Powers Act, which had been enacted by Congress, could be made the basis for such a program. Because the office of the comptroller general of the United States had put a very narrow construction on that act, the judge advocate general of the army did not feel free to accept Cutter's broad interpretation of its provisions without a supporting ruling of the attorney general of the United States. We presented this matter to Judge Patterson, who agreed to ask Secretary Stimson to ask the attorney general for such a ruling. The War Department's request for a ruling was referred to a deputy in the office of the solicitor general named George Washington. To him Cutter presented his argument and as a result, the attorney general of the United States adopted Cutter's interpretation of the statute in a sweeping opinion which gave us a solid foundation for our entire program. Cutter joyfully attached to this opinion the following salute: "George Washington, first in war, first in peace and first in the hearts of the Legal Branch."

In the meantime, with the backing of a directive of the under secretary, I made a survey of each of the supply services to determine how their procurement legal work was being handled. I found that they ranged all the way from the Ordnance Department, where effective legal service was available to contracting officers in the field, to the surgeon general's office, where apparently no legal adviser was available at any level. I was able to persuade the surgeon general that he did have need for legal services and at the suggestion of Eddie Greenbaum brought in Tracy Voorhees, a New York lawyer who had been chairman of the board of trustees of the Long Island Hospital. Tracy did an outstanding job in making legal services available to the medical department and ultimately ended his public career as under secretary of the army.

The drafting of the procurement regulations almost foundered at the beginning. It took some tact and diplomacy to rescue the project from a false start which was initiated by an officer in General Somervell's office who did not have the faintest idea of what he was doing. We had to redraft everything he did. Fortunately, we were able to argue that since the procurement regulations were to be War Department-wide in their effect, participation of the air force was necessary, although, in truth, the Supply Services had been equally critical of the regulations prepared in General

Somervell's office. Thanks to Cutter's careful supervision and the expert work of a number of the lawyers whom we had been able to bring into the office, the procurement regulations became widely recognized as an indispensable tool in guiding the procurement program. Under the skillful editorship of Richard Grossman, a Chicago lawyer who had joined the Legal Branch, this publication became a weekly loose-leaf service which kept the lawyers in the field abreast of all important developments in the department's procurement policies.

Notable among those who worked on revising the procurement regulations was a young New York lawyer who came to us from Eddie Greenbaum's firm. His name was Ben Kaplan, and to him we entrusted the sections dealing with contractual provisions. He succeeded in devising forms which while preserving uniformity where War Department policies made it imperative to do so, at the same time permitted flexibility in many instances where Washington approval had previously been required for even the slightest deviation. Ben soon got on friendly terms with the lawyers in the field who were doing the actual drafting of contracts. When they were in doubt as to whether Washington approval was needed, they simply called him, and only very rarely was his judgment questioned.

First War Powers Act Relief

Another area in which the Legal Branch had major administrative responsibilities was in what came to be known as requests for First War Powers Act relief, and here again we were fortunate in finding someone whose judgment in this uncharted area turned out to be practically faultless. Nicholas Shriver, a young Baltimore lawyer with a reputation for being a hardheaded skeptic who was still open to reason, was just the man to see that relief was granted only where and to the extent truly necessary to protect contractors from unforeseeable and crippling losses. Here again I can recollect no case in which his judgment was overruled.

There was one case, however, which I handled myself at the express direction of General Somervell. After the war broke out, William Knudsen had joined Judge Patterson's staff in a lieutenant-general's uniform. He roamed all over the country, visiting manufacturing plants where critical items were being produced, and consulted in his inimitable fashion with the men in charge. One of my friends who accompanied him said that it was uncanny the way he would walk into a plant and turn to the plant manager and say, "What's the matter with that press over on the far aisle? It doesn't sound right to me." Sure enough, something had gone wrong there and the plant manager would explain that orders had already been given to correct it.

At headquarters General Knudsen was famous for the fact that he never wasted a word and would never read any memorandum that was more than a page and a half long. For one job he suggested the name of a man in Boston and said that he expected to be in that city on the next day and would find out whether the man was available. The following day Greenbaum's telephone rang, and when he picked up the receiver, he heard this: "Greenbaum? Knudsen. O.K. Goodbye."

On one occasion General Knudsen went out to Detroit and undertook to settle a controversy over a fixed price contract to produce some experimental vehicles. At the insistence of the Ordnance Department, the prime contractor had entered into a subcontract with Reo Motors to manufacture the vehicles known as Trackless Tanks on a cost plus a fixed fee basis. The prime contractor now wished to cancel the subcontract. General Knudsen insisted that Reo be given an opportunity to complete the job, and when it was pointed out to him that the cost would inevitably exceed the original contract price, he stated that both contracts would be renegotiated so that prime contractor and subcontractor would each receive his costs plus fair compensation for his work. In the end, the vehicles were not accepted and the Detroit Ordnance District proposed to terminate the prime contract for default. In that event the contractor would have gone into bankruptcy and Reo's ability to perform other important war contracts would have been jeopardized. The whole matter had been referred to the office of the chief of ordnance, where it was under consideration when the contractor chose to employ Tommy Corcoran, who, characteristically, went directly to General Somervell. The chief of ordnance then advised General Somervell that in view of Corcoran's intervention, he would prefer to leave the matter entirely in the hands of headquarters.

At General Somervell's request, I talked to General Knudsen, who confirmed all that the contractor had said. In view of that fact, it seemed to me that First War Powers Act relief was appropriate, and I reported this to General Somervell, who asked me to put my recommendation in writing, which I did, knowing full well that I would probably be called some day before a congressional committee to explain why this matter had been handled in so unusual a fashion. And that is exactly what did happen.

Labor Relations

Another area in which the Legal Branch became involved was labor relations. Back in 1941 I had been consulted from time to time by one of Judge Patterson's team who was an expert in this field. His name was Edward McGrady, and he was the one man to whom labor and industry leaders all looked for advice when a knotty labor problem arose. Somehow he had managed to keep the confidence of all parties, and as a result, he became involved in a great many baffling situations which threatened the defense program. Assigned to assist him were two very young men, and when he found out that I had done some labor work, he insisted on my participation in a number of conferences where attempts were being made to get knots untied.

As a result of that experience, I became convinced that each legal branch should have available the services of a lawyer who had experience in this field and could concentrate on labor problems. In my own office I found that the man who came nearest to filling this assignment was a lawyer from Houston, Texas, named Dillon Anderson. Dillon had been a partner in what was then one of the leading law offices in the country, where he had done a good deal of labor work representing the managerial side. He had recently been transferred to the Legal Branch when his boss, the famous "Al" Wedemeyer, had gone overseas.

Dillon ultimately left the Legal Branch for a high staff position in the United States Army Forces in the Middle East with headquarters in Cairo, Egypt, and the next thing I heard was that he was sipping coffee with the Sheik of Kuwait. Subsequently, he was appointed by President Eisenhower to the important position of secretary of the National Security Council, a position which at that time was supposed to be held by someone with "a passion for anonymity." Of course that was changed when Henry Kissinger was later appointed to the same job.

Pricing Policies

Judge Patterson's commitment to Leon Henderson to control inflation through pricing policies proved to be a tough assignment. This was really the responsibility of the Purchases Division, but at the outset Al Browning looked to the Legal Branch for help, which he got primarily from Cutter, Bowie, and a young Texan named Benno Schmidt, who had come to the Legal Branch from the War Production Board. Benno had been a teaching fellow at Harvard Law School and had managerial talent of a very high order. During the brief time he was in the Legal Branch, he repeatedly demonstrated an extraordinarily mature grasp of the art of administration and frequently volunteered advice to me, for which I was most grateful. Unfortunately, he made a similar impression on others, and when McKeachie was sent to London to set up a purchasing office for the European Command, he asked Benno to go along with him and we lost him.

My staff prepared a tentative statement of pricing policies and procedures which was discussed at a conference held at Tryon, North Carolina, to which defense procurement agencies and contractors were invited. There the proposal was approved substantially as we had drafted it. Bowie and I attended the conference, where we met, among many other industrial leaders, an impressive man named Ernst Mahler of Neenah,

Wisconsin, who was an executive of Kimberly-Clark, which was then one of the largest manufacturers of paper products in the United States. My recollection is that the conference was also attended by Paul Hoffman, who later directed the Marshall Plan in Europe.

One consequence of the Tryon conference was the strengthening of the Purchases Division. Two very able men were added to the roster. One of them, Bill Foster, later became under secretary of commerce, deputy secretary of defense, and director of the United States Arms Control and Disarmament Agency. The other, Glen Lloyd, was a Chicago lawyer who later became chairman of the Board of Trustees of the University of Chicago and one of the founders of the Aspen Institute. These two men took over responsibility for the administration of the purchasing policies agreed to at Tryon.

Reconversion

Undoubtedly, the most complex and difficult task which the Legal Branch had to perform was to prepare regulations prescribing the procedures to be followed when contracts were terminated before completion of performance where neither party to the contract was in default. As early as the spring of 1942, Cutter had begun to study this problem along with John Kenney of the navy general counsel's office (later he became under secretary of the navy) and Stan Teele of the War Production Board (later dean of the Harvard Business School). The more this high-powered trio explored the subject, the more complex it seemed. In the summer of 1943, Cutter produced a first draft of what was later to be known as PR 15 to try out on the supply services. As the importance of the subject came to be realized—and, indeed, the prompt settlement of terminated contracts and the orderly disposal of surplus property were essential not only while the fighting continued but also when it ended—the subject began to receive attention in other quarters, and every agency wanted to have a finger in the pie. The comptroller general was particularly insistent that his office be allowed to audit settlements of terminated contracts before they became final, a suggestion which the procurement agencies strenuously resisted on the ground that such an audit would create endless delays.

When it became apparent that the issues would have to be settled by legislation, I called on Bowie to draft a more complete document which the War Department then published as a regulation known as PR 15. This was a comprehensive treatment of the procedures to be followed in the event of termination of contracts for reasons other than default. At the same time another very able lawyer in the Legal Branch, Joseph F. Johnston of Birmingham, Alabama, undertook a thorough study of the related problem of disposing of excess or surplus property. He later was the principal draftsman of a regulation on this subject which was published as PR 7.

The comptroller general immediately denounced PR 15 as an invitation to defraud the government, and hearings were held at which Judge Patterson spoke before the Military Affairs Committees of the House and Senate in words written for him by Bowie and by Kenneth Royall of the Fiscal Division. General Royall was a lawyer from North Carolina who had been at the Harvard Law School with Judge Patterson. He was a very astute lawyer with an accurate understanding of the workings of congressional committees. He later succeeded Judge Patterson as secretary of war and was the first secretary of the army.

Our next problem was to achieve unity between the procurement agencies, primarily the War and Navy departments and the Maritime Commission, as to what the form of the legislation should be. This was finally achieved after a dispute between the Legal Branch and the navy general counsel's office was settled by submitting to the arbitration of John J. McCloy, who next to Judge Patterson was the principal assistant to Mr. Stimson. Jack was a very able New York lawyer who gave a rather amusing account of how Patterson and his naval counterpart, Jim Forrestal, had each explained to him why the position of the other service was totally unreasonable, each laying the blame on the chief lawyer of the other, that is to say, me for the War Department and Struve Hensel for the navy.

Once that decision was reached, Bowie drafted a bill which was presented to Congress on behalf of all the procurement agencies and which in spite of the comptroller general's fulminations was adopted substantially as Bowie had written it. There was a short period, however, in which it looked to us as if we were being sold down the river. Lewis Strauss, who was then the navy's liaison with Carl Vinson, the chairman of the House Committee on Naval Affairs, made a deal without consulting any of the rest of us which in our view would have created great complications in administering contract settlements.

Fortunately, the president, prior to that time, acting on the recommendation of the so-called Baruch-Hancock Report, had created in the White House an Office of War Mobilization and Reconversion. The War Department's liaison with the Office of War Mobilization was a young Cleveland lawyer named Horace Chapman Rose, who was attached to the Legal Branch. At Judge Patterson's request, I had assigned Chappie to be the War Department's chief lobbyist when the Baruch-Hancock Report was being prepared. Mr. Baruch had frequently been consulted by Judge Patterson, who thought that as a result of his experience in World War I,

Mr. Baruch knew more about how to mobilize the industrial power of the United States than any other person. The Judge was delighted when the president, tiring of the disputes between the procurement agencies and the War Production Board and War Manpower Commission, turned to Mr. Baruch for advice. The Baruch-Hancock Report recommending the creation at the White House level of the Office of War Mobilization and Reconversion was just what the Judge had hoped for, and much credit was given to Chappie Rose for helping to achieve that result.

Through Chappie's skillful diplomacy, a meeting was arranged at the White House in which Lewis Strauss was called in to explain what he had done. I acted as spokesman for all the rest of those who had been working on drafting the bill (including John Kenney, who was obviously in an embarrassing position, since he agreed with us entirely but was outranked by Strauss). John Hancock acted as arbitrator and decided that the administration would support the bill as drafted by Bowie, and Strauss was directed to straighten things out with Carl Vinson. John Hancock later congratulated me on what he said was "an expert bit of bloodletting."

Ironically, when the president signed the bill, he invited Lewis Strauss to be present and handed him the pen with which he had written his signature. When the boys heard that one, they were fit to be tied. But Lewis Strauss could not understand why they were so scornful. He claimed that his lobbying with the Naval Affairs Committee had been very important in getting the bill through the Congress. No doubt he was effective in that capacity, since he later became secretary of commerce and chairman of the Atomic Energy Commission and sat on the famous board which denied security clearance to Robert Oppenheimer, whom Strauss himself had chosen as director of the Institute of Advanced Study at Princeton. Many years later I met Lewis at dinner in Washington and he spoke of the White House meeting at which he said he had been roughly treated by Bill Draper. I did not undertake to correct his faulty recollection.

In the final result, the independent Office of Contract Settlements was created and Chappie Rose ultimately became its director. Thereafter, he served as assistant secretary and under secretary of the treasury.

Joe Johnston's studies of the surplus property problem also bore fruit. The publication of PR 7 stimulated other procurement agencies to grapple with the problem, and here again, the Baruch-Hancock recommendations recognized the need for an independent agency to assume the task of disposing of surplus equipment, machinery, and facilities which would be scattered all over the world when the fighting stopped. Legislation drafted largely by the Legal Branch was passed, creating an agency which was headed by Will Clayton, a Texas industrial giant with whom I came to have very pleasant relations.

Patents

In drafting the procurement regulations, we discovered that the treatment of patents presented some very ticklish problems. Like most lawyers, I knew very little about the subject; nor did there seem to be anyone in the Legal Branch who knew much more than I did. At an early meeting of the chiefs of legal branches, I discovered that each of the services, including the air force, had developed its own method for handling patent problems and that there were wide discrepancies in the treatment of individual contractors, even within the same service. The Patents Division of the judge advocate general's office, which contained the specialists who were supposed to deal with these problems, was well aware of the situation but had apparently never been able to do anything about it.

After talking with the chief of that division, Cutter and I decided that what was needed was someone who had the capacity to reconcile conflicting interests. In the Legal Branch was a lawyer named Thomas O'Gorman Fitzgibbon, who had taken a leave of absence from the Davis firm in New York to serve in the War Department as an expert consultant. We decided that Tom, with his Irish urbanity, would be most likely to be able to serve as conciliator. His wide experience in reorganizing financially troubled railroad systems had taught him how to line up opposing interests, and we hoped that this would make up for his lack of familiarity with the patent field.

However, we soon discovered that some of the managers of our leading defense contractors had a deep interest in this subject. As soon as the new procurement regulations were published prescribing uniform patent clauses, howls of protest were heard from those contractors who had theretofore succeeded in extracting special concessions for themselves from the services. I realized that we had stumbled into a hornet's nest when Judge Patterson asked me to come to his office, where Bob Gross of Lockheed, one of the leaders of the aircraft industry, was protesting vehemently that the new procurement regulations were outrageous. Adding to this the fact that responsibility for prescribing procedures for handling cases arising under the new Royalty Adjustment Act had been assigned to the Legal Branch, it became apparent that we needed the help of an experienced patent lawyer.

Fortunately, Tom Fitzgibbon was able to recruit a Harvard classmate of mine, W. Houston Kenyon, Jr., of New York, who agreed to come down to Washington on a temporary basis to help straighten things out. Houston sized up our situation very quickly and took hold in a statesmanlike fashion. From that time on, I never had to think about patents except on the rare occasions when he wanted me to back him up in a dispute with one of the other interested agencies. I welcomed the opportunity to get to know him and his wife, Mildred, who was a writer and a friend of Barbara Ward's. My impression is that Mildred had succeeded her as the Washington correspondent for the *London Economist*. Barbara Ward had married the governor of Ghana while that country was still under British tutelage, and I remember her account of the Ghanaian youth culture, which, regrettably, was all too much like that of the United States. Apparently every teen-age Ghana girl wanted a Fiat, a "Fridge," and a "boyfriend," in that order.

Revision of Regulations Relating to Property Control

Early in 1942 we were asked to make a study of the War Department regulations relating to property accountability, responsibility, and pecuniary liability. These regulations seemed to block every avenue to modernization of procurement and supply procedures. The old-line lawyers and finance officers of the army considered this set of regulations to be untouchable. As a result of studies made in the Legal Branch, I became convinced that the regulations were not required by law and could be changed. We then succeeded in convincing the Legal Branch of the Fiscal Division and the office of the judge advocate general that there was no legal obstacle to the elimination of the pecuniary liability of an officer for property losses over which he had no control, and that this step should be taken. There followed a series of War Department circulars and manuals, in the preparation of which the Legal Branch played a guiding part. These publications eliminated one of the most arbitrary and onerous features of the War Department system of property control and greatly added to the flexibility of procurement and supply procedures.

The Railroad Strike

The most spectacular performance of the Legal Branch came during the Christmas season of 1943, when the rail unions scheduled a nationwide strike to begin on Christmas Eve. Mr. Stimson was directed by the president to take over the railroads and called on General Somervell and General Gross, the chief of transportation, for help. I was designated to act as his counsel. Fortunately for me, Joe Johnston had been in the office of the general counsel of the Seaboard Railway, and he and Tom Fitzgibbon put me in touch with the general counsel of the American Association of Railroads. All the lawyers, working around the clock, devised a procedure which avoided the legal pitfalls encountered by other government agencies which had attempted to use the requisitioning power as a means of blocking labor stoppages. I believe it was General Somervell's brilliant idea to put the presidents of all the major railroad systems into uniform and gather them all together in a meeting. I have a photograph of the assembly, and such a collection of corpulent colonels had never before been seen. As I remember it, by far the most impressive of the newly found colonels was the president of the Pennsylvania Railroad system, who generally spoke for the rest of them.

In the end, the entire railroad system of the country slipped in and out of government ownership without a ripple and left the slate completely clean of legal consequences. General Somervell and General Gross were delighted, and from that time on, the reputation of the Legal Branch extended throughout the War Department. As a result, we began to be called upon to help out in programs which had nothing whatever to do with procurement.

At about this time I got a letter from Benno Schmidt saying that people in London were talking about our performance. Moreover, I happened to run into Justice Frankfurter and Dean Acheson on one of their morning walks. They stopped and spoke to me about what they had heard about the work the lawyers in my office had been doing. Justice Frankfurter specifically asked me to send him a copy of PR 15 and when I failed to do so promptly, followed up with a note in which he repeated that request. How he had heard about it, I never found out.

On February 5, 1944, I wrote a letter to Benno Schmidt in which I summed up my feelings about this experience:

> The seizure and subsequent return of the railroads was the most interesting experience which I have had for a long time. It brought me in contact with the Attorney General, the Solicitor General, Mr. Byrnes, Mr. Clement of the Penna. RR, General Somervell, General Gross and others. The best part was that I attended several long conferences with Sec. Stimson and thus had the opportunity for the first time to get to know him. He reminded me a great deal of my father and some of his friends and I greatly enjoyed the association. In addition it was pleasant to have taken a part of some importance in a venture which was wholly successful from the point of view of the War Department. Joe Johnston rose to the occasion magnificently and was a tower of strength in every way and I could not have done without him.

Lucius Dubignon Clay

Sometime early in 1943, as a result of one of the periodic reorganizations of the Army Service Forces, Lucius D. Clay was named as director of materiel of the Army Service Forces. As such, he ultimately took charge of six divisions: Purchases, Production, Requirements, Renegotiation, Readjustment, and International Aids. He also served as Judge Patterson's personal representative on key committees of the War Production Board and as such landed in the middle of some of the hottest controversies in which Judge Patterson became embroiled. A native of the state of Georgia, General Clay had as a boy served as a page in the United States Senate. From that humble position, he rose by way of West Point to become one of General Somervell's brilliant team and, as director of materiel of the ASF, was one of the key figures in the War Department's procurement program. From there he went on to the White House, where he served as deputy to Jimmy Byrnes in the Office of War Mobilization and Reconversion, and after the victory in Germany he joined the staff of General Eisenhower as his representative on the Allied Control Commission and as military governor of the United States Zone of Occupation of West Germany, where he gained worldwide fame during the Berlin airlift in 1948.

When Clay was named as director of materiel of the Army Service Forces, he asked that I be designated as his general counsel. General Styer compromised by taking me out of the Legal Branch and naming me as legal assistant to the director of materiel in charge of all legal work of all the divisions which were under General Clay's command. The Legal Branch was assigned to the office of the director of materiel, and Ammi Cutter was named as the chief of the branch. As a result of this reorganization, additional lawyers came under my direct supervision and at one time the total, including air force officers specially assigned to the Readjustment Division, as well as the lawyers in the legal branches of the Supply Services and air forces, for whose guidance I was nominally responsible, amounted to several hundred.

In the case of the Renegotiation Division, Charlie Pengra departed after the division had gotten on its feet, so to speak, and was succeeded by Jim MacIntosh of the Philadelphia firm of Morgan, Lewis & Bockius. Jim took hold and ran the show pretty much on his own, although I was available for consultation and to back him up when he needed help, especially when congressional hearings were being held.

The Readjustment Division was organized to take over all reconversion activities of the War Department. In the organization of this division, I was called on to conduct a complicated and difficult negotiation with the army air forces and the fiscal director in order to obtain uniformity of administration in this increasingly important field. Here I came to know Colonel William H. Draper, who had been specifically charged with cooperating with the Navy Department in the preparation of a joint termination regulation. The Readjustment Division was responsible for all the activities in connection with plant clearances after contracts were terminated and for coordination of War Department activities with those of the Office of Contract Settlement, the Surplus Property Administration, and the Office of War Mobilization and Reconversion.

During this period I attended weekly meetings of General Clay's staff, and after the railroad takeover I was also invited to the meetings of General Somervell's staff, where I listened to the discussion of plans for the redeployment of men and materials all over the world so as to concentrate on the defeat of Japan. Here I listened to a fascinating account of the worldwide activities of the United States Armed Forces, stretching from the South Seas to the Aleutian Islands and from the Middle East to China. As the end of the war in Europe came closer, the emphasis shifted to preparations for what promised to be a desperate battle in the Pacific.

Through all this I listened to Clay and acquired a new perspective on the tasks which had been and still remained to be done. His brilliance and statesmanlike qualities became more and more apparent. We often talked about Judge Patterson, and I remember particularly one occasion when we were discussing a proposal for reorganizing the War Department. General Clay made the observation that military personnel had to be relied upon rather than civilians. I said, "Well, that does not fit in with my own observation," whereupon he said, "You don't know anything about it. You've just been here in war time under men like Patterson or Forrestal. Now those men worked. I have seen many Assistant Secretaries of War before, but none of them ever did any work in the way those fellows did. This is not typical at all, and no organization that assumes that you are going to have people like Patterson or Forrestal in those positions will work—you simply can't assume that."

Having had the opportunity to see the program through Judge Patterson's eyes, it was now my privilege to see it through the eyes of probably the most gifted military man in the entire procurement program. Somervell was certainly a superb executive, but for sheer long-range, statesmanlike wisdom, I believe that Clay was his superior.

Chief Counsel

In a letter dated December 30, 1947, to President Conant of Harvard University, Howard Petersen, then executive vice-president of Fidelity-Philadelphia Trust Company in Philadelphia, wrote that I had "held a position which can best be described as Chief Counsel for the procurement or industrial side of the War Department." Judge Patterson, in a letter of May 25, 1946, addressed to Grenville Clark, described my responsibilities as covering "the entire field of industrial production for war,—legislation, programs with other agencies, Army regulations, procurement programs, in fact everything having to do with arming and equipping the troops." Thanks to Colonel Young's advice to stay out of uniform, I had finally managed to fill in all but official title the role which was offered to me in January 1942 by Judge Patterson.

By the end of the year 1944, that job had been practically completed. Those of us who had been engaged primarily in procurement had done their work. How well was illustrated by a remark by General Marshall, who is reported to have said that all that was now needed was to tie a set of barrage balloons to the British Isles to keep them from sinking into the sea from the sheer weight of the armaments which had already been piled up there in preparation for the invasion of Europe.

As the troops under General Eisenhower fought their way to Paris, those who had been engaged in the procurement program became spectators, and as a consequence some of our best men began drifting away. General Clay took a busman's holiday in order to untangle a monstrous traffic jam which was strangling the movement of supplies from the French ports to the fighting forces. Not long after his return, he was called to the White House as deputy director of the Office of War Mobilization and Reconversion and was succeeded as director of materiel by Howard Bruce of Baltimore. I had known Mr. Bruce as a successful industrialist who had taken an active interest in Maryland politics. His building of the Baltimore National Bank from the ashes of the old Baltimore Trust Company had been widely regarded as the major achievement in the Baltimore business community during the Great Depression. For about a year I worked with him and was astonished at the ease with which he stepped into General Clay's shoes.

About this time Dean Acheson asked me to come over to the State Department as his assistant in handling congressional hearings. I talked to my friend Alger Hiss, who was in the State Department, and he warned me that the job would probably involve stepping on the toes of many of the important people in the department. As a consequence, I was relieved when Judge Patterson put his foot down and said that he still needed me in the War Department.

In the spring of 1945, just before the final victory in Europe, I got a call from Vernon Miller, who told me that the firm of Marbury, Gosnell and Williams was on the verge of dissolution. Jesse Slingluff, Jr., and Van Wolf had enlisted in the recently organized Army Specialist Corps and gone south for training. Charlie Evans was about to accept an offer to join Clarence Miles's firm, and Mr. Rawls was in increasingly bad health. Vernon asked me whether I planned to return to the firm and, if so, whether I could fix a definite date. I talked to Mr. Bruce and Judge Patterson, and both of them finally agreed that under the circumstances I could plan to leave the War Department not later than September 1, 1945. I later learned that Mr. Bruce told Clarence Miles to lay off Charlie Evans and to leave the clients of Marbury, Gosnell and Williams alone. Inasmuch as Mr. Bruce had great influence with many of Clarence's best clients, his intervention on my behalf was very effective.

The war in Europe ended on May 11, 1945. Shortly thereafter I was told that I had been selected as the War Department representative to accompany a delegation of the House Military Affairs Committee which proposed to investigate the way in which the War Department was conducting the liquidation of the war in Europe, the Middle East, and North

Africa, now that the fighting had stopped. My job was to see that the committee members got all the information they needed. Immediately upon my return from that thirty-day trip, I wrote an account which occupies the next chapter in this narrative.

Coda

The reader may wonder what had become of my family during the years I have described in this chapter. I am afraid that like many other wartime families, they had been sadly neglected. The burden of raising four little ones had fallen entirely on my wife. From the outset, it had been apparent that it would not be feasible for me to commute daily from Baltimore, and Mrs. Wheeler had stepped into the breach and told Natalie that I should regard the Wheeler residence as my Washington home. Natalie did not want to leave Baltimore, primarily because she felt dependent on our pediatrician and did not know to whom to turn in Washington. So for two and a half years I lived as a guest of Mrs. Wheeler during the week and enjoyed the fine collection of American art which Mr. Wheeler had gathered over many years.

One near-tragedy happened early in June 1942, when Bob Bowie and I were riding as passengers in a car driven by Chappie Rose's brother Nelson. I gave him directions which he found confusing, and as a result he turned directly into the path of an oncoming streetcar. The next thing I knew I was in the Provident Hospital in Washington, recovering from a concussion. My cousin Dr. William B. Marbury had been called in and reported to me that one of the nurses told him that when I first came into the hospital, I kept saying, "My name is William L. Marbury and I have a wife and four children." Fortunately, no one received any permanent injuries, and both Bob and I were able to get back to work within a few days.

All during this two and a half years, Natalie was struggling with an almost total absence of domestic help. At one time she really seemed to be sinking under the strain and our physician, Dr. John Eager Howard, put her in the hospital. Her family and mine stepped in to help, and the children's nurse, Katherine Lentz, who had retired because of ill health, came back for a short period.

I took Natalie on a brief vacation to Hershey, Pennsylvania, where we decided that we would have to find a home in Washington where I could be of some help to her. Fortunately, I was able to locate a small house for rent on Legation Street near Chevy Chase Circle as well as a young black girl to serve as cook and housemaid. We were also very fortunate to find an excellent pediatrician in Dr. John Washington. I was also able to arrange for the transfer of Luke and Ann to the Potomac School in Washington, where they made a very happy adjustment. I tried to make a similar arrangement for Yandes at St. Alban's School, but they were not interested in taking a temporary wartime student. On the recommendation of Henry Callard, the headmaster of the Gilman School, where Yandes had been a student for several years, we decided to send him to the public school in Chevy Chase.

In September 1944 we moved to Legation Street and soon managed to resume a fairly normal domestic life. Natalie was able to reestablish some of her former Washington contacts, but we made no effort to pursue an active social life, as she was obliged to devote most of her time to looking after Susan, who was only three years old, and I had almost no time for any social activities. We did, however, manage to see something of the Wheeler family and of the members of my family who were still in the area. This proved to be very helpful on the occasion when Susan swallowed a bottle full of nose drops and went into a coma. I came home to find Natalie distracted and while Susan finally gave some signs of recognizing me, it was clear that she needed emergency hospitalization. So Natalie and I took her to the hospital, where we were met by Dr. Washington. In the meantime, I called up Dr. Billy Marbury's wife. She was not herself available, but their daughter Lucy Marbury immediately came out to Legation Street and took charge of the rest of the children while Natalie and I stayed in the hospital with Susan. She was kept in the hospital overnight and allowed to return home the next day, fully recovered. All things considered the move to Washington turned out to be quite successful, and it seemed a pity that we had not made it sooner.

XV ❧ Congressman Marburg

On May, 29, 1945, I left the National Airport at Washington on a trip to the European and Mediterranean theaters of operation in the company of a subcommittee of the House Military Affairs Committee, of which Carl T. Durham of North Carolina was the chairman. Mr. Durham had been for many years the proprietor of a drugstore at Chapel Hill, North Carolina. His general outlook and behavior were entirely true to type. He was temperate and mild in his manner, interested in the plain people with whom he came in contact, simple and unassuming, and friendly in disposition. He was not disposed to be critical, but on the contrary, was inclined to praise good work when he saw it and was not ashamed to feel and express astonishment at the efficiency with which our armies overseas had conducted the gigantic enterprise in which they had been engaged for three years. I think that Mr. Durham's attitude set the tone for the whole committee. I cannot remember a single occasion when any member showed wounded vanity due to a lack of recognition of his importance; nor did a question of precedence ever arise.

Taking it as a whole, the group was typically American. Most of the members talked like boys let out of school, and the junior officers who accompanied us from time to time on the trip found the atmosphere most congenial. There was, however, a genuine seriousness of purpose on the part of every one of them. They really wanted to know how our boys were being handled, and I think that they found out a great deal about it while having a whale of a good time.

The Trip Over

Our flight to Goose Bay, Labrador, was without incident. This was my first trip in a four-engine plane, and it did not take long to discover that we

---

This entire chapter was dictated by me in 1945 immediately after my return from the trip which it describes. A few changes required by the lapse of time have been made, none of which materially alters the sense of the text.

were in for an unusually comfortable ride. In what seemed a relatively short period of time, as I looked down at the clouds I caught a glimpse of sparsely timbered land covered with a thin blanket of snow. This was Labrador and we were in sight of our first stopping place. As we maneuvered down to the field in the twilight I could see snow-covered mountains in the distance, and the post looked lonesome in its setting of stunted evergreen trees and frozen rivers.

After a perfect landing, we walked over to the Hotel DeGink. I was surprised to find that the temperature was mild, in spite of all the ice and snow. I walked around without a topcoat and was not uncomfortable, although I was very glad that at the last minute I had seen fit to change into a winter woolen suit.

We had a very pleasant meal in the Hotel DeGink. At the table next to ours was a group of young pilots, some Polish, some English, and some of our own air forces. I remember that one of our boys called off some sort of a toast in Polish which brought quite a ceremonious response from the Polish officers. It was all very Kiplingesque, but I was a little surprised to find a touch of formality, as though this kind of camaraderie was something not seen every day. Later I came to understand that friendly association with soldiers of other nations was not a very common experience for our boys.

After dinner we went down to the river to have a look at the pier where supplies were unloaded during the summer months. Here the tankers came two hundred miles up from the ocean carrying the winter's supply of high-octane gas. The storage capacity was ten million gallons, and as the field was handling 125 four-engined planes every day and expected to continue to do so while redeployment was under way, it was evident that enormous supplies of fuel were required.

Our guide told us that within the past month, the facilities of this little port had been threatened by a rise in the river, which was frozen solid. The threat had been removed by dropping a few 500-pound bombs on the ice from a B-25, whereupon the ice had immediately started to move and the river to recede.

The rest of the post was divided between the Canadian and the American areas. Each looked much like the other, with good roads flanked by low buildings, comfortably built and strong enough to stand rough weather. We saw a nice little hospital which we were told was almost always empty. Aside from a few cases of appendicitis and a few ankles broken in skiing accidents, no one got sick on the post, in spite of temperatures averaging twenty degrees below zero during the winter months.

About ten o'clock that night we took off for London. After we had been out about an hour and a half, I started back to the rear of the plane to get a drink. Suddenly I saw the full moon down below me and realized that the plane was turning around. In a few minutes the pilot came back and told us that we were returning to Goose Bay because of trouble with the number one engine. We landed after midnight to find that the engine had to have a new cylinder head. Had we gone on, the engine would probably have caught fire and things would have been rather bad. The job was a long one, so we all turned in for a good night's sleep at the Hotel DeGink.

The next morning, after a luxurious shower and a late breakfast, I walked out to look over a long line of bombers that were standing on the apron, awaiting clearance to fly to Stevensville in Newfoundland. Many of the boys were standing out in front of their ships passing the time away, and I talked to a few of them. Most of them had flown to Goose Bay by way of Casablanca and the Azores. However, one of the squadrons which we saw had come by way of Prestwick and Iceland. One of the planes showed 140 bombing missions completed, but most of them had less impressive records and some had not flown any combat missions. These were the new planes which had gone into service just about the time the fighting stopped.

At 1:15 P.M. we set out once more for our destination overseas. On the way down Hamilton Inlet we flew for about an hour over some of the mountains of Labrador. We could look down through the clouds on stunted spruce and muskeg with frequent stretches of bare rock.

Our chief pilot was quite a talker. He had seen many years of service with the commercial airlines and was an old hand at the game. He evidently had a low opinion of the Air Transport Command which he did not hesitate to share with us. A man hardly got to understand the weather up here before he was moved somewhere. On the other hand, if he was kept too long in one place, he got to be a nervous case, so the problem was practically insoluble. This was particularly true of the stations which were established as part of the Crimson project in the summer of 1942. At that time we were experiencing great difficulty with submarines and were casting about for a way of flying pursuit ships to England. A route was then laid out from Hudson's Bay over Baffinland and Greenland to Iceland. It was never used except for an occasional flight to visit the weather stations, but the airfields were still available for emergency landings.

After we had been out about nine hours we had a very glorious sunset and for about an hour our carpet of clouds became a beautiful thing to see; an endless ice pack with ice mountains rising in the distance. As the light failed, we saw every conceivable shade of gray reflected in the cloud formations. I was slightly confused by the fact that the sun went down in the general direction of the North Pole. When the sun rose a few hours later, it seemed to be practically in the same place.

As we arrived over Ireland, the clouds began to scatter so that we could see the fields below us, blue-black in the darkness. Soon we reached

Belfast. Here, in the rapidly increasing light of the rising sun, the city and its fine harbor stood out distinctly.

England

We landed at Bovington, England, which is thirty miles from London, just thirteen hours after we had taken off from Labrador. Here we were greeted by a colonel from the Visitors Bureau. I never saw a man so typical of the hunting set in all my life. After watching him I thought I would take a chance and ask him if he knew Marshall Exnicios. It turned out that they had hunted together. Furthermore, the colonel had a farm near Chestertown and knew my sister and brother-in-law. This made me feel quite at home, but I was soon disillusioned by my first meal, which was a pretty sad affair. After gulping that down, we were driven to the Cumberland Hotel, which is situated opposite the Marble Arch. On the way we came past Regents Park and the surrounding area, which furnished the scene for so many society novels written during the first half of this century. There were troops on every hand and huts and entrenchments in all the parks. We began to count the houses where the windows had been smashed or interiors gutted and were shocked to realize how great had been the damage.

After lunch we were loaded into a bus and taken to see the bomb damage, guided by a driver who worked for the Visitors Bureau. She was the finest type of English girl, with a determination to do well in her job even if it meant struggling with the humor of Americans. Her husband had been recently killed in Burma and all of her belongings destroyed during the blitz. She and her daughter lived with her parents and were carrying on in the best British style.

Although we were supposed to be in search of bomb damage, we spent most of the time looking at the usual tourist sights. This trip confirmed the impression which had been gained on the way in from Bovington that London, while basically unchanged, had suffered tremendous damage. We noticed that the streets were dirtier, the buildings dustier looking, and the women dowdier than ever. Even the men were, in general, less smartly dressed. Except in the area around St. Paul's, the bomb damage was not immediately evident, and it required a careful inspection to see that in almost every block there was material destruction. On the whole one could understand the weary air with which Londoners said, "When London is rebuilt, *if* it ever is."

During the course of the ride, our driver had occasion to tell us that the coupons allowed to her were enough to give her just exactly one complete set of clothes for the year: one hat, one coat, one suit, one pair of stockings, one pair of shoes, etc. How young children were kept in clothing was simply beyond my comprehension. Most of the women seemed to be wearing suits made out of some special material issued by the government, known as "utility cloth." It seemed to accept different kinds of dyes but was truly dreadful to behold.

On the way back to the hotel, I stopped by the office of the general purchasing agent, where I saw Phil Smith and some of the other boys who had been in the Purchases Division. Phil had had an interesting piece of work to do with the d'Olier Group and had been through a good bit of Germany. He said that the strategic bombing had been very successful in destroying industrial targets. I learned from him that Benno Schmidt was in town and staying at the Cumberland, so I immediately got in touch with him. He was dressing to go out to dinner with a daughter of Lord Curzon's who, he assured me, was a most charming woman. I asked him to stay over the following morning to attend a hearing which had been arranged by Colonel McIntyre. I knew from the conversations which had taken place on the plane that the committee was particularly interested in the disposal of returned lend-lease items, also in the sale of surplus properties, in the manner in which surpluses were determined, in the relationships with UNRRA (United Nations Refugee and Relocation Agency) and in the valuation of lend-lease and reciprocal aid. On all these subjects Benno was expert, and I felt certain that his presence at the meeting would be helpful, as indeed it proved to be.

After dinner I walked around the neighborhood. In the midst of Harley Street were two houses blown to bits, and this was typical of what I saw elsewhere. Many times an impressive facade covered a charred ruin or a house blasted from the rear. Queens Hall was gutted, as was the Portland Hotel, a wonderful relic of mid-Victorian luxury. The lack of street lights, the absence of traffic after 10:00, the theaters opening at 6:15 and emptying at 9:30, the long twilight, and the lack of laughter except from a few of our boys on holiday, all combined to produce a strong impression of a tired city resting after a long pull.

One marveled at the terrific effort by which the city of London had been saved from destruction by fire and starvation. I was told that for two long years every man and woman in the Islands had worked at some essential task for twelve hours a day and then had gone to bed expecting to be roused at least once during the night for special duty of some kind. All had taken their turn as fire warden or working in the shelters in addition to their other daily tasks. After two years they relaxed and worked only ten hours a day. It is easy to understand why the last few months of bombardment by the V-1s and V-2s seemed almost too much to bear. On top of this, one must remember that the food, while adequate, was very unappetizing. Even if the English could cook, which they most indubitably cannot, it would have been difficult to make much of the rations which they had available. Eggs scrambled in fish oil are something that have to be tasted to be believed.

Friday morning I breakfasted at the Grosvenor House and enjoyed myself reading the London *Times*. When I was last in England I had tried to read the *Times* but found that it took all day. The shortage of newsprint had brought about a pleasant relief; the *Times* could be read easily within an hour and glanced through in twenty minutes. The style, however, was still the same.

After an abortive shopping expedition I returned to the Hotel Cumberland for the committee's first hearing. Most of the questions were answered by Benno Schmidt; others were answered by the young officer who was in charge of the general purchasing agent's office in London, by the colonel who was representing G-4 of the United Kingdom Base Command, and by myself. Between us we managed to outline the basic facts about the quantities of supplies which had been shipped to the European Theater, the quantities which remained on hand, the methods followed in connection with reciprocal aid procurement, the methods of determining excesses and surpluses, the disposition of captured property, and the procedures prescribed for the disposal of surplus property. One of the statements made I subsequently found to be erroneous, namely, that a preference was given in the disposal of surplus property to American industries. I knew of no basis for this statement and subsequently ascertained that it was unfounded. Otherwise it seemed to me that the hearing went off very well; as a matter of fact, the information developed here impressed the committee very much.

We then went to the American embassy to keep an appointment with the ambassador. Mr. John Gilbert Winant was an amazing-looking man, with long black hair which fell off his forehead in a sort of mane. He looked like a character out of one of Eugene O'Neill's plays, and his speech was almost like that of a poet; so fervent was he in his intensity that he literally stammered. A stenographic report of his conversation would sound incoherent, but the impression made on his audience was very fine. Some of the committee asked him questions which were sufficiently pointed to arouse my interest. His performance reminded me of General "Hap" Arnold in his appearances before Congress during the early days of the war.

Mr. Winant was one of those who believed that the Russians were looking for a long period of peace. He said that they had been through a terrible twenty-five years since the revolution and were worried about the contrast between the living standard of their people and that in some of the Western countries. He cited the fact that when the Russians were finally persuaded to allow our pilots to operate from Russian bases, they at first insisted that no American publications be brought along. When we refused to agree to that condition, they insisted that every publication be numbered and given to them to burn when our men had finished with it.

Immediately after lunch that day we drove to Southampton. It was a pleasant drive through some pleasant country, made especially enjoyable by the fact that our driver was an attractive girl of good education. She had been a professional musician and before the war had played the harp in an orchestra. After 1940 she had been required to engage in an essential occupation and had finally graduated to driving a staff car. We talked about music, the stage, about the work that had been done by the Women's Land Army (whose members were deeply admired by all these girls because they had gone out and worked hard in the fields at the sacrifice of their figures and complexions and received little credit for it), about the fire wardens and the blitz, the V-bombs and their nasty habits, and so on. Our driver was quite used to the insatiable curiosity of Americans and had come to take it all philosophically. She did not seem surprised to find herself discussing her personal plans for the postwar future with a perfect stranger.

On the way back we paused at the outskirts of Southampton to visit a camp through which the troops passed who went up and down from London on what was known as Continental leave. They came into the port and were immediately sent up to this little staging area for processing. Here they were fed, checked as to clothing, papers, and so on, and started on their way. This uninspiring job was being done with a style and dash which was truly remarkable. The commander of this installation was a man who believed in doing every job well, and he had inspired his subordinates with the same feeling. Practically all the menial work was done by German prisoners of war, who were happy because they were busy. The kitchens were clean and there were no smells. The meals being served were good. We left there with a feeling of some pride that men could be found to do that kind of a job in just that kind of a way.

On the trip back I found that by diverting a mile or two I could go to Ashford and meet my cousin Kernan Slingluff's new English wife. When I arrived at the village I called her up and stopped in to see her for about ten minutes. She told me that Kernan had left that morning for the States. This was when I first learned that he had been released from the German prison camp at Buchenwald where he had been taken during the last days of the war.

The outstanding feature of the trip through England was the visual demonstration of the efficiency with which our surplus supplies had been disposed of. This was the part of England that had been so weighted down with equipment that General Marshall exclaimed that barrage balloons were needed to keep the land from sinking. Yet literally nothing was to be seen of all that vast mass of material.

The next morning, after sauntering a bit about the town of Oxford, I stumbled into a clerical bookstore known as Mowbrays. I was told that nearly all the parsons in England came here to get books for their Sunday schools and religious societies. The atmosphere of black cloth was very noticeable and quite pleasant. I asked my way to the Bodleian and immediately won the heart of the clerk. After a while she showed me a beautifully illustrated little volume which she had been keeping for nearly a month on an order which was never followed up. When I asked whether I could buy it she got permission from the proprietor to let me have it.

After leaving Mowbrays I noticed a store with an exhibit of camping equipment in the window. One little fellow about six years of age came along leading his mother by the hand and pointed to something in the window. She went inside and the clerk produced a whistle. The boy looked extremely anxious until his Mother had paid for it, then a beatific smile spread over his face and he went out of the store so obviously delighted with himself that I could not resist buying one of the whistles myself on the chance that it would please one of my own small fry.

I wandered down the street, past the Sheldonian Theater, and entered the court where the Bodleian Library is housed. I venture to state that no uninstructed person would ever suspect that the most famous library in the English-speaking world is housed somewhere in that ancient court. Having been given exact directions, I entered a doorway and mounted the stairway. The library looked very much like the Peabody and smelled exactly like it. It was quite evident that strangers were not expected, nor was there any preparation made to greet them. As the library was closing, I did not have time to try to make the acquaintance of the librarian or to be shown around. There was, however, a sort of exhibition room in which some old manuscripts and incunabula were on display. In one of the cases I noticed a set of illustrated volumes beginning with some illuminated manuscripts of the Middle Ages and ending, *mirabile dictu,* with a copy of the book which I had just bought at Mowbray's. This made the day as far as I was concerned.

I then wandered back through the college grounds and had a light lunch at a tearoom in the High. Somehow Oxford bucked me up. There was much less of the listless air which had been noticeable in London, and I was quite charmed at the combination of clerical and academic atmosphere which was still so greatly in evidence.

As I was walking down the High after lunch, Charlie Clason, a member of the subcommittee who had been a Rhodes scholar, drove by in a big staff car. He was all by himself and asked whether I would care to roam around with him. He took me all through Christchurch College, showing me the portraits by Romney, Gainsborough, etc., and then took me down to the spacious kitchens where the meals for the students had been prepared for centuries. We then went into the chapel which, as I recall it, is the smallest cathedral in England. It has tombstones, stained glass, and all the usual trappings, but with a special charm of its own, due to its very small size.

Afterward we walked down to the Isis to see the boats. Each of the colleges used to have a boat for purposes of recreation, but the Christchurch boat had sunk beneath the waves and had been replaced by a brick boathouse. While we were looking this over, a young fellow in rowing costume told us that a race would be run in about an hour. As it turned out, this was Eights Week and we were just in time to see the last of the bumping races. It was a pretty sight although far from the colorful occasion customary in peacetime. While there was something of a crowd along the towpath, the scene was rather sober in both dress and behavior. I was amazed that there were enough boys to man the crews and on inquiry learned that there were more than two thousand boys at Oxford. The policy of the government was to permit draftees with the proper qualifications to attend two terms at college before going into combat training. In addition, of course, there were a certain number of men who during the many years England had been at war had been discharged for disability.

From there we drove up to Boar's Hill to visit Sir Francis Wiley and his wife, Lady Margaret. He was formerly secretary of the Rhodes Trust and was at the time of our visit 80 years of age. He was very lively and interested in world affairs and discussed the problem of Russia with us at great length. These old people had neither servants nor fuel and I thought the house bitterly cold. They prepared their own food, made their own beds, blacked their own boots, wrapped their own packages, and in general went without all the minor services which elderly people of wealth and social position could reasonably expect to enjoy; all this not only without complaint but in the best of good spirit. They seemed to be entirely comfortable and were entertaining three guests at tea when we arrived. They were living examples of the way in which the English people bore up under the strain of the war.

On Sunday we visited the headquarters of the 8th Air Force at High Wycombe. We then drove through some beautiful country to Steepleholm, an airfield which was the headquarters of a famous group of pursuit fighters. Twenty-nine of these boys were aces, and all of them were enthusiastic about their jobs; to them it was sport, and I was told that all but two of them had volunteered to go to the Pacific. At lunch I listened to their conversation with great interest. The whole atmosphere reminded me very much of my high-school days. The dining room had been decorated by one of the staff with just the type of murals which high school boys would enjoy. However, it soon was evident that shooting for keeps had made an imprint on their characters. One boy casually mentioned the fact that he must have been responsible for the slaughter of a good deal of livestock in France. He had been given orders to "shoot everything that moves," and he had taken these orders quite literally. I did not pursue this subject, although my imagination immediately conjured up images of bicyclists and women driving oxen from the field.

After lunch we were taken through the briefing room, where the boys proceeded to go through the motions of preparing to escort a group of bombers on a mission to Berlin. We got a pretty vivid picture of how the briefing was done and what the boys were expected to do. We then went out to the control tower and watched them take off; of course this was only a training flight, but it was very picturesque nevertheless. We then returned to the briefing room and saw some moving pictures taken from planes of this group while they were engaged in strafing missions and air battles with German pursuit ships. One lad with nine kills to his credit sat beside me and explained what was going on. He had a slightly babyish look about him and seemed very soft and gentle. It was hard to believe that he had earned the Distinguished Flying Cross and was one of the finest pilots in the group.

All these boys were very proud of the part they had taken in the defeat of Germany. None of them liked strafing work, because the best of pilots may be shot down along with his less skillful companions. For this type of work they preferred the P-47 but for fighting in the air they were unanimous in preferring the P-51.

There was still some skepticism among these boys as to the value of ground strafing, although they realized that the damage done to transport had played a decisive factor at many stages of the advance in France and Germany.

While the committee was in the briefing room the boys who had gone up on the training flight proceeded to indulge in a little fancy diving overhead, much to the chagrin and embarrassment of their young commanding officer. The wing commander explained to us that the boys were pretty restless. He said he had made a point of taking all live ammunition away from them the moment operations ceased, for fear that they would go out and shoot up all lighthouses, buoys, etc., in the neighborhood.

The boys told us various tales about the efficiency of German espionage. A number of them had been taken prisoner in Germany and had been faced in their first examination with interrogations designed to develop information from them which showed an extraordinary familiarity with the details of their daily lives. One boy had been told almost every detail of his training and had been asked about a petty feud that was going on between two of the pilots belonging to his group. Some of this information could have been gained from interrogation of captured pilots, but the boys were inclined to think that some of it must have been obtained by direct espionage.

From there we moved on to Bassingbourne, the headquarters of one of the most famous bombardment groups. Here the *Memphis Belle* was stationed and from this field took place the first great raid on Schweinfurt, when sixty bombers were lost. Here I suggested that we might see how the lend-lease accounting was handled at a field installation. The records were kept in good style and the valuations, while based on a good deal of guesswork, seemed to be arrived at in a reasonably satisfactory way.

The drive to High Wycombe and subsequently to Steepleholm and Bassingbourne was enlivened by numerous exchanges with the driver of our car. This woman seemed to me to typify the so-called Cliveden Set. Before the war she had apartments in Paris and New York as well as London, and had led a life of complete idleness. She seemed to despise everyone except those who fitted into her own small group. She began on the subject of the Russians and made it perfectly clear that in her view the sooner we got on with the job of giving them a good licking the better for all parties concerned. She was somewhat taken aback when we indicated to her that we saw no reason for the United States to engage in a war with the Russians.

Her most interesting observations were on subjects with which she was more familiar, that is to say, the effect of the American occupation on social distinctions in England. She thought that the effect would be very profound due to the fact that the Americans had penetrated into the most remote areas of the island and with their generous allowances of money had brought the country girls into contact with aspects of social life which they would normally never have seen. Many of them had been taken by Americans to the best theaters, restaurants, and hotels—places which they would otherwise never have dared to enter. This was going to change the whole outlook of these people and modify their habits as well as those of the wealthier classes. It is only fair to say that she did not express any great dissatisfaction with this result; in fact, in this respect she showed an unexpected breadth of view. She said that many of the women were tired of working in factories and would be glad to return to domestic service but on different conditions from those that had previously prevailed in England. They would have to have regular hours and regular days off, privileges which before the war were entirely unknown to the domestic economy of the English household.

She also held forth on the practices of the upper classes with respect to the education of their children. She explained that among her friends, boys were usually sent to boarding school at the age of seven or eight but girls were never sent until they were at least eleven years of age. The separation of these children from their parents seemed perfectly natural and proper to her, and for the American custom, with which she was quite familiar, she had little respect. She thought that our children were on the whole badly behaved and suffered from excessive egotism as the result of the privileges which they were given in the family environment.

France

From Bassingbourne we flew across the channel to Cherbourg. Our plane was a C-47, piloted by a young fellow from Arkansas who seemed to me to have a pretty strong strain of the Ozark mountaineer in his makeup. At Cherbourg we made our first landing on a metal landing strip, and the tremendous racket which took place afforded us a little excitement.

The hotel was very unprepossessing looking but turned out to be clean, and the food, while nothing to write home about, was a relief after our English experience. After dinner we walked around the town trying to orient ourselves a little, and I tried to brush up on my French. The town looked dusty and dirty; the harbor alone redeemed the otherwise slatternly appearance of the place. French soldiers were much in evidence guarding German prisoners of war. I saw one amusing incident when one of our black servicemen stopped to help some German prisoners of war load a truck just to display his own superior strength. It amused me to think how this demonstration of racial superiority would have been relished by the Nazi Propaganda Ministry.

The following morning we left for a visit to Utah Beach. We drove down the Normandy coast in rickety staff cars over roads that were in pretty bad condition. Everyone noticed the hedgerows which had proven such an obstacle to our advance in the early days of the invasion. We passed through Caen and St. Mère l'Eglise, which seemed practically destroyed, and stopped for a moment to visit a nicely planted cemetery where many of our men are buried, and then we drove down through the meadows to the beach.

We were fortunate in being under the guidance of a colonel of the Engineers who had led the first assault wave to land on this beach and who gave us a most vivid account of the operations during the first few days and of the difficulties which developed. That a large army was supplied over these beaches for many weeks seemed almost unbelievable. The countryside reminded me somewhat of that in Southern Maryland. If one can imagine a total tonnage far greater than that handled by the port of Baltimore being put ashore in Calvert County from vessels standing out in the bay under constant attack from land, sea, and air, one can form some conception of the task which was accomplished at the Normandy beaches by our service troops.

One definite impression, subsequently reinforced throughout our trip, was of the lavish use of concrete in German fortifications. It was quite evident that the Germans had a worse case of Maginot-line psychology than the French, and there is good ground for believing that this was their undoing on the peninsula. Had they not relied so heavily on these fortifications there is every reason to suppose that we would have found much greater difficulty in obtaining a safe lodgment. On the whole I was left with the impression that the crossing was a great gamble which might have resulted in another Dieppe.

We returned to Cherbourg for lunch on a drive which took us through a part of the peninsula which had not been greatly damaged. The complete absence of abandoned equipment was very noticeable, and it was apparent that a remarkable clean-up job had been done throughout the peninsula. I had expected to see dumps of abandoned supplies of all kinds but during several hours of driving we saw nothing of the kind. We noticed a good many cattle in the fields as well as much poultry. This was evidence either of the restraint of our troops or of the ingenuity of the peasants in concealing their belongings. As far as the Germans were concerned, it seemed that they relied on this area as a productive source of food and had disturbed the countryside very little. After the invasion there was no time for them to loot. In the afternoon we drove around the port of Cherbourg. I was with the port commander, who quite evidently regarded the tour as a disagreeable chore.

After the tour of the port we drove up in the neighboring hills to visit a German prison camp. The physical aspect of this camp was very good; the site was pleasing, the drainage excellent, the shelter provided seemed adequate, and there were some neat buildings. Unfortunately, although there was considerable activity in some shops, most of the prisoners did not seem to have very much to do. We later discovered that this was not typical, but the initial impression made on the committee by the sight of so many inactive prisoners was not favorable. The physical condition of the prisoners was strikingly good, although many of them seemed to be mere children, boys between the ages of 13 and 18. Most of them looked very sad and woebegone. They had heard of terrible destruction in Germany and had no idea whether they still had homes to go back to or whether their families were still living.

I had a brief conversation with a lieutenant colonel from the provost marshall's office who was in charge of all the prisoner of war camps in the Normandy Base Section. This man had been an investment banker in Pittsburgh. He spoke German and professed to some knowledge of prewar Germany. He reported that the prisoners were docile and good workmen, but that it was necessary to deal with them on an authoritative basis. Those who made the mistake of treating the German prisoners with kindliness were repaid with insolence; there was no middle ground between arrogance and servility.

In the evening the committee divided up into groups and went around to several of the camps where there were English-speaking prisoners. I did not go on these parties but had reports from all of them. Apparently the experience was an interesting one. The men interviewed included factory owners, schoolteachers, shoemakers and a fair cross-section of lesser fry. All were deeply conscious of the catastrophe that had overtaken their country and were worried about their families. Those who came from Russian-occupied territory were particularly so. None of them seemed to have any sense of personal guilt, and practically all of them thought that the attack on Poland had been justified. All of them were critical of the Nazi regime but not of Hitler. They claimed that he had been surrounded by incompetent people but laid no blame to him for what had happened. Most of them seemed to have no conception of what the future would hold but were deeply fearful that a Communist revolution would take place. As I heard the reports, it seemed to me that the propaganda of the German government had been completely successful and that the task of reorienting these people would be a forbidding one.

Le Havre

Tuesday morning we drove to the airport and departed by plane for Le Havre, flying first over Utah Beach, where we had been the day before, and then over Omaha Beach, where I could see the bluffs up which our Maryland troops had to fight their way in those first bitter days. Below us we could see the remains of the famous "mulberries," those floating harbors which the Royal Navy had towed over from Southampton. Here also there was more wreckage than we had seen on Utah Beach.

The approach to Le Havre across the bay was very picturesque but as we flew over the city, the port seemed to be in ruins. As soon as we landed we were taken on a tour of the harbor installations. I ventured to speak French with our driver and found to my surprise that he could understand me and that I could understand most of what he said. He informed me that many thousands of people had been killed by the Allied air bombardment during the final assault. We could see for ourselves that the damage done to the facilities of the port by this bombardment and by the German demolitions was simply staggering, and it was therefore with much astonishment that we learned that the tonnage then being handled by the port was much greater than before the war. It developed that the "duck" had turned the trick. We climbed aboard one and rode out to the *John P. Poe* where we watched the stevedores unloading a cargo into a fleet of these amazing amphibians. As soon as they had a full load, they moved in to shore, climbed right up the bank, and proceeded to a warehouse about half a mile away. The port commander told us that the Germans had thought the port completely unusable and that the duck had taken them by surprise; they called it our secret weapon.

After completing our tour of the harbor, we lunched at the home of a local magnate where the port commander had his headquarters. From the terrace in front of the house, we were able to see a large part of the city and harbor, and the heavy destruction was plain to be seen. We were told that the local people had at first been bitter toward our troops and had shown open hostility. The destruction of life and property by the bombardment had been terrible; moreover, many of the people had been living comfortably and making money off the Germans. This attitude had since been modified, however, and relations were just beginning to be more pleasant.

The Ramp Camp

After lunch we took a long motor ride through the countryside to the Lucky Strike Camp (also known as the Ramp Camp) where Allied military prisoners released from German prison camps were received and readied for their return home. The drive was a very pleasant one, through picturesque country which seemed to be pretty well farmed. Many signs indicated that it was not safe to walk off the road because of mines and we were told that cattle and farmers were constantly tripping these mines with fatal consequences.

The Ramp Camp itself afforded one of the most interesting experiences of the trip. It had been prepared only very recently and was still incomplete when nearly seventy thousand men came pouring in. Aside from the physical problem of handling such a tremendous influx, the commander and his staff had a very special problem in morale. The men were in a very strange state of mind; most of them seemed to think that they were going to be released from the army, and they were anything but soldierly in their attitude. I rode in the camp commander's jeep and got quite an earful. He complained that the men refused to get their hair cut, would not salute, would not button their jackets, would not discard the fur hats they had gotten from the Russians, and insisted on sunbathing naked where they could be seen by the Red Cross girls. He was deeply embarrassed because the men, many of whom were junior officers, made no effort to salute General Koenig, the commander of the U.K. base who was riding in the jeep ahead of us. Every now and then he could not restrain himself and would bellow at some second lieutenant, "Take that hand out of your pocket and salute that general." He would then turn to us and say, "Look at that—if I try to discipline him he would write to his Congressman." And then he went on, "I tell you what I would like to do to them—I'd court martial them all and make them explain why they were taken prisoner. We can't say so, but a lot of these fellows were taken prisoner simply because they did not fight. Now they think they are privileged characters. There are only two things to do with them, get them out of the army as fast as you can for the sake of the morale of the others, or discipline them strictly and waste no time about it."

In spite of his worries it was apparent that a pretty good job was being done. As they came into the camp the men were given a thorough processing. The first step was to take their clothes away from them and give them a bath, then a thoroughgoing physical examination, then new clothes and medical treatment if necessary. All were placed on a bland diet and most of them gained a pound a day.

At this camp we got our first indication of the true talent of the American soldier for griping. The older officers in the army worried about an outfit unless the men griped. Whether for this or for other reasons, the American soldier did not hesitate to complain whenever he got a chance, and these boys were especially expert in the art. When they were invited to talk to their congressmen they let loose with a number of complaints about the food, about the fact that they were being detained in this camp, about the fact that English wives of soldiers were getting home ahead of them, about the isolation of the camp and the lack of things to do, and so on.

The California delegates were violently assailed by their constituents who had read that the California legislature was about to pass a statute permitting the adoption of the illegitimate children of married women without notifying the woman's husband. This provoked so much indignation among the absent husbands that the California members of the committee wired the governor to kill the bill. A number of the men asked about promotions for men who had been imprisoned for more than one year, but the great majority wanted to get out of the army. This led to some discussion, in the course of which the camp commander told the boys that he thought it quite likely that they would be discharged when they got home.

There was much indignation expressed over reports that the United States might quarrel with Russia. These men all seemed to feel that the sensible thing for us to do was to get out of Germany and turn it over to the Russians, who knew exactly how to handle Germans. The officers in charge of the camp reported that those who had been liberated by the Russians had come back with nothing but respect and good feeling for the Russian soldiers. Many of them had tales of ruthlessness to tell, but these were repeated in most cases with a good deal of admiration.

Just as the interviews were ended, General Koenig walked in and, after being introduced, said:

> Gentlemen, we are going to show you everything that goes on here. This camp has just recently come under my jurisdiction and it is unquestionably the biggest headache in the entire command. You will hear many complaints,

some of which may be well founded. I should appreciate having you pass them on to me so that we may improve where we can. However, we are working under great difficulties with men who are in a peculiar psychological state of mind and I hope you will take that into account when you listen to their complaints. I myself have investigated many of them and found them to be baseless. Complaints about the food, for example, must be weighed against the fact that the average man is gaining a pound a day. Even if they don't like it, the statistics show that the food they are getting is what they need.

This statement put the committee in a good frame of mind and prepared them to listen to the gripes of their constituents without getting unduly excited.

General Koenig expressed the opinion that the movement of Germans toward the area of British and American occupation would ultimately be reversed. He thought that many Germans would find the Russian occupation more satisfactory, because the policy of the Russians was to benefit the common people to the greatest extent possible. They intended to break up the large land holdings, to turn the industries over to committees of the workers, and to restore control of government functions to the people themselves. General Koenig had seen these things happening in Roumania, from which he had recently returned, and he expressed the very definite opinion that the Roumanian people, as a whole, were responding favorably to the changes which Russian occupation had produced.

Belgium

From the Lucky Strike Camp we flew to Liege, where we were put up at a comfortable hotel on the main square. During the entire ride we were over fertile and beautifully cultivated land. The country immediately around Liege is rolling and marked by huge surface coal mines which can be seen for many miles. At the hotel I discovered that the billeting officer was Lieutenant Colonel Robert Hall, a Baltimorean who was a friend of my family's. He was very eager to talk about home and we had a very pleasant time together. After dinner we went out in a jeep to see the town. We first drove around and viewed the damage done by the V-1s and V-2s and then went up to a promontory from which the entire city and surroundings could be seen. Here were the grounds intended for a World's Fair to be held in 1940.

Bob Hall gave me a graphic account of the days of danger during the Ardennes push. Liege, of course, had been the great supply base; vast quantities of ordnance and communications equipment of all kinds had been scattered through the hills near the city. After the bombardment from the V-bombs began, the city suffered very considerable damage. The bombs went up and down the river bank in regular patterns, creating terror and spreading much ruin, but they had practically no effect on military operations and damaged very few of our supplies. Nevertheless, our supporting troops withdrew behind Liege and all preparations were made by our supply services to destroy our stores. and retreat. Had this taken place, and it very nearly did, there is little doubt that the final defeat of the Germans would have been postponed for six months to a year.

We came down from the high promontory and drove back in the hills to the area were the great supply dumps had been maintained. Here we could see redeployment in full swing as along the road an entire division of airborne troops were bivouacking for the night. As to the relations between the Belgians and our troops, I got a very rosy picture. Bob Hall was both intelligent and agreeable and in speaking of him everyone emphasized his gentlemanly qualities. He spoke fair French and as a consequence had made many friends in Liege and planned to send his daughter there after the war for part of her education. He told me that the Belgians were warm in their praise of the American soldier and deeply grateful to our country. Now that the war was over they were of course most anxious to get back to normal and would be glad to see the day when our troops were withdrawn, but there was no feeling of hostility from any quarter. Other officers with whom we talked tended to place greater emphasis on the desire of the local population to be rid of us. I thought that most of our boys seemed to have something of a chip on their shoulders, but I was later to learn that their attitude toward the Belgians was friendly in comparison to the feeling of the average officer or GI for the rest of the people of Europe. "Travel is so narrowing," said G. K. Chesterton more than thirty years earlier.

Germany

The following morning we drove to Cologne. I rode in a command car at the tail of a long convoy, and this alone was quite an experience. These cars are miserably rough, and when driven at breakneck speed are downright frightening to ride in. For some reason our convoy traveled at a terrific pace through Liege and for the first half-hour or so I was convinced I was going to be hurled into the street at any moment. However, the surrounding countryside was very pleasing and reminded me of Western Maryland.

When we crossed the border we all got out and had our pictures taken and we began to feel that the real adventure was under way. Shortly after that we drove through the remains of the city of Aachen. It seemed the ultimate in destruction, with long vistas of rubble and wreckage. We saw some people here and there living like rats in the ruins, and once we saw a school bus filled with children. I was interested in studying the faces of the Germans who were walking along the sidewalks. Some of them seemed sad and dejected, others sullen, and others just bewildered. There were mainly only old men, women, and children to be seen.

As we came out of Aachen we struck one of the famous German Autobahn highways and rode comfortably through the countryside. The fields seemed in a good state of cultivation, and poppies were blooming in a profusion the like of which I have never before seen, although I gained the impression that a good part of the harvest might be lost through lack of manpower.

The next town through which we passed was Duren. This was formerly a town of about forty thousand people containing a number of large paper mills. It was the scene of the greatest devastation which I witnessed on the entire trip. The land seemed to have been heaved up by some great spasm, and we were told that ten thousand people lay buried under the ruins. In the language of the prophet Isaiah, the besom of destruction had indeed swept over this land.

After driving through some more beautiful country we entered Cologne and drove through to the Cathedral square. Here again you could look through long vistas of rubble and ruin. I had heard people speak of the marvelous preservation of the Cathedral, but the principal impression made on me was the great damage which had been wrought. All of the windows were shattered, much of the delicate tracery had been mangled, and the floor was littered with pieces of broken stone and glass. Many stones had been shaken from the high ceiling of the nave, and one felt that at any moment others might fall. There was a verger there who was too dispirited to bother to show us around. He did tell me that some of the best windows and most famous articles in the church had been placed in a bomb shelter which had been built in a corner of the church.

Here we got our first lesson in inflation. All of us had some of the German marks which had been printed for use by our soldiers. Some postcard vendors were asking the equivalent of fifty cents in this money for a postcard. I bought one for two cigarettes; another man foolishly paid an entire package of cigarettes for two of them; still another man got one of the cards for a stick of gum.

We walked over to the river and saw the bridge which had been constructed by our engineers. This was the famous bridge built in less than seven days. I had heard General Somervell tell the story of his first visit to Cologne, when he asked how long it would take to bridge the river. The reply was "two weeks." General Somervell said, "Caesar did it in ten days. Is it possible that we haven't learned anything in two thousand years?" When the bridge was built the officer in charge cabled General Somervell, "We have beaten Caesar by three days."

Next we were taken to one of the most forbidding jails it has ever been my privilege to enter. It had all the usual stink of a jail but with a special quality of its own: it also smelled of blood. It was here that the Germans had murdered many of their political prisoners. When we entered it there were a few Germans under arrest who were being examined by our counterintelligence command. One of them, who seemed to be very ill, had been responsible for the deaths of many Jews. Here also were held in solitary confinement about seventy Russians who had been arrested for murder, rape, arson and other crimes of violence.

During the days immediately following liberation, thousands of people—foreign laborers, many of whom had been held in a condition of slavery—roamed up and down the Rhineland. They were loose on the world with no idea of where to go or how to feed themselves. We were shown a series of weapons which some of these wanderers had improvised. One was a pistol made out of a rifle which had been sawed off at both ends. How anyone could fire such a weapon without tearing his hand to pieces was more than I could understand. One of the first tasks of our military government was to concentrate these so-called displaced persons into areas where they could be fed and housed. This was an extremely ticklish operation.

We were guided through the prison by Colonel Echols, a brother of General Oliver Echols's. Their father was Reddy Echols, professor of mathematics at the University of Virginia when I was there. Colonel Echols was very soldierly and quite Virginian. He was the thinnest man I had ever seen, with a deep bass voice and a very practical mind. I asked him whether the Russians had been advised of the imprisonment of these men who were in solitary confinement. He said that they not only had been advised but had requested that this be done. He added:

> When we picked these men and women up who were roaming around this country, we sobered them up, took their guns away, and told them they would have to behave. Most of them did so but there were about three hundred who were just bad eggs. We arrested them and asked the Russian liaison officer what to do with them. He said, "Shoot them." I told him that we were not shooting Russians; then he said, "Oh, well, put them in solitary confinement until we can arrange to take them back to Russia." And so that is what we did—over two hundred of them have already been sent back to Uncle Joe.

I asked him what happened to the men when they got back to Russia. He said:

> I only know what I have been told. We send them along with the record which we make at the time we lock them up. I have heard that as soon as they reach Russia, they are called before a tribunal and the record of our proceedings is read. The prisoner is then given a chance to explain himself, and if he

cannot give an adequate explanation he is ordered to be shot. I have been told that 85 percent of those who have been sent back were shot within 48 hours.

After leaving the prison we drove through what was left of the city to a camp on the outskirts where about seven thousand displaced persons were located. This enclosure looked a good deal like a concentration camp and had the smell of unwashed bodies and of garbage. It was crowded with men, women, and children who all seemed happy and cheerful and on friendly terms with the American soldiers who were standing guard at the gates. I asked Colonel Echols what the Russians thought about this camp. "Oh," he said, "they are very apologetic about it." When I expressed surprise, he explained that the camp was occupied almost entirely by Russians. He went on:

> They are apologetic about the condition of the place because it is not as clean and neat as it should be. That is entirely within their own control. They do their own cooking and policing of the grounds and are really responsible for the entire operation. We have an UNRRA group who help out—for instance, they helped them equip the nursery—but the primary responsibility is with the Russians, and they are taking it very seriously. They devote approximately three hours every morning to what they call "political education." I don't know just what goes on there but apparently they are trying to teach these people to behave so that they will be respected abroad as the American citizen is respected. They are teaching them everything—how to eat, how to wash, how to read and write, as well as the elements of political organization. They have actually conducted classes in how to use toilets; many of these people have never seen one before and live more or less like animals. They are very decent people; friendly, fun-loving, and apparently willing and anxious to improve, but they are extremely ignorant. The Russian government is determined to make a good impression on the world and is extremely severe with those who bring discredit on Russia and the Russian people.

As we walked about the buildings and looked at the people, it struck me that they were very like our own mountaineers or "Okies," and that the atmosphere of the camp was very like that of a mountain mission. Our own land has many like them, although many generations of education and democracy have cut down the number.

It must not be forgotten that these people had been in slavery, and I mean quite literally. Men, women, and children were taken from their homes just like the Africans, and were transported to foreign lands and assigned to owners who treated them as so much livestock. They were housed in wooden barracks, crowded together, fed enough to enable them to do manual labor, and otherwise treated very much like animals. When liberation came, they behaved very much like animals. They looted, burned, and raped, and they drank all the liquor they could find.

Our troops were obliged to gather them together into camps, disarm them, and keep them under strict guard. As soon as possible the Russian army sent officers to help take charge of them and from that time on there was pretty good order. In the meantime, our army and the Russians were demonstrating their ability to meet a nasty and ticklish problem in a harmonious fashion, which was profoundly encouraging to all who recognized that our relations with Russia hold the key to the future of the world.*

After leaving this camp we were driven to a handsome villa which had a lovely garden and a very pleasant swimming pool. Here we were served an excellent lunch by two very good-looking German waitresses. This naturally led to the discussion of the ban on fraternization. Opinion on this subject was predominantly influenced by the natural resentment of the soldiers, relieved from desperate fighting, against any rule which prevented them from making love to good-looking women. While this was the crux of the matter as far as the average GI was concerned, there were other aspects of even greater significance. For example, our guide through the prison and the principal aid to the head of the Visitors Bureau was a young German Jew. This boy was dressed in an American uniform but without insignia. He insisted he was not a German and that he was going back to the United States with our army. He was apparently completely loyal and according to the statement made to us was really indispensable. Yet, we were told that a strict interpretation of the rule would prevent any friendly conversation with this boy. Accordingly, I began to inquire as to the reason for the continuation of the ban after the end of the fighting. The only explanation given was that it was intended as a measure to humiliate the Germans and make them feel conscious of their guilt. I very much doubt, however, whether it had any such effect. On the contrary, when the Germans observed that the rule was clandestinely violated on every hand, they immediately felt contempt for our lack of military discipline.

Bremen

From Cologne we flew to Bremen, arriving in the midst of a thundershower. The first part of the trip took us over Dusseldorf, Essen, and other cities of the Ruhr. The destruction of the Krupp works seemed complete, and this was typical of conditions throughout the region. After my return home, I heard estimates of Germany's ability to restore normal prewar production which seemed utterly fantastic in the light of what I had seen.

---

*The reader is reminded that this language was taken from my account written in 1945. I would like to emphasize that this is still my belief.

At first glance the city seemed in relatively good condition. There were some large buildings standing apparently intact; there was a good deal of traffic in the streets, directed by German policemen in uniforms which looked exactly like those of Nazi officers; and there was a general air of activity and competence. However, a closer inspection showed that most of the buildings were damaged, and we were given estimates varying between 75 percent and 90 percent as to the proportion of buildings within the limits of the municipality which were unfit for occupancy. The shaded street of well-built villas on which General Vaughan lived furnished a fair example of the damage that had been done. In approximately ten blocks there were only four houses which had not suffered severe injury, and by far the greater part of these were unfit for habitation.

Here we sat down to a delicious meal, beautifully cooked and served. On General Vaughan's staff were a number of officers of the 29th Division, including the acting division commander, General Bryan. He was a great friend of Craig Maclanahan's and had also known my brother. We talked about some of my friends in the 29th Division, and he tried to get hold of them for me. I did succeed in reaching Jack King by telephone, but the connection was bad and he later wrote to his father that he had received an unaccountable call from a "Congressman Marburg." As I tried to send a number of messages through him to my friends in the 29th Division, I have no doubt that they were much mystified.

From General Vaughan and his staff we learned that the port of Bremerhaven was almost undamaged. Bremen is an old city, one of the Hansa towns, with a long tradition of independence. General Vaughan felt that Bremen's international outlook and tradition of independence had made it relatively easy to find men who could be trusted to take charge of the city's affairs. A new burgermeister had been appointed, but in the case of the Port Authority, many of the old members had been retained after clearance by our counterintelligence.

Perhaps on insufficient grounds, I was somewhat skeptical about the policy we were following here. I could not help wondering what our Russian friends would think of restoring control of the city so rapidly to people who had been in influential positions before our occupation. It was not easy to believe that a man who was unsympathetic to the Nazi party would have been permitted to retain a post on so important a body as the Port Authority.

After dinner we were taken down to the Rathaus, where we were met by the new burgermeister, an elderly man with a Vandyke beard and the general appearance of a scholarly physician. We were conducted through the building and given a little lecture on the historical significance of what we were seeing. The burgermeister's estimate of the intellectual capacity of his audience was evidenced by the obvious way in which he tried to emphasize the removal from the walls of the Rathaus of all physical traces of the Nazi regime. He also bore down heavily on the commercial relationships of Bremen with the United States during the years before the war. The whole thing did not come off and made us all feel uncomfortable and a little sore. However, we were all cheered up when he took us down to the Rathskeller. The burgermeister told us that on the twenty-seventh day of April, a little more than a month before our visit, the Rathskeller had been closed to the public for the first time in six hundred years: a symbol of the completeness of the defeat of Germany.

I was very much struck by the isolation of our troops at Bremen. It was obvious that General Vaughan and his staff did not have much confidence in the Germans upon whom they felt obliged to rely. Their protestations of freedom from Nazi connections were so frequent and so vehement as to create disbelief. It was also quite apparent that the Germans looked upon our soldiers as semibarbarians. Generally speaking our high-ranking officers spoke no foreign language; a few of them knew and appreciated the better brands of liquor and the choicer vintages, but almost none of them knew anything of German literature or history. To the Germans this indicated a lack of culture which bred in them a thinly disguised contempt.

One rather amusing incident arose during the tour of the Rathaus. The furnishings were in a rather heavy North German style, and the large mural paintings reminded me of the Soviet art exhibited at the New York World's Fair. One of the paintings apparently represented the slaughter of the innocents, but the figures were all dressed in the court costumes of medieval Germany. Some verses inscribed in large Gothic characters apparently explained the picture, but they were too obscure to decipher. The burgermeister, when requested to explain the painting, simply ignored the request and murmured that the painting was of no historical interest. Apparently the subject matter of the painting was a source of embarrassment to him.

Nordhausen

The following morning we left Bremen and flew to Nordhausen, which is not very far from Berlin. This flight through the heart of Germany emphasized the impression received on the previous day that German agriculture was in sound condition. The fields of Germany and the little villages that were scattered throughout the countryside were on the whole untouched by war. Our troops devastated every place where they met resistance, but otherwise, except for the large cities and industrial areas, Germany was relatively untouched. The forests especially were, and are, a great national asset. We flew over parts of the Black Forest and other famous wooded areas, and the evident care with which the German timber was grown, harvested, and replanted was deeply impressive.

Nordhausen illustrated dramatically the outstanding features of Nazi Germany. This little town, set in a beautiful rolling countryside, had an instant appeal to the eye of the average American. It was evident that the people were industrious, orderly, and thrifty, as well as clean, but behind this appealing facade lay one of the most terrifying and revolting proofs of the degradation of the modern German state and of its total prostitution of scientific and industrial talent.

Inside a large hill or small mountain just beyond the borders of the town had been constructed a vast underground factory where twenty-five thousand people had been employed in the manufacture of V-1 and V-2 bombs and of aircraft engines. The plan of the factory seemed to be simplicity itself. Two long, parallel tunnels ran through the mountain, connected at short intervals by corridors. The tunnels had a length of approximately three and a half miles, the corridors of approximately one-quarter of a mile. Into one tunnel entered raw materials and supplies of all kinds, which were transported by rail to the corridor where they were to be used. The other tunnel was a long production line. Each corridor delivered components or sub-assemblies at the appropriate spot in the production line until the completed articles emerged from the second tunnel just a short distance from where the materials and supplies originally entered. The tooling had to be seen to be believed. There was every variety of machine tool of the most modern design in quantities such as I had never imagined. I saw four huge presses, each larger than any that I had ever seen in an aircraft or automotive factory, and hundreds of turret lathes, milling machines, and drills, all apparently in tip-top condition.

This great establishment was erected almost entirely by the labor of conquered people who worked and slept here in conditions worse than those endured in chattel slavery. We were told that during the construction of the plant nearly ten thousand workmen had sickened and died. When the plant had finally been constructed the management changed their policy; it was thought that the efficiency of the plant would improve if the turnover due to sickness and death were diminished, and accordingly an eight-hour day was instituted and the workers were housed out of doors. They were given quite decent accommodations, with a swimming pool and other recreational facilities and a well-equipped infirmary. As long as the slaves put in their regular eight hours at work they were permitted to live here with their families. When, however, their usefulness as workmen ended because of illness or misbehavior, they were promptly removed to a camp at the other end of town where they were systematically starved until malnutrition or disease carried them off. Their bodies were then piled into open trucks and carted through the streets of Nordhausen for all to see.

Nordhausen made a profound impression on the committee. The weapons which were being produced were, of course, most fascinating. Our guide had acquired a fair knowledge of the scientific principles embodied in these weapons and gave us an interesting description. The size of the rockets was a surprise to many of us who had not realized that they were so large. The feeling that we were looking at something which in its later development would have a transforming effect on world politics was strong among us all. It was something of a relief to indulge in a little authorized looting, and most of the committee members appeared at the exit laden with apparatus and tools of all kinds.

The general flavor of our trip through the factory was enhanced by the extraordinary character of our guide. He was a regular army colonel who had led an infantry regiment in combat but had been passed up for his star. He talked freely, emphatically, and indiscreetly, and laid down the law to the committee on all kinds of subjects. He explained to them that strategic air bombing was a complete waste of time and that the only effective work done by the air force had been in breaking up rail transportation.

He told us that over the radio that morning the news had come that the province of Thuringia (which includes Nordhausen) was to be occupied by the Russians. He said that this would mean that he would have a panic on his hands before the day was out. Everyone would try to move westward in order to remain in American-occupied territory. It would be his task to prevent this and he did not look forward to it. He said it was folly to turn over all these machine tools to the Russians, and he outlined his plan for taking all the machine tools in Germany and distributing them free of charge to every machine shop in the United States. To the suggestion that this might destroy our machine tool industry he responded, "No machine tools will be built after the war anyway." He had some very contemptuous words for 30-year-old air corps generals and seemed to think little of the navy.

Weimar

We flew on to Weimar, where, upon descending from the plane, I was put in the car with the acting corps commander, who happened to be Major General Smith, the commander of the 76th Division. On the way out to Buchenwald camp we talked together and I discovered that his division was located at Choemnitz, right beside the Russians. He said that relations were excellent; that the Russians were most courteous and scrupulous in keeping agreements. This they did so carefully that General Smith was put to it to see that his men were equally observant.

I asked him whether he had any information as to conditions in Russian-occupied territory. He said he had some information that indicated that the relations between the Russians and the population were good. While the war was still on there had been many instances of savage behavior by the conquering Russians, but since the fighting had stopped a different policy had been pursued. He said that he and his staff had been invited to a horse show at Dresden and had noticed some thousands of people in the stands applauding the feats of the cavalrymen. Upon inquiry it developed that a general invitation had been issued to the people of the community to attend the show. There was still great fear among the population, but this was steadily diminishing as the correct conduct of the Russian troops continued.

The Buchenwald camp had been cleaned up and there was little in the physical appearance of the place to indicate the horrors which had taken place. However as guides there were former prisoners who supplied us with information which seemed to be genuine, and many of our troops were in a position to verify the facts. Our guide was a Hungarian mechanic who was half-Jewish and who spoke fairly good English. From what he told us I gathered that the conditions at the camp had not been particularly bad until the last few months. There had always been a special area where the sick people were sent but the others in the camp were not fully aware of what was going on there. Toward the end, however, the gruesome practices became more flagrant. The camp, which was self-governed, was divided into areas, each of which was required to supply a certain number of people each week with the certain knowledge that these people were to die. If the deaths in the so-called "hospital" were insufficient to meet the schedule for the crematorium, then other prisoners were garrotted or shot each week until the full schedule was met.

The hospital itself was an incredible building. Here the weak were crowded like chickens in a coop, sick men being forced to lie side by side on a shelf in a space about four or five feet long and two feet deep. Operations were performed without anethesia on a wooden ironing board placed in a corridor in the middle of a room. These operations were performed by those of the prisoners who had had medical training. These men sought to the last to save their fellow prisoners from the inevitable; an amazing example of the professional conscience at work.

Wiesbaden

From Weimar we flew on to Wiesbaden, where we were to spend the night at one of the old luxury hotels which, although partly destroyed by bombs, was still habitable. Here we were given a sumptuous banquet by General J. L. ("Jakey") Devers. It was evident that the kitchens of the hotel had not been affected by the war, and from the hors d'oeuvres through to the frozen soufflé, the entire meal, including the choice of wines, was impeccable. It was my good fortune to sit opposite General Devers at dinner and hear him expound his views. Devers was certainly a most remarkable man; positive, energetic, robust, keen in his understanding, and rich in his experience. He commanded in England before Eisenhower. He was later in command in Italy, and finally he commanded the 12th Army Group, which included the French troops as well as our own 7th Army under General Patch. His talk was notably free, at times approaching the boundaries of indiscretion.

Devers spoke with admiration of General Eisenhower, whom he characterized as a man of outstanding courage. In his opinion, the most courageous decision made by Eisenhower was to make the crossing on D-Day in the face of the opposition of the British navy. Except for Lord Louis Mountbatten, whom he called "Nicky," Devers thought the British High Command lacking in boldness; on many occasions he had been assured that measures which he desired to take were impossible; only Mountbatten had supported him.

General Devers expanded on the subject of the difficulties of dealing with the French. He had the greatest admiration for the younger French army officers; around them, he said, would be erected the new France, and there was every reason to believe that it would be a great state. At the same time the older regular army officers afforded him a great deal of amusement. They looked on all American officers with condescension because of the Americans' lack of training. In dealing with the Frenchmen it was necessary to take their pride constantly into account. Thus, at Stuttgart it was reported to him that the "Ghoums" (French African troops) had raped ten thousand German women. General Devers had a quiet investigation made and discovered that the reports had been exaggerated but that there was enough foundation to require immediate corrective action. Instead of going to the head of the French army, he went straight to the commander at Stuttgart and laid the situation before him. This indirect appeal to the commander's pride had its immediate effect; the necessary measures were taken to prevent any recurrence of the offense.

General Devers said that it was necessary at all times to be on your guard against injury to Russian sensibilities. Mrs. Churchill had described to him an experience she had had at Sevastopol, which she visited with the Prime Minister after the Russians had captured it. Upon seeing the terrible destruction she had expressed sympathy to her Russian hosts. She soon found that this had been an error. They stiffened up and said coldly, "Come back in ten years and you will find a greater city than ever before."

During the course of the conversation Devers spoke of the excellence of our performance in France. He said that we had nothing to apologize for except the breakthrough at the Ardennes, where we had been asleep at the switch. Devers went on to say that the double envelopment in the

Ruhr had been masterly and had left the German general staff completely incredulous.

In speaking of the Russians, Devers stated that in his opinion the principal obstacle to the development of harmonious working relations was the extent to which everything in Russia bottlenecked through Stalin. He said that in many instances the inability to get decisions produced irritating dilemmas, but apparently nothing could be done about it. This had been noticeable in military affairs as well as in affairs of state. Stalin was unquestionably the commander in chief of the Russian armed forces in a very real sense. It was said that he had had a number of generals shot for negligence and boasted of it after he had a sufficient quantity of vodka under his belt.

After dinner I had some conversation with the judge advocate of the 12th Army Group. He was charged with the prosecution of war criminals and was greatly disturbed by his inability to take proceedings in some flagrant cases. He said that there were nearly three hundred cases which he was prepared to prosecute at once for crimes well known in the community. Washington had so far failed to grant authority to proceed, although a wire from Eisenhower had been supported by a request for favorable action by Justice Jackson. The effect of the failure to act in these cases on the community and on our relations with the Russians was most injurious. The Russians suspected that the criminals would not be punished and were simply being protected by being taken into custody by our troops. I promised to do what I could about this and in talking after my return to Jack McCloy learned that the failure to give the authorization had been due to a jurisdictional conflict between the judge advocate general's office and other units of the War Department.

The night which followed was one of the most unpleasant of my recollection. Wiesbaden breeds an especially savage kind of mosquito and there were no screens on the windows and no netting; furthermore, the bed sheets were too short to cover the head without uncovering the feet. It was a miserable night for all.

Frankfurt

We left the hotel to drive to Frankfurt, where we had an appointment to see General Eisenhower at 10:30. As we drove into Frankfurt we saw great destruction. Unquestionably these German cities had been taking a terrible pasting for many months. The only large building fit for occupancy was the office of the I. G. Farbenindustries, a building quite equal, if not superior, in elegance to any industrial offices I have ever seen. One member of the committee muttered that it seemed strange that the headquarters of this vast international cartel should stand undamaged by bombs.

He strongly suspected that this was no coincidence and referred darkly to similar examples which had occurred during the last war. I discovered later that the building had actually been damaged and had required a good deal of reconstruction before General Eisenhower could move in.

The interview with General Eisenhower was interesting, not because of what he said, but because it revealed his skill in handling a group of men who were totally unfamiliar to him. Within a very short time he had made the force of his typically American personality strongly felt. The committee was given the distinct impression of an unaffected, straight-forward man of keen intelligence; he used homely speech occasionally interspersed with mild profanity. He spoke of his trip to Berlin (from which he had just returned) and of his first meeting with the Russian generals. In answer to questions as to the possibility of developing satisfactory working relations with the Russians, he replied that with patience and sympathy it could undoubtedly be done. He confirmed what we had already learned, that at the lower level of military operations, cooperation was relatively easy because of the good will and reasonableness of both sides. He said that there was more difficulty at the higher level, in part because of the organizational structure of the Russian government and in part because of the fears and suspicions that were generated by uncertainty as to the ultimate objectives of our respective national policies. There were also psychological problems to be recognized. As an illustration, he cited an amusing incident that had occurred during his visit to Berlin. In preparing for the meeting he had decided, in view of the great formality of the occasion, to have his aide in full dress. The Russian generals, who in comparison with ours dress like peacocks, immediately assumed that the aide was the most important person present and asked General Eisenhower to introduce them. When General Eisenhower explained the status of the gorgeously appareled individual, the Russian generals were silent at first and then said casually, "Ah yes, yes, we used to dress our aides that way too."

A very good illustration of his skill was in the handling of the issue of non-fraternization. By the time of this interview the committee members had unanimously agreed that the non-fraternization ban should be ended, and when General Eisenhower invited comment, Mr. Durham raised that issue. The General started off talking vigorously, explaining why he had that morning determined to modify the ban in its application to little children. He spoke rapidly and convincingly, and the committee members were scarcely aware of the fact that what they were listening to was a defense of the existing policy. But so it was; and very skillfully done indeed. Upon analysis the defense reduced itself to the argument that it was necessary to bring home to the German people a sense of their guilt. That was the only explanation which I ever heard advanced for the continuation of the ban, and General Eisenhower was the only man who ever advanced it without indicating his own personal skepticism regarding its validity.

As another illustration of his skill, I remember that the committee members began by complimenting the General on what they had seen and learned of the operations of the army in the European Theater. The General in a very gracious manner turned the subject into a discussion of the great wisdom of the committee members in taking the time to make these visits; he said that while they would doubtless benefit themselves, the army and the country would be the real beneficiaries. Without ever departing from the aspect of soldierly frankness, he created the impression that the members of the committee were sacrificing themselves in the public interest by taking this trip. I had heard that President Roosevelt was a past master at this sort of thing, but I venture to state that General Eisenhower could stand right beside him.

After the interview was over I had lunch with Bill Draper and Bob Bowie and got a brief insight into their problems. There was, of course, the customary organizational confusion. SHAEF (Supreme Headquarters American Expeditionary Force) had not as yet been abolished, and the military government was still in the hands of the tactical commanders. The Allied Control Commission was supposed to be planning and developing an organization, but the plain fact was that decisions were being taken from day to day which would affect the nature of the organization to be created and largely determine its policies. There was likewise confusion arising out of policies emanating from Washington which seemed inconsistent. One policy was to make the Germans live on their own resources and to pay reparations; the other policy was to prevent the reconstruction of Germany's war-making potential. Unless we were to allow millions to die of starvation and freezing, it was necessary to restore as rapidly as possible certain fundamental aspects of the economy, such as the mining and distribution of fuel and the processing and distribution of food. How these steps were to be taken without restoring to a considerable degree the industrial potential was something that defied understanding.

Certain stubborn statistics simply were inescapable. Thus, the SHAEF area of occupation had always been a food deficit area; the productivity of the mining regions had been reduced by 85 percent; the flour and paper mills had been largely destroyed; all means of transportation were at a standstill; there was no mail service and no telephone. To restore transportation it would be necessary to have locomotives and other rolling stock, to have steel rail, and to import petroleum products or manufacture them synthetically. If anyone was willing to sell oil to the Germans there was no exchange with which to pay for it, yet the reconstruction of synthetic plants would fly directly in the face of the policy against the revival of essential war industries.

We then discussed the problem of harmonizing our policies with those of the Russians. This also involved great difficulty. The Russians were apparently destroying all industrial potential in their area of occupation by simply removing all tools and equipment. Their zone of occupation produced food surpluses, which they could exchange for enough consumer goods to maintain a minimum standard of living for the population, and the Russians saw no reason why the Germans should have a standard of living better than that possessed by their victims in the area which had been overrun in 1941. Manifestly there was a problem in reconciliation of policy. This would require recognition by the Russians of the necessity for the development in the SHAEF area of productive capacity for enough goods to supply that area with its minimum needs, including the goods needed for exchange for the necessary supplies which had to be imported.

Later I sat in on a brief conference between General Draper and some members of the staff of Ambassador Ed Pauley. One of them turned out to be Ernst Mahler, who advanced the interesting idea that we should accept reparations in the form of the services of German scientists. He pointed out that in the field with which he was most familiar—the manufacture of paper—the Germans had developed entirely new methods far in advance of anything known to us. He said that the German people had brains and energy which would inevitably find employment in some form; his suggestion was that their energy and brains be put to work for us.

Thereafter I went to dinner with General Clay and Bob Bowie. General Clay was living about twenty-five miles in the country outside of Frankfurt. Through the broad picture windows of his living room the ancient tower of Schloss Koenigstein could be seen rising in the distance from the top of a high hill; to the right was a wooded hillside of great beauty. The landscape is like that in the neighborhood of Gettysburg, Pennsylvania, but the buildings which are scattered here and there through the hills are older and more beautiful. General Clay's villa was requisitioned from a Dr. Arndt, who had, I believe, formerly been connected with the Zeppelin Company.

I found during the course of the conversation that General Clay thoroughly agreed that it was of the highest importance that uniform economic and political policies be established for the government of Germany throughout the entire area occupied by the Allied troops. He believed we could work out such arrangements with the Russians provided that the Control Commission was allowed to do its job without interference. He was very much alarmed by the impatience of the press about the job that was being done in Germany. While he did not refer to this fact, I had been somewhat surprised to meet ex-Congressman Joe Starnes (then Colonel Starnes) at Frankfurt and to be told by him that he was General "Beedle" Smith's adviser on the policies to be followed in connection with the occupation of Germany. It seemed quite clear to me that there was a conflict here which could only lead to confusion. General Clay expressed the opinion in no uncertain terms that the Reparations Commission would have to take its policies from the Allied Control Commission; otherwise the task assigned to him by General Eisenhower could not be carried out.

I asked him whether there was anything I could do to be of assistance to him when I got back to Washington. He said the best thing I could do would be to send a cable to Washington saying I was staying in Frankfurt, as head of the Legal Division. If I would do that he could put me to work the next day and there was a great deal to be done. I told him that it was no longer possible for me to accept that invitation, but that had I received it two months earlier and been in possession of the knowledge I now had, I would hardly have known how to refuse. It seemed to me so evident that the development of a plan for the government of Germany which would be acceptable to the Russians and avoid the pouring out of more of our depleted resources was of such outstanding significance to the future of the world that an opportunity to help accomplish such a result could be declined only on the most serious grounds.

Late that evening I was driven to the nearby VIP guest house at Koenigstein. Early next morning, while driving me in a jeep to the nearby airfield, my driver told me a story about the Russians which was typical of many that I heard. Apparently there was a school nearby which had been taken over as a camp for displaced persons, mostly Russians. There they were in the charge of a Russian officer who, strange to say, seemed to lack the ability to maintain discipline, with the result that the neighbors' fields and orchards were visited by trespassers, mostly Russian D.P.s, who stole most of the fruits and vegetables. When the Russian officer in charge was appealed to, his only suggestion was that some of the trespassers be shot; he said that would stop all the trouble.

The sensation of staying at a VIP guest house was a new one for me. It was like visiting one of the larger English country houses or one of our Long Island establishments, except that my hosts were officers of the United States army. The atmosphere of the dining room at breakfast was unique. There were various English generals and civilians, each sitting at a separate table enjoying the usual isolation which is so dear to the Briton.

France Again

The trip from the airport to Rheims took us over the gorge of the Rhine and almost directly over the city of Luxemburg. The country had a beauty which was more appealing to me than any I had ever seen. The rolling hills covered with tremendous forests, the large pasture lands, the fine fields, and the villages nestling here and there in the valleys presented a picture of a fat land flowing with milk and honey. I marveled at the frantic folly of a people who could be discontented with such a lot.

At Rheims I had the opportunity to talk with General Thrasher for a profitable hour. The general was in charge of the salvage operation being conducted by the Quartermaster Corps at Rheims. He was very proud of the use he was making of German prisoners. He said that the prisoners made excellent workmen and that practically all of them wanted to stay with the United States Army and go to the Pacific. The men who lived in the Russian-occupied area and the others who did not have families had no desire whatsoever to return to Germany. They felt that their country was irretrievably ruined. General Thrasher was very eager to take these men to the Pacific; he felt that doing so would relieve our soldiers from much dull labor and would be a great aid to our military operations.

In our brief tour of this installation we were able to understand General Thrasher's enthusiasm. It was evident that the German prisoners were working like beavers, that they were contented, and that a fine piece of work was being done in avoiding waste of materials and in producing items that would be useful in equipping our army and those of our allies. There was a spirit of energy and enthusiasm among General Thrasher's staff which was notable. The committee was profoundly impressed.

We lunched at the headquarters of the commanding general of the Oise Intermediate Sector. This office had belonged to a French prince whose wife owned one of the famous champagne factories. It reminded me strongly of an exclusive girls school—the whole atmosphere was very institutional. After lunch we were taken to a briefing room where General Roy Lord, who was in charge of the redeployment center, gave us a rather comprehensive statement of the plans which were in process of execution for the handling of the redeployment of the troops. Undoubtedly the period of readjustment and redeployment, when troops are awaiting new assignments or discharge from the army, is a critical one; if the men can be given the opportunity for useful instruction and pleasant diversion, and if the paper work in connection with their reassignments or discharge is efficiently handled, then they move on with a respect for the army and a good feeling which will be reflected in their future attitude toward the needs of the military establishment.

One thing that struck me was the fact that in spite of the efficiency of the Assembly Area Command and of the excellence of its plans, the plans had not yet been embodied in working instructions. The importance of this was emphasized when we reached Marseilles and visited the staging area where troops were being held awaiting direct shipment to the Pacific. Nothing could have shown more clearly the need for what was being planned at Rheims. In the absence of such handling, the men who were the subject of the direct redeployment in Marseilles were a very disgruntled lot.

Paris

From Rheims we flew to an airport near Paris, whence we were driven to St. Cloud, where we were to spend the next few days at the "Brown House." This had been the headquarters of the Gestapo during the German occupation and had later been Eisenhower's headquarters. Now it had become a VIP guest house. The style of the architecture is Germanic and strongly reminiscent of the mountain chalets to be found in the Tyrol. I wandered past sunken lily ponds with little bronze figurines, old stone walls covered with climbing roses, box hedges marking off squares where vegetables were growing, flower beds planted in unstilted, almost haphazard, patterns, and wisteria vines in full bloom. The trees were particularly beautiful and of many varieties, Norway spruce, ash, elm, and copper beech, all located in a very natural way.

Soon after our arrival we drove in to a formal dinner which had been arranged for us by General John Clifford Hodges Lee, who was in command of the Communications Zone. I was introduced to General Lee's staff, including the chief signal officer, Major General Rumbough, whom I immediately recognized as the man who had taught me geometry at the Boys' Latin School in Baltimore in 1915 and 1916. We had a lot of fun recalling old times.

At dinner a remark I made about the appointment of General Omar N. Bradley as veterans administrator led to a discussion of the qualities of some of our principal military leaders. One of the senior officers said that General Bradley alone of all our military leaders had had experience in directing the actual operations of an army of more than a million men. General Eisenhower was principally engaged in political and diplomatic tasks, although certain basic decisions had, of course, been made by him. Devers was more like Eisenhower and was no match for Bradley as a tactician. There was general agreement that if we put a large army in Asia, Bradley's absence would be severely felt.

At the end of dinner General Lee made an extremely gracious speech of welcome. He had great social talents and made a very good impression. I had heard much criticism of him, but for myself inclined to the view that he was one of the finest officers in the army.

As we came out from dinner it was not yet dark and it was suggested that a short tour of the city be undertaken with me as guide. Twenty-one years ago I had been in Paris for a few weeks and I was naturally most uncertain as to my ability to find my way around. To my amazement I discovered that the city was as fresh in my mind as Washington. The city was quiet and rather dark in the twilight but it seemed even more beautiful than I had remembered it.

The next day was spent resting and writing letters until mid-afternoon, when Charlie Clason and I drove out to Versailles. In comparison with my last visit this was a very sad sight indeed. The grass was uncut, the trees and shrubs untrimmed, the fountains and reflecting pools all dry. Within the palace most of the paintings had been removed and all that remained were the rather depressing murals. The trip was not wholly a failure, however, because it gave me an opportunity to see the French family group on a Sunday afternoon walk. We saw them walking, talking, and laughing together with that look of contentment and affection that is so characteristic of the French bourgeois family. It is surely one of the most ironical of paradoxes that the French people, who next to the Jews afford the very best example of successful family life, are known to us as an immoral people. The explanation, of course, lies in their completely realistic approach to the instincts and behavior of human beings. They recognize facts and openly adjust their arrangements accordingly.

In the evening we stopped in for a few minutes at a cocktail party being given by Ed Pauley. The Pauley party reminded me of some of the passages in John Dos Passos's novel about the first Versailles peace conference. I had only a glimpse of Pauley but it was distinctly not prepossessing. He looked like a combination of successful politician and businessman trying to translate his success into social prominence.

From here we went on to the Folies Bergère. It had not changed in twenty-one years except that instead of being crowded with American college boys and girls on holiday it was filled with junior officers and enlisted men and an occasional girl in uniform. The comedians were fairly good in the typical burlesque style and the kids laughed hard, but in general the show was terrible.

Monday morning was set aside for a presentation by General Lee's staff. Through what seemed to me to be an error in judgment, the subject of UNRRA was raised, whereupon some of the committee immediately got off on one of its favorite hobbies. It was quite evident throughout the European Theater that many of the army officers lacked understanding of the function of UNRRA and were inclined to belittle it. Some of the committee for some reason had come with a rather strong prejudice against UNRRA and were consequently eager for any confirming evidence of incompetence or inefficiency. The subject was one with which I had almost no familiarity, and I could do little to keep the record straight. Furthermore, it was not my affair except that I did not like to see our people stick their necks out and mislead the committee into unjustified criticism of another organization.

In the afternoon we went to a cocktail party at the American Embassy. I noticed out of the corner of my eye some astonishing-looking females dressed in the most amazing-looking hats it had ever been my privilege to see. Some of the congressmen were clustered around these girls, exhibiting Southern gallantry to an extent that was a sight in itself. After the party, it was explained to me that Marlene Dietrich and Madeleine Carroll had been among those present.

In the subway I ran into a young Cleveland GI who was trying to find his way to a swimming pool. He had been given written directions which he was trying to follow, but as he spoke no French, the going was pretty tough. He welcomed me like a long-lost brother and told me everything he had been doing for the past twenty-four hours. The highlight had been a visit to a night club where he had paid $40 for a bottle of champagne and had accidentally stepped on the toe of a major general. We got to be quite good friends before we came to the end of the ride.

On the Left Bank I spent one of the pleasantest afternoons in my recollection. I walked up the street to the hotel where I had stayed twenty years ago and looked in the doorway. It looked exactly the same, with what appeared to be the same cat asleep on the desk in the office. The antique stores were still filled with beautiful things but I soon discovered that the prices were as high as, if not higher than, those in New York.

It was especially noticeable that during the afternoon I did not see a single American uniform. Very few of the boys ever got out of their rut, and their impressions of France were based on an extremely narrow acquaintanceship. From what I saw, the army did nothing to break down the natural isolationism of a young man in a foreign land. On the contrary, through segregation and the attempt to reproduce a homelike atmosphere to the greatest extent possible, the natural hostility of our boys toward foreigners seems to have been exaggerated. From the standpoint of troop morale this may have been the wiser course, but in the long-range view, it seems unfortunate that our troops should return from foreign lands with so little understanding of the countries and peoples they have visited and with so much unwarranted contempt for their habits and customs.

Marseilles

The following morning we flew down the valley of the Rhone to Marseilles. For some obscure reason I had thought of Provence as semitropical and teeming with life. These arid, barren hills were completely foreign to my preconception of the area. When we landed at the airport the reason for our rough trip was immediately apparent. The mistral, that celebrated wind which descends on the Mediterranean from the mountains, was blowing with a steady gale. The air was filled with red brick dust which soon covered everything like a finely sifted snow. We drove a considerable distance into the port of Marseilles over rough roads through clouds of this fine dust.

After lunch we drove around the port. This was our first look at a Mediterranean population, and even the brief ride impressed us powerfully with the feeling that we were looking at something new in the way of human beings. The way that they swarmed in the streets and hung on the sides and front and rear ends of the street cars, their sudden unpredictable dashes through crowded traffic, the variety of their costumes and the swarthy appearance of many of them, all contributed to that impression. As we studied these people we could understand the reputation of this seaport as one of the wickedest cities in the world. The port commander told us that there were forty-two thousand registered prostitutes and that the French authorities proudly asserted that there were at least as many who had failed to register: a total of more than 10 percent of the population. The district which used to surround the docks was one of the sinkholes of humanity. Into this area the German soldiers never dared penetrate, and throughout the occupation Maquis and members of the Forces Françaises de l'Intérieur (FFI) found it a safe hiding place. After a number of German soldiers had been murdered while trying to make arrests in this area, the Germans brought a flight of bombers over and leveled it; they were still finding bodies in the ruins at the time of our visit.

The visit to the port installations proved of unusual interest. The Germans had done an even more thorough demolition job here than at Le Havre, and the achievement of the engineers in restoring the port to usefulness was outstanding. We were especially interested by an operation which the Transportation Corps was conducting on one large pier, where German prisoners were assembling freight cars for use on the French system. The operation was being conducted with impressive efficiency, and the rolling stock produced was literally worth its weight in gold. We were told that German prisoners made ideal workmen.

The port commander advised us that the operation of the port was at first impeded by serious labor troubles. The men would work only short hours, insisted on every holiday, and stopped work for trivial causes. When repeated appeals to the French government got no action, he suggested, half-jokingly, that the management of the port be turned over to the Communists, by which he meant the labor unions, the leaders of which were affiliated with the Communist party. Much to his surprise this step was taken. The results were immediate and astonishing; all labor troubles ended and the port began to hum and had continued to do so ever since. The port commander made the general statement that virtually the entire population of Marseilles were Communists.

In the afternoon we drove out through terrific dust to see some installations on the hills outside Marseilles. Here was a very large prisoner of war enclosure and near it the staging area for those troops who were

being directly redeployed to the Pacific. Our drive around the POW enclosure was remarkable for the evidences of discipline. As our convoy approached, whistles began blowing and the prisoners gathered and stood
in formation. We had not seen this elsewhere, and it made an impression
on the committee. As a matter of fact, throughout the Marseilles area the
superficial evidences indicated a stricter discipline than we had seen here-
tofore. There was more saluting and it was done with more snap and pre-
cision. I thought that General Rattay might be something of a martinet
and made it my business to inquire, as did some of the members of the
committee, but the unanimous report was to the contrary. General Rattay
was apparently universally respected and liked. He was in fact a very impressive man with a glittering eye, a fierce mustache, and a somewhat broken accent. We were told that he had been born in Roumania, and there
was a touch of Teddy Roosevelt about him which was quite engaging.

The general had been the representative of the War College in Germany during the years immediately before the war and had a pretty wide
knowledge of European conditions. In his opinion the re-education of
the German people would not present any great difficulties if 15 percent
of them were summarily dealt with. He thought that the mass of the German people were non-political animals; so long as the government maintained order and enabled them to work, they took no interest whatsoever
in political affairs. Entire responsibility for the policies which had been
pursued by the German nation during recent years belonged, in his opinion, to the general staff and the leading politicians, industrialists, and educators.

The staging area here at Marseilles was located in terrain like that
which surrounds some of our camps in Florida and Arizona. It was barren and dry and constantly choked with dust. I gathered that construction work was still going on; furthermore, the entire installation was
designed to house troops for a few days only. The principal recreational
facility was an amphitheater located in what appeared to be an abandoned quarry. Here the members of the committee met with their constituents and took the worst oral beating of the trip. These boys were mad,
and they wanted to tell their congressmen all about it. To begin with,
many of them were being sent to the Pacific without any furlough. Some
of them had more than the requisite number of points for discharge but
were being held in because of specialized skills. They complained of the
food, of the latrines, of the handling of the garbage, and of the physical
facilities of the camp in general.

I was very much delighted with the committee's reaction to all of
these complaints. There were some points which they called to General
Rattay's attention, but on the whole they were not disturbed and seemed
to consider that such conditions were inevitable. They felt sorry for the
boys but did not blame the army.

The Riviera

Leaving Marseilles we turned slightly northward and flew behind the mountains to Cannes. We landed at Cannes at five o'clock and drove eastward through Juan les Pins to the Hotel du Cap, near Antibes.

The Hotel du Cap was my idea of the perfection of luxury. It was an old hotel, built about 1880, rather small, but with large rooms and high ceilings, and plumbing that was both modern and lavish. It looked out over a beautiful garden to rocks which jutted out into a sea of the most perfect blue. On the horizon the mountains of Provence loomed softly to complete a vision of surpassing loveliness. Except for the chief of chaplains and his party, we were the only persons who were enjoying all this comfort as we sat on the terrace through a long and delicious dinner. I was convinced that no choicer spot for idleness and play existed anywhere in the world. It had been a favorite spot of royalty as well as of the merely rich. The proprietor proudly showed me some photographs of his famous patrons, among them the step-daughter of my cousin Pinckney Tuck.

We were so near to Monte Carlo that some of the members of the committee could not resist the temptation to visit it, so after dinner we started out on a trip that turned out to be straight out of *My Friend the Chauffeur* by C. N. and A. M. Williamson. Three of us climbed into an ancient Delage landau in the full expectation of making a fairly quick trip, but it was not long before we had a rude awakening. Our driver started off in reverse and stalled the car two or three times, and when he finally got started it was soon apparent that his driving experience was very limited. The Delage itself, while well built, had a motor which would have been more readily adapted to a sewing machine. As we raced along at 25 miles an hour, I thought of my mother's description of "scorching" on a bicycle.

We drove along through Antibes to Nice, where we stopped for a little while to visit one of the night clubs which were being operated for the enlisted men who were there on furlough. Nice has the reputation among the GIs of being a little bit of heaven, and it is easy to see why; everything has been done to make this place attractive to them and, except for a shortage of transportation and sporting equipment which was probably inevitable, I heard of nothing which anybody wanted and failed to get. There were even quite a few girls.

I rode up front with the chauffeur and, having decided that nothing could make him drive more dangerously, I initiated a conversation in halting French. He told me that there were a few of the rich who were collaborationists or inert, but in general the people had been eager to do what they could. He said that the people were strongly democratic but anti-collaborationist. The air was soft and perfumed and the sky full of stars and the rocky precipices looming above created an atmosphere of romantic charm.

We entered the principality of Monaco about eleven o'clock, and only a dim light indicated that the casino was not closed. When we entered the doorway we saw a scene that was truly depressing; room after barely lighted room with empty tables and a few dejected-looking attendants standing around. In one back room there were about thirty people playing at two tables of roulette and one of baccarat; and that was all. As men in uniform were not allowed to play, I took a crack at one of the roulette games. My first play was successful and immediately two harridans dressed in evening clothes and plastered with jewels began to follow my lead. Of course I lost every other turn and was soon wiped out. These old witches had apparently hung on through the war following first their systems and then their hunches, quite oblivious to the collapse of the world around them.

We left ahead of the others but about halfway between Antibes and the Cap our motor died. The driver told me that he was out of gas and promptly disappeared into the darkness. After fifteen minutes I decided to walk on ahead but after having walked about a quarter of a mile I came to a fork in the road and found that there was nothing to do but turn back. Finally, after three-quarters of an hour, the driver returned. Al Browning told me to tell him to put his foot on the starter, and the car promptly started. We went on for another mile when it died again. The driver shrugged his shoulders and said, "You see, we *are* out of gas," but Al insisted that we try once more. This time we were on a hillside and when the driver took his foot off the brake we started to drift backward. Charlie Clason started to holler and tried to climb out of the car, while I got to laughing so hard I could hardly stand up. However, we started on again and so we progressed with the motor dying three or four more times until finally, at 2:50 A.M., we arrived back at the hotel, exhausted almost as much by laughter as by the long day, which had begun at 6:50 the previous morning.

The following morning I spent swimming off Eden Roc. I remembered that during the days before the abdication I had seen a private movie taken of Edward VIII and Mrs. Simpson swimming at this place. I was especially interested at the time, as I remembered Mrs. Simpson very well from the time my father and I had represented her. Now the place was crowded with young officers (with a few WACs and nurses to complete the picture) who soon after breakfast began arriving from Cannes by bicycle, jeep, and every other known form of conveyance. It was a pleasure to see these fine-looking youngsters instead of the dissolute crowd of idlers which ordinarily infests this kind of place.

During the morning a professional photographer brought a French cutie to pose on one of the diving boards. She wore an absolute minimum of clothes, and I mean a minimum by European and not American standards. Cameras appeared in some miraculous way from nowhere, and I remarked to Al Browning that the boys would certainly have something pretty good to take home with them. One of them said, "The trouble is, it's too good; I will have trouble explaining this to my wife, in fact I don't intend to try."

These boys and girls had come from all over Europe. One lad who had been in Rheims recognized me and introduced himself. He had left Bremen only a few days before and had come to the Riviera for a rest. Generally a trip to a rest center is not charged up against leave, but this seemed to depend upon the orders given in the particular case. In any event, I was told that practically everyone had a chance to come here if he wanted to do so; since the fighting had stopped it had been the policy to give everyone the chance to take a rest wherever he wanted to go. Many preferred to go back to London where they had friends; others went on to Paris; still others to rest centers in the mountains or at other beaches. Here on the Riviera, everyone was happy.

Italy

After a leisurely lunch we drove once more to the airport at Cannes and took off for Naples. The weather was hazy and there were a few fluffy clouds in the sky, but the water was of the purest blue. In spite of the haze we could see the Alps rising in the distance.

As we drove on toward the Italian coast I could not help thinking of the young Americans of whom we had seen so many during the past two weeks. Their manners were simple and unaffected, and they were friendly and good humored and healthy looking. In general they made a good impression throughout Europe, especially on the young people who had been thrown in contact with them. On all hands I heard the desire expressed to come to America, and I felt sure that this was attributable in part to the fact that our troops spoke well for our country. At the same time, they had to some extent spoiled this impression by public drunkenness and by failing to recognize the sharp distinction which the European draws between women of good reputation and the rest of the sex. In these respects they were not as well disciplined as the Germans, whose conduct seems to have been more correct, but in spite of this fact, there can be no doubt that the Germans were more disliked.

What the total effect would be on the youth of our country of the years spent in warfare seemed to me to be a grave question. Army life was very brutalizing, and I heard stories from the most authentic sources of conduct on the part of some of our units which would not make pretty stories for the *Ladies Home Journal*. In some areas where communities resisted to the last, their final surrender was not accepted but the localities were destroyed and their inhabitants shot. Where sniping was met with, the doughs did not hesitate to throw everyone out of upstairs windows without stopping to try to establish guilt. In the rage of battle they looted, ripped paintings to pieces, smashed objects of art, and behaved as ruthlessly as even General Patton could wish. On leave the great majority of our boys got drunk and chased every woman they saw. Our young pilots were trained to kill and destroy, and their casual conversation showed it. They were not concealing tenderness under a shell of toughness; they were tough through and through. Yet, beside this calm willingness to kill and think nothing of it lived a loyalty, a sense of fun, and an affection for one another which was wholly admirable. I thought that if our youth could only retain in civil life the splendid cooperative spirit of combat, we could think of the time spent in the war as not wholly wasted.

Naples

We reached the coast of Italy a considerable distance north of the Tiber. As we approached Naples we could readily see that the harbor deserved its reputation for beauty. This impression was rapidly qualified as we drove through the city, for Naples was dirty and bedraggled looking. I had often read with some impatience of the feats of Mussolini in cleaning up Naples and keeping the beggars off the streets, but I must admit that if he succeeded in doing that, it was something in the nature of a minor miracle.

Our hotel, the "Parco" (said to be in the British style, no doubt because of having more than one bathroom), was very pleasantly situated on the side of a hill with a magnificent view of the bay of Naples and of Vesuvius. As I entered the lobby I inquired how to get in touch with Colonel Perrin Long. A brigadier general standing behind me overheard my inquiry and promptly took charge of me. He turned out to be General Leon Fox, who had gained fame for his work in suppressing epidemics of typhus, first in Naples and later in the Balkans. I was told that he was the most decorated officer in the Mediterranean Theater, but he wore no ribbons and there was an intensity and simplicity about his manner, together with an unassuming modesty which was most engaging. When he learned that I was from Baltimore he said that his wife had come from "a little place you would never have heard of—Chestnut Ridge." I told him I had been born on Chestnut Ridge.

That evening we spent looking at some jewelry which was shockingly overpriced and in watching the sun set over the bay of Naples. The Isle of Capri lay beautiful in the distance and the water was as divinely blue as the poets tell. The following morning we drove out to the palace at Caserta, the headquarters of Field Marshal Sir Harold Alexander and of General Joseph T. McNarney, his deputy. The ride to Caserta was the most breakneck of all the many wild rides we took on this trip. The MPs had been told that we had an appointment for ten o'clock and they meant to see that we kept it.

The visit to Field Marshal Alexander was chilly. After we had been introduced, he looked at us helplessly and said, "Isn't it distressing—we seem to have only three chairs, I suppose we won't be able to sit down." I thought the committee looked a little nonplussed at this strange greeting and it was quite evident to me that the field marshal had no intention of having any long visitation by delegations and protected himself by the simple practice of not having any seats for them.

I had heard that the field marshal was a cousin of the king's and that he fancied himself as something of an amateur artist, on the Churchillian model. Certainly he looked the part; in fact he was as unmistakably British as Eisenhower was American. On the other hand, he soon showed both energy and a keen wit. He was quite frank in answering the questions put to him by members of the committee. He said that his trouble with Marshal Tito over Trieste was only one of the difficulties involved in his complex command. Tito was in his opinion one of the truly great leaders who had arisen out of the war, but he was playing his hand for more than it was worth, and it was necessary to call him up short. However, he had scored a material gain for his country while accepting what appeared to the public as a humiliation. He contrasted this with the French, who had just agreed to withdraw from Italian Savoy under strong pressure from the field marshal. They had finally agreed to make a complete withdrawal on condition that it would be made to appear to the public that they were doing so voluntarily. The field marshal spoke warmly of the work being done by UNRRA and expressed the opinion that the Italian economic situation was not too bad, provided that political conditions could be stabilized. He remarked that there would be food enough and also enough industrial capacity in Italy to avoid national bankruptcy.

After this interview I saw Colonel Perrin Long of the Johns Hopkins Medical School, who had been the chief medical consultant of the Mediterranean Theater. With him was Colonel Eldridge Campbell, another old friend from Baltimore. We talked about mutual friends and exchanged Baltimore gossip during a large part of the visit. Perrin told me several facts of interest. He said that in his opinion Italy would have enough to eat. Agriculture was efficient and had not been seriously affected by the war. Colleagues of his who were interested in the study of diseases caused by malnutrition had found very little material to work on in Italy. There was undernourishment but not real malnutrition.

After the hearing we had cocktails in the grotto, followed by a beautiful luncheon in the garden of the palace. I sat next to Colonel Murray

Mitchell, who said that the great political problem immediately facing the Italian government was the incorporation of the recently liberated northern provinces. At this luncheon I first heard the statement, frequently repeated thereafter, that the withdrawal of our troops would precipitate something of a convulsion. I gained the impression that the British were trying valiantly to hold things together but that only a rapid improvement in economic conditions could give them any hope of success.

After luncheon we drove around the port of Naples and saw some of the destruction which had been effected by our bombing and by the German demolitions. This was the first port at which our engineers had shown what they could do to reopen a wrecked port. Here we saw piers which used sunken vessels as a foundation and other ingenious tricks which caused the Germans to change their tactics when they sought to demolish the port facilities at Le Havre and Marseilles.

The visit to Pompeii was profoundly disappointing. Except for the obscene paintings (which quite lived up to reports) the long walk in the hot sun produced little of interest. It appeared that everything of special value had been removed to the museum at Naples which was now closed. There were of course exceptions to this rule; the house of the Vettii had some beautiful frescoes and was quite interesting, as were the remains of the stadium, the forum, the temples, and the Court of Justice.

We then drove on to Sorrento, where we were to dine at the Aubergo Grande Excelsior Vittoria. Here many of the crowned heads of Europe used to come for visits and here Caruso died. This was another of the rest hotels available to our officers and was filled with boys and girls who were having a good time. The music was good in the sentimental Italian style. I suppose we heard "Take Me Back to Sorrento" at least ten times during the evening. The town itself was extraordinarily charming and medieval. There was even an odor which probably had been there since the middle ages.

On the way back to Naples we were again impressed with the contrast between the extraordinary beauty of the scene and the degraded poverty of the human beings and of their habitations. It was like traveling through the worst parts of Baltimore, only it extended for mile after mile. It was perfectly evident that the lives of the masses in southern Italy lacked almost every element of decent comfort. Dirt, filth, disease, and poverty were present on every hand. It was no wonder that these people were not content with the prospect of restoration of the old regime. Some blamed the sordid condition of the population on the poverty of the soil, but what I was able to see of the agriculture of the surrounding country failed to bear this out. I think it more probable that the social system of Italy, with its strong relics of feudalism, was responsible for a condition which must have been intolerable. After a visit to Naples there was little difficulty in understanding the rise of fascism.

Rome

After spending a day at the island of Capri we headed for Rome. Shortly after takeoff we circled over the crater of Mt. Vesuvius. In the morning we had seen some steam rising from the tip of the cone, but as we passed over it I could see nothing but masses of rock of a sort of lavender hue. From here we flew into the heart of the Appenines, passing over the Volturno River and the surrounding territory where some of the heaviest fighting of the Italian campaign took place. I was astounded to discover that the Appenines were so barren of vegetation. Of Cassino there is nothing to be seen except stones lying about on the ground. The monastery was still an impressive ruin but I was sure that it could never be restored to its ancient glory.

Upon landing in Rome we were convoyed through the city at a rapid pace, with three motorcycle policemen riding ahead and two behind. It was simply infuriating to dash at such speed through a city every stone of which I was eager to see. By the time we arrived at the hotel I was thoroughly out of temper for the only time on the trip. As soon as we had time to freshen up we were driven to the Ambassador Hotel for an official dinner, which proved to be very tedious. I was seated among a group of chaplains and whiled away the time by starting an argument on the probable effect of war experiences on the religious life of the soldiers. The nephew of one of the committee was a captain in the air corps who had been on some eighty missions as a pursuit pilot and had strong feelings on this subject. He got rather indignant with me for suggesting that the piety of a boy faced with immediate danger was emotional and not very deeply rooted. He insisted that he had never prayed so fervently in his life as when on a mission. He told a story of the naval aviators who, after releasing their bombs, used the expression "All right, J.C., take over."

I think that several of the chaplains were inclined to some skepticism as to whether any permanent results would follow from this temporary feeling. Most of them agreed that the early training of the boy was apt to be controlling. It was quite evident to me that these men found it difficult to face the fact that some of the behavior of our soldiers was pretty ruthless. We discussed the order to the pursuit pilots to "shoot everything that moves." Price's nephew said that he himself had always qualified this by common sense and had not taken a shot at a farmer driving a team of oxen. On the other hand, he admitted that many of the boys had applied it quite literally. I do not think that the padres had faced up to the difficulty of reconciling this sort of thing with Christian principles. Historically wars have given a strong impetus to religious life, but this war may have been different.

Our next stop was at the Red Cross headquarters, which was housed in a building which used to be one of the showplaces of Rome. It belonged to a princely family which had contributed a long line of famous men to Italy, including one or two popes. Some members of the family were still living in an apartment on the top floor, but the balance of the building had been requisitioned by our army for the Red Cross and was being operated as a recreation center for our troops. The sight of hundreds of boys from American farms and cities sitting about in the magnificently decorated rooms listening to radios or turning the pages of magazines sticks in the mind. The lady in charge was a masterful type whose general appearance and volubility reminded me of my cousin Neely Bowie. She guided us through the rooms of the palace and finally led us to a courtyard where she forcibly injected coffee into the entire committee. She had a low opinion of the owners of the palace who, according to her story, had been detected stealing electric current from the Red Cross. At 5th Army headquarters I learned that Prince Rospogli had been very active in developing the resistance movement in northern Italy and had been quite resentful of the requisitioning of his home.

We stopped for a few minutes to look in on a Communist meeting which was held amid the ruins of an ancient market place and temple. The theme of the speaker was that the ruling classes of Italy had brought disaster to the people and that control of the government should be taken from their hands. As far as I could gather, the tone of the speaker was moderate and his arguments were not couched in a violent or inflammatory style. The crowd, which was made up nearly equally of men and women, looked like clerical or professional people; factory workers distinctly did not predominate. The speaker, we were told, was one of the most aggressive and brilliant leaders of the Italian resistance movement and was regarded as perhaps one of the most forceful men in modern Italian politics.

We returned to the hotel for lunch with Admiral Stone, the head of the Allied Control Commission. He had with him a civilian who was in charge of UNRRA in Italy. At this luncheon we received the first coherent picture of the problem which was facing Italy. The country was producing enough to feed itself; the industrial facilities, most of which were located in the northern plain, were relatively unharmed; but transport did not exist and there was desperate need for trucks and fuel of all kinds. With these and with raw materials, the successful rehabilitation of the Italian economy was within the bounds of reasonable possibility. Of course, the establishment of political order was a necessary condition, the principal obstacle to the fulfillment of which was the tug o'war between the British interests, which resisted social change, and the Russian, which sought to promote it. The sentiments of the masses of the people were thought to lie somewhere in between. Some breaking up of the hold of the church and of the wealthy families on the nation's resources was desired by most people; on the other hand, the program of the Communist party was too radical and, in spite of superior leadership and organization, the Communists had been losing ground in recent months. Unfortunately, the moderate, middle-of-the-road sentiment was completely lacking in leadership.

Monday morning a private audience with Pope Pius XII had been arranged for us. I scarcely had time to grasp the feeling of the Vatican as we drove up through the privacy of its streets to the courtyard where visitors are received. However, our progress from the doorway to the pope's study would not soon be forgotten. We marched at a dignified pace through room after room filled with statuary, mural paintings, busts, medallions, mosaics, and carved furnishings, all outlined against walls of red damask. In some of the rooms guards in colorful uniforms saluted us with great formality. The succession of so many rooms, so much alike, could not fail to impress the most cynical visitor. The War Department representatives stood outside the pope's study while the members of the committee went in ahead of us. After they had been with him for about twenty minutes we were summoned to join them. The members of the Roman Catholic faith knelt and kissed his ring; the rest of us bowed and were warmly greeted.

It was immediately evident that the pope was putting an intense effort into the interview. He did not speak English readily and found it difficult to understand, but he made you feel that your presence was a source of special gratification to him. Surprisingly enough I was strongly reminded of General Fox; perhaps it was the single-mindedness and transparent spiritual quality that produced this impression. After a few preliminaries, he read us a statement which he had prepared. This was written in English and it was apparent that he did not find it easy to read. When this was completed, he gave each of us a rosary and blessed those which we had brought with us. He then blessed the entire company and after chatting a little while, we departed.

The members of the committee were delighted with their experience. The pope had been extremely cordial. He had asked where each was from and in many cases had recalled visits to their home states. He seemed genuinely delighted to see them and had made them feel that they had conferred a privilege on him by the visit. There was a little by-play between Bob Sikes of Florida and the two representatives from California which he seemed to appreciate and enjoy. He asked them for their impressions of Italy and told them that he was much disturbed about the years that lay ahead and about the violent emotions that were still seething in the community. He said that in this respect the women were perhaps worse than the men. When he learned that one of the committee was from Puerto Rico he addressed him in Spanish, which the committee member said was excellent and much more fluent than his English. We were told that the pope was able to address 42 nationalities in their own tongue—surely an unparalleled feat of scholarship. We were also told that every afternoon he walked and meditated in his garden for two hours and thus achieved some relaxation from his heavy labors.

After leaving the pope's study the committee had its picture taken and we were then conducted on a walk through the Sistine Chapel and the Vatican Museum. This was the most tantalizing experience of the trip. To get a mere glance of one of the choicest collections of beautiful objects that has ever been gathered together was a really painful experience. It is true that we were afforded a vision of beauty that cannot be matched anywhere else in the world, but it was like a mirage in the desert to a thirsty traveler.

We were to have lunch with Ambassador Alexander C. Kirk, so we proceeded to the Palazzo Barberini. The words *splendor* and *magnificence* are entirely appropriate in describing this place; every private residence I have ever seen pales into insignificance in comparison. Mr. Kirk had taken one of the smaller apartments (only 42 rooms) and furnished it with his own belongings, which are surpassingly fine, as he has the most impeccable taste and apparently almost unlimited funds with which to gratify it. The succession of beautifully furnished rooms through which we walked was almost equal to the apartments of the Vatican. I am willing to put the dining hall up against any room which I have ever entered. Busts of Barberini popes (of whom there have been quite a number) stand in niches against a background of sky blue. On the ceiling there is a very famous and beautiful mural painting. The table at which perhaps twenty were seated did not nearly fill the room.

I got into a discussion with a young colonel who was in charge of the Visitors Bureau at Rome. He told me that Mr. Kirk entertained in this fashion twice a day. After luncheon, when the guests departed, he worked until eight o'clock with a short interval for tea with his staff. From then until about half past ten he entertained again; then he returned to work until about four or five o'clock in the morning, when he would drive out to his villa in the country. He would usually go to bed about six and arise at noon and then repeat this performance.

The colonel said that his service in Rome was like being in fairyland. He had come from Memphis, Tennessee, and the lavish existence of Mr. Kirk and Myron Taylor was something the like of which he never expected to see, much less to participate in. He seemed to have a great admiration for Mr. Kirk, who he said was universally respected. Mr. Kirk thought that it was of first importance to the future peace of the world that the influence of the United States be raised to the highest possible point and had suggested to President Roosevelt that we keep one million men in Europe under arms for an indefinite period.

I had a little talk with Mr. Kirk himself. He had heard that I was a friend of the Baltimore Garretts and sent his warmest regards to Mrs.

Garrett. He thought that in spite of certain peculiarities she was the most brilliant and glamorous woman he had ever known and regarded her relationship with Mr. Garrett as something to be treasured in recollection. He said that his purpose was to protect the Italian people against the imposition of a social order which they did not desire, and he made it clear that he was referring to the program of the Communist party. He said that if our people were prepared to do their part and contribute enough of their substance to keep the Italian people from freezing and starving, it should be possible to establish a government that could succeed in rebuilding the Italian economy without a preliminary period of chaos and anarchy.

After lunch we drove outside of Rome to the Replacement and Training Command at Cecchignola. In this place, which had a long history, Mussolini had erected a military city and had begun the buildings for a World's Fair which he intended to pull off in 1942. The military city was pretty efficiently constructed and it turned out to be very useful for our program of converting service troops and air force enlisted men into infantrymen in twelve weeks' time. After all the high-flying magnificence which we had been experiencing, it was a treat to get down to earth again and see our men doing a solid piece of work.

On our return to the city we visited the Fosse Adreanali, where the Germans had murdered more than three hundred political hostages in reprisal for an attack on some German troops who were marching through Rome. Many of the victims had been prominent and I recognized one or two names of political figures. The cave was filled with coffins of various kinds, and while we were there some mourning females were paying visits of respect. In Italy apparently they do not bury the dead as we do. The bones of the Italians are eventually conveyed to mausoleums, and individual lots are not known. I had heard of the smell of the charnel house but this was the first (and I hope the last) time that I ever had to experience it.

Of all the incidents of the trip, the visit to Rome was the most unsatisfactory; there was so much here that demanded to be seen yet which there was no time to see. Rome is not like Paris; its beauties are not so plainly displayed. The finest treasures are to be found within buildings, many of which are not much to look at from the outside. Actually the superficial appearance of the city came to me as a complete surprise. Of course, I expected the Tiber to be yellow, but I had never envisioned a city all in brown, with burnt orange, sepia, tan, and mud the predominant colors. Even the relics of ancient Rome have a different aspect from what I had imagined. They are on a much smaller scale, and lacking in the splendor which I have always associated with the Roman Empire.

One of the staff at the embassy who had lived in Rome before the war assured me that the city was essentially unchanged; shabbier, poorer, suffering from a shortage of consumer goods and an inflation of values, and politically insecure, but still not very different from what it always had been. Music still stood next to religion as one of the greatest solaces of the people, and the opera, which we were unable to attend, gave a performance every day.

Lake Garda

From Rome we flew to an airfield near Verona. As we came into the plains of Lombardy, we immediately noticed the change in the landscape as the all-pervasive brown began to give way to green. This impression was heightened as we drove from the airfield to Gardone, the headquarters of the 5th Army, through some very attractive countryside, with frequent views of Lake Garda.

Gardone was a hospital center for the Germans and Italians and later for our troops. It was also the headquarters of the 5th Army, and it was from here that our drive up the Brenner Pass was directed. Here the foothills of the Alps come down to the borders of Lake Garda to create some of the most beautiful scenery in the world.

We then were driven up the western shore to Riva at the northern end of the lake. The ride was over a road which was cut out of the side of cliffs and which dips in and out of tunnels through solid rock. Here and there villages nestled on the shore below the road; the hillsides are covered with terraces with odd-looking wooden frames upon which some kind of fruit grows; and the mellow-looking buildings, with their attractive lines, add to the idyllic beauty of the scene. This is one place where nature and man seem to have combined to produce a perfectly harmonious result.

We were interested to find that the Italians had moved a lot of machine tools into these tunnels and had tried to produce aircraft engines here. The result was a production line about ten miles long with breaks as large as half a mile. Contrasted with the Nordhausen factory, this looked like a measure of desperation.

On this ride we stopped at a modest villa where Mussolini lived with Clara Petacci for the last eighteen months of his life. It was from here that he fled toward Switzerland in his last abortive dash for freedom. His wife lived down at the other end of the lake on an island near Gardone. This arrangement seemed perfectly satisfactory on all sides. At the beautiful little mountain town of Riva we boarded Mussolini's private yacht and cruised back down the lake to Gardone. It was a delightful experience made even more interesting by the graphic account given us of the campaigns which had been waged along the borders of the lake.

We had dinner on the terrace, where I sat beside an officer who had been at the Pentagon in 1942. Ladue had some interesting observations to make on the political situation in northern Italy. He said that the fact that the Communist party was financed with Russian money had been established beyond all doubt, and that they were by far the most aggressive political organization in Italy and had the ablest leadership. On the other hand, he was convinced that there was a strong attachment to the monarchy among the farmers. He said that the damage done to industry by strategic bombing was very slight, but that the transportation system had been completely wrecked.

After dinner we walked down the road in the light of a full moon to the villa where d'Annunzio had lived during the last years of his life. Here he had built into the side of the mountain a full-scale model of a destroyer as a memorial to the heroes of Fiume. Behind it, the Italian government had nearly finished an amazing tomb where d'Annunzio's body was to lie in state. In the moonlight these fantastic buildings seemed to have the plausibility of a dream; they created an effect which would, I am sure, have been pleasing to the poet himself. After this expedition we took a spin on the lake in an E-boat by way of a nightcap.

The following morning the E-boat ferried us across to an airstrip where we were to take off in L-5s up the valley to Bolzano and then over the Brenner Pass into Austria. The L-5 is the little two-seater observation plane built by Stinson and is not much bigger than a Piper Cub, so I was a little nervous at the prospect of what seemed to me to be a pretty nasty flight. I asked my pilot, a Tennessee boy who spoke a broad mountain dialect, about the weather, and he said it looked fine to him. He added, "Last night when we heard we were going to take you folks on this trip, we began to sweat—the weather up there in the Brenner is generally rough enough to scare us even—so when I looked out this morning I was certainly relieved." With this as an appetizer we bounced up in the air and headed across the lake for the Upper Adige Valley.

My pilot had done a good deal of flying up this valley during the campaign and he knew where to look for trouble. He pointed out a number of places where the railroad had been cut by bombing and also indicated the location of some of the antiaircraft gun emplacements. I was very much impressed by the excellent job that had been done on the railroad. However, he told me that the Germans had shown an extraordinary ingenuity in maintaining operations; every evening they repaired the damage that had been done, even floating bridges in place from concealment up stream. They had a device by which a section of a bridge could be sunk below the water during the day so that from the air the bridge appeared to have been wrecked; at night the section was brought up to the surface again and traffic was resumed.

As we approached Bolzano, I noticed that the bomb damage seemed to be confined to the old section of the city and that the new areas where the mills and industrial offices were located seemed relatively untouched.

The old section of Bolzano was very rich in association and possessed a marked charm; in fact it was an almost perfect specimen of the Tyrolean architectural style, showing both Germanic and Italian influence, so that it seemed a great pity that the bombs had not found their way to the newer and more garish buildings which had been erected under the Fascist regime.

Here also we visited a camp where displaced persons were being sorted out and classified. The place was a bedlam, with people of all nationalities milling about, loudspeakers roaring in a variety of languages, UNRRA workers darting about, counterintelligence officers holding interrogations, and moving picture cameras grinding away to record the entire proceedings. This reproduction on a small scale of the scenes which had been taking place in the Rhineland afforded one of the most fascinating spectacles that I have ever seen and I would have liked to spend the entire morning there, but our pilots were impatient to get on with the trip over the Brenner while the weather, which is notoriously treacherous in this area, remained favorable, so we regretfully left the camp, passing on our way out a trailer as long as a flatcar loaded with prisoners of war and towed by a wood-burning truck that puffed along for all the world like a little alcohol-burning steamboat that I played with as a child.

The following two and a half hours are beyond my power to describe. We ascended the valley to Merano and then up a narrowing pass until we were surrounded on all sides by mountains. As we rose higher and higher the snow-covered Alps came into sight and we passed above the tree line. It was amazing to see goats pasturing right at the feet of glaciers and occasional shepherd's huts nestling on hillsides so steep that they could not hold a loose pebble. I was struck once again with the ability of men to wring a livelihood from the most unlikely parts of the earth. Apparently the inhabitants lived healthy and comfortable lives in a land where one would suppose that starvation would be inevitable. At last we rose high enough to cross over the top of the pass into Austria. Below could be seen the yards of Brenner, which had been thoroughly pasted by our bombers. The air was cool and the atmosphere seemed very thin. Every now and then something reached out a lazy paw and tipped our plane sideways or bounced it up and down. We would approach a mountainside and look down a sheer cliff and I would experience something of that vertigo which frequently oppresses me when I look down from tall buildings in New York. We were at the snow level and could see the beginning of those little rivulets which far below became rushing torrents. Because of the cold, we had closed in the cockpit, so I was interested when my pilot let down one of the flaps and began to take a picture of a saw-toothed mountain. I shouted over the roar of the motor and wind and asked him if he knew the name of the mountain; it looked to me like one of the Dolomites, which I had seen when I visited Cortina d'Ampezzo in 1924. He shouted back, " 'Deed, I don't know, sir; I've never been up here before. We aren't allowed to fly in these planes up this far." This was very comforting.

Just about that time I glanced to the left and saw one of the other planes headed directly for me. It was so close that I recognized Pinero's beret. I shouted to my pilot and tried to call his attention to what seemed to me to be an imminent collision, but by the time he turned around, the other plane had sheared off. After we got down, Pinero told me that his pilot had been looking in the other direction until he had poked him in the back.

Venice

When we got back to the hotel I was very tired, but we had to pack and leave immediately for Venice. As we came into the landing field at the Lido, I discovered that as a result of my morning's experience, I was sweating out the landing in a way that I had never done before. I hoped that we could go to our rooms and have time to relax, but a sightseeing tour had been planned for us and there seemed no method of escape, so once more I drifted up and down the Grand Canal. I am afraid that the committee was more impressed by the general air of dilapidation than by the architectural beauty of the palaces that we saw along the canal. None of them had been repaired for fear of destroying their authentic quality, and as a result they looked as though they would soon crumble away and fall into the water.

In the evening we went over to dine at one of the big hotels on the Lido. This was the only place on the whole trip where we saw British and American soldiers together in a rest center, and there was not too much fraternization at that. The party went in for some systematic drinking and stayed until after midnight, by which time I was too tired to enjoy anything. I felt a little like the young American pilot I saw sitting all by himself on the veranda with four drinks lined up in front of him which he took one by one. I never saw anyone look more solemn and I have no doubt that he was drinking for some companions who would never be with him again.

The following morning I wandered off through one of the side streets in search of silk cloth which I did not find. I had been warned that silk had gone into the black market, and this proved to be the case. However, I ran into a store where some fine books were on display and I saw two pink-cheeked young New Zealand officers, fine physical specimens, discussing a book of reproductions of famous works of art. Their accent was more American than British and I was strongly reminded of some of the boys from the better New England schools who used to be seen around Harvard Square. The presence of the troops added a novel note to the normally sticky atmosphere of Venice in midsummer.

The following morning, after a last whirl at a post exchange, we took off on a long and extremely dull flight down the Adriatic coast to Bari. We were then taken to the staging area at Goia where the "Green Project" was in operation. Here bomber crews came with their planes for their final processing before taking off for return to the United States. We followed through the whole procedure from beginning to end, including the medical examination where the boys had to strip and go through the line feeling like they had lost all individual personality. It was painfully obvious that these men could not compare physically with the combat infantrymen we had seen at Garda, and I could not help wondering whether any effort was made to keep them in good physical shape.

Back at Bari the traffic proceeded without any sort of direction or order. Carabinieri, very handsome and erect in their colorful uniforms, passed proudly along the sidewalks through innumerable soldiers, children, and ordinary civilians, all busily intent on their own affairs, chattering and gesticulating, and paying not the slightest heed to the bellowing and bawling of the tenors and sopranos which came through the windows of the neighboring apartments. I was told that Bari had been one of Mussolini's favored spots. Here, on the site where the Crusaders had embarked for the East, he was building a great port to connect Italy with its empire, and here he erected a great stadium, known as the Bambino Bowl, to reward the community for having the highest birthrate in all of Italy. His dream of re-creating the glories of ancient Rome, the evidences of which are to be found throughout Italy, was strikingly exemplified in the structures to be seen throughout this area.

Bari and its surrounding country did not bear out the idea which I had so frequently heard expressed that southern Italy was, to quote Mr. Hoover's memorable phrase, an "effective poorhouse." On the contrary, I thought I saw here the basis for a prosperous community. The agriculture of the region was in some respects quite primitive—thus we saw horses treading out the grain, almost as in biblical times—and the means of transportation, especially the railroads, seemed absurdly antiquated, but every nook and cranny of this land seemed to be providing its full measure of fruit or vegetables, grain or corn. Aside from fuel and transport, the principal lack was political stability. Without this, inflation, stimulated by a desperate shortage of consumer goods, seemed likely to get out of hand.

The relations between our troops and the people of the city were not good. Most of the Italians barely tolerated our presence and their dislike was heartily reciprocated, even by those of Italian descent. I had an opportunity to talk with several enlisted men whose parents had come from Italy and who had some command of the language. Without exception they were eager to get back to Brooklyn, Cleveland, Des Moines, or Chicago. To them Italy was unspeakably backward. As one boy remarked, "You don't have any idea what a good life we lead until you come over here and see how these people live. Thank God, my father had sense enough to leave here before I was born." From that sentiment I never heard a single dissent throughout my trip.

From Bari we flew down the heel of Italy over country which seemed to me to disprove once and for all the frequently expressed opinion that the south of Italy is lazy and shiftless. Certainly that was not true of the farmer of this region in 1945.

Greece

We crossed the Adriatic to the coast of Epirus and then headed down over the mountains where the Greeks fought so valiantly against Italy in the campaigns of 1940 and 1941. Except for the African desert this seemed the most sterile soil over which we passed during our entire trip. Rocks rose in great masses with no covering except an occasional bush and here and there patches of yellowing brown soil.

We landed at Eleusis, where we were met by Lincoln MacVeagh, the minister. He told us that we were to enter Athens through the pass which was used by processions on their way to the sacred temple where the Eleusinian mysteries were practiced. Mr. MacVeagh spoke quite freely of the troubles of Greece and of the political uncertainty which existed. The emotions of the community were still very much disturbed by the revolution of the previous December, which had been even more terrible in some respects than the German occupation. He said that the partisan movement, which had enlisted the sympathies of almost the entire population as long as the Germans remained in occupation, came under the control of the Communist party soon after liberation and sought by violence to impose radical social and economic changes on the entire nation. These changes were resisted by the element which had been dominant before the war and which in this resistance commanded the support of a majority of the people.

Unlike in Italy, the ruling classes of Greece had not been discredited by association with the Nazis and Fascists. The Metaxas government, while unquestionably a dictatorship, had not been very corrupt and had gained the support of the entire population by its successful resistance against the Italians. Thus when the partisan movement had come under the control of the Communist element its greatest popular support was alienated. Since the suppression of the December revolution by British troops, the conservative elements had apparently overplayed their hand somewhat, with the result that popular sympathy was again shifting toward the Left.

I asked Mr. MacVeagh whether he had reliable information as to conditions in the Balkan countries which were under Communist domination. He replied that a good deal of information was coming through which indicated that the Communist party was quietly effecting a program of revolution without violence. Thus the ownership of land was being strictly limited and the larger estates being divided up; there was a deliberate currency inflation designed to destroy the rentier class, and many business enterprises were being taken from the control of their stockholders and placed under committees chosen by the workers and by the state. He emphasized that communism in its current form was not to be confused with the abolition of privilege. On the contrary, he believed that the privileges of rank had never been greater than they were at present in Russia.

Mr. MacVeagh reported that the Russians were not interfering in Greece as far as he had been able to determine, but he pointed out that the Russian press, in reporting on conditions in Greece, voiced only the partisan version of events. Mr. MacVeagh thought that reconstruction of Greece could not get under way until an elected government took over. During the Metaxas regime all the polling lists had been destroyed and the reestablishment of the mechanisms of democracy would not be easy, especially in view of the violent feelings which were still abroad.

The Germans prior to their departure had stolen or sunk a great part of the coastal shipping which furnished the principal means of transport. In addition they had completely wrecked the railroad system and taken away all motor vehicles. Then the revolution had interfered with measures which would otherwise have been taken to restore communications and delayed UNRRA in getting to work. UNRRA had now begun to do a fairly good job, although the absence of coastal shipping was still a severe handicap. Mr. MacVeagh thought that with the restoration of adequate transportation and the establishment of a stable government, the country would still be capable of maintaining a fair standard of living.

Athens

At the Acropolis, our guide was a young archaeologist named Arthur Parsons who had spent most of his mature life digging in Athens. He was slow to speak and careful in his statements but his fund of information about Greece was extraordinary. We had arrived on the Acropolis amid the full glare of the afternoon sun. Here even more than in Rome I was impressed by the absence of vivid color; indeed, a white mosque which stood on a hill in the distance was the only jarring note in an otherwise monotonous repetition of every shade of brown. Even the marble of the Parthenon was not white but creamy gold and so it was with the other ruins which were pointed out to us. The fields had been harvested and the drought had dried up the countryside. The air was hazy with heat and there was no such play of light and shadow as I had always associated with this part of the world.

Parsons was not apt to develop the obvious and volunteered information only on controversial questions of archaeology, which I am frank to say were not of great interest to me. I found, however, that his views on the current political situation were grounded in an intimate knowledge of the feelings of the people of Greece. He said that the British occupation was recognized as necessary but at the same time was regarded as a humiliation. The sympathy of the people was unquestionably with the forces which had led the resistance movement but the people had not liked the extreme elements which had gained control at the time of the December revolution. As far as an election was concerned, he was sure that many of the people were completely inert politically and would not exercise the franchise with any intelligence, especially as there was a lack of political information available and the means of communication were extremely poor. He felt that there was danger that the moderate views of the average Greek could find no effective expression in the midst of the conflicting ambitions of the extreme parties which were being supported on the one hand by the Russians and on the other by the British.

From the Acropolis we drove to Piraeus, which smelled worse than any place we visited on our whole trip. In the course of this drive we fell into a discussion of the attitude of the Greeks toward the German soldiers. Apparently the Greeks, who are innately modest, were shocked by the German habit of going around in nothing but shorts. In general, however, the German soldiers had behaved correctly and had even let the women alone, perhaps because of their peculiar racial doctrines. Many Greeks compared the conduct of our men unfavorably both because of their attitude toward the women and because of their public drunkenness. However, they really hated the Germans and liked the Allies, especially the Americans.

After our return from the harbor we went to a cocktail party at the Ministry. Here I had a chance to talk at greater length with Mr. MacVeagh. He said that while he was in Cairo he had seen a good deal of the Russian diplomats who were stationed there. They were extremely suspicious of the British because they could not discover what the real aim of the British policy in the Middle East was. They had expressed themselves quite freely on the subject and said that they found it very difficult to get along with people who could not say what they wanted. Mr. MacVeagh said that Egypt was in an explosive condition. With resources adequate to support a population of three million, the country actually had to support eleven million—of whom 95 percent were paupers. The remaining 5 percent were vastly wealthy and as irresponsible a class as could be found anywhere. The Russian minister had said to MacVeagh, "The British are afraid that I will disturb things here by making propaganda. There is no need for me to make propaganda; the situation speaks for itself and the natives are beginning to understand it."

MacVeagh said that the great question of the future was whether the Russians would attempt to sever the British lifeline to the East. The protection of the Suez and of the communications with India was the object of a great deal of the maneuvering that was going on. I suggested that the Russians, having suffered two catastrophic invasions and a social revolution during the past thirty years, would now want a period of peace, and that if they could be insured against the possibility of a third invasion by a coalition of Western powers, it should not be necessary for them to threaten the lifeline of the British Empire. Mr. MacVeagh said that this, of course, was what everyone hoped would happen but that we could not close our eyes to the fact that the foreign policies of the Soviet government were very like those of czarist Russia. He added that communism in Russia was scarcely more than a name; that there were class distinctions of the most marked kind quite equal to any known in the past; and that in many ways, the old habits were reasserting themselves.

In discussing the revolutions which were taking place in the Balkan states, he agreed that the ruling classes had shown a sense of irresponsibility and an inability to improve the lot of the masses of the people such as to deprive them of any great sympathy. He made the remark that the British had only themselves to blame for Marshal Tito.

That evening I dined with Pinero in an open-air restaurant and got a good meal at a fair price. I was persuaded by Pinero to purchase a mouth organ, and his judgment was later confirmed by my eight-year-old son Luke who said, "Oh, I wonder who that simply lovely mouth organ is for?" Naturally enough he got it.

Egypt

From Greece we flew down the Aegean, in sight of Crete, until we reached the Nile delta. The Isles of Greece were not too distinct in the haze and Crete was just tantalizing. We could see the dominant peak streaked with snow where legend has it that Zeus was born, but of the rest of the island, where the most dramatic campaign of the entire German war was fought, nothing could be distinguished from so great a distance.

The delta of the Nile struck us all with astonishment. From the air it presented a picture of vitality such as we had not seen for many a day, and the lush richness of its teeming fields was extraordinarily welcome to eyes which had become accustomed to so much arid sterility.

Payne Field where we landed is on the edge of the desert just outside of Cairo. Here we were met by General Giles and the American minister,

Pinckney Tuck, who is a first cousin of my father's. Tuck drove me in to Shepheard's Hotel and on the way we had a pleasant talk about family matters and about the things which I had seen in Germany. After resting in my room, I came downstairs and had tea on the terrace. This spot had been called the crossroads of the world and it certainly lived up to its reputation. As I sat there I could see the uniforms of almost every Allied nation, American, British, Australian, Polish, Palestinian, South African, New Zealander, Indian, and even Fuzzy-Wuzzies looking like they had just been brought down from the jungle.

Egyptians in their red tarbooshes and Arabs in their white burnooses were everywhere to be seen. As I sat there a distinguished-looking Arab in most beautiful linen robes with golden circlets on his brow came out of the door attended by the manager of the hotel, who was positively fawning on him. He climbed into his waiting Rolls Royce and drove off for all the world like a Park Avenue dowager leaving a fashionable reception. Veiled moslem women and turbanned Hindus passed, and camels and donkeys mingled with every sort of vehicle from carts to smart limousines; I even saw a little Arab on a scooter darting in and out of the traffic. In a little while a wedding party came by with the bride and groom simpering in an open barouche piled high with flowers.

During the course of the evening at the Menon House, Colonel White, who was the G-4 of the United States Air Force in the Mediterranean (USAFIME), told me that there was really desperate need in that theater for a liquidation commissioner to get on the job immediately. He said that some of the fixed installations were going rapidly back to jungle and that much of the property might vanish or depreciate in value unless something were done to liquidate it promptly. I gathered from him and from other sources that there was a substantial amount of property in the area which should be declared as surplus.

Later on we drove up between the pyramids and then down to the temple at the foot of the Sphinx where we got out of our cars and looked at these wonderful structures by the light of a full moon. It was an unforgettable vision with the Sphinx rising mysterious and majestic in the silvery moonlight and the pyramids glistening against the backdrop of a purple sky through which the stars shone like flames. The shadows seemed full of color and the gleaming sands reached to the horizon. A few wandering Arabs and some fiercely barking dogs added just the right note of menace to the scene.

The following morning we drove out to see the pyramids by daylight and were shown around by a very competent guide. I was most impressed by the huge size of the stones, and the way in which solid rock was carved into a right angle. Then we returned to the center of town, where we visited the Egyptian Museum. Here we were allowed only twenty minutes to examine the contents of the tomb of Tutankhamen. The variety and character of the objects removed from that tomb are simply incredible. The lavish use of gold, the beauty of workmanship, and the freshness of their appearance is matched only by the number of individual items.

All too soon my companions grew weary of these sights, so we moved on to the Red Cross snack bar where we lunched with the GIs on hamburgers and Coca-Cola. Immediately afterward we were taken up to the Citadel to see the alabaster mosque. Our guide gave a dignified and graceful explanation of the usages of the Moslem faith and we were all deeply impressed. The mosque had an odd air of Methodism about it; the alabaster pillars and walls were of great beauty but the most impressive feature of the building was its spacious emptiness. After enjoying a fine view from the Citadel, we drove down through some very ancient ruins and through a cemetery known as the City of the Dead to the old Arab quarter, where we had a glimpse of one of the early Coptic churches. From here we returned to the center of town in a hair-raising drive through the streets of Cairo.

As we came out of the bazaar a bunch of little Arab boys crowded around us and one of them asked, "Where you from, Yank? Chicago?" I said, "No." "New York?" "No." "California?" "No." "Texas?" "No." "Where you *from*, Yank?" in complete amazement.

He was a cute rascal about twelve years of age who had learned his English at the American Mission. Perhaps they taught him not to beg, because he was the only one who did not pester me for some form of handout. While we were standing there one of the little boys bumped into an old Arab who took his cane and struck the boy in the face and continued to beat him until the boy ran screaming out of reach. None of the other Arabs paid the slightest bit of attention to this scene of violence; as a matter of fact this was but one of a number of such instances which brought home to us that the Egyptians were a pretty dangerous kind of people. The *suffragi* at the hotel, for instance, had a way of bowing which indicated dignified acquiescence in your desires combined with a complete contempt for your stupidity. If they were not outrageously tipped they were insulting. The same attitude was felt everywhere, and I was left with a strong impression of a population which harbored a thinly concealed anger toward the European and American invaders.

That evening I went to the Tucks' for a drink and then on to dinner at the Cecil Lyonses'. The drive across the river and down the island was most attractive. The river itself was very beautiful at Cairo and the picturesque sailing vessels that tacked up and down the stream added an exotic note which was very appealing. Mrs. Lyons was the daughter of Under Secretary Joseph C. Grew, and both she and her husband, who was in the Foreign Service, had made many choice purchases in all parts of the world, so that their apartment was a delight to the eye.

I learned a good deal more about the thieving habits of the *suffragi* than I did about political and economic conditions. The ladies had learned, from bitter experience, that any theft, however minor, must be immediately punished or greater thefts would follow. There was much discussion about a laundry which had burned down. Mrs. Tuck was convinced that the owner had deliberately burned up the laundry after first stealing the wash. She said that she had had to put all her linen in storage because it was disappearing so rapidly. With the wages they were paid, the servants could not afford to clothe themselves in view of the tremendous prices which were being charged for all the necessities of life. Even an empty wine bottle could be sold for two dollars.

As we sat on the porch in the moonlight, I began to understand just why the British were so sensitive of any attempt on our part to interfere with their commercial monopoly in this area. The Arab states were like dry tinder, ready for the spark, and the British had the unhappy example of the French in Algeria and in Syria and Lebanon to prove it. At that time the British had managed to preserve stability in the states bordering on Suez by maintaining a monopoly on trade which gave them a stranglehold on the local governments. Thus, they could rule indirectly with a minimum of outlay, and guarantee the communications of empire. Any disturbance of this situation threatened imminent disaster and would be consented to by the British only under duress. Hence their refusal to permit us to sell our surpluses in this area.

All agreed that Cairo was in a highly explosive condition; in fact, Mrs. Tuck said she felt exactly as she had while they were interned in Germany. Every time her husband went out of doors she worried until he got back safely, and the fact that he had been raised in Cairo and knew Arabic quite well did not give her much comfort. I mentioned what Mr. MacVeagh had told me in Athens and they agreed entirely with his statement. Mrs. Tuck said that the attitude of the small group of immensely wealthy people who owned nearly everything in Egypt was unbelievably stupid. One princess had told her that it was very fortunate that the infant mortality rate was so high (something like 60 percent), because otherwise they would never be able to feed the population. Another acquaintance had lost twenty-five thousand at cards in one night at the club. At the same time the people were really desperate for the ordinary necessities of life.

Palestine

We landed at the Lydda airport and proceeded directly to Tel Aviv, a modern Jewish city which managed to look both American and Arabian at the same time. The drive to Jerusalem was a very interesting one. The soil of the plain around Tel Aviv was apparently quite rich, and there were oranges, lemons, tobacco, corn, and sugar in great profusion. As we gan to climb up the hills toward Jerusalem, the soil became more and more rocky until all that we could see were stony terraces out of which a certain amount of vegetation appeared to be growing in direct defiance of the laws of nature. We passed through some Arab villages which presented a picture of primitive squalor very strangely in contrast with the modernity of Tel Aviv. Here we saw three camels tied together and led by an Arab on a donkey; they were carrying such enormous loads of straw that it was easy to believe that one more straw could break the camel's back.

Upon our arrival at Jerusalem we went to the YMCA, a very handsome building built with American money. We then were driven to the Church of the Holy Nativity in Bethlehem. This ancient basilica, built in the time of the Emperor Justinian, was completely satisfying. The beautiful marble columns, the mosaic floor, the altar, and the ancient frescoes combine to create an impression which is worthy of the holiest spot in Christendom. There is unique agreement among the Christian sects that this was the actual birthplace of Christ, and the Russian, Greek, Armenian, Coptic, Roman, and Protestant churches all conduct services here. As we entered, a Greek Orthodox service was coming to an end with antiphonal readings by bearded priests wearing huge black hats like bakers' caps and by boy choristers. As that service ended the Roman Catholic service commenced and the music of Gregorian chants came through the door from a side chapel. My attention was attracted by a party of black soldiers in British uniforms, and as we approached more nearly, I was fascinated to discover that they looked exactly like the pictures I had seen of some natives in the jungles of Africa. They had high, prominent chests, swayed backs, and pierced ears with lobes falling almost to the shoulders, and they were almost blue-black in color. Their guide chanted to them in some strange dialect as though he were crooning. It was perfectly evident from the expression on their faces that they were deeply affected by the images, the decorations, the chanting, and the whole atmosphere by which they were surrounded. This was especially apparent in the crypt where we were shown the manger in which had been placed a little image of the Christ Child, and I noticed that the guide had great difficulty in getting them to leave there.

From Bethlehem we returned to Jerusalem, where we visited what was supposed to have been the garden of Gethsemane and then went on to the Mount of Olives. I could not help feeling that there was a certain amount of propaganda and commercialism connected with these spots, and I found that this feeling was widely shared by the other members of our party, especially Pinero. However, the sight from the Mount of Olives of the Dead Sea lying far below with the mountains rising straight from its shores was well worth the trip.

After a brief stop at King Solomon's quarry, which seems to be the principal shrine of Masonry, we were taken to the famous Wailing Wall. The loud praying of some of the worshippers seemed almost like exhibitionism, and this impression was heightened by the movements which accompanied the prayer. The whole effect was to travesty the dignified religion of the Hebrews, and our Jewish guide reacted as Henry Mencken might have done to a camp meeting of Holy Rollers.

The trip up through the Arab quarter from the Wailing Wall to the church of the Holy Sepulchre beggars my powers of description. Looking back upon it, I think that from a visual point of view this was probably the most extraordinary thirty minutes I have ever spent. Only the trained perception of an artist could possibly retain all that we saw during that time. I remember a group of Arab children, not one over 4 years of age, carrying cans of water on their heads; a cafe where four Arabs were playing dominoes while the radio blared strange music; a grocery store where vegetables were on display and I picked up a handful of those lentils for which Jacob sold his birthright; a shop selling cosmetics of English manufacture; a meat store with the carcasses, black with flies, hanging from the ceiling; a store where bolts of gayly colored cloth were on display; an Arab carrying a pile of chicken coops higher than his head; UNRRA and Red Cross workers talking intently together; fastidious-looking Jews in Western dress; an orthodox Jew with blonde beard and curls and pink cheeks striding along like a soldier; a hooded Franciscan with a black beard; a group of priests of the Greek church in conical hats and veils; soldiers of all colors and costumes; Syrians, Lebanese, Egyptians, Armenians, Greeks, Italians, and Jews; and a motley rabble of children, chickens, ducks, dogs, and donkeys all pouring along the offal-littered street amid a Babel of chatter. I could easily understand why the Arab population preferred to live here rather than to find quarters in modern Jerusalem. In their minds cleanliness and comfort were inadequate compensation for dullness and boredom.

At this point our Jewish guide turned us over to a Franciscan brother who was from Topeka, Kansas. He seemed quite young and had a high, piping voice. A rather scraggly beard added to the general wistfulness of his appearance. Of the church itself I will say very little. It is supposed to be located on the site of Golgotha, but I had my doubts and was not surprised to learn that the authenticity of the location is much disputed. The interior decoration is of the late nineteenth and early twentieth century in the most execrable taste, the Madonna of the Jewels being perhaps the worst example of all. It was perfectly apparent that most of this show had been recently organized, and the effect was far from convincing. The evidences of antiquity which were so plain at the Church of the Holy Nativity were lacking here, and I could not avoid the strong suspicion that my credulity was being played upon.

From here we returned to the King David Hotel, one of the most comfortable establishments on our entire trip. Here, after freshening up, we went to the American consul's apartment and had a pleasant hour, returning later for dinner at the hotel. There I sat next to the local representative of the Foreign Economic Administration (FEA), who was charged with the task of disposing of surplus property. Under cross-examination from me he confessed that they were making little headway against the attitude of the British. I expounded my own personal view that we were butting our heads against a stone wall and should not attempt to assert any interest in that area except for certain specific concessions, such as landing rights at Payne Field, Eleusis, and Lydda, pipeline and docking privileges, etc. This view struck him as very shocking.

North Africa

Bengazi was extremely interesting. Here Mussolini had carried out one of his finest ideas by constructing a beautiful city and by developing on a neighboring plateau a farming colony which was a model of successful colonization. Bengazi itself, although terribly damaged, still showed the signs of having been a handsome place. The colors of land and water and sky were vivid and pure. The palace, which had been occupied by Graziani, the impressive city streets with every wall adorned with the face of the Grand Senoussi (the chief of the local Arabs, who preferred to live in luxury in Cairo), and the beautiful beach, all remain with me as a vivid impression.

At Algiers we landed in the darkness and drove in to the Hotel Aletti, where I slept on a bed so dirty that I preferred not to turn back the sheets. The following morning we took a short drive up the hills through the residential section of Algiers and got a good view of the harbor. Here we passed about two hundred small boys from an orphanage school and noticed that all of them looked pale and undernourished. For some reason the distribution of food had broken down in Algiers and there had been serious rioting as a consequence. Everyone here was more miserable than at any time during the war. The weather here was disagreeably hot and humid, much more so than in Cyrenaica or Tripolitania.

From Algiers we flew inland over the cities of French Morocco to Casablanca. The countryside was mostly mountainous and extremely forbidding. Occasionally, however, we came upon beautiful and fertile land and saw some very interesting-looking cities. In particular the city of Fez remains in my mind, with its pink palace and its tall minaret of light blue that shines out against the surrounding territory like a beacon. I had never seen any city from the air which offered more of an appearance of romance and splendor. These cities were gleaming white against a background of lush vegetation, and I found here all the blinding brilliance and exoticism that I had been disappointed not to find in other parts of the Mediterranean world.

Casablanca was a fitting climax for our trip. We were entertained for lunch at a villa which had belonged to a noted collaborationist, and I have never seen a finer example of modern architecture and interior decoration. We were served a lunch which exhibited the French cook at his very best, and after that toured the city in the company of the military police. Inside the Medina, the walled city which is a prohibited zone for all troops, we were taken up to a heavily guarded gate behind which lay the white streets and walls of a village devoted entirely to brothels. Apparently this area was regularly made available to the French troops under the strictest medical supervision. Here women found guilty of solicitation on the streets were sentenced to serve for various periods of time, and some of them apparently had taken up permanent homes here, as we saw many little children running about the streets. As it was not yet mid-afternoon, there was not much activity in the place, but as we walked through accompanied by a burly MP some of the women were bathing in a public trough without a stitch of clothes on. I had heard of these places but never expected to see one, especially in such respectable company.

The Trip Back

At 3:30 we left Casablanca in a luxurious C-54. Our companions for the trip were the crew of a Catalina bomber who had been overseas for about eighteen months flying from English and North African bases. The bottom had been knocked out of their bomber the week before as they were taking off to fly back to the States. All except one had escaped without injury and were now going back in luxury.

Until we reached the Azores there was little to be seen, as we were traveling over a carpet of clouds most of the time. Our landing there was made on instruments in the midst of a local storm and was one of the most exciting events of the trip. It took us nearly three-quarters of an hour to come in, and we could see a number of other planes circling around awaiting their turn. For nearly twenty minutes we were in a fog so dense that nothing could be seen and I could not avoid a little apprehension that we might collide with some other plane.

The Atlantic flight was completely uneventful. We could see nothing below us so we passed the time in talking with our sailor companions. We canvassed the merits and demerits of tattooing, the problem of women in foreign countries, the characteristics of the "mighty Catalina," and many other topics which served to while away the time until at last we arrived at the Washington airport around 11:00 A.M., almost exactly thirty days to the hour from our time of departure.

Slingluff home on Chestnut Ridge in Baltimore County

*My grandmother, Mrs. Charles Bohn
Slingluff (Valerie von Dorsner), and her
daughters, Valerie and Ella Slingluff,
sometimes called the "Potsdam Guards"*

The author at age 1 on the lawn in front of the Slingluff home in 1902

My father, William L. Marbury, on his hunting mare, Sorrel

My sister, Valerie von D. Marbury, my mother, Silvine von D. Slingluff Marbury, my great aunt Silvine von Dorsner and my aunt Valerie von D. Slingluff in the Dorsner studio in Munich in 1913

The author at age 20

The author and his wife,
Natalie Jewett (Wheeler)
Marbury, leaving on
their wedding trip on
December 3, 1935

The author and his three children, Anne, Susan and Luke, at 43
Warrenton Road in Baltimore

The Legal Branch at Headquarters Army Service Forces in the War Department 1942–1945
Top row, Benno C. Schmidt, W. Wadsworth Watts, Charles O. Pengra, W. James
MacIntosh, Scott Rigby, Gregory Prince; Second row (including top row of center
group), John M. Wisdom, Richard Merrick, Benjamin Kaplan, Thomas J. Reidy, George
Whittaker, James Murtaugh, W. Houston Kenyon, Joseph F. Johnston, Thomas O'G.
Fitzgibbon, Henry Parkman; Bottom row (including bottom row of center group),
Stanfield Johnson, H. Chapman Rose, Max Felix, R. Ammi Cutter, the author, Robert C.
Barker, Dillon Anderson, Robert R. Bowie, Joseph Howorth

The Tax Amortization Board appointed by Assistant Secretary of War, Robert P. Patterson, in 1941

General Somervell and his newly minted colonels who ran the railroads during the Christmas Eve strike in 1944

Inscribed photograph of General Lucius D. Clay

*The author on survey trip
with members of a
subcommittee of the House
Committee on Military
Affairs in June 1945*

Ruins of Duren, Germany in June 1945

*Ruins of Cologne Cathedral in
June 1945*

*Furnace at Buchenwald where Jews
were cremated after first being
garroted or shot*

General Dwight D. Eisenhower with survey subcommittee of the House Committee on Military Affairs in June 1945 (the author in background)

The Secretary of War, Robert P. Patterson, presenting the Presidential Medal for Merit to the author in 1945

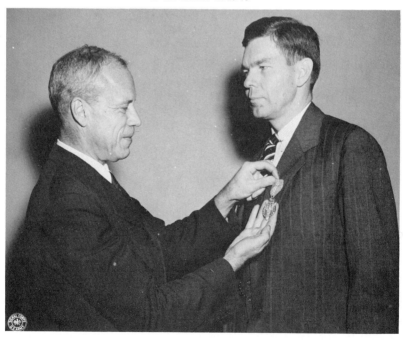

The Harvard Corporation in June 1947—Charles A. Coolidge, Roger I. Lee, Paul C. Cabot, Treasurer, James B. Conant, President, Harry Shattuck, Grenville Clark and the author

R. Ammi Cutter and the author at the summit of Mt. Lafayette, N.H. on August 26, 1947

The Harvard Corporation in June 1965 — Seated, Paul C. Cabot, Treasurer, Charles A. Coolidge, Nathan M. Pusey, President; Standing, R. Keith Kane, Francis H. Burr, Thomas S. Lamont and the author

American Bar Association Committee on Standards of Judicial Conduct — F. R. Franklin (Staff Assistant), Professor E. Wayne Thode (Reporter), Whitney N. Seymour, Justice Potter Stewart, the author, Chief Justice Roger J. Traynor, Judge Ivan Lee Holt, Judge Irving R. Kaufman, Professor Robert A. Leflar; missing, Dixie Beggs and Judge Edward T. Gignoux

*Procession at Harvard Commencement
in June 1970 at which the author
received an honorary LL.D.*

Award to author of honorary LL.D. from Harvard University in June 1970

The author when Chancellor of the Episcopal Diocese of Maryland in 1965, together with Bishop Harry Lee Doll, Bishop Noble C. Powell and Presiding Bishop John E. Hines

The author in his office at Piper & Marbury in 1984

The author speaking at the 75th Anniversary Meeting of the Lawyers'
Round Table in Baltimore on April 1, 1986

At wedding of daughter, Anne Wyatt-Brown—Yandes, Susan, Anne,
Mrs. Marbury, the author, and Luke Marbury

*The author with his grandsons—Top row, Robert R. Marbury, Hugh Jewett Marbury;
Bottom row, Edward Marbury Briscoe and William Marbury*

*The author's wife, Natalie J. Marbury, and her four children, Anne,
Yandes Wheeler, Susan and Luke*

I came home with two impressions uppermost in my mind. The first was the paramount importance of ending the fear of the British that Russia had designs on the communications of the British Empire and, on the other hand, of convincing the Russians that they had no reason to fear a third invasion at the hands of a coalition of Western powers. It seemed clear to me that if these fears could be allayed, there would be an end to the maneuvering which was keeping all Europe and the Mediterranean in a condition of political instability which forbade economic rehabilitation. I believed that Germany was the key to the solution of this problem.

My second impression was of the damage which might come from the failure of our troops to understand and appreciate the good qualities of the foreign peoples among whom they had been obliged to live during the preceding few years. Homesickness, combined with lack of education and a deliberate policy of segregation, had contrived to create in our boys a contempt for the people of the British Isles, of Europe, and of the Arab states which did not promise well for the future of our relations with the rest of the world. Since it can no longer be a matter of doubt that we must, as the poet Auden has said, "Love one another or die" it is doubly regrettable that the next generation to come to political power in this country had received such a conditioning. It meant that the task ahead, which was grim enough in all conscience, would be that much more difficult.

XVI ❧ The Bomb: Behind the Scenes

When I got back to my office in July 1945, Judge Patterson explained to me that a new weapon was about to be tested which if it functioned as expected would probably end the war and usher in a new era in world history. Needless to say, it was the atomic bomb, which was designed to employ the energy released by splitting the uranium atom. I recognized this at once as being what Charlie Pigott had talked about in the 1920s when he was visiting at 159 West Lanvale. During the war he was commissioned in the navy and early in 1943 I had dropped by his home in Washington and casually asked him whether anything further had come of his ideas about nuclear fission. He told me that the subject was one which he could no longer discuss.

Judge Patterson said that more than two billion dollars had been spent in developing a weapon which was now about to be tested. Mr. Stimson had recently appointed an Interim Committee, of which Mr. Stimson himself was the chairman, to advise the government on what to do in case the test of the weapon proved to be successful. The alternate chairman of the committee was George Harrison, the president of the New York Life Insurance Company, and the committee included Vannevar Bush, head of the Office of Scientific Research and Development (OSRD); James B. Conant, president of Harvard University; Karl T. Compton, president of MIT; Ralph A. Bard, under secretary of the navy; William L. Clayton, assistant secretary of state; and James F. Byrnes, who had just resigned as director of the Office of War Mobilization. At the insistence of Bush and Conant, a group of four scientific advisers had been named, including Robert Oppenheimer, who had been in charge of the installation where the weapon had been constructed, Ernest Lawrence, Enrico Fermi, and Arthur H. Compton, the last three being eminent nuclear physicists.

The Interim Committee had recommended that the War Department be prepared to introduce a bill in Congress as soon as the existence of the new weapon became public, and a special committee had been appointed to arrange for the preparation of this legislation. The members of the subcommittee were Harrison, Bush, and Conant; General Leslie Groves, who had been the military head of the Manhattan Engineering

District which had been responsible for the development of the weapon, and Robert Oppenheimer had been asked to serve as consultants to the subcommittee. Mr. Stimson had asked Judge Patterson to assign Kenneth Royall and me to be the legal advisers of the committee and to draft whatever legislation they recommended.

I immediately got in touch with Kenneth Royall and found that he had already had a meeting with General Groves, where he had been given an outline of the points which the Interim Committee thought should be covered in the legislation we were to draft. Since the final test of the weapon was to take place very soon, the time for drafting the bill was short, and it was necessary to work at top speed. Royall asked me to prepare the first draft. In this emergency I turned to Frank Rowley and asked him to assign me the best legislative draftsman in the Legal Branch. He named Oscar H. Davis, who was later appointed judge of the United States Court of Appeals for the District of Columbia Circuit.

Oscar and I then went to see General Groves. I was immediately struck with the general's self-assurance. It was obvious that he had thoroughly mastered the subject and was familiar with all the discussions that had taken place in the Interim Committee. Oscar then prepared a draft of legislation designed to meet what we understood to be the goals set by the Interim Committee, and we submitted this to General Royall, who suggested some clarifying changes. The draft was then submitted to Van Bush and Jim Conant. The heart of the bill called for the creation of an agency on the model of the Tennessee Valley Authority, with power to take over the vast enterprise which had been created by the Manhattan Engineering District and to control any future development which would involve the release of any substantial quantity of atomic energy. Provision was made for the appointment of a commission with full powers to develop and control military, industrial, and medical uses of that energy.

Somewhat to our surprise, in the light of what we had been told by General Groves, Bush and Conant both felt that some of the grants of power to the commission were too sweeping, and we revised the draft to narrow them sufficiently to meet their views. In the meantime, Conant attended the first test of the bomb device and reported that it had proven to be successful beyond all expectation and that within a few weeks the air force would be able to drop a bomb on Japan with the explosive force of twenty thousand tons of TNT. This added to the urgency of our task.

On August 11 the first bomb was dropped on Hiroshima. Mr. Stimson sent to the White House a draft of what was generally referred to as the War Department Bill. In the meantime, arrangements had been made for the introduction of the bill in the House by the chairman of the Military Affairs Committee and in the Senate by Senator Johnson of Colorado. All that was needed was a message from the president requesting these gentlemen to introduce the bill as an administration measure. Because of objections to the bill raised by some members of the White House staff, this message was delayed until October 7.

In the meantime, the country had been stirred up to a state of near-hysteria which continued after the surrender of Japan on August 14. At one extreme were those who feared that the secret of the bomb would not be adequately protected; at the other were the members of the academic community who had chafed under the strict security regulations imposed on them by General Groves. Accustomed to the freedom of academic discussion, the young scientists who were working in this field regarded the prospect that they might continue to be subjected to this kind of surveillance in their laboratories as simply intolerable now that the war was over.

These young scientists had found a champion in Jim Newman, who was in the Office of War Mobilization and Reconversion at the White House. The director of that office was now John Snyder, with whom I had worked in 1940 and 1941 when he was head of the Defense Plant Corporation. Snyder had been selected to succeed Jimmy Byrnes as head of OWMR by President Truman, and as time went on it became apparent that OWMR was going to play an important role in determining the policies followed by the Truman administration in the development of atomic energy. Now, with the backing of John Snyder, who obviously had the ear of his old Missouri friend in the White House, Jim Newman was in the driver's seat.

I left the War Department early in September to return to law practice in Baltimore. Shortly thereafter, I got a call from Malcolm Sharp of the University of Chicago Law School, who had been one of the editors of the *Harvard Law Review* in 1923. He told me that a group of Chicago scientists were looking for a lawyer to represent them at the congressional hearings on atomic energy and he wanted to know whether I would be available. I explained to him that I was one of the draftsmen of the War Department Bill. Thereafter Malcolm called me to say that he quite understood my position and that his Chicago friends had asked Ed Levi (later dean of the Chicago Law School and president of Chicago University, as well as attorney general of the United States) to represent them.

When the message recommending the War Department draft finally came from the White House, Mr. Stimson and Judge Patterson thought that the way was clear for the prompt enactment of the War Department Bill, which was simultaneously introduced in both houses of Congress and became known as the May-Johnson Bill. Accordingly, Judge Patterson appeared before the Military Affairs Committee on October 9 believing that he had the support of the White House in recommending the prompt enactment of this legislation.

At Judge Patterson's request, I came back from Baltimore and was present during the committee hearing. Testimony against the bill was given by Dr. Leo Szilard and Dr. Harold C. Anderson, both of whom were identified as members of the faculty of the University of Chicago. Testimony in support of the bill was given by Arthur Compton and by Robert Oppenheimer, who presented a telegram signed by himself and by Enrico Fermi and F. V. Lawrence urging the prompt passage of the bill.

In the meantime, however, it had become clear that the opposition to the May-Johnson Bill was building up to formidable proportions. At one luncheon I sat beside Edward U. Condon, who was then the head of the Bureau of Standards, and heard him say to Jim Conant, "I believe I speak for the scientific community when I say that your attitude on this bill will determine whether you are with us or against us." I remember saying to him that I was willing to bet that after all the shouting was over, a bill would be passed using different language but saying substantially the same thing as the May-Johnson Bill.

By the time the House committee had completed its hearings, it had become evident that the scientific community believed that the May-Johnson Bill had been framed largely by General Groves as a means of continuing military control over the development of atomic energy. When the report of the House Military Affairs Committee recommending the passage of the May-Johnson Bill, with clarifying amendments, appeared at the end of October, the clamor had grown to such an extent that I was moved to write a letter to the *New York Times* which was published in full on November 11, 1945. That letter read in part:

> As one who participated in the drafting of the May-Johnson Bill (HR 4280), I have been amazed to read some of the extravagant statements which have been made by its critics. . . .
>
> As soon as it became apparent that the release of the first atomic bomb was imminent, the Secretary of War, with the approval of the President, appointed an Interim Committee to advise him on the steps which should be taken to insure that the potentialities of this new source of energy would be developed for good and not for evil.
>
> At early meetings of the Committee it became apparent that three things need to be done as soon as possible. First it is necessary to insure the successful continuance of the projects which are now being conducted under the supervision of the Manhattan Engineering District of the War Department. The first step has been successfully taken in the development of the most powerful weapon known to man, but it is recognized that this is but the beginning. If (to borrow the words of General Marshall) the security of the United States of America is to remain in our own hands, leadership in the field of atomic weapons will have to be maintained. For this purpose new legislation is obviously necessary, as the imminent lapse or repeal of war powers will make virtually impossible the successful prosecution of the projects now under way, as well as those for which a future need may appear.
>
> Second, it is necessary to take prompt steps to protect the nation against the hazards inherent in the release of atomic energy. Until our knowledge of

nuclear physics is vastly extended, it seems unthinkable that the release of atomic energy in substantial quantities should be permitted, except under strict control.

Third, it is necessary to prevent the disclosure of information which can properly be classified as a military secret. Those who have worked under the supervision of the Manhattan Engineering District have gained much information of great military value. Up to this time the War Department has determined by regulation the extent to which this information can be communicated, and violation of those regulations has carried criminal penalties. With the return of peace a special problem will be presented. Many persons may leave the service of the War Department and take with them the information which they have gained. Some of this information will be such that publication should not and probably could not be prevented, but there will be much information of a character which nearly everyone will agree should be communicated only in accordance with policies established by the Government after full consideration of the needs of the national defense.

In order to meet the needs which I have outlined, legislation is clearly required to confer upon some governmental agency a large measure of the authority now being exercised by the Manhattan Engineering District under war powers. It was the view of the Interim Committee that the exercise of such great powers in time of peace should not be committed to military control, and for this reason the Committee proposed the creation of a commission to be appointed by the President. . . .

More controversial are those sections of the Bill which are designed to meet the second of the needs which have been outlined. In order to protect the public against the uncontrolled release of atomic energy, it was necessary to vest in the Commission powers adequate for that purpose. A large measure of control could be obtained through transfer to the Commission of the physical properties now in the possession of the Government and operated under the control of the Manhattan Engineering District. . . .

There has been much discussion of the extent of the regulatory powers conferred upon the Commission by Section 13 of the Bill. This section, it has been charged, empowers the Commission to stifle all development in the field of nuclear physics. I believe that anyone who reads Section 13 of the Bill in its entirety will agree that it does not authorize the Commission to control research or experimentation in the field of nuclear physics, unless there is involved the release of atomic energy in amounts which the Commission believes would constitute a national hazard, or would be of military or industrial value.

The provisions of the May-Johnson Bill which provoked the greatest outcry, and led to the most extravagant charges, are those designed to prevent the disclosure of military secrets. Section 17 of the original Bill authorized the Commission to establish and provide for the administration of security regulations covering the communication of information relating to or connected with research on the transmutation of atomic species, with the production of nuclear fission and with the release of atomic energy. It does not appear to have been generally understood that this section did not authorize the Commission to prevent or limit the dissemination of information developed as a result of research and experimentation which was not subject to the Commission's control under Section 13, or that of its predecessor, the Manhattan Engineering District. That, however, is the clear meaning of the language and this has been emphasized by the action of the House Military Affairs Committee, in limiting the authority of the Commission to make such regulations to cases where required by the national defense or by considerations of military security.

This provision will not satisfy those who believe in complete freedom of exchange of scientific information, nor will it satisfy those who believe that future discoveries of military significance, which may be made by scientists no longer in the employ of the Government, should be subject to security classification. The real question is whether a better method can be devised to meet the views of the great majority who believe that military secrets should be protected without sacrifice of scientific progress. To the Interim Committee, the only solution possible in the present state of knowledge seemed to be to delegate to the Commission the authority to make necessary regulations with a clear exemption of those fields in which no limitation of communication was desired. It must be conceded that a great deal will depend upon the wisdom and forbearance of the Commissioners, but those who have wrestled with this problem may be permitted to doubt whether any more acceptable solution can be found.

A final criticism relates to the failure of the Bill to prohibit or encourage the communication of information regarding atomic weapons to other nations. The failure of the Bill to touch upon this subject was deliberate. The Interim Committee felt that prompt legislation was urgently needed for the reasons previously advanced, and that consideration of the international aspect of this problem should not be permitted to delay the setting up of the machinery necessary to make effective whatever policy might finally be determined upon after full public discussion.

Whatever judgment may ultimately be passed on the activities of the Interim Committee, I hope that I have said enough to make clear that it has faced many difficult problems which permit no ready answer, and that discussion of its work need not be conducted in the mood of denunciatory violence which has been so commonly evidenced during the past few weeks.

By the time this letter appeared, the president had been persuaded that the War Department Bill should be stopped. Mr. May, the chairman of the House committee, who had introduced the bill, was told that the administration did not want the bill to be brought to a vote until after hearings had been completed on a substitute measure which had been introduced by Senator McMahon. This bill was written by Ed Levi and Jim Newman. Characteristically, Judge Patterson stood his ground and in his appearance before the Senate committee stated his preference for the May-Johnson Bill, as a result of which he was told by the president to take his instructions from the White House. The Senate hearings continued and were not completed until April of 1946, when a bill was reported to the Senate and passed unanimously with President Truman's support.

About that time Judge Patterson called me on the telephone and asked me if I would give him my views on the McMahon Bill. Apparently he was trying to make up his mind whether to oppose the Senate bill when it came up for consideration in the House or whether to indicate his acquiescence. How he could oppose the bill in the face of the White House endorsement was not clear to me, but, at any rate, at his request I wrote him a letter dated April 26, 1946. At the conclusion of that letter, I said:

> My analysis of this bill leads me to the conclusion that it . . . would be wise for the War Department at this time to endorse the McMahon Bill, pointing out that it accomplishes all of the fundamental objectives which the Interim Committee had in mind in drafting the May-Johnson Bill.

The McMahon Bill passed the House by nine votes and became the Atomic Energy Act of 1946. In most of the extensive literature which has dealt with this subject, including especially President Truman's memoirs, the passage of the McMahon Bill is described as the final defeat of an attempt by the War Department to continue military control of the development of atomic energy. That was simply not so.

For me the most valuable part of this experience came from sitting at the table with the members of the Interim Committee, particularly Bush, Conant, and Oppenheimer. Oppenheimer had an absolutely lethal ability to detect weakness in other people's reasoning and no hesitation in exercising his powers in that direction. Bush was more cautious and had a more statesmanlike approach to the novel task which the sudden acquisition of this overwhelming power had thrust upon the United States. But of all the members of the Interim Committee, I found Jim Conant to be the most sensible, in that he could match wits with Oppenheimer and was as farseeing a statesman as Bush. Moreover, his ability to handle people seemed equal to that of George Harrison. I have never had a more challenging experience than sitting at the table with these men and discussing the strategy which should be followed in preparing and presenting the legislation which all of them believed to be necessary.

XVII ❖ Settling Down Again

My separation from the War Department had been set for September 1, 1945, and proved to be quite ceremonious. First there was the farewell luncheon at the Pentagon, where busy officers endured with patient expressions on their faces the encomiums which were bestowed upon me as a departing member of Secretary Patterson's staff. I especially noted, with some irony, Judge Patterson's remark that I had "characteristically stayed on the job until it was done." Since the date of my departure had been tentatively fixed several months before the capitulation of Japan had actually taken place, this seemed to me to be something of an overstatement.

On another occasion Judge Patterson pinned on my chest the Medal for Merit and handed me an elaborate citation signed personally by President Truman. Natalie and the children and my mother joined me in Judge Patterson's office for this ceremony. When it was over Judge Patterson gave the boys a complete set of model tanks, and for some time thereafter they would refer to "the day we got the tanks."

Finally, there was the farewell dinner which Howard Bruce gave for his entire staff at Belmont, his home in Howard County. On that occasion he startled me by introducing me as the next solicitor general of the United States. When I asked him after dinner to explain that introduction, he expressed great surprise and told me that Governor O'Conor had been asked by the White House for political clearance on my appointment and had been given to understand that the matter was settled. That was the first and last that I ever heard of it, and as the appointment went to Phil Perlman, I assume that someone persuaded the White House that Perlman had a better claim to what had begun to be regarded as a political plum. As I had committed myself to return to Baltimore in September, I was relieved not to be put on the spot where I would have to turn down the appointment.

When I got back to the firm in September, I soon realized that my return had been just in the nick of time. One of the conditions which I had made in my negotiations with Vernon Miller and Charlie Evans called for notifying Bill All that there would be no place for him in the reconstructed firm of Marbury, Miller and Evans. We anticipated, of course, that he would look for another connection, but we did not foresee that in doing so he would represent that our firm was moribund. This he did, however, and as soon as I got back I had to spend quite a little time in mending fences.

Aside from interviewing men returning from the service, I found that I was spending an inordinate amount of time trying to extricate myself from the coils of Washington. In addition to attending the hearings on atomic energy legislation, I responded to an appeal from Tracy Voorhees for advice on how to handle my friend Dr. Perrin Long, who was now out of the army and installed as a full professor at the Johns Hopkins School of Public Health. Perrin was scandalized by the incidence of venereal disease among the occupying troops in the Mediterranean and North African theaters and was trying to bring pressure to bear on the surgeon general and the secretary of war to enforce the army's official policy for the elimination of prostitution in the occupied areas.

Looking over my correspondence during this period, I find that I was called to Washington in May of 1946 to help draft a reply to an outrageous attack on the War Department's handling of contract settlements which the comptroller general had made in testimony before the so-called Mead committee. Thereafter I thought that I was at last free to make plans for an extended vacation in Canada which I had promised to Natalie and the children. The boys and I were to leave from Baltimore on the first of August and planned to drive my old Plymouth all the way to Chester, Nova Scotia, stopping in Maine to pick up Natalie and the girls, who were staying with Grace McNeal, one of Natalie's friends who was running a camp for girls near Sargentville known as Camp Four Winds.

As it happened, I was in New York on the Friday before we were to leave, when a nationwide rail strike was suddenly called. I got the last train south out of Pennsylvania Station, but the conductor said it would not run beyond Philadelphia, so I went to the Bellevue Stratford, planning to get to Baltimore in the morning by bus or rented car. At two in the morning I was roused from my bed and told to go to the airport, where a plane was waiting to take me to Washington to attend a meeting of War Department lawyers who were planning to take over the railroads. Apparently they were looking for a repetition of the 1943 takeover and thought that I could tell them how to do it. When I explained that I was scheduled to take my two boys to Maine, I was informed that this would be taken care of.

I arrived in Washington about five in the morning and reported to the War Department, where I was told that the strike had been called off. Meanwhile, an army sergeant had been detailed to drive my Plymouth to Bangor Airport, and I was told that a plane would be standing at the old Baltimore Harbor Field Airport the following morning to fly me and the two boys to Bangor. I got home with what I thought was exciting news for the boys. They looked at me glumly and said that they had said goodbye to all their friends and what were they to do for the next twenty-four hours? Incidentally, when we got to Bangor, I found that the sergeant had driven the Plymouth at top speed, with the result that my synthetic rubber tires were obviously about to blow out. By some miracle they lasted until I got to Camp Four Winds, where by another miracle I was able on a Sunday morning to get a complete set of prewar rubber tires at a country store, thanks to Grace McNeal, who was treated by the natives as one of their own.

That was not the last time that I was asked to go back to the War Department to help tie up loose ends. I did turn down a number of opportunities, including an appointment as assistant secretary of war to succeed Howard Petersen. I also declined a rather tempting opportunity to spend thirty days in Europe interviewing the men who had been in charge of the procurement programs for the British, the Germans, and "hopefully" the Russians. In particular I was told that Hitler's chief of war production, Albert Speer, had a most interesting story to tell, but I begged off.

I also turned down an offer from Sydney Mitchell to study government procurement for the Hoover Commission on Organization of the Executive Branch and an offer from Arthur Hill to become general counsel of the National Security Resources Board. In addition, I turned down an offer to go to Palestine as a member of a commission appointed by President Truman to make recommendations as to the recognition of the State of Israel. Similarly, I declined an opportunity to represent the War Department at congressional hearings on proposals for the adoption of a program of universal military training.

Finally, I turned down a request from Dean Acheson, who asked me to come over to Washington to see him. He told me that Mr. Baruch had announced his intention of resigning as the representative of the United States on the commission of the United Nations which was trying to arrange for international control of atomic weapons. Apparently Mr. Baruch had gotten nowhere with his mission and was tired of butting his head against a stone wall. It so happened that about this time Alger Hiss came to Baltimore to receive an honorary degree from the Johns Hopkins University, and I told him in confidence that Acheson had suggested that he and Judge Patterson and Jim Forrestal were all prepared to recommend my appointment in Mr. Baruch's place. I told him that I did not see how I could possibly undertake anything like that and still hope to develop a law practice at the same time. Alger urged me to try to make arrangements whereby I could have a deputy who would do most of the work. He said that Mr. Baruch and his deputy, John Hancock, had both been very stiff-necked in dealing with the Russians but that he believed some real progress could be made if I would take the job. I declined, however, and the job was given to General Fred Osborne, who got nowhere with it.

Another offer came to go with Paul Hoffman and Howard Bruce, who were organizing the European Cooperation Administration, which was to administer the Marshall Plan which had been announced at the 1947 Harvard Commencement Exercises. This was really tempting, but again it seemed to me that my plain duty to my family and my partners made it impossible to accept the assignment.

Thanks to my Baltimore friends, I was making some progress in re-establishing my local identity. In February 1946 Howard Bruce told me that Governor O'Conor wanted me to accept the chairmanship of a commission which he had been directed by the legislature to appoint to conduct a survey of higher education in the state of Maryland. The governor had delayed appointing the commission for more than six months and was now under pressure from the *Sunpapers* to act. I knew the *Sunpapers* were out to break the hold that President H. C. "Curley" Byrd had established over the University of Maryland, and I gathered that the job which the governor was offering me was a hot potato and that whatever the commission did would be bound to create controversy. However, Mr. Bruce thought that, properly handled, this might be an opportunity for me to alert the whole state to my return from the wars.

I went to the governor and had a frank talk with him. I said that I would not be interested unless we were given technical assistance of the best quality available. He promised that we could select our own advisers, and I accepted. In the end it was agreed that the American Council on Education would be given a contract to make a thorough survey and to present the facts, leaving the commission to make recommendations for any desired action by the legislature or the governor's office. The council designated Professor John Dale Russell of the University of Chicago, later United States commissioner of education, to conduct the study, and he did a remarkable job in preparing the report of the survey.

The commission members then decided that we would lay it on the line and not try to stay out of trouble. We did, however, make an exception in the matter of the treatment of black graduate students. A majority of the commission felt that the time had come to open the graduate schools of the University of Maryland to black students. However, our Southern Maryland member was strongly of the contrary opinion, and at his suggestion President Byrd was called in and asked his opinion as to the effect such a recommendation would have on the university. He stated flatly that in his opinion it would result in student riots and in the loss of essential financial support from the legislature. So on this point we compromised by recommending the strengthening of Morgan College and the continuation of out-of-state scholarships for black students. A dissent by Carl Murphy, the editor of the *Afro-American,* expressed his general concurrence with the report except as to the graduate schools, on which he took what in retrospect was a clearly sound position that "colored" people, as he called them, had a constitutional right to attend courses at the University of Maryland "which were not afforded at a state institution of higher education for colored students."

With that one single exception, we did not shrink from making a number of recommendations which made our report politically difficult to accept. Tom Pullen, who was the state superintendent of schools, told me that it was perfectly obvious that I had no political expertise. He said that I had stepped on everybody's toes and that opponents of the recommendations would all gang up on me and kill the whole program, which is just what they did. However, in 1981, Professor Malcolm Moos of the University of Maryland wrote a book in which he described the report of the Marbury Commission as "the finest, most scholarly and candid analysis ever made of Maryland's higher education situation." He further pointed out that a great many of the principal recommendations made in the Marbury Report had ultimately been adopted.

Sometime in 1946, Mr. Conant asked me to serve on an ad hoc committee to help in the selection of new members of the Harvard Law School faculty. This was during the last few months of Jim Landis's tenure as dean of the law school. Things had gone badly with him, and shortly thereafter he resigned as dean of the law school, and Henry Friendly, who was then a judge of the United States Court of Appeals for the Second Circuit, Herbert Goodrich, who was a United States Court of Appeals judge for the Third Circuit as well as director of the American Law Institute, and I were invited to Cambridge, where we were asked for our suggestions as to persons who might be considered for appointment to the faculty of the law school.

At the meetings of this committee, I made the acquaintance of several of the members of the Harvard Corporation other than President Conant and Grenville Clark, both of whom I had worked with in the past. The other members of the corporation were Harry Shattuck, William Claflin, Charles Coolidge, Henry James, and Roger Lee. I was quite conscious of the fact that they were apparently sizing me up, but I did not understand why until I happened to run into people in various parts of the country who told me that I was being seriously considered for appointment as dean of the Harvard Law School. Apparently Judge Patterson had written a rather extraordinary letter recommending me to Grenville Clark, and I heard from friends in Florida and Texas that I was one of the leading candidates. In the end, Erwin Griswold was chosen as dean, apparently much to Judge Patterson's disgust, and at a luncheon meeting of the Harvard Law School Association at which he presided, during the annual American Bar Association meeting at Atlantic City in August of 1946, Judge Patterson spent most of the time when he was supposed to be introducing the new dean in praising my work at the War Department.

Somehow during this period I was gradually beginning to fit together the pieces of a law practice. Judge W. Calvin Chesnut had been helpful by inviting me to deliver one of the principal speeches at the state bar association meeting in June of 1946. The speech I made at that time attracted some attention in Philadelphia and in Richmond, and I heard from people like George Gibson, who was then one of the leading partners in the Hunton Williams firm. In addition, Mr. Bruce suggested that Governor O'Conor employ me as his personal counsel in an election contest arising out of the United States senatorial elections in the fall of 1946. Governor O'Conor, who could not again succeed himself as governor of Maryland, had decided to run in the primary against George Radcliffe and had managed to win the Democratic nomination for the United States Senate. At the general election he was opposed by a Republican from Frederick County named Markey, who demanded a recount when it appeared that he had lost by only 165 votes. The recount was conducted by the staff of a senatorial committee on elections which was dominated by Republicans, and it was generally felt that somehow or other they would manage to throw out enough O'Conor ballots to change the result. O'Conor had employed Clarence Miles to represent him at the recount, but Clarence was not very anxious to count ballots, and Howard Bruce suggested that I undertake that job. As it turned out, it was unspeakably boring most of the time, but I was able to frustrate the Republican-dominated staff at hearings which were held in Washington, and in the end O'Conor triumphed by a slightly increased margin. O'Conor was profoundly grateful for the time which I devoted to this trying task, which, needless to say, attracted a lot of attention from the media. My wife remembers that he called me at home every night while the recount was going on.

In April 1947 I was astonished to get a call from Grenville Clark asking me whether if elected to the Harvard Corporation I would be willing to serve. He said that he had no authority whatsoever to make any proposal to me, but that he and several other people were considering promoting my candidacy and did not want to waste time if I would not accept even if elected. I made inquiries of my Harvard friends, who all seemed quite incredulous that I should be considered for the post, which apparently had always been reserved for first families of Boston. They thought that the fact that I was not a graduate of Harvard College would make it utterly impossible to expect the overseers to ratify my appointment. Feeling that there was very little likelihood that it would come to anything, I indicated to Mr. Clark that I would accept the appointment if offered.

I later learned that about the time that Mr. Clark had spoken to me, Mr. Henry James had announced that he expected to retire from the Corporation, whereupon Bill Claflin, the treasurer of Harvard (who with Paul Buck had really run the place during the war while Jim Conant spent nearly all his time in Washington), proposed a young businessman who exactly fit the description of the typical member of the Corporation, in that he belonged to an old Boston family, was very wealthy, and had been an active alumnus of Harvard College. Conant and Clark felt that if Claflin were successful in getting his candidate elected to the Corporation, Conant's position would become impossible. Apparently, Claflin had proved to be very reluctant to let go the reins when Conant came back from the wars and had already managed to make Conant extremely uncomfortable.

During the summer months of 1947, I had planned to take my family to the North Carolina mountains, but because of an outbreak of polio, our pediatrician insisted on a change of plan and we ended up in a cottage at Randolph, New Hampshire, across the road from Ammi Cutter's summer cottage. Here, under the tutelage of Ammi, the Marbury family learned to walk the mountain trails of the Presidential Range and were introduced to all the privileges of membership in the local mountain club. We found among our neighbors some of the leading Harvard professors, including President and Mrs. Conant, who regularly spent their summer holidays in the area. During the next month we saw quite a little of the Conants, but nothing whatsoever was said on the subject of the Corporation.

In October the Corporation turned down Claflin's candidate and by a vote of five to two elected me to succeed Henry James. Claflin did not give up. He had many friends on the Board of Overseers and was reported to have said that if the overseers consented to my election, he and Charlie Coolidge, his neighbor and good friend who was then a senior partner in the firm of Ropes & Gray, counsel to the university, would resign from the Corporation. Apparently Mr. Conant had let it be known that under the circumstances he would feel obliged to resign if the overseers did not consent to my election. At that point Judge Patterson had jumped in, and he and Grenville Clark together conducted an elaborate campaign in which they collected letters from people who knew me, including Douglas Arant, George L. Harrison, Dean Acheson, Judge Herbert Goodrich, Howard Petersen, and Jack McCloy. Mr. Conant had also obtained copies of the report of my Committee on Higher Education and circulated these. Of all this I had heard no word, and as time went on I assumed that nothing more would come of it, when suddenly in January 1948 I got a telegram signed by Judge Patterson congratulating me on my election "by a unanimous vote." This aroused my curiosity, and I made inquiries among my Boston friends, who told me what had happened. Coolidge did not resign from the Corporation. Claflin did resign, but only after he was asked to do so by Conant. The rest of the Corporation welcomed me with open arms and from then on, on every other Sunday when the university was in session, I journeyed to Boston on the Federal Express and attended an all-day meeting at which, in addition to dealing with the university's investments and physical plant, the Corporation discussed many questions of policy, including all important administrative and academic appointments.

Mr. Shattuck introduced me to the Society of Fellows, and I especially remember that at my first meeting there I was seated at a table with three young men, Cord Meyer, McGeorge Bundy, and Jack Sawyer, all of whom later made their mark not only in the academic world but, in the case of Meyer and Bundy, in national and international politics, as well.

I attended my first Harvard commencement in June of 1948. I had arrived in Boston on the preceding day and suddenly realized that I had left my silk hat on the Federal Express. I knew that I would have to walk through the Harvard Yard on commencement day with the president and fellows and the overseers, all arrayed in silk hats which they lifted as they passed John Harvard's statue in the middle of the Yard. Fortunately, at the suggestion of Grenville Clark, I had been elected to membership in the Somerset Club, so I went there and consulted the chief steward. He asked me what size hat I wore and in a few minutes produced a silk hat of old-fashioned cut which fit me very comfortably. When I asked how on earth he had been able to do this, he said he remembered that Mr. Appleton had left his hat at the club during the commencement exercises in 1907. This was the same man who was reported by the press to have insisted that firemen who responded to an emergency call enter the club by the rear door, on the ground that only members and their guests were privileged to use the front door. When asked whether this actually happened, he replied, "Well, you see, Sir, the fire was in the kitchen."

Membership in the Somerset Club was generally confined to scions of old Boston families whose roots went back to pre-Civil War days. My friend Bobby Cutler had told me that he had recently overheard at the club a disgruntled alumnus complaining, "Harvard is really going to hell under Conant! Have you seen who were elected as Class Marshals? A Jew, a Negro, and a Roman Catholic, and they say that this fellow Marbury is not even a College man!"

As Joe Alsop has pointed out, for sheer pageantry there is no ceremony in the United States which can touch the commencement exercises at Harvard. By the time it was all over, I realized that once again in my life I was sitting in the catbird seat. Not only was I among the academic elite of the country, but the members of the Board of Overseers and the candidates for honorary degrees, who gathered for dinner at the president's house the night before commencement and lunched on commencement day at the Fogg Museum, were as interesting a company as could be found anywhere in the world. During the years I served on the Corporation, I sat beside such people as Chancellor Adenauer, Nils Bohr, Jack Kennedy, Martha Graham, and Wallace Stevens, to name only a few. I also especially remember Cardinal Cushing, who when he met Paul Cabot (who had been elected treasurer to succeed Bill Claflin) said, "Well, Cabot, I didn't think I would ever make it."

By June of 1948, my law practice had begun to make a strong comeback. Thanks to the War Department and Don Swatland, I had been chosen to handle key litigation involving the constitutionality and interpretation of the Fair Labor Standards Act, and cases which I had successfully argued in the Supreme Court and other federal courts had attracted a good deal of attention. At the suggestion of Ammi Cutter, I had been elected as a member of the American Law Institute in 1946, and when I attended the first annual meeting after my election, I found that I had just been elected to the council of the institute, a rare honor, as the council then included a number of the outstanding lawyers and judges of the country, notably, George Wharton Pepper, Augustus Hand, Learned Hand, Henry Friendly, Herbert Goodrich, and Harrison Tweed, all of whom participated actively in the council's discussions. At Harry Tweed's request, I agreed to serve with him on a committee of the institute to collaborate with the American Bar Association in organizing a program for continuing education for lawyers, which has since developed into a nationwide operation.

By the end of July I was looking forward to spending a relaxed month in Alder Creek, New York, in a cottage I had rented across the road from the Kernan homestead, and I had the feeling that at last I was getting a fairly firm grip on life after the turmoil of the war years.

XVIII ✤ Alger Hiss: The Puzzle Opens but Never Closes

On the third day of August 1948, the Baltimore evening papers carried scare headlines announcing that at a hearing before the Un-American Activities Committee of the House of Representatives, Alger Hiss, then president of the Carnegie Endowment for International Peace, and his brother Donald, then a partner in the Washington law firm of Covington and Burling, had been identified by a writer on the staff of *Time* magazine named Whittaker Chambers as members of an "apparatus" of the Communist party which operated in Washington, D.C., during the years 1934 to 1938. The next morning I wrote to Donald Hiss as follows:

> Dear Donie:
>
> If you and Alger are party members, then you can send me an application.

I sent a copy of this letter to Alger Hiss with a note saying:

> I know that you will have received offers from hundreds of friends who can do much more for you than I. However, if there is any service that I can render, just let me know.

My acquaintance with Alger Hiss began when he was a very small boy. His mother, Mrs. Charles Hiss, a widow who lived in our neighborhood in Baltimore, used to shepherd her flock to Memorial Episcopal Church every Sunday, where they occupied the pew right in front of the Marbury family. From time to time I heard of Alger Hiss's shining career as an undergraduate at the Johns Hopkins University. My brother-in-law Hugh Jewett, who was a classmate and fraternity brother of Alger's, has told me that Hiss was by all odds the most admired member of the class, not only for his intellectual accomplishments but even more for his good manners and personal charm.

I first came to know Alger Hiss really well during the summer of

This chapter is adapted from an address to the Fourth Judicial Conference held at Hot Springs, Virginia, on June 4, 1977, which was originally published in *Maryland Historical Magazine* 76 (1981): 70.

1926, when both of us spent a week at an old-fashioned house party in upstate New York. He had then just graduated from Johns Hopkins, having won many honors—indeed, one of his classmates told me that the undergraduates all claimed that the college administrators treated Alger as if "he had a mortgage on Gilman Hall," where the offices of the university were located. Before the house party was over, I understood why he was so highly regarded by his classmates. During Alger's law school years we always met during holidays when he returned to Baltimore, and by the time he had graduated in 1929 we had become close friends.

Every year Professor Frankfurter selected two students from the graduating class of the Harvard Law School to serve as law clerks, one to Justice Holmes and the other to Justice Brandeis. In 1929 the Holmes appointment fell to Alger Hiss. Sometime in October or November of that year I saw him in Baltimore at his mother's home, and he confided that he was planning to marry. It turned out that the girl was Priscilla Fansler, who had been at Bryn Mawr College with my sister. She had been married to Thayer Hobson, a New York publisher, had borne a son, and had recently been divorced.

A digression is in order at this point. Priscilla was only one of Alger Hiss's feminine interests. There was a great deal of the knight-errant in his make-up, and the girls to whom he attached himself from time to time were almost always in some sort of difficulty. His friends were at times quite concerned for fear that he would involve himself with someone who was unstable in order to rescue her from her troubles. Priscilla Hobson was clearly in trouble, although apparently not unstable. I have heard that when she told Alger that she was planning to marry Thayer Hobson, he went to Philadelphia, rode up on the B&O train with her to Jersey City, and rode backward and forward on the ferry for two hours during a driving rain, trying to persuade her not to go through with the ceremony. All to no avail; he came down with pneumonia and she went ahead with the wedding. According to reports which I have since heard, her marriage to Hobson was brief and stormy, ending with his abandoning her and her child in order to get a Mexican divorce. She was, therefore, clearly a damsel in distress, and that Alger Hiss should come to her rescue was strictly in character.

On December 11, 1929, Alger Hiss and Priscilla Hobson were married in the Washington apartment that he was sharing with Charles Willard, who was then working on the staff of the Wickersham committee. Jesse Slingluff and I were among the few invited guests. Somewhat to my astonishment, Priscilla, who during her college years had professed to be a Quaker, consented to be married by a Presbyterian minister.

The next summer, when I was recovering from a surgical operation, Alger and Priscilla invited me to spend a week at their cottage at Montserrat, north of Boston. Alger was obliged to be away during most of the day, attending to Justice Holmes, who was spending the summer at Beverly, nearby. The old man's eyesight was not very strong, and Alger's principal job seemed to be to read aloud to him. Because of Alger's absence I saw a good deal of Priscilla, and I carried away an impression of a rather assertive woman who had no intention of letting Alger "steal the show." It almost seemed as if she resented the attention his friends paid to him. Like Anthony Trollope's Mrs. Proudie, she would interrupt when he was asked for his opinion and answer for him.

As soon as his term as law clerk ended, Alger went to work with the firm of Choate, Hall and Stewart in Boston. I had two classmates who were practicing law with that firm, and both gave enthusiastic accounts of Alger. Neither of them, however, seemed to find Priscilla easy to get along with. She later told me that she was very unhappy in Boston, that her only real friend was Marian Frankfurter, and that both of them felt completely overshadowed by their husbands in the society of Cambridge.

After they had lived in Cambridge for about a year, Priscilla determined that she could stand it no longer and abruptly moved down to New York. She and Roberta Fansler had together gotten a grant from the Carnegie Fund to write a report on the history of the teaching of art, and she insisted that she could not do the necessary research in Cambridge. Alger was heavily involved in preparing for the trial of an important case for the Gillette Company and felt obliged to continue where he was for the time being. For several months he commuted to New York on weekends but finally gave this up and resigned his position at Choate, Hall and Stewart in order to move to New York.

In 1933 Jerome Frank, later a judge of the Court of Appeals for the Second Circuit, was appointed counsel for the Agricultural Adjustment Administration, which was then being organized pursuant to one of the early New Deal laws. He asked Alger Hiss and Lee Pressman to be his assistants, and they both accepted. During my visits to Washington, I saw Alger from time to time. I gathered that there was bitter feuding in the AAA, with Chester Davis acting as a bridge between two factions. Secretary of Agriculture Henry Wallace seemed to lean first toward one side and then toward the other. I was told that Alger was the only lawyer whom everyone trusted and that as a result he was overworking himself and had contracted a case of pneumonia. I remember that I shocked him deeply by saying that in my opinion his health was more important than any work he was doing. He thought this very cynical.

In 1934 Senator Nye was chairman of a committee conducting an investigation of the munitions industry—what nowadays would be called the military-industrial complex. At the request of Senator Nye, Alger Hiss was temporarily lent to the committee and served as its counsel. In that capacity he attracted a good deal of notoriety by his cross-examination of some national figures, notably Bernard Baruch.

Toward the end of July 1935, I saw Alger and Priscilla at the home of my sister Mrs. Wethered Barroll, on the Eastern Shore of Maryland. I was spending the weekend there, and Alger and Priscilla came up from Chestertown in order to see me. At that time the constitutionality of the Agricultural Adjustment Act was before the Supreme Court. The solicitor general, Mr. Stanley Reed, was overwhelmed by the flood of litigation which the New Deal legislation had provoked, and when Alger Hiss offered his services to prepare the brief in support of the act, Mr. Reed accepted eagerly. However, in order for the appointment to be made, it was apparently necessary for Alger to be endorsed by his senators. He was at that time still a registered voter in Maryland, and he asked me if I could get the endorsements of Millard Tydings and George Radcliffe. This I was able to do. In the course of my letter to Senator Radcliffe, I wrote: "I should like to add that this is not a perfunctory letter. I have known Mr. Hiss intimately for many years, and there is no one who stands higher in my esteem and affection."

In the autumn of 1935 I became engaged to be married. A few weeks before the wedding was scheduled to take place, I received a call from Miss Perkins, who was then the secretary of labor. She told me that her general counsel, Charles Wyzanski, was leaving and that Professor Frankfurter had suggested my name. I reminded Miss Perkins of the biblical ruling that a newly married man was always excused from military service for a year so that he might "comfort his wife" and told her that I hardly felt it would be an auspicious time to try to succeed Charlie Wyzanski, who had worked at his job for at least eighteen hours a day. Subsequently, Charlie told me that Lee Pressman had been a leading candidate for the job but that Alger Hiss had suggested my name in preference to his. It should be noted that it has since been established that Lee Pressman was at that time a member of the Communist party.

Alger and a few of my other close friends were invited to the church ceremony when Natalie and I were married, and I remember that both he and Priscilla were there. During the years immediately following our wedding, our friendship with the Hisses continued to be close. My wife had known Alger through her brother Hugh for many years before our marriage, and she had always been very fond of him. I am sure that we dined with the Hisses in Washington on at least one occasion, and I remember that they came to dinner with us in Baltimore. When our second child, a daughter, was baptized, I asked Alger to be her godfather, and he came to Baltimore for that purpose and spent the night in our home.

By that time Alger had transferred to the State Department. While he was still in the solicitor general's office, he was assigned to work on a case involving the constitutionality of the Trade Agreements Act under which reciprocal trade treaties were to be negotiated with foreign nations. Francis B. Sayre, who as assistant secretary of state was then responsible for the implementation of the act, had worked with Alger on the brief in that case, and after the Supreme Court had upheld the act he asked Alger to come to the State Department as his assistant.

I had a number of talks and correspondence with Alger about neutrality matters during 1938 and 1939. My position was quite isolationist and his was the opposite. I remember his saying that he did not think that war would be the end of our civilization and that we must stand for collective security even at the risk of another war. At the time of the repeal of the Neutrality Act I had some correspondence with him. This was shortly after the war in Europe had begun, and a letter from him shows that he was not following the Communist party line at that time. The summer of 1940, when I began to work part time for Judge Patterson, was the period of the Hitler-Stalin Pact, when followers of the party line were accusing Great Britain and France of an imperialist attack on Germany. Alger Hiss was a strong advocate of aid to Great Britain and France.

In March 1942, I began to work at the War Department full time and I managed to stop in to see Alger from time to time, although we were both so busy at work we could hardly find time for enough sleep, much less social contacts. However, during the summers of 1943 and 1944 I lived at the home of Judge Patterson in Georgetown. Alger was living right around the corner, and I used to drop in quite frequently and chat with him and with Priscilla. We often talked about Russia. I remember that on one occasion I expressed strong views as to the ruthless and tyrannical character of the Soviet government, which provoked some mild protest from Priscilla. Alger expressed his entire agreement with what I said.

During this time I dropped in to see Alger at the State Department occasionally, and we went to lunch together. I remember discussing with Alger his move in 1944 to the Office of Special Political Affairs in the State Department. At that time the war was far from over, and I expressed some surprise that he should be interested in working on postwar problems at such a time. He said that collective security had always been his principal interest.

At the Office of Special Political Affairs, Alger was working with Leo Pasvolsky on the preparatory work for the Dumbarton Oaks Conference, where the foundations of the United Nations Organization were laid. Alger took a prominent part as secretary of the conference. Thereafter, he accompanied Ed Stettinius, who was secretary of state, to the Yalta Conference and was given the responsibility of representing the United States delegation in the discussions relating to the organization of the United Nations.

In June of 1945 the conference was held at San Francisco, where the organization of the United Nations was finally agreed upon. Alger acted as secretary of the conference, and his performance in that capacity was outstanding. Dr. Isaiah Bowman, president of the Johns Hopkins University, was one of the delegates at the conference. He had been an adviser to the State Department throughout the war period and had come to know and admire Alger. I served with Dr. Bowman for many years on the Board of Trustees of the Peabody Institute of Baltimore, and he told me that Alger had made a tremendous impression at San Francisco, that he was respected and liked by all the delegates, "including the Russians," and was being prominently mentioned for the post of secretary general of the United Nations Organization.

After he got back from San Francisco, Alger showed me an entire book of photographs of Hiss in action taken by Time-Life photographers, one of which appeared on the cover of *Life* magazine. The result was that his name was on everyone's tongue in Washington. I was especially impressed by the fact that he did not attempt the social circuit but kept steadily at work. When we met he would direct the conversation to my activities rather than his own.

In September 1945, I resigned from the War Department and returned to the practice of law in Baltimore. About a year later Alger Hiss told me that he planned to resign from the State Department. He gave as his reason the changed atmosphere in the department under Jimmy Byrnes, who had been appointed by President Truman to succeed Ed Stettinius as secretary of state. What he did not tell me was that Secretary Byrnes had sent for him and informed him that some members of Congress were saying that he was a Communist. Byrnes told him that the congressmen gave the FBI as their source, and at his suggestion Alger went voluntarily to the FBI and was interviewed by J. Edgar Hoover's deputy.

On February 22, 1947, the Johns Hopkins University conferred an honorary degree on Alger Hiss in recognition of his outstanding contribution to the organization of the United Nations. He was also invited to speak at the annual meeting of the Johns Hopkins Alumni Association. While he was in Baltimore I had lunch with him, and he told me that he had been offered and had accepted the presidency of the Carnegie Endowment for International Peace. John Foster Dulles was then chairman of the board of trustees of the endowment, which included among its members John W. Davis and Arthur Ballantine.

Shortly thereafter Judge Patterson told me that he was resigning as secretary of war to return to the practice of law in New York. During the course of the conversation I mentioned Alger Hiss's name, and the Judge thereupon said, "There has been a terrific uproar in the State Department about that fellow. Jimmy Byrnes says that some congressmen have been charging that he is a Communist. Byrnes looked into it and found that it is all based on a story told by one man, and it all comes down to a question of veracity as between this man and Hiss." I asked him if he knew who the informant was, and he said that Jimmy Byrnes had not mentioned his name. I then said that if it were a question of veracity, I would have implicit faith in Alger Hiss. About a year later Judge Patterson told me that Alger Hiss had been working with him on a committee organized by Clark Eichelberger in support of the European Recovery Program (the Marshall Plan), to which the Soviet Union was bitterly opposed. Judge Patterson said: "Hiss is a good man."

Which brings us back to August 3, 1948, when Whittaker Chambers appeared before the House Un-American Activities Committee and charged that Alger Hiss and his brother Donald had been members of a Communist apparatus between 1935 and 1938. The day after I wrote the two letters which I quoted in full at the beginning of this chapter, I got a telephone call from Alger Hiss. He said that he had asked and been granted the privilege of appearing before the committee to reply to the charges made by Whittaker Chambers and would like to have me accompany him as counsel.

I said I would be glad to go with him, and we arranged to meet at the offices of Covington and Burling on the following morning. At that meeting Alger said that to the best of his knowledge, he had never seen Whittaker Chambers. Together we prepared a brief statement for him to make and then rode up to the Capitol. Alger read his statement and then submitted to questions from the committee.

Chambers in his testimony before the committee had claimed to have known Alger and Priscilla Hiss as friends. Alger flatly denied that he had ever heard of Whittaker Chambers except that sometime in 1947 he had been asked by two FBI interviewers whether he knew him. He said to the committee, "So far as I know, I have never laid eyes on him." When shown a photograph, he said, "I would not want to take oath that I have never seen that man. I would like to see him and then I think I would be better able to tell whether I have ever seen him."

On the whole, Alger handled himself very well before the committee, and at the end of the hearing Mr. Rankin of Mississippi, who had the reputation of being its most bigoted member, came down and shook his hand. Richard Nixon, then a delegate from California and a member of the committee, later claimed that at the end of the hearing the rest of the committee was prepared to drop the Hiss investigation altogether and that he persuaded them not to be so precipitate.

The following morning the *New York Times* carried a front-page story in which I was prominently mentioned as one who had accompanied Alger Hiss to the hearing. I immediately wrote to the editor, explaining my presence and saying, "I have known Mr. Hiss since boyhood and I would as soon believe that the editor of the *New York Times* is a Communist."

Diplomatic Interlude

On August seventh I left for upper New York State, where I expected to spend the rest of the month on vacation. Shortly after my arrival, I received a telephone call from William H. Draper, Jr., then the under secretary of war, asking me to come to Washington immediately. On the following day I met him and several representatives of the State Department, who explained that they were organizing the United States delegation to the Second Session of the Signatories of the General Agreement on Tariffs and Trade, commonly called the GATT, which was to be held at Geneva from August 15 to the middle of September. The State Department had agreed that the War Department could have a representative on the delegation to press for most favored nation treatment for the occupied areas of Germany and Japan, and that was the job they were asking me to undertake. They suggested that I talk to Herbert Feis, who was familiar with the whole background. From him I learned that the proposed assignment would not be an easy one. At the session of the GATT held the preceding year, Harold Neff had tackled the assignment but had met unyielding opposition from the British and French delegations as well as from the Chinese. Moreover, the support from the State Department had been lukewarm.

It seemed clear to me that I also would fail unless the State Department was prepared to go down the line for me. I therefore insisted that our ambassadors be specifically instructed to take the question up with the governments to which they were accredited and to press for support of the position which I was being asked to take. I was assured that this would be done and that arrangements would be made for me to have a personal interview with Lewis Douglas, our ambassador to the Court of St. James, and Jefferson Caffrey, our ambassador to France.

Armed with a diplomatic passport, I was put on a plane for London which left on the morning of August 11. In London, I was given a few minutes with Mr. Douglas. He was very pleasant but soon turned me over to a second secretary, who told me that he had arranged an appointment at the Foreign Office that afternoon. There a minor official, whose name and rank I have forgotten, explained to me that the French were opposed to the whole idea and that the Foreign Office was reluctant to oppose them on this particular issue.

On Sunday afternoon I flew to Paris and was driven straight to the embassy. I remember that the streets were deserted, as this was the Feast of the Assumption, when every Frenchman goes on holiday. Accordingly, I was surprised to find that the ambassador was waiting in his office, and even more surprised to learn that my visit was his only reason for being there. Mr. Caffrey listened to my story in complete silence and then said, "Mr. Marbury, I think I understand what you wish. I will do what I can."

On arrival at Geneva I found the British noncommittal, the French polite but uncooperative, and the Chinese actively hostile. All of them disclaimed having received any new instructions bearing on the point in which I was interested. There the matter rested for two weeks, during which I spent my time reading in the library of the Palais des Nations and walking around Geneva and its suburbs.

I was beginning to consider seriously whether to give up the job as hopeless when suddenly the head of the French delegation burst into our office and handed me a telegram from the Ministry of External Affairs in Paris which simply said, "Get in touch with Marbury of the American delegation and cooperate with him." Of course, I was delighted to explain to him just exactly what the telegram meant. He was incredulous but said he would get in touch with his ministry and let me hear further. In the meantime I asked him for a copy of his telegram and showed it to the head of the British delegation, who did not conceal his astonishment. He also asked for a copy and within forty-eight hours told me that he had been instructed by Whitehall to go along with the French.

I later learned that Mr. Caffrey had succeeded in persuading the French minister of external affairs to support the War Department's proposal. No one knew how he accomplished this, but I was told that he and the minister were both botanists and horticulturists and that they spent every Sunday afternoon walking together in their gardens, with results which sometimes bordered on the miraculous.

I got in touch once more with the head of the Chinese delegation, but he remained thoroughly obdurate. He told me that in his opinion China needed at least fifty years of economic protectionism "just as your country did when you were beginning to industrialize." In the meantime the last thing in the world the Chinese wanted was to promote the industrial recovery of Japan.

My proposal was promptly placed on the agenda for discussion. The head of the British delegation said that the Foreign Office had raised the question of whether my proposal conflicted with other proposals for economic cooperation which were being discussed with Ambassador Douglas and with General Lucius D. Clay, who was then military commander of the American Zone of Occupied Germany. General Clay was in Berlin, and I was authorized by Washington to go there to discuss the matter with him.

At that time the Berlin blockade was on, and I was told to go to Frankfurt and fly in on one of the "airlift" planes, which were the only means of communication with the beleaguered city. On arrival in Frankfurt I went to the airport and was put aboard a plane which taxied out to wait its time to take off. Flights were then being scheduled at three-minute intervals, and if you lost your place, that was just too bad. Through some foul-up, that is exactly what happened, and after waiting for fifteen minutes, the pilot announced that we had missed our turn and that the next passenger plane would not fly until the following morning. I told him that I had an appointment with General Clay for noon on that day, and in about half an hour I was told that I would be permitted to get on the next plane but that I would have to sit in a sealed compartment on top of a pile of mail sacks. I did just that and as a result saw nothing whatsoever until I arrived in Berlin at Templehof Airfield, but I got there in time for my appointment with General Clay.

I explained my mission to the general, who told me that he had just received a communication from Bill Draper saying that I was coming. He said that he doubted very much whether most favored nation treatment would at that time be particularly helpful to Occupied Germany. He and Lewis Douglas were engaged in attempting to negotiate bilateral and multilateral agreements under the aegis of the Organization for European Economic Cooperation, and this seemed to him to be much more significant for the rehabilitation of Germany. However, he said that he would take care to see that nothing was done to cross wires with what I was trying to do at Geneva and would see that Douglas reassured the Foreign Office.

He then launched into a description of the troubles he was having with Washington. In the preceding June he had succeeded in getting the commanders of the British and French zones of Occupied Germany to agree with him on a joint program which would substitute a single new currency for the old German reichsmark on the basis of one for ten. He told me that the leading German politicians had all advised him privately that the German economy could never recover unless drastic measures were taken to wipe out the fiscal commitments which were strangling it. For example, he said that more money was being paid in pensions by the state railway systems in West Germany than was being paid to the operating personnel. Similar conditions existed in the schools and other government activities. Obviously, a wholesale repudiation of these obligations would work great hardships, and the politicians told him that for this reason they would be obliged publicly to protest against what they were privately advising him to do.

A different kind of protest had come from the commander of the Russian Zone. General Marshall's famous speech at the Harvard commencement in 1947, at which he proposed the European Recovery Program (which was later known by his name), had met with immediate opposition from the Russians. Refusal to cooperate with the Western powers in a unified currency reform was a logical step in the Soviet government's attempt to block the Marshall Plan. So the commanders of the Western zones had been obliged to go ahead without the Russians and to limit the circulation of the new West mark to their zones.

The question had then arisen as to what currency was to circulate in Berlin. It was obviously desirable that there be only one currency there, but the Russians insisted on having sole charge of the bank which was to issue that currency. General Clay believed that if this were allowed, the other three occupying powers would become simply guests of the Russians in Berlin. Disregarding his objections, the Russians had sent a letter advising that a separate currency reform was being put into effect for their zone and that they would issue new East marks for circulation throughout Berlin. The three other occupying powers thereupon made the new West mark legal currency throughout Berlin. The Russians, who had begun the breakup of the quadripartite government of Berlin as soon as the Marshall Plan was announced, seized upon the currency issue as an excuse for withdrawing their sector of Berlin from all contact with the sectors which had been assigned to the other three occupying powers. At the same time they cut off all access to Berlin except by air.

Throughout July and August negotiations had been going on, and the British had finally persuaded Washington to allow the East mark to be accepted as the sole currency for Berlin and to agree that the regulation of the circulation of that currency should rest solely with the Soviet-German Bank of Emission in Berlin, provided that the Soviets would agree to remove all restrictions which had been imposed on transport between Berlin and the Western zones and would further agree that there should be no discrimination against holders of West marks; that equal treatment should be given to currency, banking, and credit facilities throughout Berlin, foreign countries, and the Western zones; and that currency should be provided to meet Allied needs in Berlin. General Clay told me that he thought this was totally unworkable but had been unable to persuade Kenneth Royall, who was then secretary of war, to allow him to oppose the proposal.

The general said that he was meeting with the other three commanders at lunch to discuss the British proposal. He asked me to come to dinner that night at his home. In the meantime he would assign an aide who would show me anything I wanted to see in Berlin. I asked him if I could go into the Russian sector, and he said that I could if I did not object to spending the night in jail.

I arrived at General Clay's home to find that neither he nor Mrs. Clay was there. Shortly thereafter he came in, looking very cheerful. It appeared that the Russian commander, General Sokolovsky, had refused to listen to the British proposal and that his manner had been so contemptuous that the British commander, General Robertson, had withdrawn his proposal, with the result that General Clay had not been obliged to say anything at all. About an hour later Mrs. Clay came in, full of apologies. She had been out on the lake sailing and had gotten becalmed and was drifting toward the Russian Zone when some young Americans who were rowing a boat on the lake discovered her plight and hauled her back to safety.

The other guest at dinner was an economist, and I listened to much inside talk about the organization problems of the Marshall Plan and the embryo efforts to organize Western Europe into an economic union. The following day I returned to Geneva, but this time I did not have to ride on the mail sacks. After I got back, a working party began to draft the necessary papers to give most favored nation treatment to Occupied Germany. I relied entirely on John Leddy, who was obviously respected by all the other members of the working party and who finally came through with a polysyllabic formulation which sounded like the work of a Harvard graduate student of political science. The Britisher then remarked, "As usual Mr. Leddy appears to have found a solution for our problem. Now if I may be permitted to translate his proposal into English, I suggest the following . . ." In simple, clear diction he then rephrased Leddy's proposal in about half the words.

At the next plenary session the report of the working party was adopted, and my mission had ended in at least partial success. I left for home with the definite feeling that my only real contribution had been made in Washington and Paris prior to my arrival in Geneva.

The Hiss-Chambers Libel Suit

In Geneva we were all stunned when a late arrival from Washington reported that the Thomas committee had reopened public hearings, that Alger Hiss had been confronted by Whittaker Chambers, and that the general impression was that Alger Hiss had equivocated as to their past relationship. As time passed, more and more ominous reports began to come in about the progress of the investigation and even the Swiss newspapers carried articles on the subject. I remember sitting up one night in my hotel room drafting and redrafting a letter to Alger expressing my dismay at having deserted him in his time of trouble. In Berlin the Hiss case was mentioned and I was distressed to hear General Clay say that he had not been surprised by Chambers' charges, since in his contacts with Hiss over Chinese matters, Hiss had consistently taken positions which were helpful to the Chinese Communists.

I returned from Geneva on September 12 and went immediately to Cambridge for a meeting of the Harvard Corporation. Together with Grenville Clark, who was a senior member of the Corporation, I spent the night at the residence of President Conant. Most of the talk was about the Hiss case. I learned that Alger in his last appearance before the committee had challenged Chambers to make his accusation under circumstances where he could not claim the privilege of a witness under subpoena from a congressional committee. Chambers had responded by stating in a radio interview that to his knowledge Hiss was once a member of the Communist party and might still be one. Both Conant and Clark felt that this left Hiss no alternative except to bring a libel suit against Chambers. They said that his failure to do so had already been taken as an admission of the truth of Chambers' charges, and they feared that a flood of similar charges against political and academic figures would soon follow, which would have a very serious impact on our foreign policy and on academic freedom generally. Clark was especially emphatic in urging me to get in touch with Alger immediately and urge upon him the importance of bringing suit promptly.

While I was in Cambridge I had a talk with Judge Wyzanski, who told me that Alger had been advised not to sue Chambers. When I got back to my office I found a letter from Alger saying that in my absence he had employed Edward McLean of the firm of Debevoise, Plimpton and McLean of New York City to represent him and that he was planning to bring a libel suit against Chambers if he could get "enough unprivileged material" to justify such a suit. He asked me to let him know as soon as I got back to Baltimore.

I called him on the telephone and in the course of the conversation asked him about the libel suit. He said that he wanted to bring it immediately but that Mr. Davis and Mr. Ballantine had advised him to go slow and that Ed McLean agreed. I said that in spite of the eminence of those gentlemen I felt differently, and he asked me to come to New York and discuss the matter with them.

In the meantime Alger sent me copies of statements for publication made by prominent people, all expressing complete confidence in his integrity. Among them were Judge Patterson, who had been secretary of war, Will Clayton, who had been under secretary of state, and Devereux Josephs, who was president of the New York Life Insurance Company and who had been president of one of the Carnegie Funds. I noted that Eleanor Roosevelt, who had worked with Alger as a delegate to the first conference of the United Nations, had given a very thoughtful and perceptive interview on his behalf to the *Christian Science Monitor.* I was especially interested in letters from Francis B. Sayre, Leo Pasvolsky, and Stanley Hornbeck, who had been Alger's immediate superiors in the State Department. Alger had been working for Hornbeck during the time when Hornbeck had been meeting with General Clay on problems relating to China, and I was therefore especially interested in what Hornbeck had to say. I quote the entire letter, which was dated September 2, 1948:

Dear Alger:

In pursuance of what I volunteered to you when we talked last week, I want you to know that, having known you well for ten years and having had a very close association with you in the Department of State during the years from 1939 to 1944—when you were my assistant and one of my "sparring partners"—I should be glad to testify in any form that I have never known or thought of your having been engaged in any doubtful or questionable activities, or of your having given indication of radical leanings or sympathies; that I at no time have suspected you of being a communist or a "fellow traveler"; that short of conclusive proof, I would not now believe that you ever were either of these or that you ever have been knowingly a member of any "corp" chosen, favored or used by Communists in service of communist, subversive or disloyal purposes; that I have never in any connection found you to have been other than truthful; and that I consider you a gifted, high-principled, devoted and loyal citizen.

With cordial regards and all best wishes, I am,

Yours ever,

(signed) Stanley K. Hornbeck

As Hornbeck was known throughout the department for his anti-communist views, I found this very reassuring. However, I found that my associate Franklin Allen, who had been following the Thomas committee proceedings, was very much disturbed. There was no doubt that in his appearances before the committee in my absence Alger had handled himself very badly. He had adopted a rather arrogant attitude and had repeatedly fenced with the members of the committee. He had written a letter to the chairman which reeked with hurt pride and indignation, and had grudgingly admitted association with Chambers under the name of George Crosley, but only after examining Chambers' teeth and asking him to read aloud some passages from a document.

Richard Nixon had shown himself to be a skillful prosecutor. At a secret session he had examined Chambers and had developed a number of details which indicated that there had indeed been a close relationship between the Chambers and Hiss families. When Alger was called back to the stand, Nixon examined him in turn on all these points and demonstrated that Chambers had been generally pretty accurate in a number of his assertions with regard to the Hiss household and the habits of the Hiss family. For example, Chambers had said that he and Alger were both bird watchers and that Alger was very proud of the fact that he had once seen a prothonotary warbler along the old C&O Canal in Georgetown. Without knowing of Chambers' testimony, Alger testified that he was a bird watcher and that he had seen a prothonotary warbler in that vicinity.

Chambers said that the Hisses had never known him under any name except that of "Karl," which he said was his party name. When finally confronted with Chambers, Alger had admitted knowing him under the name of George Crosley as a free-lance journalist who was down on his luck. He acknowledged that he had sublet his apartment in Washington to Chambers in 1935. Alger said that at the time he rented his apartment to Crosley he had also "thrown in" an old Ford automobile for which the Hiss family no longer had any use. Chambers had testified that in 1936 Alger had delivered an old Ford to a dealer who was a party member and who had agreed to turn it over to another member of the party. The certificate of title was produced and showed that Alger had signed a transfer in 1936 but not in 1935.

While there thus seemed some very disquieting evidence in the record, it was nevertheless apparent that the issue was still primarily one of veracity between Chambers and Hiss. Bear in mind the fact that Chambers did not accuse Hiss of espionage. On the contrary, when specifically questioned about that at his first appearance before the Thomas committee, Chambers replied that the objective of the apparatus to which Hiss belonged was not espionage but rather infiltration of the government, although espionage was certainly one of its eventual objectives. In 1935 membership in the Communist party was not illegal, and it was well known that a number of people, particularly in academic circles, were party members. For this reason alone Chambers' lurid story of conspiratorial secrecy seemed incredible on its face. While I was reluctant to advise an action which would be opposed by Alger's board of trustees, it seemed to me inevitable that if he failed to sue Chambers, his reputation would be so irretrievably destroyed that the endowment would have to dispense with his services anyhow.

Accordingly, I went to New York and spent an entire day in interviews, the first with Alger and Priscilla Hiss at their apartment, where I spent the night, then with Mr. Davis and with Mr. Ballantine, and finally with Judge Patterson. I warned both Alger and Priscilla that if there were any skeletons in the closet of either one of them, they would certainly be discovered if suit were filed, and they both assured me there was no cause for worry on that count. However, I found my interview with Priscilla somewhat mystifying. I had asked to see her alone after Alger had left for the office, and we talked for nearly an hour. I got the impression that she felt that in some way she was responsible for the troubles which had come to Alger. However, she stoutly supported Alger's story of his association with "George Crosley" and flatly denied that either she or Alger had ever been connected with a Communist party apparatus.

I am afraid that in my meeting with Mr. Davis and Mr. Ballantine I spent most of my time trying to persuade them to withdraw their objections to the filing of the suit. I did secure from them what I took to be a commitment that if the suit were filed, no action would be taken to remove Alger as president of the endowment until the case had been tried.

Alger Hiss then had to make the decision as to whether to be guided by my advice or by that of Ed McLean. One of McLean's worries arose out of the fact that the New York courts appeared to draw a distinction between an accusation that a man had once been a member of the Communist party and a charge that he still was a member. Chambers in his broadcast had been careful not to assert that Alger was still a Communist. It seemed to me, however, that coming immediately after the congressional hearings, Chambers' broadcast amounted to a charge of perjury and was therefore clearly libelous.

McLean also was troubled by the fear that a libel suit would not come on for hearing until too late to do any good. I pointed out that since Chambers was then living with his family on a farm in Carroll County, Maryland, we could probably make venue stick in Maryland and also establish diversity of citizenship, which would confer jurisdiction on the federal District Court in Baltimore. At that time our federal District Court would try any case that was at issue within 60 days if the parties did not seek delay.

A meeting was scheduled to be held in my office on Monday, September 22, to reach a final decision as to whether to bring suit. Alger arrived accompanied by a lawyer named Harold Rosenwald, who had known him at the Harvard Law School and who had volunteered his services during the congressional hearings. No sooner had the meeting begun than Alger announced that he had made up his mind and that he wanted suit brought immediately. I again warned about skeletons in the closet and mentioned the case of Oscar Wilde, but Alger brushed this aside, saying that he had nothing to hide. After discussion it was agreed that suit should be brought in Baltimore and that my partner Charles Evans and I should appear as counsel and have primary responsibility for the trial of the case. Charlie had been deputy state's attorney for Baltimore City for a number of years and had a wide trial experience, primarily in criminal cases. Ed McLean agreed to continue as counsel and offered to prepare a draft of the complaint.

A general discussion followed as to what should be included in the complaint, and all agreed that it should be kept as brief and simple as possible. We believed that Chambers could not afford to raise any technical defenses and would be bound to defend on the ground that the statements which he had made before the Thomas committee and in the broadcast were true. The question of the amount of damages gave us much concern. Alger was not looking to profit by his lawsuit but wanted public vindication. I thought that a jury might well hesitate to inflict heavy damages on Chambers and if we claimed a large sum and got a relatively small verdict, we would fail in our primary purpose, so we agreed to claim only fifty thousand dollars, which would be substantial enough to hurt but would not bankrupt Chambers. Such were the times that we believed that fifty thousand dollars would be enough to cover the costs of the trial.

On September 27, 1948, suit was filed in the United States District Court for the District of Maryland. Immediately after the suit was filed, Chambers handed a statement to the Associated Press in which he said, "I welcome Mr. Hiss's daring suit. I do not minimize the audacity or the ferocity of the forces which work through him." This language seemed to us to be clearly libelous, and we promptly filed a supplementary complaint seeking an additional twenty-five thousand dollars in damages.

There followed a period of frenzied activity. Grenville Clark wrote long letters making recommendations as to strategy and tactics. Thomas Eliot wrote from Boston to say that he had once been panhandled by a man who looked like Chambers and used a name something like Crosley. A publisher named Roth (who later became famous when the Supreme Court undertook to define obscenity) volunteered that Chambers had offered for publication a number of pornographic poems under the pseudonym George Crosley. At least three different people stated that they knew that Chambers had been under treatment for mental disorders. One of them named as his psychiatrist the famous Dr. Kubie. All of these reports had to be run down. None of them proved to be helpful.

At the same time we were conducting an investigation of Chambers to develop any facts which might bear upon his credibility. Because of the impact of the Thomas committee hearings on the public mind, the burden was really on Alger Hiss to prove that the charges made by Chambers were false. True, the Maryland law of libel as it then stood did not impose that burden on plaintiffs, but nevertheless it seemed quite clear to all of us that Alger Hiss would never get a verdict in his favor unless he was able to convince the jury that he was not and never had been a member of the Communist underground. So we were up against the lawyers' bête noire—proving a negative.

We hoped to accomplish this in two ways. First, by proving that Alger's character and conduct throughout his life had been totally inconsistent with Chambers' story and, second, by establishing that Chambers was unworthy of belief. In that connection we proposed to show that throughout his career Alger had earned and won the trust of men and women whose integrity and judgment commanded respect and that he had frequently and effectively opposed the Communist party line during his career as a public servant. On the second point, we hoped to be able to prove that a number of the statements made by Chambers to the Thomas committee were untrue and that his character and conduct throughout his life made his testimony unreliable. In the end, we hoped that the jury would see the issue as one of veracity between a valuable public servant of spotless reputation and a renegade Communist who, on his record, could not be believed under oath.

Thus, the case called for a thorough examination of Chambers' entire life history, including a study of everything he had ever written as well as a check on the details of the story he had told to the Thomas commit-tee. On the Hiss end, it involved interviewing a large number of people. I personally interviewed many different individuals, including Dean Acheson, Chester Davis, Stanley Hornbeck, Leo Pasvolsky, Charles Wy-zanski, Ed Stettinius, and others with whom Alger had worked over the years.

In the meantime I was preparing to examine Whittaker Chambers on oral deposition. One subject I definitely did not intend to get into, and that was Chambers' homosexual activities, which it now appears that he confessed to the government before he took the witness stand at the crim-inal trials in New York City. Early in October, Charlie Wyzanski had writ-ten to report that, according to John Cowles, the gossip among news-papermen was that Chambers was a homosexual. Harold Rosenwald called my attention to the fact that Chambers had translated a novel called *Class Reunion,* in which a character with a history much like that of Cham-bers succeeds in destroying the shining career of a former classmate of the same sex because of unrequited love, of which the injured party is quite unaware.

In the course of one of our discussions, I brought up this subject with Alger. At that time he told me, in strict confidence, what has now been proclaimed to the whole world, that his stepson, Timothy Hobson, had been discharged from the navy because of a homosexual episode. He said that he had reason to think that the Thomas committee knew of this and would not hesitate to bring it out if the subject of Chambers' abnormality were ever brought up. He added that there had been rumors of a homosexual relationship between Timmy and Chambers, which were outrageous, but because of Timmy's vulnerable record, neither he nor Priscilla would allow Timmy to testify, as he was eager to do.

On November 4, 1948, I began the examination of Whittaker Cham-bers at my office in Baltimore. Chambers was represented by Richard F. Cleveland and William D. Macmillan of the firm of Semmes, Bowen and Semmes. For two days we reviewed his life's history, and an extraordinary story it was. Much of it you will find outlined in a book which Chambers later published under the title of *Witness.* Among the interesting facts brought out in his testimony were the following: that he had at different times used a variety of aliases; that he had been forced to withdraw from Columbia University for publishing in the college newspaper an article which, by the standards of that age of innocence, was considered to be both pornographic and blasphemous; that he had written and published a lesbian poem; that he had taken books from the Columbia Library and not returned them until it was discovered that he had accumulated nearly a roomful; that he had lived in a house in New Orleans which was also occupied by a prostitute known as One-Eyed Annie; that he had made false affidavits in order to obtain a job with the Railroad Retirement

Board; and that he had written a letter to Mark Van Doren in which he boasted that he had gained readmission to Columbia by lying to the dean about his intentions.

Speaking generally, Chambers confirmed everything of a derogatory nature which our investigation had turned up. He specifically reiterated the testimony which he had given before the Thomas committee that he had no evidence that Hiss had committed any act of espionage.

At the end of the second day of testimony, it was apparent that in the absence of some written evidence which would corroborate Chambers' story, no jury would ever believe it. Chambers himself stated in *Witness* that he "had realized from the tone and the maneuvers at the pretrial examination how successfully the Hiss forces had turned the tables with the libel suit" (p. 734).

Accordingly, I made demand on him to produce anything whatsoever which he had in his possession in the way of written evidence which would substantiate his story, and particularly any communications from Alger or Priscilla Hiss. Chambers wrote in *Witness*, "This time Cleveland warned me that if I did have anything of Hiss's I had better get it" (p. 735).

According to the story which he later told on the witness stand in New York, and embellished in his book, he had a vague recollection that he had at one time turned some papers over to his wife's nephew in New York for safekeeping. He accordingly went to New York and asked for the papers and was delivered a dusty envelope. To his utter amazement, he discovered that the envelope contained what appeared to be copies of documents which he claimed that Hiss had delivered to him from time to time during the year 1938. There were also two rolls of developed microfilm, three cylinders of microfilm which had never been developed, and four memoranda in Alger Hiss's handwriting.

In *Witness* Chambers said that he extracted the films and then delivered the rest of the papers to Cleveland for safekeeping. He felt that he needed time to make up his mind whether to destroy the papers and the films and commit suicide. For this reason he says that he decided not to come back to my office for further oral examination on November 16 but sent his wife instead to give her testimony, while he sought divine counsel as to where his duty lay. He then made up his mind to retain all his films for the time being, without telling Cleveland that he had done so, and to tell Cleveland to introduce in evidence the typewritten papers and the handwritten notes which he had entrusted to him.

In the afternoon of November 17 Chambers appeared in my office and, with a flourish, produced a package of papers. Four of the papers were handwritten memoranda. The balance appeared to be typewritten copies of communications received by the State Department in Washington from various foreign service officers overseas during the first three months of 1938. I examined the handwritten memoranda and found that they appeared to be in Alger's handwriting and purported to summarize documents, some of which might well have had a secret or restricted classification.

Chambers then launched into an explanation of how the papers had come into his possession. He said that either in August or the early fall of 1937 Alger had attended a meeting in New York which Chambers had arranged with a Russian Colonel Bykov, who went by the pseudonym of Peter and who spoke no English. Through Chambers as interpreter, Peter asked Alger whether he would be willing to turn over to Chambers for transmission to him copies of documents which came across Alger's desk at the State Department. Alger agreed to do this, and thereafter there was a fairly constant flow of such material, which Alger would bring home in his briefcase and which Priscilla Hiss would copy on her typewriter. In cases where it was not feasible to bring home documents which appeared to be of special interest, Alger would make notes of their contents in his own handwriting.

I was shocked when I recognized what seemed to be Alger's handwriting. There was, of course, always the possibility of forgery, but barring that, it was obvious that the handwritten memoranda really meant the end of the libel suit. I had spent most of my professional life as a litigator and had participated actively in the defense of some fairly important libel cases, and I was fully aware of the devastating effect that these memoranda would be certain to have on Alger's suit. I was also conscious of the need for careful handling of a situation which might well result in a criminal prosecution of Alger.

It seemed clear to me that it would be unwise to attempt to proceed further with the examination of these papers until I had a chance to consult with Alger. For all I knew, the documents might have been sheer fabrications, which Alger could immediately identify as such by examining the photostatic copies. Accordingly, I said that I would need time to examine the original papers, and it was agreed that in the meantime they should be kept in the safe deposit box at Semmes, Bowen and Semmes, subject to our right of inspection. Cleveland then turned over to me the photostatic copies, which I handed to Harold Rosenwald and told him to take them to Alger at once. In the meantime I proceeded for the rest of the afternoon to examine Chambers on other points.

As soon as the examination was ended, Charlie Evans and I discussed what we ought to do. The documents together with Chambers' explanation of them were certainly proof that Chambers had engaged in espionage. They also proved that he had lied to the Thomas committee when he had denied any participation in such activities. If Chambers were indicted for perjury, then the libel suit would become academic. Clearly the Department of Justice had far greater resources than we to find out whether these typewritten papers were copies of genuine documents of a classified nature. They were also in a far better position to investigate and determine how Chambers had gotten possession of them. Moreover, Charlie Evans felt strongly that we were under an obligation to tell the Department of Justice what had happened.

When I talked to Alger on the following day, he had already been shown the photostats by Harold Rosenwald. He confirmed that at least three of the handwritten memoranda appeared to be in his own handwriting. He said that he had probably made them for his own use in reporting to Mr. Sayre and that anyone could have pilfered them from his desk. He denied ever having seen the typewritten papers before, although he acknowledged that the contents appeared to be similar to that of papers which had passed over his desk. He said he could not imagine how Chambers could have gotten hold of them. I said that in view of that statement it seemed to me that he could have nothing to lose by turning the papers over to the Department of Justice, and he agreed entirely. While I sat at his desk, he tried to call the attorney general in Washington but found that he was out of town. He then agreed that I should call him on the following day.

I returned to Baltimore that night and the following morning tried to reach the attorney general by telephone but found that he had left his office and was not expected to return. I then spoke to Phil Perlman, who was the acting attorney general, and asked him whether he could arrange to see McLean and me on the following day. Perlman said that he would get in touch with the head of the Criminal Division of the Department of Justice and tell him to call me.

Later I received a call from a Mr. Campbell, who indicated that he was head of the Criminal Division of the Department of Justice and that he had been instructed by the attorney general to come to Baltimore immediately. When he arrived I explained the circumstances and gave him the photostatic copies of the original papers which had been produced at the deposition on the afternoon of November 17. Cleveland told Campbell that the originals were in his possession and had been placed in a safe deposit box. Campbell then asked that the taking of further depositions be suspended for a period of two weeks and that the utmost secrecy be preserved in the meantime so as to enable the government to make as complete an investigation as possible. He agreed that at the end of two weeks he would get in touch with me and let me know what the government intended to do.

During the following week I heard nothing from Campbell, and I began to have a great deal of concern about what might happen if, in fact, the papers turned out to be copies of genuine State Department documents. In that event, it seemed to me that it would be quite likely that Alger and not Chambers would be indicted. After thinking the matter over, I called Alger and said that I wanted to see him and Priscilla together. They were planning to visit the Eastern Shore of Maryland and agreed to come over to Baltimore to my house for lunch on Sunday, November 28. Their little son Tony came with them.

After lunch I talked to Alger and Priscilla and said that I feared that Alger would be indicted and might be convicted. Priscilla looked stunned. Alger said that he knew that he was innocent and had confidence that the truth would prevail. I told him that even so, they had better prepare for the worst. I suggested that he should think about what lawyer he would like to have defend him in case he were indicted, and he asked me to discuss it with Ed McLean and Judge Patterson. I suggested that he and Priscilla make every effort to locate papers written on her typewriter so that they could be compared with the papers which Chambers had produced, since this would be the best possible way of establishing that Chambers was lying.

I went to New York to see Judge Patterson. He was very much shocked by the developments and advised us to try to line up Lloyd Stryker, who was then New York's best-known criminal lawyer. On December 3, I wrote Alger a letter in which I reported on my visit to New York, in the course of which I said:

> As you no doubt know, I spent several hours with Harold and Ed McLean on Wednesday. We had a full discussion of all phases of this matter and arrived at a tentative program of action. We also had a brief conference with Judge Patterson and got his advice on what to do in case there should be any action by the New York grand jury. Incidentally, I may say that his reaction to the new developments in the case confirmed my feeling that I did not overdraw the picture when I talked to you and Prossie on Sunday.
>
> I am troubled by the fact that your inability to explain what became of the typewriter which Prossie had in 1938 might be construed as an attempt to cover up something. This inference could be rebutted by the voluntary production on your part of papers which were typed by her on that particular machine. I think that she should make every effort to locate some such papers. Perhaps the manuscript of the book which she was writing on the history of the teaching of art could be located.

On December first a columnist writing in the *Washington Post* reported that there had been developments in the libel suit which had shown who was lying. He compared the developments to the dropping of a bombshell. On the same day a report appeared that someone in the Department of Justice had issued a statement saying that the grand jury proceedings in New York were at a stalemate and that the Hiss-Chambers inquiry was about to be dropped. I promptly called Mr. Campbell, who told me to pay no attention to that statement and assured me that there would be an announcement very shortly.

On December third, on the very day I wrote the letter to Alger Hiss describing my visit to Judge Patterson, the Department of Justice announced that new evidence had been produced which would be laid before the New York grand jury. That same evening, I got a call from Frank Johnstone at the office of the Federal Bureau of Investigation in Baltimore, who said that he wanted to interview Mr. Hiss in Baltimore on the following day. I reached Alger at midnight, and he agreed to come to Baltimore immediately. The following morning he arrived, and we went to the FBI office and remained nearly all day, during the course of which he was served with a subpoena to appear before the grand jury in New York.

During the long interview with Mr. Johnstone, a number of questions were asked about the typewriter. Some of those questions related directly to whether any copies of State Department documents had ever been made by Priscilla Hiss. Alger denied that there was any possibility of this. At the end of the interview, Alger signed in my presence a statement, from which I quote the following:

> During the period from 1936 to some time after 1938, we had a typewriter in our home in Washington. This was an oldfashioned [sic] machine, possibly an Underwood, but I am not at all certain of the make. Mrs. Hiss, who was not a typist, used this machine somewhat as an amateur typist, but I never recall having used it. Possible samples of Mrs. Hiss' typing on this machine are in existence, but I have not located any to date, but will endeavor to do so. Mrs. Hiss disposed of this typewriter to either a secondhand typewriter concern, or a secondhand dealer in Washington, D.C., some time subsequent to 1938, exact date or place unknown. The whereabouts of this typewriter is presently unknown to me.

I remember that while we were talking about the typewriter I said that we were extremely anxious to locate it, since we were confident that we could then demonstrate that the papers which Chambers had produced in my office had not been typed by Priscilla Hiss. Of course, if it turned out that they had been written on that typewriter, then Alger would indeed be in serious trouble, and my recollection is that I said so and that Alger did not demur to this.

The following morning I ran into William Curran, then Baltimore's leading criminal lawyer, who said, "I thought there was something in the Hiss case, but this business about the pumpkin has reduced the whole thing to a farce." I had no idea what he was talking about, so I immediately bought a newspaper and learned, to my astonishment, that Chambers, in the presence of members of the staff of the Thomas committee, had opened a pumpkin on his farm from which he had produced microfilm which contained photographs of secret State Department documents which he said Alger Hiss had handed over to him.

The circumstances which led up to this deliberately sensational scenario have been the subject of a number of accounts. After reading them all, I think it is reasonably clear that Chambers had become convinced that the Department of Justice intended to suppress the papers which had been turned over to Mr. Campbell in my office. Through a lawyer named Vazzano, he dropped a hint to the chief investigator for the Thomas committee that he had some valuable information. On December first the investigator came to the Chambers farm. Chambers told him that he had produced some documentary evidence at the Baltimore deposition but wasn't allowed to talk about it. That same night, after a meeting of the Thomas committee, Nixon signed a subpoena and the investigator was instructed to serve it on the following day.

In the meantime, Chambers went out into the garden on his farm, opened a pumpkin which was lying there, and inserted some microfilm which he had withheld when he delivered the typewritten papers to Cleveland on November 16. When the Thomas committee, accompanied by a cameraman, arrived at ten o'clock at night on December 2 with the subpoena, Chambers took them into the garden and solemnly went through the farce of opening the pumpkin in their presence and extracting the films. At the same time he turned over to them a set of photostatic copies of the typewritten papers which had been produced at the deposition. The next day the committee investigators prepared press releases, accompanied by photographs of the pumpkin, which were made available to the media for publication on December 4. The resulting nationwide publicity must have exceeded even Chambers' wildest hopes.

A day or two later, a telephone call came in from McLean in New York. He said that among some papers which had been handed to him by Priscilla Hiss back in October he had found two documents which had been typed by her in 1933. Our experts, who had been employed to look at the papers which had been produced at the deposition, announced that the newly discovered papers were undoubtedly written on the same typewriter—a Woodstock—and probably by the same typist. When I heard this, I felt certain that Alger Hiss would be indicted.

However, the FBI agents knew nothing about this and were still searching for the typewriter. Apparently they had interviewed every second-hand dealer in the District of Columbia without success. Finally, they located some other papers which Priscilla Hiss had typed on her Woodstock and compared them with the typewritten papers which Chambers had produced at the deposition on November 17. Independently they reached the same conclusion that our experts had reached, and on December 14 they reported this to the Department of Justice. Mr. Campbell, who up until that moment had planned to ask the New York grand jury to indict Chambers for perjury, turned completely around and asked for an indictment of Alger.

On December 15, 1948, the last day of the term of the New York grand jury, Alger Hiss was indicted on two counts. First, that he had lied on December 15, when he denied under oath that either he or Priscilla in his presence had ever turned over to Chambers any State Department documents; and, second, that he had lied when he denied having seen Chambers between January 1, 1937, and the Thomas committee hearing in 1948.

Thereafter my role became a very subsidiary one in the unfolding Hiss-Chambers drama. While the indictment did not technically abort the libel suit, it was perfectly clear that it would be impossible to try the libel suit until the criminal trial had been disposed of. That was now the responsibility of Ed McLean and Lloyd Stryker, who had both agreed to represent Alger at the New York trial.

The case came on for trial in New York, and the prosecutor, Thomas Murphy, made the cardinal error of saying that the central question in the case was whether Chambers or Hiss was telling the truth. Stryker seized upon this and devoted his entire case to showing that Chambers had repeatedly lied throughout his life, whereas Hiss had a spotless reputation for integrity and reliability. Stryker played down the importance of the typewritten papers, which he conceded had been written on the Hiss Woodstock. These tactics were successful in persuading four jurors that there was a reasonable doubt as to Alger's guilt, and the jury hung.

At the second trial a Boston lawyer named Claude Cross succeeded Stryker as the leading counsel. Our office continued to run various errands at his request, and I agreed to appear as a witness for Alger. My testimony related primarily to my past associations with Alger and was essentially that of a character witness. This time Murphy pitched his case primarily on the typewritten documents which had been introduced at the Baltimore deposition. The jury voted unanimously for conviction. There followed an appeal to the Court of Appeals for the Second Circuit, which affirmed the conviction (185 F.2d 822), and a petition for certiorari was denied. Judges Augustus Hand, Swan, and Chase sat on the panel of the Second Circuit which affirmed the Hiss conviction. A more respected group could not have been found in the federal judicial system, and it was, accordingly, with some astonishment that I read the remarkable statement which appeared in the first volume of Justice William O. Douglas's autobiography: "In my view no court at any time could possibly have sustained this conviction."

On March 22, 1951, Alger Hiss went to prison. At that time he was represented by Chester T. Lane, who wrote to me suggesting that I request that the libel suit be dismissed without prejudice, and Cleveland responded by moving that the case be dismissed with prejudice for want of prosecution. Judge Chesnut heard the matter in chambers and, after consideration, entered an order on April 6, 1951, dismissing the case with prejudice. That was the end of the Hiss-Chambers libel suit.

Aftermath

One curious by-product of my connection with Alger Hiss was an invitation to deliver the Godkin Lectures at Harvard University. I declined the honor on the ground that the Hiss case had preempted the time which I would need to prepare lectures worthy of the occasion. I could truthfully have added that I lacked the scholarly qualifications to prepare them. To me it still seems that my selection was an emotional reaction of the Harvard community to the charges against Hiss rather than a recognition of intellectual achievement on my part.

Otherwise, the events of August 1948 marked a watershed in my career. Up to that time the road to national prominence in some capacity appeared to be open. To the strong backing of Judge Patterson and General Clay had now been added the friendship and support of Jim Conant. Thus, I found myself being looked over by the trustees of Columbia University, who were searching for a new president of that institution. I do not mean to suggest that their choice of General Eisenhower was a difficult one, but I was reliably informed that until he had definitely indicated that he was available, my name was very seriously considered. This explained a mysterious visit which I had from the chairman of the Board of Trustees of Columbia, who caught me at a hotel in New York City one morning and insisted that I lunch with him and several other Columbia trustees at the Downtown Club where they were ostensibly seeking my advice on some of their current problems. Later on, when the Board of Trustees of the Johns Hopkins University were looking for a new president, the chairman of that board himself told me that I had been strongly recommended by Jim Conant.

As the Hiss case began to attract more and more national attention, I noticed that I was no longer being bothered by efforts to persuade me to leave my law practice. The reason became quite clear when Tom Cabot, who had recently taken on a job for the State Department, asked me to go along with him and without consulting me submitted my name to the department for clearance. He was told that because of my connection with Alger Hiss, there might be a serious problem.

I think I can honestly say that I was not much concerned by Tom Cabot's report of his unsuccessful effort to obtain clearance for my appointment to a position that I had no intention of accepting. I was more concerned with the rapid fulfillment of the prophecy which Conant and Clark had made in September 1948 as to the effect which the Hiss case was likely to have on academic freedom. Shortly after the grand jury indicted Hiss, a highly respected Baltimore lawyer drafted a bill which was adopted by the Maryland legislature, making it a criminal offense to be a member of an organization which advocated the overthrow of the government of the United States by force or violence. The Ober Bill aroused considerable opposition in academic circles in Maryland.

As Frank Ober was a friend and distant relative of mine, I managed to stay out of that particular controversy, but thereafter things really began to heat up. In March of 1950 Senator Joe McCarthy made his famous speech at Wheeling, West Virginia, in which he announced that he intended to name a consultant of the State Department as "the top Russian spy in the country." Jim Conant asked me if I had any idea to whom McCarthy was referring. I told him that I had a rather definite idea that it was Owen Lattimore, who was at that time a director of the Page School of International Law at the Johns Hopkins University. I had been present at a meeting of a private club in Baltimore at which General "Al" Wedemeyer at my request had spoken about his mission to China. Professor Lattimore, who was present as a guest of one of his colleagues at Johns Hopkins, questioned Wedemeyer very sharply and after the meeting Wedemeyer asked me if Lattimore was a "Red."

Sure enough, on March 24, 1950, McCarthy appeared before a subcommittee of the Foreign Affairs Committee of the United States Senate and charged that Owen Lattimore was "the top Russian spy in the country and a former boss of Alger Hiss in a spy ring in the State Department." The Lattimore case then moved to the center of the national stage. While Lattimore succeeded in completely disproving McCarthy's charges, his belligerent attitude was so offensive to the members of the subcommittee that he ended up under indictment for perjury. He did manage to obtain a dismissal of that indictment without actual trial, but, to quote the Duke of Wellington, it was "the nearest run thing you ever saw in your life."

The indictment of Lattimore produced a profound reaction in academic circles. Even prior to that point there had been suggestions that witnesses called before congressional committees investigating subversive activities should take the shelter of the Fifth Amendment. I found these suggestions very alarming. During the month of December 1952, some junior members of the Rutgers faculty were called to testify before a congressional committee investigating subversive activities and refused to answer questions, invoking the Fifth Amendment. Their dismissal from the Rutgers faculty produced widespread protests that the exercise of a constitutional right should not be made the basis for dismissing professors.

It seemed to me that the academic profession was headed for a confrontation which could do untold harm to institutions such as Harvard, and acting on my own initiative, without consulting the other members of the Corporation, I wrote a letter to Professor Zechariah Chafee, who was then widely recognized as one of the foremost champions of civil liberties in the United States. I pointed out what seemed to me to be the dangers involved in what looked like a coming confrontation and urged him to take the lead in trying to dissuade the members of the Harvard faculty from invoking the Fifth Amendment. I suggested that in almost every case there was no probability that a candid statement of prior connections with the Communist party would result in a criminal prosecution of the witness and that the use of the amendment solely to avoid naming names seemed to me to be unjustified.

Professor Chafee replied that he had consulted Arthur Sutherland on this subject and that they had both agreed to make a statement urging the faculty not to take the Fifth Amendment. On January 13, 1953, the *Harvard Crimson* published the Chafee-Sutherland statement on the Fifth Amendment. To my great gratification, it followed in general outline the views which I had expressed in my letter to Professor Chafee. As far as I could tell, it was generally regarded by the faculty as a definitive statement.

In the meantime, Conant had called a meeting of the faculty to discuss the announced intention of a committee of the House of Representatives known as the Velde committee to investigate the loyalty of teachers in all educational institutions which received federal funds. At the conclusion of that meeting, he appointed a faculty advisory committee to assist the Corporation in deciding how to deal with questions which might arise in connection with such an investigation of Harvard University.

Late in December 1952 Conant had been told that President Eisenhower wished to nominate him as ambassador to Bonn and as United States representative on the Allied Control Commission for Germany. This was still nominally the governing body of the city of Berlin, although that commission had not really functioned since 1948, when the Russians broke up the quadripartite government of Berlin and established complete unilateral control of their sector of that city. Jim and Patty Conant were both deeply interested in the opportunity to help guide West Germany into the path of democracy, and so he consented.

Early in January 1953 he announced his intention to resign as president of Harvard University. At his suggestion the Corporation appointed an administrative committee under the chairmanship of Paul Buck to perform the duties of the president. From that moment Charlie Coolidge, as senior fellow of the Corporation in the absence of the president, became the most influential member of that body. My own position, which had been enhanced by my relationship with Conant, was correspondingly diminished. That I had been of some influence in shaping Conant's views was definitely proven at the hearing on his nomination, where, as he wrote to me on February 4, 1953, the whole question of Communists at Harvard was "exhaustively explored." In his letter to me he said that he had generally followed my line in giving his testimony.

Judge Morris A. Soper, an outstanding federal judge, supported the view taken by Mr. Conant and went even further by suggesting that any member of a university faculty who took the Fifth Amendment thereby automatically forfeited his right to teach students. On February 28, 1953, Professor Arthur O. Lovejoy, a noted defender of civil rights, asserted that membership in the Communist party was evidence of unfitness for membership in a university faculty.

On February 26, 1953, Wendell H. Furry, an associate professor of physics at Harvard, was called before the Velde committee and declined to answer questions as to his membership in the Communist party on the ground that his answers would tend to incriminate him. On the same day I received a telephone call from Paul Buck, who said that I was the only member of the Corporation he had been able to reach; all others were on vacation. According to my distinct recollection, he said that he had taken part in a meeting of representatives of the Association of American Universities at which it had been agreed to recommend to the governing boards of each member university that any faculty member who invoked the Fifth Amendment be suspended from teaching with pay pending further investigation. I told Paul Buck that in my opinion no such action should be taken without the prior approval of the Corporation.

During the next few days, I was in frequent contact with Paul Buck and with Oscar Shaw. We agreed that the Faculty Advisory Committee must be consulted before any final action by the Corporation but that in the meantime Charlie Coolidge and I should interview Professor Furry as soon as Charlie got back from vacation.

On March 4, as I was greeting guests who arrived at my home for dinner, I received a telephone call from Joseph Alsop, a prominent journalist who was a member of the Harvard Board of Overseers. He demanded to know whether the Corporation proposed to take any action against Professor Furry. I informed him that the Corporation was considering that very question. He then gave me a long lecture on the evils of congressional investigations as they were presently being conducted. I suggested that I had some knowledge of that, since I had been responsible for representing the War Department at a number of such investigations. This seemed to irritate him, and he proceeded to harangue me until I told him that I couldn't listen any longer, as my guests were waiting for their dinner.

On Saturday afternoon, March 7, 1953, Charlie Coolidge and I had an interview with Professor Furry. During the course of that interview, Professor Furry volunteered the information that during the years 1943 and 1944 he had been asked by the FBI for information about candidates for employment in highly classified work and had falsely denied that they were members of the Communist party.

It so happened that the overseers were meeting shortly thereafter, and Charlie Coolidge and I appeared to report on our interview with Furry. We received the very definite impression that the overseers felt that no statement should be issued until the Corporation had concluded its investigation and Professor Furry had been given an opportunity to supplement his previous testimony before the Velde committee. A number of the overseers apparently felt that due process required further hearings by the Corporation to be conducted somewhat more formally and that findings of fact should be made. Moreover, some of the overseers expressed strong opposition to bringing pressure to bear on Professor Furry to name persons who had to his knowledge been members of the Communist party, although other overseers disagreed with equal vehemence.

On March 16 Charlie and I interviewed Furry again and subsequently met once more with the Faculty Advisory Committee. It became apparent that a majority of the Advisory Committee thought that invoking the Fifth Amendment could not be considered to be grave misconduct warranting dismissal of a tenured professor from the faculty of the university, and that while the false statements which Furry had confessed to making to the FBI in 1943 and 1944 did amount to grave misconduct, his dismissal was not necessarily required in view of the passage of nine years and the voluntary disclosure by him of these incidents.

On March 24 the Association of American Universities issued a statement which included the assertion that "invocation of the Fifth Amendment places upon a professor a heavy burden of proof of his fitness to hold a teaching position and lays upon his university an obligation to reexamine his qualifications for membership in its society." The significance of this statement was enhanced by the fact that it bore the signature of Paul Buck as chairman of the Administrative Committee of Harvard University.

On March 26, Leon J. Kamin, a teaching fellow and research assistant in the Department of Social Relations, invoked the Fifth Amendment before the Jenner committee. On the same day Mrs. Helen Dean Markham, an associate in anatomy at the Harvard Medical School with the rank of assistant professor, also invoked the Fifth Amendment before the Jenner committee.

On April 22 Charlie Coolidge sent a memorandum to the members of the Corporation dealing primarily with the case of Dr. Jacob Fine, who held a term appointment in the Medical School and was a member of the staff of the Brigham Hospital. Dr. Fine had taken the Fifth Amendment before the Velde committee, and when asked to appear before the Corporation had declined to do so and had submitted a long explanation of the reasons for his refusal to answer any further questions.

On April 23, 1953, Professor McGeorge Bundy wrote a long letter to Paul Buck in which he undertook to discuss all of the issues raised by the invocation of the Fifth Amendment by members of the Harvard faculty. This very thoughtful letter was widely circulated, and Paul Buck advised the Corporation that it was generally regarded as an accurate expression of the views of a majority of the faculty. In it Professor Bundy conceded that if a member of the faculty who had invoked the Fifth Amendment refused to be candid with the Corporation and to deny present membership in the Communist party, dismissal might be an appropriate remedy; if, on the other hand, he dealt candidly with the Corporation and made it clear that he was no longer under Communist domination, then, in Professor Bundy's opinion, dismissal would not be warranted. He went on to say that "without supposing that there will be no exceptions, I offer the opinion that Harvard should consider the use of the Fifth Amendment in cases such as those which have lately occurred as a serious obstacle to appointment or reappointment to the University."

On April 24 Charlie Coolidge prepared a draft decision in the case of Professor Furry. From this it seems clear that the Corporation was largely in agreement with Professor Bundy as to the proper treatment of faculty members who had taken the Fifth Amendment but was still undecided as to whether Professor Furry's false statements to the FBI in 1943 and 1944 required his removal from the faculty in the light of his unwillingness to testify as to all his past connections with the Communist party.

At about this time, at the suggestion of Ed Mason, then Dean of the graduate school of public administration and one of the sagest minds on the faculty, which we were told had been approved by Professor Furry, the Corporation decided to notify the FBI of the incidents which had taken place in 1943 and 1944.

Matters now began to move rapidly. On May 4 the Corporation met and considered a memorandum from Paul Buck suggesting that Furry be reprimanded and that the faculty be asked for an opinion as to whether his conduct required that he forfeit "his full and equal participation in the deliberations of the faculty and the Department of Physics." The members of the Corporation decided that it was their responsibility and not that of the faculty to make this decision and, after discussion, tentatively decided to remove Professor Furry because of grave misconduct in lying to the FBI and thereafter failing to testify candidly to the congressional committee. They also decided tentatively to remove Mr. Kamin.

At this point a new question was raised by Professors Purcell and Ramsey. They contended that at the first meeting which Charlie Coolidge and I had with Professor Furry, the professor had been assured that the information which he gave us about his false statements to the FBI in 1943 and 1944 would be kept confidential.

On May 11 a meeting was held of the Faculty Advisory Committee; all of the members except George Berry were present. At that meeting the members of the Faculty Advisory Committee in attendance strongly urged that Professor Furry not be removed.

That evening the Corporation met with the Board of Overseers at dinner. Charlie Coolidge outlined the four pending cases and undertook to summarize all of the relevant arguments. It soon became apparent that quite a few members of the Board of Overseers felt very strongly that Professor Furry should not be dismissed and that most of those in attendance would not be upset if the Corporation decided to retain him. On the following day I wrote a letter to Charlie Coolidge, in which I said:

> After yesterday's meetings it is quite clear to me that the Corporation cannot dismiss Professor Furry. Whatever we may think, we cannot act effectively if after full discussion the vast majority of the faculty, headed by the Provost, would regard our action as unfair and unjust. This is particularly true when they would be supported by a substantial number of the Board of Overseers.
>
> If in Furry's case we are to ignore conduct so serious as that to which he admits, then I think we can hardly take a stern position in the cases of Mr. Kamin and Mrs. Markham. The result must be that we take no action against any of them.

The following day Charlie Coolidge prepared a final draft of a statement to be issued by the Corporation in regard to the Furry, Kamin, and Markham cases. Furry's false statements in 1943 and 1944 were held to be grave misconduct, but in view of his volunteering this information to the Corporation, probation for a period of three years was found to be more appropriate than dismissal from the faculty. His taking the Fifth Amendment before the Velde committee was regarded as misconduct but not grave misconduct, in view of the fact that he had been candid with the Corporation and had specifically stated under oath that he had not been a member of the Communist party since 1951 and had never attempted to indoctrinate his students. In the cases of Kamin and Markham, their taking the Fifth Amendment was held not to be grave misconduct, and no further action against them was deemed to be appropriate. With the approval of the members of the Corporation, this statement was submitted to the Faculty Advisory Committee and with the committee's endorsement was presented to a full faculty meeting on May 19, where it was greeted with cheers.

In the meantime, Dr. Fine was given a hearing before the members of the Corporation, at which he presented a long statement explaining his reasons for refusing to answer any questions about his connections with the Communist party. Charlie Coolidge then prepared a preliminary draft of a statement finding Dr. Fine guilty of grave misconduct and stating that he would not be reappointed when his term expired on June 30. According to my recollection, George Berry presented a draft of this statement to Dr. Fine, who then changed his mind and stated that he had never been a member of the Communist party, had never attended any secret political meetings or advocated the overthrow of the government by violence, and had no hesitancy in taking in good conscience the teacher's oath. Accordingly, on June 4, the trustees of the Peter Bent Brigham Hospital and the Harvard Corporation issued a joint news release stating that the two governing boards had decided to take no action against Dr. Fine.

Both before and after the Jenner committee hearing, Mrs. Markham issued press releases in which she made statements implying that the Harvard Corporation approved her refusal to testify. On June 17, Herbert A. Philbrick testified under oath before the Jenner committee that Mrs. Markham and her husband had been members of the Communist party in 1947. This testimony was denied in a press release by Mrs. Markham and her husband.

On July 16, after consulting the Faculty Advisory Committee, the Corporation reopened her case and gave her an opportunity to be heard, but in the meantime suspended her with pay until further order. This provoked an extensive correspondence between Charlie Coolidge and Erwin Griswold, who protested this action very strongly. On September 1, 1953, the Corporation issued a news release stating that Mrs. Markham had been given a year's notice that she would not be reappointed and that in the meantime her suspension was terminated.

Nathan M. Pusey took office as president of Harvard University on September 1, 1953. At about the same time, Senator Joseph McCarthy of Wisconsin, as chairman of the Senate Committee on Governmental Operations, embarked on an attempt to demonstrate that the army, and particularly the Fort Monmouth installation of the Signal Corps, had been infiltrated by the Communist party. This was the investigation which ultimately led to his censure by his senatorial colleagues. However, when he began this investigation, he was still riding high and commanded widespread support from the public and the news media.

Senator McCarthy had an old political score to settle with Mr. Pusey, who, as president of Lawrence College in Appleton, Wisconsin, had opposed his reelection to the Senate in 1950. To those familiar with the techniques of the junior senator from Wisconsin, it was no surprise that he attempted to drag Mr. Pusey and Harvard into his investigation of the army. This he did by summoning Professor Furry and Mr. Kamin to testify at a secret session of his committee held on November 6, 1953. According to a broadcast by Cedric Foster, Mr. Pusey received a telegram from Senator McCarthy on that date announcing that Professor Furry had been called before his committee and had refused to answer questions, invoking the protection of the Fifth Amendment. According to the broadcast, Senator McCarthy stated that Furry had refused to answer these questions: "Did you ever turn over to the Communists secret data on the radar project during the war while working for the United States Signal Corps?" "Did you know there were Communists working on that project while you were there?" "Did you ever attend Communist meetings and did you ever indoctrinate Harvard students in the Marxist philosophy?" McCarthy gave a copy of this telegram to the press, stating that the situation at Harvard University was "a mess" and declaring that he couldn't understand how any father or mother would wish to send a son or daughter to Harvard University, "where they would be open to indoctrination in Communist philosophy."

According to Foster, Mr. Pusey replied to this telegram with a telegram of his own:

> My information is that Dr. Furry has not been connected with the Communist party in recent years. My information is also that Dr. Furry has never given secret material to unauthorized persons, nor has he sought to indoctrinate students. Since there are conflicting reports concerning what Dr. Furry said before your Committee at the private session . . . and since you have not made the complete testimony public . . . I am quite unable to comment on the significance of his latest refusal to answer questions, nor can I say whether any further action will be taken by us concerning Dr. Furry.
>
> Harvard University is unalterably opposed to Communism. It is dedicated to free inquiries by free men. I am in full agreement with the opinion publicly stated by my predecessor, Dr. Conant, and the Harvard Corporation . . . that a member of the Communist party is not fit to be on the faculty, because he has not the necessary independence of thought and judgment. I am not aware that there is any person among the three thousand members of the Harvard faculty who is a member of the Communist party. We deplore the use of the Fifth Amendment but we do not regard the use of the Constitutional safeguard as a confession of guilt.

Senator McCarthy replied to Mr. Pusey in a telegram dated November 9, which is so characteristic that it is worth quoting in full:

Dr. Nathan Pusey, Pres-

Harvard University Cambridge Mass-

If a witness before a congressional committee and under oath is asked whether he is a member of the Communist party and he refuses to answer and tells the committee that a truthful answer would tend to incriminate him, this can mean only one thing, merely he is a Communist because if he were not a Communist the truth could not in any conceivable manner incriminate him. Even the most soft-headed and fuzzy minded cannot help but realize that a witness refusal to answer whether or not he is a Communist on the ground that his answer would tend to incriminate him is the most positive proof obtainable that the witness is a Communist. You and the Harvard Corporation can of course continue to keep Fifth Amendment Communists teaching the sons and daughters of America. However, Harvard will learn how reprehensible and unAmerican the mothers and fathers of America consider this attitude. Your statement that "Harvard is unalterably opposed to Communism. It is dedicated to free inquiry by free men" is ludicrous in the extreme when in the next breath you indicate that you still as of today are retaining as a teacher a man who refuses to state under oath whether he has given secret radar material to members of the Communist party and also refuses to state whether he has sought to indoctrinate his students in the Communist philosophy. You state that your information is that Furry never gave secret material to Communists or sought to indoctrinate his students in Communism. Will you please inform me as to where you received this information. If you got it from Furry prior to his appearance before our committee, then he was guilty of perjury in that he testified under oath that you never questioned him in regard to Communist activities and expressed no interest whatsoever in whether or not he was a member of the Communist party-

Joe McCarthy USS-

Senator McCarthy's crusade against Harvard University and its new president reached a climax on January 15, 1954, when he staged a hearing in Boston before the television cameras, at which Leon J. Kamin and Wendell H. Furry were called as witnesses. The transcript of the proceedings was immediately published. From this it appeared that although both witnesses had waived their privilege under the Fifth Amendment, both of them had refused to identify persons whom they had known as Communists when they were members of the party. They persisted in this refusal in the face of Senator McCarthy's threats to have them cited for contempt.

The storm of publicity which followed produced strong reactions among all elements of the Harvard community. On January 20, I wrote a memorandum stating my views as follows:

1. Do nothing for the present—this would exclude threats to Furry, although he should, in fairness, understand that the Corporation cannot commit itself to retaining him if he is convicted of contempt.

2. If he is indicted, grant him a leave of absence with pay.

3. If he is convicted, let us make our decision in the light of circumstances as they then appear.

4. Let Kamin's appointment expire on January 29.

According to my recollection, after further discussion the Corporation determined to proceed in the manner I had suggested and asked me to communicate with President Lowell Reed of the Johns Hopkins University to find out exactly what Hopkins had done in connection with the Lattimore case.

On May 27, 1954, the Harvard Chapter of the American Association of University Professors issued an invitation to all members of the faculties of Harvard University to attend a ceremony at which citations were issued in appreciation of "the spirit, character, and courage of the Governors and Administrators of Harvard in dealing with the many challenges to the integrity of the University and its Faculties over the recent years."

On December 17, 1954, Professor Furry was indicted for contempt of the Senate. His colleagues in the physics department joined in forming a Furry Legal Aid Committee to raise funds for his defense. Furry succeeded in having the indictment against him dismissed on the ground that the questions asked of him were not within the proper scope of inquiry by the committee.

XIX ❖ How to Hold Russia at Bay

During the summer of 1950 we were once more vacationing in Randolph, New Hampshire, when the Cutters invited us to dine with them. The other guests were Tracy Voorhees and his wife. After dinner Ammi and I listened to Tracy, who as under secretary of the army had just returned from surveying the military situation in Western Europe. What he had found there he summed up in a quotation from General Alfred N. Guenther, who was then deputy chief of staff for plans and operations of the army. Guenther told Tracy's committee, "All the Russians need to march through to the channel is shoe leather."

Tracy said he was convinced that nothing was holding the Soviet Union back except the fact that the United States still had a monopoly of atomic weapons. The well-authenticated report of an explosion of an atomic weapon in Russia in the latter part of 1949 had made it clear that this monopoly would be short-lived. The three of us agreed on the need for a citizens' committee to press for action by the government to deal with this situation. We also agreed that the ideal chairman would be Jim Conant, and Cutter agreed to invite him to meet Tracy at dinner during the following week. Because I had to return to Baltimore, I could not attend that dinner, but Ammi informed me that Jim had been deeply impressed by Tracy's presentation. In his autobiography (*My Several Lives,* pp. 505–19) Jim has explained how that dinner led to the organization of the Committee on the Present Danger (not to be confused with a recently organized group which has appropriated the same name).

In October 1950 a meeting of the organizers of that committee was held in New York City. Conant, Voorhees, Cutter, and I were present, as was Judge Patterson. We proceeded to draft a letter to General Marshall, who by that time had become secretary of defense. Voorhees and I were appointed to present this draft to Bob Lovett, who had recently been named deputy secretary of defense, for his comment, with the request that he discuss it with General Marshall. This we did, and Mr. Lovett replied very promptly that the general would welcome the organization of such a committee. After considerable polishing, and with some editorial assistance from Robert E. Sherwood, the playwright, a letter was sent to

General Marshall on October 24, 1950, over Mr. Conant's signature and those of a group of prominent citizens.

Attached to this letter was a proposed statement of the committee's position which contained the following:

> In our view, the necessary supplement to the present atomic supremacy of the United States is an allied force in being in Western Europe sufficiently strong to furnish east of the Rhine effective resistance to military aggression. . . . The European members of the Atlantic alliance have expressed their willingness to supply the larger part of the required manpower and some of the required equipment, provided that the United States will undertake responsibility for procuring the rest of what is needed and will make a very substantial contribution of troops.
>
> To make such a contribution . . . the people of the United States . . . will have to maintain a very substantial U.S. ground force of several hundred thousand men, under arms in Europe for a long period. This would of course be in addition to the strength required for our strategic reserve in this country and our military obligations elsewhere in the world. We believe that such a program will probably require universal two year service of our young men, both to train a manpower pool should war come, and to make possible a rotation of personnel to maintain our requisite military strength.

General Marshall replied promptly to the letter, inviting all the members of the committee who could conveniently do so to meet with him on November 20 to discuss a possible public statement on the principles and purposes of the committee. However, Bob Lovett reported to Tracy Voorhees that the general seemed to be leaning in the direction of universal military training rather than a program for universal military service. The organizers of the committee discussed this and came to the conclusion that they should stand upon the position embodied in the statement accompanying the letter of October 24 to Secretary Marshall in favor of universal military service for two years. Although they were familiar with the arguments in favor of universal military training as a long-range policy, they could not see how the immediate manpower requirements of their program could be met unless training was followed by immediate service on active duty in the armed forces.

Judge Patterson was particularly emphatic in urging that the committee take a firm position. He pointed out that the report of the Compton commission advocating a program of universal military training had met with little favor. He personally believed that UMT was no answer to the real need, which was to eliminate the exemptions and deferments which characterized the existing selective service as administered by General Hershey. Furthermore, it would not prevent the calling into service of veterans of World War II which was then taking place as a result of the invasion of Korea.

The meeting in General Marshall's office was attended by Judge Patterson and Messrs. Bush, Clayton, Baxter, O'Brian, Wriston, Dodds, and Voorhees, all of whom had signed the letter. In addition, Howard C. Petersen, who had been assistant secretary of war under Judge Patterson and subsequently under secretary of war under Secretary Royall, Ammi Cutter, and I were present. General Marshall had with him Anna Rosenberg, recently appointed as assistant secretary of defense for manpower, and Felix Larkin, general counsel of the Defense Department, to whom had been assigned the duty of drafting the new legislation. A few days later, in a letter to Jim Conant (who had been unable to attend because of illness), I described the meeting in some detail:

> General Marshall opened the meeting by giving us a little lecture on the military situation in Korea. He made it clear to us that disaster had been avoided by "a gnat's nose" and then only because McArthur had put 35,000 untrained South Koreans into our own units. He said that the present situation along the border was very trying to the morale of our forces who were being attacked constantly from "prisoners' base" in Manchuria but that for the present nothing could be done about that. He could throw very little light on the probable intentions of the Chinese but indicated that the theory that they were not committed to a full scale intervention was still a tenable one.
>
> As soon as the General had finished his exposition (which lasted about fifteen minutes), Bob Patterson explained that it was the view of the signers of that letter that the most urgent problem was the supplying of "bodies for the line" and that we had reached the conclusion that the way to accomplish this was by the passage of legislation providing for two years' military service at the age of eighteen. He emphasized the fact that, in our judgment, there should be substantially no exemptions (other than complete physical incapacity) and that the issue should not be confused by the introduction of any long-range provision for "training" as distinct from "service." He said that a long-range training program would rouse opposition which would not be met by a simple proposal for universal military service to supply the manpower needed to meet the immediate peril.
>
> When Bob had finished, Wriston took over and expressed with considerable vigor the views of the educational world on the bad effects of the present system. He said that, as matters now stood, no educational administrator could begin to prepare a budget for next year. He added that the Trytten system of exempting high-standing students might bring intellectual achievement into disrepute and said that it was disliked and feared by practically every educator.
>
> General Marshall then launched into a long monologue. I think that he talked for nearly three-quarters of an hour. He said that the Defense Department was in the process of trying to make up its mind on the questions which had been raised by Judge Patterson. There was, of course, the immediate need for manpower which was urgent. He indicated that he was inclined to the view that this could be met by appropriate amendments to the Selective

Service Act and by lowering the draft age to eighteen. There was then the long-range problem as to which his primary concern was that we should find an enduring solution. . . .

During this long speech I could see Bob Patterson's wrath rising. When General Marshall had finished, Bob said, "Well, General, we will, of course, not go ahead with this project, if you don't want us to." General Marshall replied that he must have been misunderstood. The Defense Department had not agreed on a program, but he did not want to delay the organization of our committee which he knew would take time. Van Bush then broke in to ask the direct question whether it be helpful or harmful if our committee should come out publicly for universal military service at this time. General Marshall replied that even if the Department decided to ask for a more limited program, the fact that our committee had come out for the stronger program would help in the process of educating the public and the Congress. Bob Patterson then said that he would not be willing to advocate universal military service if the Department was going to come along afterwards and ask for some "watered down" program. He felt that under the circumstances our committee had better just mark time.

General Marshall said that it seemed to him that there was more than one way of accomplishing the objective on which we are all agreed. He asked Mrs. Anna Rosenberg what she thought, saying that she was his manpower expert. Mrs. Rosenberg replied that she was inclined to think that our committee was "on the right track."

Bob Patterson then said that any program which called merely for "training" would not meet the situation. There would have to be "service" and, in the opinion of our committee, it would be much simpler to stick to the basic issue and not confuse it with a long-range training program. General Marshall said that a program of universal military service might be simple but, in his opinion, it would not be enduring. He felt that we should try to find a solution that would outlast this emergency. Bob Patterson said that no solution which would permit prominent athletes to be excused from military service would satisfy him. He had recently called several such cases to the attention of the Surgeon General and had been brushed off with the usual "blah blah."

We then went to lunch where Van Bush opened up on them with both barrels. He told them that as a result of the meeting in General Marshall's office, our committee had come to a standstill and that it was not easy to get this sort of thing started again once it stopped. He said that we had been shocked and disheartened by the atmosphere of "defeatism" and "timidity" which seemed to us to pervade General Marshall's remarks.

They immediately fell over themselves to say that it had all been a terrible mistake. The fact was that they had not had time to talk this matter over with General Marshall and to prepare him properly for our conference. Mrs. Rosenberg said point blank that she was satisfied that the only possible solution for the present situation was along the lines of universal military service and that she felt confident that within the next few days she would get the commitment of General Marshall and Mr. Lovett to support that program.

Mr. Larkin then stated that he had already drafted legislation which would include the following:

1. Amendments to the Selective Service Act eliminating certain existing exemptions now applicable to the ages of nineteen to twenty-six.

2. An Amendment to the Selective Service Act calling every eighteen year old boy into service at the age of eighteen (or when he graduated from high school), with the understanding that for a limited period (perhaps six months) the boys would be in training and that their actual military service as such would not begin until the end of that time. In exceptional cases, e.g., medical students, military service might be postponed.

Larkin said that he felt that this program would, in effect, provide what our committee was urging. The members of the committee who were present agreed that this would be the case, provided that it was clearly understood that the training was to be followed by a period of service. They felt that if this was made perfectly clear, then our committee would be willing to go ahead.

At the end of the meeting it was agreed that a subcommittee would be appointed to discuss legislation with the officials of the Defense Department, and Bush, O'Brian, Voorhees, and I were requested to undertake this task. We accordingly met on December 1, 1950, with Mrs. Rosenberg and Marx Leva, both of whom were assistant secretaries of defense. At the end of the meeting it was decided that representatives of the committee would be given an opportunity to examine the bill which the department intended to introduce before it was sent up to the committees of Congress. It was decided to proceed with the organization of the committee and the completion and publication of a statement of position.

The statement of position was then rewritten and released for publication on December 12, 1950. On the subject of manpower, the committee said:

The time has come for a new concept that universal service in defense of our freedom is a privilege and an obligation of our young men. To accomplish this with the least interference with education, with business and professional careers, and with family life, this service should commence at the age of 18 or upon graduation from high school, whichever is later. Two years of such military service, including training, will be necessary, and the program should embrace radically broadened standards of fitness.

The statement of the Committee on the Present Danger received nationwide publicity, and by the time Congress reconvened in January 1951, support had come from influential quarters. On December 4, 1950, the Association of American Universities, representing the leading universities of the country, adopted a resolution advocating the induction of all males at age 18 upon completion of the twelfth grade, with no exemptions except for "such extreme physical, mental or moral disability as substantially to inhibit the possibility of useful employment." However, in order to attract sufficient support for this resolution, a proviso was added to the effect that after induction "a substantial number of properly qualified young men [should] be furloughed to colleges of their choice for further education in all areas of learning before completing their required mili-tary service."

On December 5, 1950, Dr. William C. Menninger, chief psychiatrist for the army during World War II, in an address to the White House Con-ference on Children and Youth, strongly urged that at age 18 all young men be inducted into military service. On January 10, 1951, the Associa-tion of American Colleges, which represented 650 institutions, adopted a declaration asserting that "all young men should share equitably the re-sponsibility of national defense" and recommending that the age for in-duction into military training and service be 19 except "when and as long as emergency manpower shortage requires a lower age."

Of particular significance was a private communication to President Truman bearing the signatures of twenty prominent citizens, members of a study group appointed by the Council on Foreign Relations. This group was headed by General Eisenhower, then president of Columbia Univer-sity, who had just been asked by President Truman to take charge of organizing the defense of Western Europe under the auspices of the North Atlantic Treaty Organization, which was then in process of forma-tion. At a meeting of this study group held on December 11, 1950, Gen-eral Eisenhower expressed the opinion that "what we need is universal military service (as distinguished from training, which adds no men)." He added that the Pentagon was looking for a system that would work over a long period of time but observed that "the trouble with that approach is that we are now dangling on a thread over the edge of a cliff." He then wrote out in his own hand a draft of a proposed letter to President Tru-man, to be signed by all members of the study group, in which he called for the production of additional military forces at maximum speed under "a system of universal military service at nominal pay."

The Department of Defense bill was presented to the committee on January 17, 1951. It contained no clear provision which permitted the call-ing of persons at age 18 without regard to exemptions or deferments per-mitted by existing statutes and executive regulations. The Committee on the Present Danger urged that this point be clarified. However, the drafts-men of the bill insisted that the right to induct all 18 year olds without regard to existing exemptions or deferments was implicit in the provision giving the president power to induct by age groups. They assured repre-sentatives of the Committee on the Present Danger that the spokesmen for the Department of Defense would make this clear in their testimony before the appropriate congressional committees. Judge Patterson had also read the Defense Department bill and wrote to Mrs. Rosenberg expressing his disappointment at those provisions which authorized the president to permit seventy-five thousand young men to go to college after induction and before service without any firm requirement that they should later complete their military service. He added:

> As to the reserve officers' programs, the men in them who will come out with officers' commissions will be far less competent to command than the men whom they are expected to command, the men who have taken the more rigorous service. The Army had that very experience in 1941.
>
> In the second place, a great part of the value of the universal military service and training program lies in the mere fact that it is "universal." A man who has been drafted will not complain much if he knows that all are being treated alike. But if he feels that soft berths are being created for a great many whose situation on the merits cannot be distinguished from his, it is offensive to his innate sense of justice.

However, as the hearings progressed, it became quite clear that the attempt of the Department of Defense to achieve universal training and service by indirection was going to fail. The members of the Armed Services Committee were under strong pressure from the public not to give the president power to induct 18 year olds. On the other hand, little if any attention was given by the Senate to the basic issue in which the Committee on the Present Danger was interested.

Meanwhile, powerful forces were mobilizing to preserve the existing exemptions and deferments. In particular, religious groups and many of the smaller liberal arts colleges protested any change in the status quo. When the House hearings were begun, General Hershey, whose testimony before the Senate committee had appeared to endorse the program outlined by General Marshall and Mrs. Rosenberg, changed his position. He submitted a plan for educational deferments which went even further than the Trytten recommendations in granting wholesale deferments to "students in a professional school of medicine, dentistry, veterinary medicine, osteopathy or optometry," as well as to all full-time graduate students seeking a graduate degree who were "currently meeting degree requirements." The plan also proposed that deferments be granted to undergraduates who had attained specified levels of standing and to high school graduates who had been admitted to college. The Vinson committee went out of its way to express approval of General Hershey's plan.

The only recognition given to the Defense Department's program as originally presented by General Marshall was to recommend a provision for the inauguration of an entirely separate program of military training at such time as the president or the Congress by concurrent resolution should eliminate the period of service for all persons who had not attained their nineteenth birthday. However, it was specifically provided that persons inducted for this training program should not be considered to be members of the armed services.

304 / Chapter XIX

On March 31, 1951, a directive was issued by General Hershey adopting the plan of student deferment which he had proposed to the Vinson committee. In a television interview Jim Conant denounced the Hershey directive, saying that it violated "the democratic principle of equality of sacrifice. The deferring of college students is to establish a pattern in which boys who can afford to continue their education are given special privileges. We do not believe the American people wish to set apart one group of young men. The demands of the emergency require that our youth be asked to serve in the armed forces."

On April 10 the bill passed the House with a provision expressly authorizing the president to defer "any or all categories of persons whose activity in study, research or medical, dental, veterinarian, optometric, osteopathic, scientific, pharmaceutical, chiropractic, chiropodial or other endeavors is found to be necessary to the maintenance of the national health, safety or interest."

On June 1, 1951, with the approval of Jim Conant, I sent a letter to the editor of the *Baltimore Sun,* in which I said:

> The Compton proposal for universal military training is obviously irrelevant to our current needs. At a time when veterans are daily being called from their desks and forced to abandon their families and their occupations in order to meet the man-power requirements of the nation, it seems irrelevant to discuss a post-crisis program of giving six months' military training under supervision of a predominantly civilian commission to boys who will not be called upon immediately for active military service. Yet the fact is that in a vain effort to save the Compton plan for universal military *training,* the Administration has sacrificed an unparalleled opportunity to obtain universal military *service.* In the resulting confusion, the lobbies which supported the Hershey proposal have won at least qualified endorsement for their discriminatory and undemocratic measure.
>
> Thus, we now find ourselves in the situation where in exchange for a promise to consider in future a program of universal military training which has no practical significance as far as the present struggle against communistic expansion is concerned, we have endorsed a system under which, aside from the unfortunate reservists, no one will be selected for military service except those too poor to afford to go to college, too stupid to stay there, or too lacking in initiative to avail themselves of some of the other manifold avenues by which military service can be avoided.

Judge Patterson wrote:

> I am glad to have a copy of the letter which you submitted to the *Baltimore Sun* and which I devoutly hope the editor saw fit to publish without deletions. It does show signs of indignation but no more than this fouled-up situation calls for. The letter is an able paper.

On June 6, 1951, the Universal Military Service and Training Act passed the Congress. There was no provision for universal military service, and the only provision for universal military training was for the creation at some future time of a National Security Training Corps and the establishment of a commission to report on how and when it should be put into operation. Such a commission was appointed and reported in December of 1951; in effect it adopted the 1947 findings of the Compton commission. The Department of Defense then introduced a bill seeking to carry out the recommendations of the commission by establishing a limited program of universal military training entirely separate and apart from service in the armed forces. Since the bill made no provision for military service, the Committee on the Present Danger did not endorse it. The bill never came to a vote and Mrs. Rosenberg made it clear to representatives of the Committee on the Present Danger that the Department of Defense intended to do nothing further.

XX ❧ The Pusey Years at Harvard

What I have written in the immediately preceding chapters of this book should have made clear that in the early 1950s the presidency of Harvard University was bound to be something of a storm center. The rising antagonism between the Soviet Union and the West was unleashing emotions which disturbed the tranquility which the academic world had hoped would follow the cessation of hostilities in 1945. As a result, the new president of Harvard soon found himself faced with some nasty problems.

I played a very minor role in the selection of Nathan M. Pusey as successor to Jim Conant. I was assigned the task of interviewing several leading members of the faculty, notably John Finley and George Kistia-kowsky. Both of them said that the faculty wanted Paul Buck. So far as Paul Buck was concerned, it seemed to me to be the old story. The faculty knew him and wanted to take no risks. Under Conant he had been the perfect number two man who knew just how to deal with them once the essential policy decisions had been made by someone else but was quite incapable of making those decisions himself. His vacillation in the Furry case was a perfect illustration of what happens when such a man is chosen to take the lead.

When Pusey was suggested, I remembered that Ernst Mahler had been a trustee of Lawrence College, and I asked for his opinion. He said that Pusey had done a fine job at Lawrence but he doubted whether he was quite big enough for Harvard. He seemed to feel that Nate had a stubborn streak which made him reluctant to follow the advice of his trustees. I reported this conversation to my colleagues, who had in the meantime gotten high praise of Pusey from other sources.

Indeed, during the early years of his presidency, Nate handled some very thorny problems with much skill. I have already dealt at length with the Furry problem. In the case of the Arnold Arboretum also he inherited a nasty situation, and here again he conducted himself in such a way as to win praise from the Harvard faculty. As the Arboretum matter attracted wide attention among horticulturists all over the country and resulted in a lawsuit in which I was called to testify, a brief statement of the controversy seems to be called for.

On May 3, 1948, shortly after my election to the Harvard Corporation, Jim Conant brought up the subject of the so-called Bailey Plan for the coordination of Harvard's botanical activities. He stated that a report presenting that plan had been given general approval by the Corporation on January 7, 1946, at which time the Corporation was told that a contribution of one million dollars from the unrestricted endowment of the university would be required in order to put the plan into effect. He said that it was something of an academic miracle to find all the Harvard botanists in agreement on so comprehensive a proposal and that he proposed to move ahead as rapidly as possible.

The subject came up again at meetings of the Corporation held on June 1 and June 9, 1948, when further steps to implement the plan were approved. To the best of my recollection, there was no suggestion then that any opposition to the plan had developed, although Jim did say that we should keep our fingers crossed, in view of the contentious nature of botanists.

My first indication that dissension had begun to develop came sometime during the year 1949, when Grenville Clark advised me that he had been consulted by some members of the Overseers Visiting Committee for the Arnold Arboretum who were unhappy about the Bailey Plan. He said that they felt (and he was inclined to agree) that the plan was designed to further the interests of scientific botany rather than horticulture. As I remember it, he said that he had spoken to Jim Conant about it but that Jim had a blind spot as far as the art of horticulture was concerned. Clark said that there were quite a number of very influential people who were opposed to the Bailey Plan and that it looked as though we were headed for trouble.

Shortly thereafter, Professor Oakes Ames, a retired director of the Arnold Arboretum, in a pamphlet entitled "The Arnold Arboretum and Other Botanical Institutions," published a broad attack on the Bailey Plan. This pamphlet was given wide circulation and was accompanied by a letter dated January 17, 1950, signed by T. W. Reynolds, a Boston lawyer, stating that he agreed with Professor Ames's contention that the Bailey Plan involved serious breaches of trust. Professors Mangelsdorf and Bailey thereupon drafted a sharp reply in the form of a letter to Reynolds under date of January 31, 1950.

During the summer of 1950, some members of the visiting committee, acting at the suggestion of Grenville Clark, employed J. W. Farley of the law firm of Herrick, Smith, Donald, Farley and Ketcham to prepare a report on the legal validity of the Bailey Plan. Farley prepared what was called a preliminary draft of such a report, which was delivered to the visiting committee on September 29 and by the committee transmitted to the Corporation for consideration at its meeting on October 2, 1950. On that day the Corporation again voted to defer proceeding with the central botanical building pending a further review of the whole project, including the legal questions raised by the Farley report. At its meeting held the following week, on October 9, 1950, the Board of Overseers referred the entire matter to its Coordinating Committee on Biological Sciences, the new chairman of which was Laird Bell of Chicago, a distinguished lawyer who was chairman of the Board of Trustees of the University of Chicago.

Shortly thereafter, Grenville Clark resigned from the Corporation. However, he did not give up his opposition to the Bailey Plan; on the contrary, he proceeded with his usual tenacity to prepare for a long fight. His first step was to persuade the visiting committee to employ Farley and Robert G. Dodge to follow up on the 1950 Farley draft report by preparing a final report, which they submitted on March 2, 1952. In that report they stated that they had reached the conclusion that carrying out the Bailey Plan would involve the Corporation in various breaches of trust. In particular, they asserted that the proposed removal of the greater part of the library and herbarium from Jamaica Plain to Cambridge would not be compatible with the purposes of the indenture creating the trust for the Arnold Arboretum.

At this point it became clear that the Corporation would have to choose between three possible courses of action:

1. To go ahead with the construction of the central botanical building at Cambridge and transfer to that location the greater part of the books and specimens previously housed at Jamaica Plain, in the full realization that this action would be challenged in the courts;
2. To ask the court for a ruling as to the propriety of the proposed transfer; or
3. To abandon the Bailey Plan altogether.

Jim Conant strongly recommended that we proceed with the Bailey Plan. He was opposed to the idea of petitioning the court because of the delay and expense which would be involved. Because of increasing construction costs, delays already experienced had proven to be costly, and the resulting uncertainty had created morale problems among the faculty engaged in botanical activities.

After thorough discussion, all the members of the Corporation felt that they should accept Jim's firmly expressed conclusion that the proposed transfer would in the long run be in the best interests of the Arnold Arboretum. Accordingly, Oscar Shaw of the firm of Ropes & Gray was asked to study the entire file and to give the Corporation the benefit of his advice. After careful study, Shaw advised that the proposed transfer would, in his opinion, be lawful, provided that the Corporation determined that the proposed transfer of the books and specimens from Jamaica Plain to Cambridge would in the long run be in the best interests of the Arboretum.

Armed with Shaw's opinion, Jim then conferred with Laird Bell, who had been following developments in this matter on behalf of the coordinating committee. According to my distinct recollection, Jim reported to the Corporation that Mr. Bell had assured him that the coordinating committee was prepared to recommend that the Corporation proceed with the proposed transfer.

Accordingly, on October 14, 1952, a resolution prepared by Oscar Shaw was submitted to the coordinating committee recommending that the Corporation proceed as promptly as possible with the construction of the central botanical building at Cambridge and the transfer to that building of the greater part of the library and herbarium previously housed at Jamaica Plain. While the coordinating committee was considering this resolution, Grenville Clark sent a letter to Jim Conant which was read to the Corporation at a meeting on January 5, 1953. Clark enclosed memoranda prepared by the director of the Bailey Hortorium at Cornell University and by Professor Slate of the faculty of that university. In the light of these memoranda, the Corporation determined that a committee consisting of Messrs. Conant, Marbury, and Kane should consult with three eminent horticulturists, each of whom was asked whether the proposed transfer was "the best way of carrying out the terms of the trust." The committee met with these gentlemen in New York City, and each of them answered this question in the affirmative. However, according to my recollection, the interviews were more or less a formality, intended, as the Supreme Judicial Court of Massachusetts subsequently noted, primarily to demonstrate that "there was professional support outside the university for the decision of the Corporation."

On January 12, 1953, the Board of Overseers of Harvard University accepted the report of the coordinating committee and unanimously recommended that the Corporation proceed with the construction and with the transfer. On January 19, 1953, the Corporation adopted a resolution to that effect, and during the succeeding two years, the construction of the building was completed and the transfer of the books and specimens took place.

In the meantime, Grenville Clark organized a committee and proceeded to raise the funds necessary to carry on the fight in the courts of Massachusetts. Eventually, permission was given to bring suit in the name of the attorney general, and after prolonged litigation, the suit was dismissed by a vote of three to two in the Supreme Judicial Court of Massachusetts.

Grenville Clark's role in this prolonged controversy was much resented by Jim Conant. As a result, a long friendship came to an end. When in 1953 Jim resigned the presidency of Harvard to become ambassador to West Germany and high commissioner for the United States in Berlin, I found myself in the position of being the only member of the Corporation who continued to be on speaking terms with Mr. Clark. I remember meeting him at the Somerset Club and having a conversation in which we agreed to disagree about the Arboretum but to continue what had been a warm relationship ever since he had enlisted me in the fight against President Roosevelt's court-packing plan in the summer of 1937.

Whether the Arboretum suffered as a result of that litigation is at present not clear to me, but that the outcome was satisfactory to the faculty I have no doubt.

For some years after that, affairs at Harvard seemed to go quite smoothly, and I found my connection one of almost unalloyed satisfaction. Nate Pusey soon persuaded the Corporation to make sharp increases in the level of faculty compensation, to the point where the losses which had resulted from the inflation which accompanied and followed World War II were substantially rectified; he successfully planned and helped conduct the largest fund-raising campaign that any American university had ever undertaken; he was very successful in his dealings with the alumni and in organizing alumni relations; he was a good judge of people and proved to be very successful in selecting good people for key positions in the university; and, altogether, he illustrated the remark of a prominent Yale alumnus that the president of a university should always remember that he is alma mater's husband.

One of the great privileges which I enjoyed in the years I served on the Corporation was to dine frequently at the Society of Fellows. So far as I could tell, that organization was the intellectual heart of the university, and I came to know some of the most distinguished members of the faculty. Some of them said that in their dealings with Nate, they found that he did not ask as good questions as had Jim Conant. In general, however, I think it is fair to say that those with whom I talked were quite satisfied with his performance as president.

The relationship which Natalie and I had with the Conants had been very close. Jim and I seemed to react much the same way to the problems which came before the Corporation, and although I was almost totally lacking in knowledge of physics, chemistry, or biology, not to mention the more esoteric sciences, I found his analysis of the educational problems which he was attempting to solve quite easy to follow, and I read with profit the many books and articles which he had written on a variety of subjects. He seemed to think it worthwhile for me to participate in his discussions with people like Edwin Cohn and Robert Oppenheimer, although I was primarily a listener and observer who seldom ventured to hazard any remark on the topics under discussion. As for Patty Conant, both Natalie and I enjoyed every moment of her company. Indeed, to Natalie she was almost an idol, and their merry laughter when they were together was a joy to hear. The days we spent in the company of the Conants in Cambridge and later in Bonn and Berlin were red-letter days for both of us.

Under the circumstances it would not have been surprising if the arrival of the Puseys at 17 Quincy Street had proven to be something of a letdown, but Nate and Anne were fine people in whose company we took real pleasure. The fact that they were both active Episcopalians was a source of great satisfaction to Natalie, and I found that in most matters Nate reacted in what seemed to me to be just the proper way. I did observe that he was a little less skillful than Jim Conant in making other people feel that their views had been understood and respected, and once or twice I was reminded of what Ernst Mahler had said about him.

How much help I really was to him, I do not know. I do remember that I was able on at least one occasion to be of some assistance. I refer to the time when the long-standing rule against the use of Harvard Memorial Church for a Jewish wedding was challenged. This stirred up quite a little protest from some elements in the Harvard community, which I believe I helped to mollify by a statement which I prepared for the Corporation to issue on the subject. The Puseys visited us in Baltimore and seemed to enjoy themselves there, much as had the Conants. When my son attended Harvard and both my daughters later attended Radcliffe, Nate and Anne gave them just the right amount of friendly attention.

The relationship which Natalie and I developed with the Puseys was characteristic of the regard in which the members of the Harvard Corporation held one another at that time. The welcome which the senior members of the Corporation extended to us when we made our first appearance in Cambridge could not have been warmer. The senior fellow, Harry Shattuck, who was a bachelor, invited me for a weekend at a club which he owned in Dover, where I remember dining with his Richardson nephews. The conversation turned on Goethe and the merits and demerits of his English translators, and I was astonished at the erudition of Elliot Richardson, who later became a well-known international figure. Roger and Ella Lee invited us for a gourmet weekend at their Brookline home, and the Grenville Clarks gave a dinner in our honor at the Somerset Club, at which the Daniel Webster silver graced the table. Charlie and Alison Coolidge were especially generous in their hospitality, and their home in Belmont was opened to us on many occasions. Paul and Virginia Cabot invited us for a weekend at their home in Needham, and so in very short order our provincial notions of the special quality of Southern hospitality were completely dispelled.

When Keith Kane joined the Corporation, matters reached something of a peak. His wife, Amanda Kane, was then and still is probably the most widely known private citizen on the Eastern seaboard, and we all thoroughly enjoyed the Kanes' company. In later years the Tommy Lamonts from New York, the Francis H. ("Hooks") Burrs from Boston, the Al Nickersons from New York, and the Hugh Calkins from Cleveland fitted right in and helped to create a happy atmosphere, which made us all look forward to the times we got together to perform what might otherwise have been tiresome duties.

However, as the Vietnam War dragged on, students at many colleges and universities all over the country began to demonstrate. Some of them were troubled by the fact that they were managing to escape military service altogether, while their less fortunate contemporaries were getting killed or wounded in action; a few were downright revolutionaries who welcomed any excuse for activities designed to tear down what they called "the power structure," which they claimed was ruling the universities and colleges as well as the government of the nation. Buildings were seized, classes disrupted, visiting speakers shouted down or otherwise harassed, and in a few cases officers of the institution were locked in or out of their offices.

In the year 1968 an outbreak of this sort took place at Columbia University. There followed an investigation in which Archibald Cox, a professor at the Harvard Law School, was asked to study what happened at Columbia. According to my recollection, he filed a written report in which he put a good deal of the blame on the failure of Columbia's administrative officers to take firm action to stop the disorders when they first began.

Shortly thereafter, a group of radical students forcibly took over University Hall, where the principal administrative offices of Harvard College were located, and rifled some confidential files. I was called to the telephone in Baltimore and told that Nate planned to ask the Cambridge police to expel the students from the building. Since the retirement of Charlie Coolidge I was the senior fellow of the Corporation, and I was told that Nate would not take the proposed action over my objection. I asked whether the faculty had been consulted and was informed that Nate intended to call a meeting of the council of deans and leave it up to them to deal with their faculties. I said that if Nate was sure that he would have the support of the faculty, I was in no position to override the judgment of those who were on the spot. The police were called in, some force was used on a few students, the building was cleared, and within a few hours the whole place was in a turmoil.

I arrived in Cambridge on the following morning to find that classes were at a standstill, speakers were haranguing crowds of students in the Harvard Yard from hastily erected platforms, and a self-constituted committee had called a mass meeting at the stadium that afternoon, at which a list of demands was to be presented to the Corporation. None of the members of the Corporation thought it wise to attend that meeting, but the following day I went to the Divinity School, where a meeting had been called of the theological students. At that meeting several barefoot students prostrated themselves while another student delivered an oration which would have done credit to Savonarola.

As I left that meeting, I met a Dunster House student who called me by name and asked why I had not attended the meeting at the stadium. I replied that my study of Greek history had taught me that government by mass meeting did not work very well. With some heat I asked him just what he thought had been accomplished by that meeting other than to stir up student hysteria. He replied by asking, "What are *you* doing to stop this abominable war?"

In the course of the next twenty-four hours I got the definite impression that while most of the faculty deplored the action of the radicals, an overwhelming majority felt that Mr. Pusey had made a grave error in not consulting the faculty before calling in the police. Accordingly, I was not surprised when at a hastily called meeting of the Faculty of Arts and Sciences, a committee was set up to investigate the whole situation and to make recommendations for such disciplinary measures as might be needed in order to restore order in the academic community. I gathered that this action was intended as a rebuke to the Corporation and particularly to President Pusey.

In the meantime, representatives of the news media were gathering around Cambridge like so many vultures, and the Harvard Corporation was requested to designate a representative to respond to questions on a nationwide TV hookup. As senior fellow, I was given that assignment and read a brief statement, after which I was asked a few questions, which I tried to answer as briefly as possible.

However, as commencement week approached, there were rumors that the graduating class would refuse in a body to participate in the exercises. The radical student organization known as the Students for a Democratic Society (SDS) demanded that a representative of the organization be permitted to make a speech as a part of the commencement exercises. Mr. Pusey turned this request down on the ground that student speakers at the commencement exercises had already been chosen competitively and that it would set a bad precedent to allow any group to force its way onto the platform.

As we were lining up on commencement morning to begin the procession through the Yard, Judge Charles Wyzanski, who was a former chairman of the Board of Overseers of Harvard College, came up to me and said that the commencement marshals who had been elected by the graduating class had asked him to try to persuade the president to change his mind. Charlie said he had spoken to Nate but had found him adamant. Bob Bowie, who was then director of the Center for International Affairs at Harvard, was standing beside me and overheard this conversation. He reminded me of the occasion when a radical group in Baltimore had announced its intention to march on City Hall without a permit, in defiance of a city ordinance. The group had been completely deflated when a permit to make the march was granted on the application of a person who called himself by the name of Johnny Appleseed. As a result, the proposed demonstration was a complete fizzle and the community laughed at it.

I then went in to see Nate and added my voice to Charlie Wyzanski's. Nate agreed to listen to the class marshals, and they were sent for. He demanded to know whether it was the will of the graduating class that the representative of SDS be allowed to speak, and they said yes. He then asked whether they would guarantee that the speaker would not take more than ten minutes. They again said yes, whereupon he said, "Very well. It is on your head."

After we had all taken our place on the platform, when the time came for the student representatives to speak, Nate explained that the class marshals had indicated that it was the desire of the class that a student representative of SDS be allowed to speak for not more than ten minutes. Since commencement day primarily belonged to the graduating class, the request had been granted, and he called for the speaker to come forward. A boy then shambled up to the platform with a cigarette dangling from his lips and proceeded to deliver a diatribe in which he insulted the president and in general made a fool of himself. The students began to turn thumbs down and call for his removal from the platform. When the ten minutes were up, he refused to leave, whereupon the class marshals returned to the platform and took him away. Thereafter the exercises proceeded as usual.

So effective was this whole affair in taking the wind out of the sails of SDS that some students suspected that the whole incident had been planned in advance in order to discredit the radicals. At their request the Committee of Fifteen conducted an investigation, and I was asked to make a statement of my participation, which I was happy to do. So far as Harvard was concerned, that was the high point of student demonstrations, and the occasional disturbances that followed were an anticlimax.

I was scheduled to retire from the Corporation at the end of the academic year at which I reached my seventieth birthday. Keith Kane was scheduled to retire in the preceding year. While I had apparently made a complete recovery from a mild heart attack which I suffered in the year 1968, I had found the events of 1969 quite strenuous, and my medical adviser told me that I ought to hasten my departure from the Corporation. Accordingly, when we met again in September of 1969, I told my colleagues that I intended to retire in February 1970, when I would have been on the Corporation for twenty-two years.

One more task, however, lay ahead of me. It became increasingly clear that the Pusey administration was now something of a lame duck.

The faculty were no longer responding to his leadership, and several of the overseers indicated to me that the time had come when Nate should set a date for his own retirement. It was suggested that I approach him on this subject. Finding my colleagues on the Corporation in agreement, I first sounded out Anne Pusey and found that she was most anxious for Nate to resign. The events of the past year had been extremely trying for her, and she was at times alarmed for her husband's safety. In the end, I did not have to bring the matter up again, as Nate took the initiative and notified me of his intention to resign at the end of the academic year which was to begin on July 1, 1970.

And so, in the course of the next two years, Marbury, Kane, and Pusey resigned from the Harvard Corporation and were sent on their way with the customary honorary degrees.

A new generation of historians appears to have reached the conclusion that during the Pusey years, the members of the Harvard Corporation were dominated by groundless fears of a Communist conspiracy to overthrow the government of the United States by force and violence. They characterized this as the "delusion" of a group of "cold warriors." This delusion is said to have led to acts which are now claimed to have been invasions of academic freedom.

On January 7, 1951, the Committee on the Present Danger, of which President Conant was the chairman, published a statement which said:

> Certain facts are beyond dispute. A menacing despotic power, bent on conquering the world, has twice in recent months in Korea resorted to aggressive war. But these attacks do not prove that Russia—which clearly directed both—will launch a major war. Much less do they prove that Russia is ready to start such a war at this time.
>
> Europe is the next great prize Russia seeks. We learned belatedly in the First World War and again in the Second that the successful defense of the United States must be made in Europe. So in entering the North Atlantic Pact, we sought to prevent a Third World War by serving notice that an assault on Europe means war with the United States.

This statement was signed by former Under Secretary of State William L. Clayton, former Secretary of War Robert P. Patterson, the president of the Carnegie Institute of Washington, Vannevar Bush, and the former director of the Office of Strategic Services, William J. Donovan. In addition to the president of Harvard University, the signatories also included the presidents of Princeton and Brown and of the Universities of California, Chicago, Colorado, Missouri, and Washington, and of Williams and Sweetbriar colleges.

For my part I came with reluctance to accept that statement as accurate. In 1939 I had made a radio broadcast under the auspices of the Junior Bar Conference of the American Bar Association in which I said:

When I was asked to talk about American Citizenship my mind turned very naturally to what has always seemed to me to be the essence of Americanism, that is the spirit of individual freedom. . . .

This spirit underlies our most characteristic institutions. To it we owe the federal character of our government, the dispersion of power within our governmental units and the outright prohibitions against government action embodied in our fundamental laws. Within the shelter of these institutions, the spirit of freedom lives. We call them our civil liberties. . . .

Today, more than ever before, we realize the value of those barriers which we have erected against the exercise of governmental power. If we can still call our country the land of the free, it is because our fundamental law guarantees freedom of religion, of speech and of assembly; freedom from arbitrary deprivation of life, liberty or property; and equality before the law.

I have said that our law guarantees this freedom. I wish that I might add that it insures it, but no law, however solemnly enacted, can insure freedom, for freedom cannot live in the court room alone; it must live in our hearts as well. Only as we ourselves cherish it, can it take on reality. Furthermore, liberty like love, must be shared with others if it is to survive. To the extent that we deny to our fellows any freedom that we claim, we deny it to ourselves. Indeed freedom depends entirely upon our willingness to extend it to those who would deny it to us if they could. For freedom is indivisible; by punishing the intolerant, we throw away the only weapon that can defeat them. These are truths which need to be realized daily if our American civilization is to survive. . . .

Translated into practical terms, this means that when we . . . deny any man or group of men the right to express a political or social creed (whether they belong to the Communist Party or to the Nazi Bund) we destroy the foundations of our civilization.

In 1954 I wrote a letter to the *New York Times* which was published in full in which I expressed my dismay at the denial of security clearance to Robert Oppenheimer. But the fullest statement of my views on the problem of academic freedom is found in an address which I made at Tufts University in 1952. I said:

Our problem is to reconcile two familiar aphorisms, that "freedom is not for those who would destroy it"; and that freedom must embrace "the thought that we hate." . . .

It is an old maxim that *inter arma silent leges*. We all know that it takes discipline to overcome danger and the greater the danger the more rigid the discipline. Thus when our national safety is threatened, we submit to the seizure of private property, to price and wage controls, to compulsory military service and to a thousand other deprivations of freedom. We tell those who work in industries essential to our safety that they must work for a wage which they are unwilling to accept and we enforce that mandate by court order. By the same token we compel the managers of industry to pay wages which to them and to their stockholders seem unreasonable and enforce that mandate by executive seizure. All this we do to protect the safety of the State, and where that safety is clearly understood to be at stake, little dissent is heard. Alexander Hamilton summed it all up in the eighth of the Federalist papers when he said, "Safety from external danger is the most powerful director of national conduct. Even the ardent love of liberty will, after a time, give way to its dictates." . . .

So, I submit, we must face up to the fact that without liberty there can be no safety and without safety there can be no liberty. To be free, we must be prepared to assume risks, but we cannot risk all. In spite of the eloquence and passion of those who would ignore the presence of danger, if we must choose between voluntary limitation of our freedom and surrender of that freedom to those who would destroy it, the choice is clear enough. We should, of course, be very certain that the choice must be made. For we cannot escape our dilemma by preserving our own freedom while limiting that of others. . . .

On the other hand, the coming to light of strong evidences of a carefully planned conspiracy of members of the Communist party to overthrow our government by force and violence has produced a widespread conviction that the government must take affirmative action to unmask members of the conspiracy who may be employed in "sensitive" occupations. It is perhaps a compliment to the profession that teaching by general consent should be included in this category. The immediate result, however, has proved something less than gratifying. Since academic administrations are properly unwilling to undertake the function of investigation, resort has been had to other devices which some regard with almost equal revulsion. The loyalty oath in particular has stirred up a passionate controversy. . . . But it would be idle to deny that there are those who regard as undesirable any inquiry even by the government into the past or even the present activities or associations of teachers, even if these include membership in organizations known to be committed to the overthrow of the government by force and violence. Speaking for myself, I feel that the teaching profession would be well advised not to take so extreme an attitude. That those who advocate the violent overthrow of the government should not be employed in the instruction of youth is a proposition not hard to defend. This is particularly the case where teaching in elementary and secondary schools is concerned. The argument that the student should be free to come to an independent conclusion as between competing claims to truth seems strained when applied to immature minds. . . .

I do not wish, however, to end on a note of false optimism. There is, I think, legitimate cause for alarm in the extent to which hysteria seems to have taken hold upon large parts of our population. It does seem indeed at times that the lights of liberty are burning low. We can take comfort, however, in words which General Lee wrote to Colonel Marshall during the years when the land which he loved lay prostrate under military rule. These also were times of hysteria, of vindictiveness and of the test oath. Nevertheless, General Lee found it possible to write these calm words from which, it seems to me, we may all take inspiration in these times:

"My experience of men has neither disposed me to think worse of them nor indisposed me to serve them; nor, in spite of failures which I lament, of errors, which I now see and acknowledge, or of the present aspect of affairs do I despair of the future. The truth is this: the march of Providence is so slow, and our desires so impatient, the work of progress is so immense, and our means of aiding it so feeble, the life of humanity is so long, and that of the individual so brief, that we often see only the ebb of the advancing wave, and are thus discouraged. It is history that teaches us to hope."

XXI ❧ Wrestling with Racial Prejudice

While my services at Harvard required me to deal with many troubling questions, I believe that the most difficult problems I have ever been called upon to face arose out of the status of black people in the United States. As President Benno C. Schmidt, Jr., of Yale University has recently pointed out, the notion of inferiority of the Negro race was widely accepted among the "progressives" who held leading positions in the early years of the twentieth century. In the middle of the nineteenth century a French diplomat, Count Gobineau, had written a book entitled *The Inequality of the Races of Mankind,* in which he advanced what purported to be a scientific demonstration of the truth of that idea. His thesis was later developed in another book entitled *The Passing of the Great Race,* whose author, Madison Grant, was a respected professor of anthropology at Columbia University.

My father was among those who accepted the racial theories propounded by these authors, although he refined them by pointing out that there were wide differences in the tribal characteristics of the African blacks, which accounted for the fact that some of them turned out to be natural leaders. However, he believed that the great majority of those who had been brought to the United States as slaves were quite incapable of assuming the responsibilities of citizenship. It was primarily for this reason that he had been active in seeking to disfranchise what he regarded as the venal vote of the uneducable black, and he had also opposed women's suffrage, primarily on the ground that it would serve to increase the number of such voters. During his last years my father spent much of his time working to prevent blacks from purchasing homes in the Mount Royal District of Baltimore City by the use of restrictive covenants. As a boy I ran errands on behalf of the Mount Royal Association and later I successfully argued a case in the Court of Appeals of Maryland in which the court upheld the validity of these restrictive covenants.

However, Adolf Hitler, with his odious persecutions based on similar racial theories, caused me and many others like me to reexamine our racial assumptions. Moreover, I had in 1937 met Dr. Charles Houston, the dean of the Law School of Howard University. On behalf of the NAACP

Dr. Houston had demanded that the School Board of Calvert County, Maryland, abandon its policy of paying black teachers less than whites who were doing a similar job. The members of the board asked me to represent them in litigating this question, but by that time it had become clear to me that the Court of Appeals of Maryland would no longer tolerate this form of discrimination, and I so advised the board. They said they had no money to raise the salaries of the black teachers, and I suggested that they explain this to Dr. Houston and try to make the best deal with him that they could.

At a meeting held in my office in Baltimore City, Dr. Houston and a young black lawyer named Thurgood Marshall were present along with the members of the Calvert County School Board. Dr. Houston very quietly stated that the time had come when discrimination in teachers' pay based on race could no longer be accepted by the black community. My clients then pointed out that they had no money in the budget with which to raise the teachers' salaries. Dr. Houston said that his clients were prepared to accept a court order which would not become effective until the next fiscal year. The Calvert County board chairman then pointed out that if black teachers were to be paid as much as whites, they would have to demonstrate equal qualifications and that this would surely mean that a number of black teachers would lose their jobs. At this point Thurgood Marshall started to speak, whereupon Dr. Houston put his hand on Mr. Marshall's shoulder and he subsided. Dr. Houston then said:

> We are prepared for that. We are not asking for preferential treatment for black teachers and we don't want our children taught by teachers who are less qualified than those who teach white children. Furthermore, we want the black teachers to have an incentive to take whatever additional training they need to meet the same standards as the white teachers. We are prepared at Howard University to give them courses which will qualify them to meet those standards.

The members of the school board then withdrew to another room and sent for me. They told me that they were now prepared to tell the county commissioners of Calvert County that they would have to consent to a decree such as Dr. Houston proposed. In the end the matter was settled without litigation. I was deeply impressed by Dr. Houston's handling of this very delicate situation.

In 1950 I received a letter from Erwin Griswold enclosing a draft of a brief he was filing in one of the desegregation cases then pending before the Supreme Court involving the application of a black to enter a law school which admitted only white students. Erwin's brief made it quite clear that his client was entitled to admission to the law school on the basis of the separate but equal doctrine which had been announced by the Supreme Court in *Plessy* v. *Ferguson*. However, he went further and argued that *Plessy* v. *Ferguson* should now be overruled and segregation of the races totally eliminated. According to my present recollection, he quoted freely from a then recently published book entitled *The American Dilemma,* written by a Swedish sociologist named Gunnar Myrdal. I wrote to him on May 25, 1950, saying:

> As you predict, I do not like all of the brief. I find myself in substantial agreement with the proposition that a one-man law school is not the equivalent of the real thing. On the other hand, I have too little confidence in the exact nature of the social sciences to feel that the court will be justified in ramming down the throats of southern communities, as newly mined constitutional ore, the *obiter dicta* of Gunnar Myrdal. Step by step is still the right way in constitutional adjudication.

In May 1954 the Supreme Court handed down its decision in *Brown* v. *Board of Education.* That decision was bitterly criticized and along with a number of other lawyers acting under the leadership of Senator George Wharton Pepper, I signed a letter in 1956 deploring some of the attacks which were then being made on the court. I received a rather blunt letter from my friend Joe Johnston of Birmingham, Alabama, who had been of invaluable help to me in World War II. Joe took me to task for having signed Senator Pepper's letter and in reply I wrote to him on October 17, 1956, as follows:

> The bi-racial system of the South as it has developed during the last fifty years just cannot be squared with the fundamental proposition which lies at the core of our American society, that all men and women are entitled to equality of opportunity. No man willing to face facts can claim that the system of separating the races as it actually exists in the southern states today does, in fact, afford equality of opportunity to the negro.
>
> I make those assertions without apology for their dogmatism. My forebears, like yours, belonged to the plantation aristocracy. When my father was born, his parents gave him the son of one of the house servants to be his companion and body servant. To him the South of Thomas Nelson Page was a reality, and I was raised to think as he did. I went South to school and college and I have relatives and friends scattered all through the southern states. I have spent a good part of my life there because I like Southerners and their ways. I think I understand social conditions in the South well enough to have the right to speak of them with as much assurance as any other man.
>
> Of course, I am familiar with the arguments which are now being advanced by Southerners to justify the present system.
>
> First there is the contention that equal facilities are now being afforded to the negro. On this point statistical proof is available and unanswerable. Even in the physical sense, equality of facilities in the areas of education, housing and recreation may be found only in urban communities and frequently not there. Moreover, physical facilities alone do not always give equality of op-

portunity. In Baltimore we have done fairly well in giving the negroes school buildings and equipment equal to those of the whites, but the quality of instruction has been far inferior, largely because of the deficient training of the negro teachers. I believe that is generally true wherever separate schools exist.

Another argument is that the low level of achievement of the negro people demonstrates their innate inferiority and justifies separation. Fifty years ago there was some supposedly scientific support for that thesis. Today there seems to be none.

I realize that the Southern layman finds this pretty hard to reconcile with the evidence of his senses. In daily contact with the product of the negro quarters and the negro schools, he is convinced that these people must be of a lower order of intelligence than the white people of his community; if the professors think otherwise then that is to him just another proof of their lack of common sense. But I do not see how we can reject the unanimous opinions of the men and women who have spent their lives studying this subject and who have no axe to grind.

A much more potent argument rests on the undeniable disparity in the actual level of achievement of the average negro and the average white in the schools. This is claimed to justify separation, in fairness to both races. This seems to me to be an effective argument against compulsory integration on an inflexible geographical basis, but I do not think that it can possibly justify continuation of the present system. As every Southerner knows, there are and always have been a certain number of negroes who are able to triumph over the homes from which their parents are absent all day and sometimes all night, the neighborhoods roamed by unruly gangs of adolescents, and the schools taught by comparatively poorly trained teachers—in spite of these handicaps a significant number of negroes have somehow been able to prepare themselves adequately for the best education their communities have to offer. But unlike the children of the unfortunate or incompetent whites, who have demonstrated similar abilities, these superior negro children, if they happen to live in the southern states, cannot hope to realize their capabilities unless they are able to leave home and go elsewhere. It is just at this point that the conflict between the southern bi-racial system and the concept of equality of opportunity is most glaring. I do not see how that system can possibly be defended as it applies to the gifted negro or to the negro who is prepared to profit by a better education than the negro schools can give him. This is the gap in the moral armament of the South and until it is closed nobody is going to listen as sympathetically as they should to the very real problems which the South faces in giving equal opportunity to the negro.

In Maryland, in Kentucky and elsewhere the authorities have not attempted to force colored children to leave the schools where they are happy and to enter into competition with white children for which they are unprepared, nor have they attempted to force white children to attend predominantly negro schools. What they have done is to permit properly prepared colored children who wish to do so, to attend predominantly white schools in order that they may get a better education. Before admitting colored children to any white school a careful process of exploration and education has taken place through parent-teacher associations and similar organizations. In communities where great reluctance has been shown the school boards have proceeded with great caution. In some of the counties of Maryland no actual integration has yet taken place but meanwhile the leaders of both races are facing up to their responsibilities and are working toward a solution of what all recognize to be a very difficult and delicate problem.

Now, as to Senator Pepper's statement which I agreed to sign. I, myself, think that the Court moved too fast in the sweeping opinion which it handed down in the school cases. But I have no patience with the contention that the decision is political or that it is a usurpation of power. Of course, as every intelligent lawyer knows, every interpretation of the great guarantees of the Constitution is a political act and for this reason the Court must appraise social conditions and weigh the consequences of its pronouncements. But it is the duty of the Court, nevertheless, to interpret the Constitution in the light of realities, and to apply its provisions in a manner consistent with the facts. If, as I believe, it is true that the negro does not have equality of opportunity today in the schools of Prince Edward County, Virginia, then I do not see how the Court could have said otherwise.

The fact that this involved a departure from precedent does not shock me. The "separate but equal" idea had a great deal of plausibility when it was first put forward as the answer to the problem created by the Thirteenth, Fourteenth and Fifteenth Amendments. Maybe at the time it was the best possible way to make progress toward the achievement of the great ends which those Amendments were intended to accomplish. I have no doubt that if I had sat on the court that decided *Plessy* v. *Ferguson* I would have voted with the majority with a clear conscience. But I do not honestly believe that the system as it exists today after a half-century of development, does in fact actually afford equal protection of the laws to the negro and if I were on the bench I would feel bound to say so when the occasion demanded. It seems to me of the first importance that the southern leaders of the Bar should recognize this simple fact and until they do so I think that it is the duty of lawyers in other parts of the country to do what little they can to show their southern brethren that their unyielding position is one of untenable isolation.

And from another letter to Joe Johnston:

The Southerner is convinced that the Negro is innately inferior to the whites and for that reason he is determined that the races shall not mix on a basis of equality; therefore he has built a social system which separates them in every activity which might possibly throw them together as equals. To the extent that he can offer equality of opportunity to the Negro within that framework, he is willing to do so, although somewhat reluctantly, since it costs a lot of money and in view of the Negro's natural limitations he strongly suspects that a lot of this money is going to be thrown away. However, on one thing he is implacably determined, and that is that the bi-racial system must be maintained regardless of any inequality which may result.

That is certainly an advance over the state of opinion described so accurately by Taney in the Dred Scott case (for doing which he has never really been forgiven, although he told the simple truth) but I must say it hardly seems consistent with the Constitution. Whether the signers of the Declaration of Independence meant to include negroes among those entitled to inalienable rights may be a doubtful question but at any rate Jefferson's eloquence ran away with the show and it soon became clear that there was a fatal contradiction between the principles of the Declaration and the social system of the slave states. As Lincoln pointed out in his Second Inaugural, it was this fatal moral flaw in our Constitution which we expiated in the years from 1861 to 1865.

I recognize, of course, that legal fictions, even when backed by constitutional authority, are apt to lack moral sanction and that the Southerner has always been ready to follow his own ideas of proper behavior without much respect for legal compulsion. But the right to equality of opportunity is not a legal fiction it is a moral ideal and as such perhaps our greatest asset in the battle in which we are now engaged for the soul of the world. I think it is ironical that the Southerner should be blind to this and should think that he is protecting his culture when he denies equality of opportunity to the Negro. Of course, the irony is doubly bitter if the Negro really is capable of sharing in that culture on a basis of equality.

That brings me to your prediction that the South will not alter its position in the foreseeable future. I hope and believe that you are wrong. I think that Southerners will begin to have doubts about those presuppositions which you so bluntly stated in your letter to Griswold. Having myself shared them for many years, I can testify that they are not impregnable to a reasoned attack. Your assumption, for example, that the colored teachers have been as well schooled as the whites because they have as many, if not more, academic degrees just won't wash. Degrees from where? The presupposition which more than any other conditions the Southern mind—that the bi-racial system is the only alternative to miscegenation—can hardly stand up under careful scrutiny. Is there any evidence that miscegenation in Illinois or New York is proportionately greater than in Alabama or Louisiana? I should suppose quite the contrary. Is not the whole conception of "miscegenation" based on the present disparity between the cultural levels of the two races? So long as that continues intermarriage can never be socially acceptable and the mixing in schools or public parks will scarcely alter that fact. If the time does come when the cultural differences between the races have been eliminated, what is left but a matter of taste? These are some of the questions which I think the Southerner may begin to ask.

Another force working on Southern opinion is the moral isolation which, for reasons which I tried to explain in my previous letter, the South is bound to suffer so long as it remains unyielding in its attitude on this question. This is likely to have painful consequences. Among them is the steady draining away from the South of the best of its negroes and many of the best of its whites who will prefer to live in a community which does not feel itself to be misunderstood, if not persecuted by the rest of the country. For all of these reasons the Southern attitude is bound to be under strong internal pressure from now on. I realize that an emotional storm has been stirred up by the threat of Federal coercion in what Southerners regard as one of their most intimate concerns, the rearing of their children. Until that has blown over, the voice of moderation cannot be heard in the South. But it is my impression that there are many influential Southerners who recognize that the bi-racial system as it now exists is bound to go and who are looking for a way to effect its gradual liquidation. I think that it will not be too long before they will feel able to speak out and when that time comes we may find that the present impasse can be solved more quickly than you suppose.

My description in those letters of Maryland's handling of the situation created by the *Brown* case was prematurely optimistic. In the first place, the NAACP was not content to accept the interpretation which the lower federal courts originally put upon the *Brown* decision. Most of the judges took the view that while the *Brown* decision outlawed compulsory segregation, it did not require compulsory integration. Accordingly, white children need not be compelled to attend predominantly black schools, nor should black children be compelled to attend predominantly white schools. Freedom of choice could still be the slogan. The black leadership contended that this would rob the *Brown* decision of all practical significance. Thus, there was continued agitation for the use of devices such as busing.

Altogether, the years immediately following the *Brown* case were a time when relations between the races were seriously troubled. To many black people the courts still appeared to be dominated by the white power structure. On the other hand, through many parts of the South and Southwest, the federal courts seemed to be reviving a tyranny which had been laid to rest by the compromises which terminated the Reconstruction period. Reaction took a variety of forms, from the "massive resistance" of Virginia to the antics of George Wallace, then governor of Alabama.

For a time I watched these developments uneasily, taking an opportunity to expostulate with my old school and college friend Virginius Dabney, who had written an article published in *Life* magazine in which he seemed to say that the decisions of the Supreme Court were not law. On April 8, 1959, I wrote to him as follows:

> Whatever may be true of the great mass of the Negro race, there are a certain number of them who deserve a better education than they can find in segregated schools. In order to get that, they must leave home, and in many cases they do so, never to return, to the loss of the communities which they have been forced to abandon. It is the recognition of this undeniable fact which, I think, has led the judges of the Supreme Court to feel that they can no longer honestly say that separate but equal facilities afford equal protection of the laws to the Negro race.

At any rate, since Judge Marshall's time it has been established that the Supreme Court is the final interpreter of the Constitution, which simply means, as Chief Justice Hughes said, that the Constitution is what the Supreme Court says it is. It follows that those who say that the Supreme Court decisions are not law are trifling with words.

I would have preferred to see the Court postpone action in these cases until the South had had more time to adjust itself to the admission of Negroes to institutions of higher education, to which most people in the South were already resigned. I believe that in another decade the people of the Southern States would have realized that their social system could survive the abandonment of enforced segregation in the schools. I still think they will discover that to be the case, but it is going to take longer, and in the meantime, relations between the races have undoubtedly been badly disturbed.

Once again to Dabney:

It seems to me that it all comes down to this: a decision of the Supreme Court interpreting the constitution may be criticized on any ground that you please, but when you deny its force as law, you challenge our whole constitutional system. I think it is most important that the people of the South recognize this as a fact and face it without equivocation. Until they do so, they can hardly hope to succeed in persuading the people of the North to face the immense difficulties which make complete integration of the schools in this generation a practical impossibility. In particular, it seems to me that border states like Maryland and Virginia have an opportunity similar to that which they muffed so badly in the middle of the nineteenth century. If they can show their brethren how to live under our constitutional system without disorder and without disrupting the social fabric, they will make a very great contribution to the political health of the nation.

In Baltimore City the *Brown* case at first caused relatively little disturbance. This was largely due to the wise leadership of Mayor Theodore McKeldin at city hall and of Judge Roszel Thomsen as chairman of the school board. I myself made a minor contribution. At the Peabody Conservatory of Music black students had never been officially accepted prior to World War II, although many faculty members were giving them private instruction. Of course, this could not lead to a degree, nor would the students have the benefit of group class instruction.

When I became president of the Peabody Institute in 1947 I brought this subject up and found that while the members of the board of trustees were prepared to admit black students, they were reluctant to do so without the approval of the faculty. At that time the administrators at the preparatory department advised against making the change, but while the matter was still under consideration, the *Brown* case was decided by the Supreme Court and the Baltimore City School Board announced its intention to open all schools to applicants without regard to race. The Peabody Board of Trustees then decided to follow suit, and the principal of the preparatory department showed me an announcement which she was preparing to send to the faculty and to the parents of all students in the Prep. I told her not to send out any announcements. Instead, when any qualified black applicant appeared, he or she should be assigned to a teacher who was already teaching black students and should be permitted to enroll in classes for group instruction as a matter of course. This was done and, so far as I ever heard, no objection was ever made by anyone.

However, in other parts of the state, rising ferment led to racial confrontations, and even in Baltimore the black leadership of the community was agitating for a city ordinance which would outlaw racial discrimination in all places of public accommodation. In June of 1963 Mayor McKeldin appointed an advisory committee to assist the city council in framing such an ordinance. He asked me to serve on that committee, along with a group of outstanding community leaders, all of whom were also white.

At the first meeting of the committee it became apparent that some of the members had strong objections to some of the language of the proposed ordinance which had been drafted by the mayor's staff. Particularly those sections dealing with housing and real estate transactions drew protests. I then undertook to prepare a statement which every member of the committee eventually agreed to sign, with the exception of the president of the Johns Hopkins University, Dr. Milton Eisenhower, who was never able to attend any meeting of the committee. This somewhat Delphic statement was apparently satisfactory to everyone, and Mayor McKeldin and the only black member of the city council wrote me congratulatory notes. The statement read in part as follows:

> During recent months it has become apparent to us all that the Negroes of Baltimore are no longer willing to submit to the discriminations which have heretofore been their lot. They are demanding that measures be taken to eliminate these discriminations not only by voluntary action but by law.
>
> That demand cannot be disregarded without splitting this community into an insecure majority and an embittered minority. The racial frictions and hostility which such a division is bound to produce will, in our opinion, bring economic disaster to our city, to say nothing of the effect which the release of such vicious emotions will have on the welfare and happiness of every Baltimorean.
>
> The inescapable fact is that we live in a city in which more than one-third of our fellow citizens are Negroes. We believe that their demand for equal status should be met and met with good grace. To the extent that this can effectively be accomplished by the passage of a comprehensive ordinance, we favor such a course. At the same time we recognize that there are limits to the effectiveness of legal action in this field, and we do not wish to be understood as endorsing every provision of the bill which the City Administration has laid before you.

What we do wish to express is our deep conviction that equal status for our Negro fellow citizens should be achieved as promptly as possible, not only by voluntary action but by the passage of an effective and carefully drawn ordinance.

Charles H. Buck
Charles S. Garland
Robert B. Hobbs
Jerold C. Hoffberger
William L. Marbury
Emory H. Niles
L. Mercer Smith
Walter Sondheim

By coincidence, also in the latter part of June 1963, while attending a meeting of the Maryland State Bar Association, I, along with the president-elect of that association, H. Vernon Eney, was invited to a meeting at the White House where more than two hundred lawyers from all parts of the country were addressed by President Kennedy, Vice President Johnson, and the attorney general, Robert Kennedy. We were told that a lawyers' committee on civil rights was being organized under the chairmanship of Harry Tweed and Bernie Segal and the cooperation of lawyers with that committee was strongly advocated. A follow-up letter from the attorney general dated June 28, 1963, summarized what was said at that meeting.

It seemed to me that the attorney general's letter stated very clearly what needed to be done, and I, accordingly, wrote to him on July 12 as follows:

> I have already indicated to Messrs. Tweed and Segal that I shall be glad to serve on the committee which they are organizing. Insofar as the local situation is concerned, a great deal of what you suggest has already been accomplished. There is a state-wide bi-racial committee and, in many communities, there are local committees serving a similar function. In general these committees have been very effective in working out voluntary programs, although we have a spectacular failure in Cambridge.
>
> Here in Baltimore there has been trouble with an amusement park, which is not within the scope of our recently enacted public accommodations bill, but this is the subject of the litigation now pending in the Supreme Court of the United States, and until that litigation has been disposed of there is nothing which lawyers can do.
>
> Finally, I am informed that the President of our Maryland State Bar Association has appointed a committee, the purpose of which is to carry out the general objectives which you have outlined in your letter of June 28th.
>
> I feel obliged to add that I am deeply disturbed about the rising emotional tension in this State. Since the opinion in the *Brown* case, we have made great progress toward removing discriminations against the Negro race and public opinion has supported these changes. The recent enactment by the Mary-

land State Legislature of a public accommodations bill is indicative of this. I am sorry to say that I think the atmosphere has changed materially in the last few weeks. Latent prejudices are being stirred, and public opinion appears to be shifting toward resistance to further advances. I am afraid it is going to be very important for some of us with cooler heads to keep out of the fray so as to be in a position to bind up the wounds which are being inflicted by unwise actions.

In that letter I mentioned a situation which had arisen at Cambridge, Maryland, a community on the Eastern Shore, where a group of militant young blacks had undertaken to end discriminatory practices by force. This had been the principal subject of discussion at the meeting of the Maryland State Bar Association in June of 1963, and as incoming president, Vernon Eney had immediately appointed a committee to try to assist in the restoration of peace in that community. With the assistance of an extremely gifted officer of the Maryland National Guard named George Gelston, that effort turned out to be successful, and on July 27, 1964, I wrote to Messrs. Tweed and Segal a letter in which I said:

> I am happy to report that throughout the State of Maryland lawyers have been taking the lead in facing up to the problems created by the Civil Rights movement and that marked progress has been made. As evidence I call to your attention the fact that for the first time a Negro has been elected as President of the City Council in Cambridge, Maryland. The National Guard has been withdrawn from that city and there seems to be a new spirit of cooperation at work. This is in considerable measure due to the work of lawyers who have been acting in close coordination with the Maryland State Bar Association.

Another effort to deal with racial problems came in the year 1965 and is fully described in a paper which I prepared in 1966 for delivery to a group of Baltimore lawyers, from which I quote the following:

> In recent years every large city in the country has experienced in greater or lesser degree the flight of white residents from what is called the "inner city." Many people attribute this phenomenon to the decision of the Supreme Court in *Brown* v. *Board of Education.* But those of us who were raised in Baltimore in the days before World War I know that the movement of white people from the inner city began long ago and that the culprit was not the Supreme Court but the automobile. Fifty years ago I delivered a paper to a small group who used to gather in the library of Huntington Cairns. The title of that paper was "Filling Stations as a Solution to the Negro Problem," and my thesis was that the entire city of Baltimore south of North Avenue would soon be inhabited exclusively by Negroes and that the moving cause would be automobile traffic with its satellite filling stations, garages and parking lots.
> In all honesty, I should add that the paper which I then delivered showed no consciousness of the profound social significance of the change which I

was predicting. The idea that people who live in almost complete separation come to think of themselves as having no stake in the social order from which they are excluded simply never occurred to me or if it did, I did not foresee the consequences of such an alienation.

The Emancipation Proclamation was followed by a period of national chaos, which was eventually terminated by establishment of a system which substituted for slavery a subordinate status for the Negro race, symbolized by segregation. I say that this segregation was symbolic: I might even say that it was a token segregation, since Negroes continued to live and work beside white people, often in intimate contact with them. The real purpose of the system was not to effect a separation of the races but to dramatize the difference in their status. By a myriad of small measures, which were so familiar to us that we were hardly conscious of them, the Negro was obliged to acknowledge inferiority solely because of his race. It is only recently that we have begun to understand that the Negro accepted this inferior status very reluctantly and only because leaders like Booker T. Washington gave assurance that it was a temporary transitional state.

Professor Vann Woodward contends that the termination of Reconstruction by what he calls "the great compromise" was made possible as a result of the Tilden-Hayes election. According to him, it was the price the Republicans paid to hold on to the presidency. However this may be, it was perfectly evident that with the rise of a black middle class, the compromise was beginning to wear very thin by the end of World War II.

Thus, we came to the 1960s with two forces at work of outstanding significance. First, the concentration of Negroes in wholly separate ghettos or—to use the term now fashionable among them—"zoos," and, second, the rising determination on the part of the black leadership to end once and for all the subordinate status of their people. It is these two social forces which have combined to create the social dynamite which has been exploding in the Watts district of Los Angeles. I think it is clear that what we saw in Watts was not just a race riot but rather the rising to the surface of a sort of anarchistic desire to be free of restraints which were felt to have been imposed by an alien society.

Now I have no doubt that there are many Baltimoreans who would find it hard to believe that any such destructive forces are at work in this city. That, too, seems to be one of the consequences of physical separation, that the dominant race is invariably astounded at the reactions of the subordinate race. We see this in South Africa and Rhodesia today, where intelligent and educated people assure you that they have found the correct solution for the problem and one which is satisfactory to the leadership of both races. Here in Baltimore it has been repeatedly said by black and white leaders alike that there will be no repetition of Watts. Nevertheless, when we realize that there are more than 350,000 Negroes in this community, most of them living in almost complete physical separation from the white people, we have every reason to be concerned.

About a year ago the community was startled by the murder of a police sergeant in the Western District of Baltimore City. This is an area inhabited exclusively by Negroes, and the sergeant, a white man, had been attempting to make an arrest of the Veney brothers, two Negroes who were wanted in connection with the shooting of another white police officer. All of you will remember what happened after that. A special squad of police, armed with automatic weapons and batteries of searchlights, conducted a series of raids on Negro homes all over the city, but particularly in the Western District. Some of the houses raided were occupied by Negroes who were well known in their community as law-abiding citizens, with the result that indignation began to mount in the black community. Finally the local chapter of the NAACP, with the support of the national organization, filed suit in the United States District Court seeking an injunction against any further raids by the police without search warrants.

One of the witnesses who appeared before Judge Thomsen was a young Negro woman. She was obviously well educated and her manner indicated a superior and cultivated intelligence. During the course of her testimony, she characterized the behavior of the police who had raided her home as "rude and crude." In response to a direct question from the court, she said that she was not surprised at this behavior, since the police were the enemies of the Negro race.

This remark was shocking to Judge Thomsen, as it was to me, and at the Midwinter Meeting of the State Bar Association that year I took occasion to ask George Russell, whom I am sure many of you know, whether this young woman was reflecting the opinion of other educated Negroes of the professional class. He answered that, much as he regretted to have to say so, this was a widely held opinion among the people of his race at all social levels.

It seemed that the time had come to make an effort to establish some kind of dialogue (to use the fashionable word) between the Negro community and the Police Department. Counsel for the NAACP agreed to cooperate in this effort. At that time a group of employers had been meeting for more than a year with members of the black community, trying to work out plans for increasing employment opportunities for Negroes in business and industry. Among the leaders in this group were Mercer Smith, Walter Sondheim, Dr. Furman Templeton and George Russell. Bill Somerville, who had been chairman of the Human Relations Committee of the Maryland State Bar Association, was also active in this group. After consulting with them, it was agreed that George Russell should ask the group to name a bi-racial committee to act in an advisory capacity to the Police Commissioner and to request the Governor and the Mayor to give their endorsement to the selection of such a committee. The group cooperated willingly, and a statement was prepared and issued by the Governor and the Mayor which was given wide publicity. On the following day the Governor and the Mayor jointly announced the membership of the committee and another press release was issued.

The committee met very promptly under the co-chairmanship of Bill Somerville and Furman Templeton but an extraordinary incident took place which, for the time being, brought our work to a standstill. A Negro family moved into what had always been a white neighborhood in Hampden. According to newspaper reports, some white youths threw stones at the house which the family was occupying and broke some windows. This aroused natural indignation in the black community of Baltimore, which was greatly increased when WBAL television station broadcast a film which purported to be an on-the-spot recording of the stone-throwing incident. In this film a white police officer appeared to be watching the stone-throwing incident without making any attempt to deter the juvenile offenders.

Bill Somerville immediately got in touch with WBAL and asked that a special showing of the film be given to the members of the committee in the presence of the Police Commissioner and of the reporter who made the film. Such a showing was arranged, but when the members of the committee arrived at the station, they were met by the manager, who said that the reporter was in the hospital, having just undergone an emergency appendectomy. However, the manager said that he had talked to the reporter in the hospital and had learned that the film was a reenactment which had been deliberately staged by him, that no rocks had been actually thrown, and that the police officer had been stationed there after the actual rock-throwing incident and was totally unaware of what was going on.

The white members of the committee were appalled by what had taken place, realizing that it might well have provoked a riot. The black members expressed their incredulity at the manager's explanation but were assured that the reporter had been fired and was willing to make public apology as soon as he was released from the hospital.

As the result of this incident, it became crystal clear that Russell's statement to me was, if anything, an understatement. I questioned the Negro members of our committee about this very directly and received direct answers. Bishop Love said that one of the leading clergymen of his denomination had been working on the problem of police-community relations and had consented to serve on a committee appointed by the Captain of the Western District. He had suggested that the committee meet in the parish house of his church and had brought the matter up before his elders for what he hoped would be a routine ratification. To his chagrin, the elders unanimously turned down the idea, saying, "It's all right for you to serve on that committee, but we will invite no uniformed policemen to enter this church or any of its property." . . .

At the conclusion of our discussions in the committee, we reached the unanimous conclusion that it was important to establish some sort of procedure which would satisfy the black community that complaints against policemen would not simply be swept under the rug. We recommended the establishment of a Complaint Evaluation Board to review charges of discourtesy, abuse or brutal conduct by policemen.

Under procedures drafted by the Attorney General, all complaints of this character were to be reduced to writing and filed at an office to be established in the City Hall, staffed by civilians. The original complaint was to be retained in a permanent record book and carbon copies mailed within 48 hours to the Chief Inspector of the Baltimore Police Department and to the members of a Complaint Evaluation Board, consisting of the Attorney General, the City Solicitor, the State's Attorney, the Director of the Baltimore

Community Relations Commission and the Executive Secretary of the Maryland Commission on Interracial Problems and Relations, or their nominees. Within 48 hours of the receipt of his copy of the complaint, the Chief Inspector was to recommend either that charges be preferred or that the complaint be dismissed, or, in the alternative, he was to assign the investigation of the complaint to the Captain in charge of the investigative staff of police officers attached to the office of the State's Attorney of Baltimore City. In any event, the Chief Inspector was to report the action taken to the Complaint Evaluation Board. Copies of the report covering any investigation were then to be forwarded to the Complaint Evaluation Board, together with the recommendation of the Chief Inspector as to the action to be taken. Any member of the Board disagreeing with the recommendation of the Chief Inspector could file his own recommendation with the Chief Inspector, and a conference should then be held by the full Board, which would have power by a majority vote to determine whether the charges should be placed against the officer and a hearing scheduled before the Police Commissioner. The State's Attorney's office would have final say as to whether any criminal prosecution should be instituted.

According to my understanding, the Complaint Evaluation Board has continued to function in spite of occasional efforts on the part of individual members of the black community to substitute a more active civilian review board. Commissioner Donald Pomerleau, for whose appointment our committee was largely responsible, was at first quite doubtful of the value of the work of the board but later wrote me that he believed it had served a useful purpose.

While I was chancellor of the diocese of Maryland, Bishop Powell told me that Bishop Moore of New York had, without consulting him, decided to come down to Baltimore County at the head of a group of civil rights activists. The group attempted to force its way into Gwynn Oak Park, which at that time did not admit blacks. The management called in the county police, who arrested some of Bishop Moore's party for trespassing. Among them was a young black who had been searched at the time of arrest and a vial of nitroglycerin tablets had been found in his pocket. The state's attorney of Baltimore County announced to the press that he intended to ask for an indictment of the young man for illegal possession of narcotics. The young man protested that the tablets had been prescribed by a physician for a heart condition, but he had not been able to produce a prescription. At that time I was myself carrying a vial of such tablets in my own pocket and could not for the life of me remember what had become of the doctor's prescription.

I promptly drove myself out to Towson and went to see John Turnbull, who was then chief judge of the Circuit Court for Baltimore County. I showed him my vial and told him there were literally thousands of people who carried just such a vial in their pockets for heart disease. I pointed out that this case was already attracting national attention because of the presence of Bishop Moore and that Baltimore County and the state of Maryland would become the laughing stock of the whole country if it appeared that a black had been indicted for carrying tablets to relieve heart pains. He agreed and called in the state's attorney, who said he would see that the charges were dropped.

About a year later George Russell was appointed to the Supreme Bench of Baltimore City, where he distinguished himself as a very capable judge. However, at the outset of his judicial career, he issued a public statement in connection with his release of a prisoner who had been sentenced to death by a fellow member of the Supreme Bench. In that statement he explained that he was following recent decisions of the Supreme Court of the United States and of the Court of Appeals of Maryland which required the setting aside of a conviction which was based on a confession which had been obtained by the police in violation of the constitutional rights of a suspect. He made it clear that in his opinion these decisions were laudable. Judge Charles Harris, who had presided at the original trial of the convicted man, then gave a statement to the press sharply criticizing Judge Russell for his remarks.

Rignal Baldwin, who was my successor as president of the Maryland State Bar Association, sent me a copy of a letter in which he had asked the chairman of the Committee on Judicial Ethics whether both judges should be censured. I thereupon wrote a letter to the *Baltimore Sun* in which I pointed out that Judge Russell was simply doing his duty. I sent a copy of this to Rignal Baldwin, and in my letter to him I said:

> I think it would be incredibly stupid of the Bar Association to censure Judge Russell. The truth of the matter is that the Bar itself has shown no understanding of the state of mind of the Negro community and particularly its younger members. There is an increasingly widespread opinion among them that the law is administered for the benefit of the white power structure and when feelings like this become sufficiently widespread, riots are inevitable.
>
> George Russell has been willing to stick his neck out and risk the censure of his own race for the statements which he has been making, all of which are designed to establish the fact that the law protects the poor as well as the rich and the Negro as well as the white. He deserves the commendation of the Bar, and, so far as I personally am concerned, I certainly intend to do everything I can to see that he gets it.

In September of 1970, I was asked to represent Parren Mitchell, a black man who had just been told that on the preceding Tuesday he had lost the primary election for Congress from the Seventh Congressional District of Maryland to the incumbent, Samuel N. Friedel. He said that he had received reports that many voters had been turned away from the polls because the voting machines had failed or on other similar pretexts and that spot-checks had indicated that the normally reliable unofficial vote count not only was late in being completed but was riddled with errors. He said that the election-night figures had shown Friedel to be the winner by 182 votes but he was prepared to show that several hundred people had been prevented from voting for him, and he was convinced that there was a white conspiracy to steal the elections. He also said that a number of his younger supporters had said that "unless we win the election, we are going to burn down this town."

I suggested to him that he make every effort to prevent his supporters from engaging in violence and pointed out that there were a number of remedies available if the final official count showed that he had lost the election. My experience in the O'Conor-Markey fight had persuaded me that a careful recount could result in a very substantial change.

Mr. Mitchell accepted this advice and called a meeting of his supporters at which he urged them to avoid violence and to await the official report. According to an account which appeared in the *Sun* on September 18, 1970, they did exactly that, and on September 27, 1970, the official recount was compiled and checked by the election boards, with the assistance of the representatives of both Mitchell and Friedel. The final tally showed Mitchell had won by 38 votes.

During this period, under the leadership of Frank Gray, Piper & Marbury established a branch office in East Baltimore, where we undertook to supplement the work of the Legal Aid Bureau in handling pro bono cases for indigent litigants, most of whom were black. For several years this office was run under the direction of Peter Smith, who had made a reputation in representing juveniles. In the end, this experiment foundered, largely because of the unwillingness of other young lawyers to work in relative isolation. However, during the five years the branch office was kept open, the annual expenditures amounted to approximately fifty thousand dollars a year. In due course, we closed the office and made an arrangement with the University of Maryland Law School whereby pro bono work could be continued by law students under the supervision of lawyers of Piper & Marbury.

My experience with the Police Community Relations Committee was so satisfactory that I was glad to accept an invitation to serve on the local board of the Urban Coalition, a group organized nationally under the leadership of John Gardner to promote racial harmony in metropolitan communities. For several years I attended meetings of the board with a growing feeling of disappointment. The attitude of the black members was in striking contrast to that of their brethren on the earlier committee. Instead of working on plans for eliminating friction between the races, we were urged to become an instrument for confrontation. The result was that people like John Luetkemeyer simply stopped coming to the meetings and eventually so did I, but not until it was clear that this particular group was not going to accomplish anything.

XXII ❧ Under Full Sail

Piper & Marbury

During the years which followed the end of World War II, the practice of law in Baltimore, which up to that time had not changed very much since the nineteenth century, began to resemble the New York model which I had found so lacking in appeal in the 1920s. Small law offices were no longer able to give the business community the legal services which it needed in order to cope with an ever-expanding economy and a corresponding increase of government regulation. This was borne in on me when Hooper Miles, who was then president of the Maryland National Bank, asked me whether anyone in my office had had any experience in setting up executive stock options. At that time some Wall Street law firms were using this device to compensate top executives in large corporations whose shares were traded on a stock exchange. I had to admit that no one in my office had actually prepared such a program for any of our clients, although we were, of course, familiar with what had been done in New York. Hooper said that under the circumstances it would perhaps be better if the Maryland National Bank let one of the New York law firms handle it.

At that time I made up my mind that we would have to reorganize our firm so that we would no longer be under the necessity of losing business of this nature. The problem was one of manpower. I had been successful in recruiting several very able youngsters who were just beginning the practice of law. But what we needed were more men who were experienced in a wider variety of specialties. It seemed to me that the answer would have to be to merge with another firm which had already established a reputation for expertise in areas in which we ourselves were less experienced. To me it seemed that a promising prospect was the firm which for many years had been headed by James Piper.

After prolonged negotiations we finally agreed to merge under the name of Piper & Marbury, with offices in the Maryland Trust Building, where my firm had practiced since before the days of the Baltimore fire of 1904. The new firm opened its doors in 1952. There were 13 partners and

4 associates, and it was the largest firm in the city. Its clients included several of the largest banks and other financial institutions, as well as numerous public utilities and manufacturing concerns. The groundwork had thus been laid for the development of an institution which as of this writing includes 78 partners and 114 associates as well as 50 paralegals. While most of this expansion has taken place in very recent years, after the leadership of the firm passed into other hands, in the years which followed the organization of Piper & Marbury in 1952 I devoted a substantial amount of time to the development of the firm and to counseling with its members on questions of policy as well as their personal problems.

As the practice of the firm grew, I found that my personal practice was also growing. At the same time extracurricular activities became even more demanding and, as a result, during the period from 1952 to 1968 I was as busy as I have ever been in my life.

The Annapolis Banking & Trust Company

Sometime in the early 1950s I was consulted by Pierre Bernard, a graduate of the Naval Academy who after a successful career as a banker in New York City had retired to Annapolis, where he hoped to lead a quiet life. Shortly after his arrival he had been asked to serve on the board of what was then known as the Annapolis Banking & Trust Company, where a great many retired graduates of the Naval Academy did their banking. Thinking that this would help to keep him from getting bored by a life of idleness, he had consented to do so. To his dismay he discovered in fairly short order that the chief executive officer of the bank, Andrew H. Kramer, had been making loans which not only were in violation of sound banking practice but appeared to be in violation of the law.

Pierre said that several of the younger officers in the bank would cooperate in developing the facts. With the aid of Frank Gray, these young officers were interviewed and after careful study of the bank records it became perfectly clear that Kramer had been "lending" money to his family and friends without proper security and in total disregard of the law. Frank Gray and I reported our findings to the members of the board and, acting on our advice, they asked Kramer to resign, which he refused to do. Thereupon the board voted to remove him from office. Kramer then filed suit for breach of contract, but before the case came up for trial we took his deposition and then got in touch with the United States attorney in Baltimore, with the result that Kramer was indicted by the federal grand jury for violating federal criminal statutes, was tried, convicted, and sent to jail.

I came away from this encounter with great respect for Pierre Bernard, who did not shrink from what turned out to be a most demanding task of steering the bank through treacherous waters. After Kramer's departure he had taken over the leadership when the bank seemed headed straight for the rocks and had shown the kind of responsible commitment that we like to think is characteristic of the graduates of the Naval Academy. Fortunately, he still had time for some of the amenities of social life in Annapolis, and I enjoyed lunching with him at the South River Club, which, he informed me, was the oldest social club not only in Maryland but in the entire United States.

James Rouse: Vision

During his absence in military service in World War II, James W. Rouse asked Dorsey Watkins and Marty McDonough of the Piper firm to look after a small mortgage banking company which he and a friend had organized under the name of the Moss-Rouse Company. Shortly after the merger of the Piper and Marbury firms, Jim asked me whether I would be willing to serve on the board of that company in place of Marty. He said that he felt very much indebted to Marty for his wartime help, but that he found their outlooks to be incompatible on a variety of social questions.

Jim regarded the mortgage banking business as the lowest rung of what to him was a form of holy orders. Business conferences at which he presided sometimes took on the atmosphere of a camp meeting, at which he held forth with almost evangelical fervor. In a style which was truly inimitable, he combined highly imaginative business concepts with a thorough knowledge of the real estate business.

Jim was convinced that through lack of proper planning, the cities of this country had created intolerable living conditions for large masses of their populations, and that these conditions could be alleviated by rehabilitating old communities and creating new ones from scratch. Mortgage financing was a tool which, properly used, could help accomplish this highly desirable result, as was also the creation of carefully planned retail shopping centers. Properly handled, these devices would help the American people to learn to live together harmoniously in healthy surroundings. His imagination went so far as to contemplate communities which provided facilities for ecumenical religious worship. Perhaps his most visionary idea was to develop mass transportation that was so convenient that the residents of his planned communities would be willing to limit the use of their private automobiles to movements outside the community.

Before a group of supposedly hardheaded business executives and bankers Jim could describe his vision in terms so convincing that they were willing to make unheard-of financial concessions to help him with his plans. A wartime acquaintance of mine who later became the president of the Aetna Life Insurance Company told me that Jim was the finest salesman he had ever seen in action. At times I found Jim's optimism difficult to share. He could and did serenely take risks which I found daunting, so much so that I persuaded Dorsey Watkins, who had recently been appointed to the federal bench, to resign as a director of the company, which he was most reluctant to do, as he found Jim Rouse in action as fascinating as I did.

Because of my skepticism, I never really became a member of the Rouse team, although I was able to make a contribution to his work in my capacity as a lawyer, notably when I succeeded in obtaining the dismissal of a class action brought in Philadelphia in which his company had been sued for one billion dollars, a sum which at that time was quite unprecedented.

I also helped by assigning three of the young lawyers in the firm to work, first, for the mortgage company, next, for a recently organized holding company which sponsored shopping centers all over the United States, and, finally, for the Howard Research & Development Company, which developed the city of Columbia in Howard County, Maryland. Franklin Allen became an expert in negotiating shopping center leases, and Jack Jones performed spectacular services in acquiring the real estate on which the city of Columbia was eventually located. Finally, Matt De-Vito became the house counsel of the parent Rouse Company and later succeeded Jim Rouse as its chief executive officer. In my opinion it was the combination of Jim's vision and Matt's executive ability which brought recognition of the Rouse name to a point where it is now nationally and internationally known for its projects at Boston, New York, Baltimore, and Columbia, where the most celebrated of its projects are located.

Maryland Port Authority

On November 3, 1954, I addressed a letter to Hamilton Owens, the editor of the *Baltimore Sun,* where it was published shortly thereafter. As it dealt with a subject which dominated my professional career for nearly a decade, I quote it in full:

> The favorable vote on the constitutional amendment limiting the authority of the Port Commission of Baltimore must be ascribed to a lack of leadership in our community at both the state and local levels. It is scarcely likely, at this late date, that the people of Maryland do not realize the importance of the port of Baltimore to the prosperity of the state as a whole. The port is now, as historically it has always been, the heart of our economy. In a very real sense, its activities are a barometer by which the material well-being of the entire state may be predicted. All this is well understood.
>
> What is not so widely appreciated is what needs to be done to keep the activities of the port of Baltimore at a high level. Under the slogan of private enterprise the railroads have been permitted to dominate the port and the officials of our state and local government have given only the most cursory

attention to its problems. It is only fair to say that Dr. Byrd in his recent campaign did attempt to stress this vital subject, but it was evident that neither the press nor the public were in the mood to listen to him.

In the meantime we have been paying dearly for our complacency and accompanying inertia. Other communities under more aggressive leadership have greatly improved their facilities and their competitive position. Our neighbors in the Delaware River Valley now bid fair to take from Baltimore a large share of the ore traffic which has represented so great a part of the total trade of the port in recent years. While we have made no progress in obtaining even preliminary approval from the Corps of Engineers for certain minor improvements to Baltimore's channel, Congress has given its final approval to a grandiose project for the deepening of the Delaware River channel all the way to Morrisville. There is general agreement that Baltimore needs new facilities for the handling of general cargo, but no real progress in this direction has yet been made. In the meantime the freight differential on which we have leaned as a crutch for so many years has been narrowed in scope and may disappear altogether. The prospect of the opening of the St. Lawrence Seaway contributes another aspect to an altogether depressing picture.

All of these developments were foreseeable and some of them might have been prevented. More important, aggressive conduct of the affairs of the port might have produced gains to offset inescapable losses. Our present difficulties were predicted in the Knappen report in 1947, which clearly showed the need for a state agency having full authority in all matters relating to the port of Baltimore and its environs. That report emphasized that in order to do the job really needed, such an agency would have to possess broad legislative powers, superseding those of all municipalities in whose territory any facilities of the port of Baltimore might be located. These findings were ignored and a Port Commission was established which, by the very nature of its organization, was bound to be ineffective. The results of this continued adherence to the policy of drift are now apparent.

Is it not high time that Governor McKeldin and the leaders in the Legislature took this matter firmly in hand? No doubt the details of any proposal can await the report of the survey now being made by the Association of Commerce. But the basic outlines are plain. If Maryland's greatest economic asset is to be preserved, a state agency must be created which will have powers independent of the City of Baltimore and of the adjacent counties, sufficiently broad to permit it to carry on those activities which are essential to the welfare of the port. This will certainly include an adequate power of condemnation. If the matter is properly explained to the people of Maryland they will surely be willing to set aside the parochial feelings which brought about the adoption of the recent constitutional amendment and will gladly confer the necessary powers on a properly constituted state agency.

During my tour of duty in the War Department, I had come in contact with a New York banker who was a member of the governing board of the Port of New York Authority. He was very proud of the record of that agency in helping to build the port of New York to the commanding position which it still holds in world trade. He attributed this largely to the fact that the authority was independent of political and bureaucratic control. Because the port of New York is partly located in New Jersey, the legislatures of both states had been zealous to safeguard the authority's autonomy and, as a result, the authority could function with the freedom of a business enterprise, and membership on its board was a much sought after honor in the business community.

As my letter to the *Sun* indicated, there had been considerable agitation in the Baltimore community about the sinking state of the port of Baltimore, and various committees had been organized to study the problem. But as of the end of 1954, the only result had been to create a Port Commission, which consisted almost entirely of representatives of special interests. Thus, the railroads, the labor unions, the shipping lines, and the various port services each had a member to represent it on the board and, of course, virtually nothing was agreed upon.

However, shortly before I wrote my letter, the Association of Commerce had appointed yet another committee, and a leader of the admiralty bar, Robert W. Williams, who had served for four years as a member of the Federal Maritime Commission in Washington, had taken an important role in its deliberations. That group was ultimately successful in getting the support of Governor McKeldin and of the leaders of the legislature, with the result that in 1956 a law was passed creating the Maryland Port Authority on the model of the Port of New York Authority. Bob Williams was appointed as chairman of the commission which was the governing board of the authority, and his fellow commissioners were Luke Hopkins, a Baltimore banker; Paul Smith, a Hagerstown public utility executive; Avery Hall, a Salisbury insurance executive; and Ed Corcoran, a community leader from Anne Arundel County.

At the first meeting of the commission it was agreed that Bob Williams should ask the attorney general of Maryland to consent to my appointment as general counsel of the commission. Attorney General Ferdinand Sybert immediately agreed, and for the next decade, I attended virtually all meetings of the commission, including the weekly informal lunches at the Merchants Club. My first assignment was to obtain rulings from the state Law Department establishing the independence of the authority from control by any other state agency. This I was able to do, and the attorney general handed down a series of opinions to the effect that the authority had control of its own budget, could hire its own staff at salaries fixed without regard to state standards, could do its own procurement, and could select an independent firm of certified public accountants to audit its books.

Meanwhile, I was charged with responsibility for representing the authority in a number of proceedings before the Interstate Commerce Commission, the Maritime Commission, and the courts. For eighty years the rate structure which governed the movement of freight to and from the industrial heartland of the Middle West and the Atlantic ports had recognized that the port of Baltimore was entitled to a differential over the rival ports of New York and Boston. This long-established differential had recently been challenged by railroads serving the northern ports, which had reduced their rates to the same level as the rates to Baltimore. The railroads serving Baltimore had responded by lowering their rates so as to reestablish the differential, and the Interstate Commerce Commission had suspended all the rates and set the matter down for hearing. This was generally regarded as the most important rate case in the history of the port, and the members of the Port Authority instructed me to intervene in support of the Baltimore railroads.

In another rate case the Interstate Commerce Commission had permitted railroads serving Philadelphia and New York to file rates on the movement of iron ore through those ports to points in the Middle West at the same level as the rates from those points to Baltimore. This ruling had been appealed by Baltimore interests and was awaiting hearing before a three-judge court in the federal court in Baltimore. At stake was a movement of iron ore which accounted for a substantial percentage of the total tonnage moving through the port of Baltimore, and again I was instructed to intervene on behalf of the Maryland Port Authority in support of the position taken by the Baltimore interests.

Finally, one of the major shipping lines which served Baltimore as well as New York proposed to file rates which absorbed wharfage charges at the port of New York on shipments from Puerto Rico but failed to do so on the movements from Puerto Rico to the port of Baltimore. It was feared that this proposal would result in the diversion to New York of traffic which had for many years been moving through Baltimore, and I was instructed to institute proceedings before the Federal Maritime Commission to prevent this.

All of these cases presented a challenge because of their public importance and because of the fact that they took me into unfamiliar territory. Fortunately, I had the guidance of the general counsel of the B&O, Edward Burgess, and his successor in that office, Jervis Langdon. While I felt competent to handle the case pending in the federal court, when it came to proceedings before the Interstate Commerce Commission and the Federal Maritime Commission, it seemed to me that I needed the help of a Washington lawyer who specialized in that field. Bob Williams agreed, and at his suggestion I got permission from the attorney general of Maryland to employ Donald Macleay to work with me in these cases.

Aside from the rate cases, I was asked to take part in negotiations with the city of Baltimore which involved the taking over of responsibility for many port activities previously handled by the city and the transfer of several city-owned waterfront properties, notably a virtually obsolete airport in Dundalk known as Harbor Field. I was asked also to assist in negotiations for the acquisition of property in the Anne Arundel area of the port known as Hawkins Point. The negotiations with regard to these properties were long and complicated. The city was represented, by, among others, Walter Graham, Hyman Pressman, and William Donald Schaefer. At that time there was nobody on the staff of the authority who knew much more about the subject than I did. Later on, Joseph L. Stanton was employed as executive director of the authority, but he also at first had a good deal to learn about the port and its activities. Fortunately, I was able to call on my partner Vernon Miller, who had a remarkable store of learning as the result of years of practice in the admiralty field, during which he had become something of an expert on port affairs.

When Joe Stanton took charge, he also turned to me at times for help in matters which were not strictly legal. At one time he got into a controversy with Don Schaefer on the question of the taxation of port facilities owned and operated by the authority. The argument got heated and Don thought that his integrity had been questioned. At this point Joe asked me to take over, and I did what I could to sooth the ruffled feelings of the then president of the city council.

An important development was the retirement of Mr. Simpson as president of the B&O. Howard Bruce told me that they did not seem to have anybody in that organization who was ready to take over the job. I suggested to him that he take a good look at Jervis Langdon, who seemed to me to have a remarkable grasp on every aspect of the railroad business, and I was delighted when Jervis was chosen to be the next president. Later on Jervis asked me to suggest the name of a representative Baltimorean to fill a vacancy on the Board of Directors of the B&O, and I believe that I was responsible for the selection of Charles S. Garland, who was then the guiding partner in the firm of Alexander Brown & Sons.

Altogether, by the end of 1958, a very warm relationship had been established between me and the commissioners and the staff of the authority, and I began to feel that it might be possible for me to develop in the Baltimore community a usefulness comparable to that which I had succeeded in attaining in Washington during the latter part of the war. I was encouraged in this belief by a letter which I received from Bob Williams on November 18, 1958, in which he said:

> One of the great satisfactions which I have is looking back to the talks we had in the early days which resulted in your being willing to serve as General Counsel for the Port Authority. A new organization particularly needs the advice of the best possible counsel available with judgment and experience, and you have contributed in this regard to the highest degree.

Bob Williams's term expired in the summer of 1958 and, to the disappointment of all of us, he was not reappointed by Governor McKeldin.

Instead, John L. Kronau, a local contractor who had the reputation of being something of a political wire puller was named in his place. The other members of the commission were concerned about the possibility that some of Kronau's business connections might involve conflicts of interest. They asked me to discuss this with the attorney general, which I did, and I believe that he must have taken the matter up with Kronau.

At any rate, someone stirred up the press by suggesting that Luke Hopkins, as an officer of the Maryland National Bank, was in a position of conflict of interest because the commission maintained an account in that bank. Luke asked me to look up the law on that subject, which I did, and found that the Maryland law was rather murky. The attorney general agreed with me that it would be stretching the law too far to hold that the Maryland National Bank could not perform routine banking services for the authority just because Luke Hopkins was an officer of the bank. He agreed to sponsor clarifying legislation, but in the meantime we worked out a program under which all the commissioners and the staff agreed to furnish confidential lists to the secretary of the authority of all companies in which they or their families were interested as directors, officers, employees, or stockholders, so that they might be excused from participating in any way in any transaction between the authority and any of those companies. As it turned out, a conflict did arise in which John Kronau was involved, and I had to insist on a change of his plans, to which he acquiesced very grudgingly and only after seeking the advice of independent counsel.

Clearly the departure of Bob Williams was something of a cloud on an otherwise rosy horizon, but for the time being, it served to strengthen the bonds which I had established with Paul Smith and Luke Hopkins. Paul Smith was a remarkable man. Physically he was handicapped by an almost grotesquely leonine head and hands and feet that were also abnormally large and clumsy, but his mind was powerful and his standards of the highest. His company was always stimulating and to be in his confidence was a privilege. I got the impression that he was an exceptionally wise man who dominated the business community of Western Maryland by sheer force of character. Superficially, the contrast between him and Luke Hopkins was striking. Born with a silver spoon in his mouth (as the old saying goes), Luke had been educated at a fashionable school, followed by Princeton in its palmiest days. Yet he and Paul Smith immediately understood one another and worked together harmoniously. So long as these two men were on the commission, I felt very secure in my professional relationship and, indeed, up until the year 1964, all seemed to go well.

In a sense, they went too well. This was a time when railroads were attempting mergers, and on June 8, 1960, the C&O asked permission of the Interstate Commerce Commission to acquire stock control of the

B&O Railroad. This was deeply disturbing to Jervis Langdon, who felt that he had been badly treated by the C&O when he had worked for that railroad before World War II. He told me that it was his understanding that the New York Central was interested in making a connection with the B&O. Sure enough, a contest followed between the two railroads to gain the support of the business interests in Baltimore as represented by the Association of Commerce, and ultimately both sides tried to enlist the support of the Maryland Port Authority. Due in part to Jervis Langdon, I found myself in the middle of this controversy. In the end, the C&O won the support of the authority by making a number of promises, which were never kept. Included among them was the promise to establish a headquarters in Baltimore and to keep the name "Baltimore" in any merged railroad.

During the course of these negotiations I got to know Walter Tuohy, the president of the C&O, and found him very congenial. I have in my file letters from him referring to the fact that both of us had been amateur violinists, and the general tone of our correspondence shows that we were on quite friendly terms. In contrast, the chief spokesman for the New York Central was its president, Al Perlman, whose attitude was quite different. His principal argument seemed to be that the only alternative to the merger of the New York Central and B&O would be a merger of the New York Central and Pennsylvania railroads, to which I gathered he was much opposed.

After the Interstate Commerce Commission had given its approval to the C&O's acquisition of the controlling interest in the B&O, Walter Tuohy rented an apartment in Baltimore in the neighborhood in which the Langdons and I were living and told me that he intended to establish his residence in Baltimore. I still believe that had he lived, the headquarters of the combined B&O/C&O system would have been in Baltimore. Unfortunately, shortly after this conversation, he was stricken with a heart attack from which he never recovered.

The C&O management gave a big dinner in Baltimore to celebrate its arrival in the community. Cyrus Eaton, who was well known to be the power behind the throne in C&O affairs, was present. Mr. Eaton told me that in his youth he had been a claims adjuster for the WB&A Railroad, where he knew my father. He added that at that time Marbury, Gosnell and Williams seemed to him to be clearly the leading law firm in Baltimore. The business leadership of the Baltimore community had been invited to meet Mr. Eaton, and there was a big head table at which the governor of Maryland and the mayor of Baltimore, as well as the members of the Port Authority, were seated. Below the head table was another table where minor officials of the railroad were seated. To my intense embarrassment, I found that I was seated at the head table and that Joe Stanton was seated at the lower table. I asked how on earth this had happened and was told that Mr. Tuohy had personally arranged it. I sat through a very uncomfortable evening.

In the meantime, we lost the freight differential case. We had won it before the Interstate Commerce Commission, as, indeed, we had won practically every other important matter which I had handled for the authority up to that time. The Boston & Maine Railroad had promptly appealed from the ruling of the commission to a three-judge court in the United States District Court of Massachusetts. At the trial of that case, I had associated a Boston lawyer named Ted Chase with me and had gotten the impression from him that my argument in support of the Interstate Commerce Commission ruling had been well received. As a matter of fact, the law clerk of one of the judges had been so indiscreet as to intimate as much to one of my Boston friends, who reported it to me. So it was quite a shock when the court unanimously reversed the commission's ruling.

When the Supreme Court agreed to hear our appeal from the order of the Boston Court, I felt quite hopeful that we would get a reversal. I spent the next summer in preparing a brief, with the aid of my associates Franklin Allen, Jack Jones, and Paul Sarbanes. By that time Jervis Langdon had become president of the B&O and had other things on his mind, and I was under the impression that he would leave the argument in the Supreme Court to me. Counsel for the other ports, including particularly Hampton Roads and Philadelphia, had expressed their satisfaction with the brief which my office had prepared and had agreed to let me speak for them at oral argument. To my chagrin, the general counsel of the ICC insisted on making the opening argument and Jervis said he expected to follow him. As a result, the Court heard first from the Interstate Commerce Commission, second from the railroads, and third from me as counsel for the ports. By the time I got to argue the case, the Court seemed to have heard all they wanted to hear from our side, and I was left with the impression that some of the judges had not been convinced by what they had heard.

Looking back, I can now see that I should have realized much sooner that Jervis would not allow me to take charge of the oral argument in the Supreme Court. He had insisted on filing a separate brief on behalf of the railroads which presented an argument which I did not think the Court would find persuasive. Indeed, Jack Fishwick, who was then counsel for the Norfolk & Western, told me that when he first read a draft of Jervis's brief, he was so upset that he called other railroad counsel and suggested that they ask Jervis to step aside and let somebody like Dean Acheson handle the case for all the appellants. However, according to Fishwick, after reading my brief he and his friends felt better and decided to drop that idea.

When I realized that the general counsel of the commission and

Jervis were both determined to make the opening arguments, it was too late to bring in someone like Acheson. I did suggest that it might be better if I dropped out altogether, but they protested that this would be hurtful, and I realized that I could not just walk out on all the port interests which had agreed to let me represent them at the argument. So I decided, with much foreboding, to use what little time was allotted to me as best I could.

Had Jervis not, as president of the railroad, had so many other things on his mind, I think that he would have reached the conclusion that it would be wiser to let a third party choose between our competing theories and present the case to the Court. In a sense, the ICC's counsel acted as that third party, but because of his many other responsibilities, he had been too busy to read my brief and took me aback by asking me to outline my argument to him in a short conference in his office. I replied that I intended to follow the line which I had taken in my brief, which I doubt he ever found time to read.

In the middle of Jervis's argument, Justice Black inquired whether the port of Baltimore was involved in the case. Altogether, by the time I came to argue, I was seething with frustration and remember expressing to Jervis the fear that the Court might affirm the case by an evenly divided vote, since one of the judges had disqualified himself. And that is exactly what happened. This was the greatest disappointment of my entire legal career, and I was reminded of my father's loss of the Northern Central case.

From that time on, my relationship with the authority began to go downhill. Within the year Paul Smith died and Luke Hopkins resigned. True, for the time being, there was no apparent change in my status as general counsel to the authority. Railroad mergers were still in the air and a contest was brewing over control of the Western Maryland Railway. The controlling stock interest in that railroad was owned by the combined C&O and B&O but was still held in an independent trust, which they moved to terminate for the avowed purpose of merging that railroad into the C&O/B&O system. At this point Jack Fishwick came to see me and suggested that the Norfolk & Western was prepared to intervene in opposition to that motion provided that the Maryland Port Authority would join in opposing the absorption of the Western Maryland by the C&O/B&O system. He said that the Norfolk & Western was most anxious to get an outlet to the port of Baltimore and would be in a position to move a substantial amount of traffic through that port in preference to Hampton Roads. I reported all this to Joe Stanton and, after full discussion, the members of the authority and the Merger Committee of the Association of Commerce decided to give conditional approval to the termination of the trust, and I was instructed to intervene in the proceedings and ask that certain conditions be attached, to which the C&O and B&O had been unwilling to agree.

Following the loss of the freight differential case, Franklin Allen and I had a conference with Jervis Langdon, at which it was agreed to initiate a program of lowering rates to Baltimore on individual commodities, with the hope that this would substantially offset the loss of the freight differential. Apparently, Jervis had some difficulty in selling this program to the C&O, and in the end only a single rate reduction was proposed, relating to the movement of paper from points in central territory. This was promptly challenged by the New York railroads, which claimed quite correctly that it was an attempt at an end run around the Supreme Court decision in the freight differential case. However, once again we were successful before the Interstate Commerce Commission, and thus the road seemed to be open for the filing of a number of similar rate reductions on other commodities. To our surprise and chagrin, this never happened. As no appeal was taken from the commission's ruling in the paper rate case, we naturally reached the conclusion that some kind of deal had been made by the C&O.

Meanwhile, Jervis was having other troubles with the C&O management. With the death of Walter Tuohy, the C&O's attitude toward Baltimore had undergone a sharp change. Matters had come to a head over a proposal which Jervis had made to build a new coal pier in Baltimore, which would have attracted much of the export coal traffic which was moving through other ports. When his plans were vetoed by the management at Cleveland, Jervis resigned as president of the B&O. His successor was a man who appeared to have no interest whatsoever in developing the port of Baltimore.

Shortly after Jervis's departure, it became apparent that my relationship with the authority was changing. In a number of ways I sensed that Joe Stanton wished to modify the relationship which had been established in 1956 and I, accordingly, suggested to him that he take the matter up with the new attorney general, Francis B. Burch, who promptly insisted on taking back control of all the legal business of the authority. Nominally I remained as counsel of record in all open matters, but this proved to be largely a clean-up job which was virtually completed by 1967, when I formally resigned as counsel to the authority.

After 1967 I had very little contact with the authority. On one occasion, however, I was invited to a luncheon at which a proposal was advanced to merge the Port Authority into a Department of Transportation which was to include the State Roads Commission and a newly created Mass Transit Administration. I was shocked to discover that this proposal had the support of the Greater Baltimore Committee and learned that the reason was that the committee wanted to get access to the revenues which the Port Authority had, since its creation, been deriving from that portion of the state corporate income tax which had been allotted to it by the legislature. The Greater Baltimore Committee was urging the state to help finance a subway system in Baltimore City and hoped to divert some of the Port Authority's revenues to that objective.

Over what seemed to be my lone protest, this program was put through the legislature, with the result that the law creating the authority was repealed in its entirety and a Port Administration was established as a division of the new Department of Transportation. The members of the authority were all voted out of office and their powers were delegated to a new port administrator, subject to the supervision of the head of the Department of Transportation. Sometime after this reorganization had taken place, I met Walter Boyer, who had been the chief of the engineering staff of the authority, and asked him how things were going. He replied, "We have been forced into a shotgun marriage with a bankrupt."

In April 1986 the *Sun* ran an article describing the achievement of a freshman legislator who was boasting of the fact that she had succeeded in attaching to the appropriation of funds to the Port Administration a requirement that the administrator submit to a subcommittee of the legislature a report showing in detail how the appropriations were to be spent. Obviously, all the work that had been done since 1956 in establishing the autonomy of the Port Authority has now been undone.

Maryland's Use Tax

A retail store located in Wilmington, Delaware, advertised in newspapers which circulated in the state of Maryland and on a radio station whose coverage included a part of the Eastern Shore of the state. Its management refused to collect use taxes on goods which were sold to Maryland residents. Delivery of the goods was in some cases made by the use of trucks which carried them into Maryland, and at my suggestion, the comptroller of Maryland arranged to have an attachment laid on a company truck when it made a delivery in the city of Baltimore. This seemed to me the best way to emphasize the fact that in attempting to collect Maryland use taxes on such transactions, the comptroller was going too far.

The Court of Appeals of Maryland upheld the tax but on appeal I was able to persuade five justices of the Supreme Court that Maryland had violated the due process clause of the Fourteenth Amendment to the Federal Constitution. As soon as I had finished stating the facts, Justice Frankfurter asked, "Why did not your client ignore the Maryland tax collectors?" Whereupon Justice Jackson answered for me, saying, "He did and they seized his truck." John Mason Brown, the famous drama critic who was then a Harvard overseer, was preparing an essay on Justice Frankfurter and, at the justice's suggestion, sat in the courtroom during my argument. He told me later that he thought that I had won the case, and it turned out that he was right by the narrowest of margins. The decision of the Court in this case still stands, marking the limits of the taxing power of the states in an important area.

Dealer Terminations

An automobile dealer whose franchise had been terminated by the Hudson Motor Company brought suit in the federal District Court in Baltimore, claiming treble damages for a violation of the Sherman Act. My firm represented Hudson and Judge Thomsen granted my motion to dismiss before trial. This action was upheld on appeal in a decision which for many years stood as an important precedent in antitrust law.

The dealer then brought suit in the state court for breach of contract, and Jack Jones and I were successful in defending that suit before a jury. The dealer claimed that he had lost sales which he would have made had his franchise not been terminated. In response to interrogatories, he furnished a list of his prospective customers, and I arranged to have each one of them interviewed and discovered that every single one of them was prepared to say that before the dealership had been canceled, he or she had decided not to buy the car.

When the case came to trial, I made no opening statement but reserved the right to do so after the close of the plaintiff's case. When the dealer took the stand, I read him the list of prospective customers that his counsel had furnished and asked him whether he was prepared to swear that they had all indicated their intention to buy the car. He replied, "Yes, sir, they did, every one of them." I did not cross-examine him and when the plaintiff's case was completed, I made an opening statement in which I told the jury that I proposed to prove that not a single one of those alleged customers had any intention of making a purchase. I then called them, one after another, to the stand and they testified to that effect. The jury brought in a verdict for the defendant in fifteen minutes. I later learned that Hudson's Detroit counsel, who had attended the trial as an observer, had been so scandalized by my failure to cross-examine the dealer that he had seriously considered asking the court to postpone the case while Hudson got new local counsel.

State Aid to Denominational Colleges

In 1962 and 1963 the Maryland legislature, following a policy of aiding private colleges (including those with sectarian affiliation) which dated back to 1784, enacted four bills, each of which provided for the sale of certificates of indebtedness of the state of Maryland and for the payment of the proceeds of the sale to a specified church-related college for the construction of a building for educational purposes. The Horace Mann League and a group of Maryland taxpayers joined in bringing suit to prevent the payments, claiming that they would violate the "establishment clause" of the First Amendment to the Federal Constitution, which under then recent decisions of the Supreme Court of the United States had been held to forbid the establishment of any religion by a state government. In the case of three of the Maryland colleges, the building to the cost of which the state of Maryland was contributing was to be used for instruction in the sciences; in the case of the fourth college, the building was to be used for a dormitory and classrooms.

The senior counsel for the Horace Mann League was Leo Pfeffer, who had attained a national reputation by challenging legislation on the ground that it tended to aid religion. It appeared that he had chosen the Maryland legislation as a test case to determine the then open question as to the extent that a state could validly contribute to church-related institutions of higher education. This challenge had been accepted by the hierarchy of the Roman Catholic church, and the choice of counsel to represent two of the Maryland colleges, which were being operated by religious orders of that church, rested in the hands of Cardinal Shehan. I think that my selection as lead counsel for those two colleges was primarily due to the fact that at that time the principal legal adviser to the Catholic archdiocese of Maryland was Frank Gallagher, a former associate of Piper & Marbury.

In preparing that case for trial, I came in contact with quite a few of the leading figures in Catholic higher education. I was particularly impressed by the president of St. Louis University, Father Paul C. Reinert, S.J., who testified as a witness for the colleges. My friends at Harvard informed me that Father Reinert was the most respected figure of all the Catholic educators in the country, and after hearing his testimony I could see why.

During the trial of this case Mr. Pfeffer and his local counsel, Mel Sykes, undertook to prove that every phase of the education given at the two Catholic colleges was permeated by religious dogma. They came a cropper when they undertook to examine one of the teachers in the English department, Sister Mary Maura, who had achieved national recognition as a poet and who taught creative writing at Notre Dame College. When asked whether she used the Bible as a model, she replied in the affirmative. She was then asked what translation she used, to which her reply was, "As a model of English prose, the King James version is unequaled." She was then asked what other models she used in teaching her students and replied, "Principally the *New Yorker*." This remark was immediately quoted by a national magazine in an article commenting on recent developments in Catholic higher education.

Judge Duckett decided the case in our favor, saying, "It would, therefore, seem to me that the scientific education of college students is most vital to our public safety and welfare, perhaps more so than training juveniles at St. Mary's Industrial School, even though it did produce Babe Ruth."

When the case reached the Court of Appeals of Maryland a majority voted to reverse the lower court on the federal constitutional question. Although expressly finding that the statutes in question were on their face not intended to aid religion and that they achieved an important secular purpose, they nevertheless concluded that since three of the institutions involved were substantially affiliated with particular religious denominations, no state aid could be given to them, even to achieve a secular public purpose. To my great disappointment, the Supreme Court denied certiorari, although our petition was supported by a brief filed on behalf of the Association of American Colleges as a friend of the Court.

The Virginia Tuition Grant Cases: A Breathing Space for Parents

Sometime during the year 1963 I was asked to argue a case in the Supreme Court on behalf of Prince Edward County, Virginia. After the decision in the *Brown* case, the School Board of Prince Edward County closed its public schools and proceeded to grant tuition scholarships to students who were attending private schools which were opened for white students only by a recently organized Prince Edward Foundation. The parents of a group of black students who lived in Prince Edward County brought suit in the United States District Court for the Eastern District of Virginia to force the reopening of the public schools and to prohibit the payment of tuition grants to any Prince Edward County student who was attending a school to which black children were not admitted. The District Court entered an order requiring the reopening of the public schools and prohibiting the issuance of tuition grants to any students from Prince Edward County so long as the public schools in that county remained closed. The Court of Appeals for the Fourth Circuit had reversed that judgment, and an appeal from that order was pending in the Supreme Court.

I declined the employment on the ground that the use of tuition grants in so obvious an attempt to evade the ruling in the *Brown* case would jeopardize the use of public funds for secular purposes at Maryland church-related colleges which I was then representing. As I had predicted, the Supreme Court directed the Fourth Circuit to affirm the order of the district judge. It was, therefore, with some surprise that I received an invitation to attend a meeting in Richmond at which the lawyers for the Virginia State Board of Education and for the school boards of a number of Virginia counties had been summoned by the attorney general of the state. The attorney general wished to develop a strategy for handling a number of suits which had been brought following the ruling of the Supreme Court in the Prince Edward County case. These suits all involved the validity of tuition grants to private schools in a variety of circumstances. Some county school boards had adopted what was called "freedom of choice" programs which left it up to the parents to select either a desegregated public school or a private school, in which case tuition grants would be made available. The NAACP challenged the validity of tuition grants in any case where the private school excluded blacks.

I took Lewis Noonberg with me to the meeting, where we listened to the county lawyers' description of the reaction of their constituencies to the *Brown* decision, which ranged from outright defiance to resigned acquiescence. On one point all the lawyers were in agreement, viz., that white parents were simply not willing to send their children to schools where they would be in a racial minority. If that meant changing their place of residence, then they would do so, but they had to have time to make the necessary adjustments. The lawyers all recognized that their constituencies would have to live with the ruling that state-supported schools have to be open to children of all races, but the lawyers also made it clear that their constituents were counting on tuition grants to afford a flexibility which would make it possible for their children to attend schools where they would not be in a racial minority. The Virginia program of tuition grants had existed since long before the decision in the *Brown* case, and all the lawyers said that it was essential to preserve it if possible.

Lewis and I were both impressed by the pragmatic approach of the attorney general of Virginia as well as by the legal acumen of his assistant, Bob McIlwaine. At the conclusion of the conference the attorney general asked me whether I would accept appointment as a special assistant to represent the Virginia State Board of Education in all the cases then pending in the federal courts. After thinking the matter over and discussing it with Lewis, I agreed to accept this employment on the clear understanding that the state board was not committed to the position taken by any of the county boards and particularly did not propose to defend the Prince Edward County School Board, which had taken positions which the NAACP claimed were in contempt of the spirit of the order of the District Court which the Supreme Court had affirmed.

For several years thereafter Lewis and I appeared in a series of cases in the Eastern District of Virginia and in the Fourth Circuit seeking to sustain the use of tuition grants in cases where the public schools were open to all races. It so happened that two appeals were taken from different rulings of federal judges in the Eastern District of Virginia. In one case arising in Surry County, Virginia, the state board was supporting the use of tuition grants where the county school board had announced its intention to open the public schools to students of all races. The other case arose again in Prince Edward County, where it was claimed that the school board had adopted a subterfuge by announcing that the public schools would be reopened to children of all races and then closing the only opened school on the ground that there were no applicants, while at the same time continuing to use public funds to support the Foundation School.

Lewis and I filed briefs in both cases on behalf of the Virginia State board, which made it entirely clear that we were not endorsing the actions of the Prince Edward County board. To our consternation, the Court of Appeals for the Fourth Circuit consolidated the two appeals and said that only one argument from each side would be heard in the consolidated case. I told the counsel for the Prince Edward County board that I intended to refer the court to his brief while at the same time making it clear that the state board was not endorsing his position. I thought he would protest and demand the right to be heard, but apparently he thought that it would be useless to do so. The result was that I made the only argument and was reported as having appeared on behalf of Prince Edward County, which I did only on the limited question which we raised for the Surry County board.

In the light of revelations subsequently made by one of his law clerks, it would appear that Judge Sobeloff, who was then chief judge for the Fourth Circuit, was not blind to the public relations aspect of the situation and seized the opportunity to appear to be striking down Prince Edward County, which by that time had become notorious all over the country as a community which had denied even an elementary education to all black students for many years.

While the decision of the Fourth Circuit clearly forbade the use of tuition grants for the so-called Foundation Schools, it did not go so far as to outlaw all tuition grants to all schools which were not integrated. Accordingly, shortly after the decision was handed down, the NAACP brought a suit claiming that the entire Virginia tuition grant statute was invalid. Lewis and I appeared again on behalf of the Virginia State Board of Education and were successful in convincing the court that the statute was not unconstitutional on its face. However, the court held that it would retain jurisdiction for the purpose of prohibiting tuition grants to private schools wherever it appeared that the grants represented the schools' major source of support.

The attorney general of Virginia was well satisfied with the result, which, as it turned out, gave the people of Virginia about four years in which to accomplish real desegregation of the state's public school system. At the end of that period the Supreme Court affirmed without opinion two decisions handed down in the Fifth Circuit by three-judge courts. There Judge Wisdom (who had worked in my office during World War II) condemned as invalid under the Fourteenth Amendment the use of public funds which tended *in any way* to facilitate evasion of the spirit of the *Brown* decision. In the light of these cases the Virginia three-judge court, after hearing further argument, modified its previous ruling and entered a sweeping order holding the Virginia tuition statute invalid insofar as it permitted grants to students at any private school which excluded black students. Once more Lewis and I journeyed to Richmond for a conference at which some of the county lawyers were urging the attorney general of Virginia to appeal this last ruling to the Supreme Court. While indicating our willingness to take such an appeal if requested to do so, Lewis and I also made it clear that we had very little hope of a favorable result, and the attorney general agreed with us and advised the State Board of Education to be content with what had been accomplished.

Maryland Casualty Company: A Model Takeover

For well over a century the descendants of the founders of the investment banking firm of Alexander Brown & Sons have mocked the folk wisdom which teaches that nepotism and loyalty to the old school tie will inevitably bring economic disaster to any business undertaking. The sons and sons-in-law of the Brown family and of their school friends and classmates have for generation after generation been offered an opportunity to work in that firm, and in some extraordinary way that group has contrived to produce, with the aid of a few outsiders, leaders who have kept the firm at the apex of Baltimore's business and cultural life. During the first half of the twentieth century the outstanding figure in that firm was undoubtedly B. Howell Griswold, who had married the daughter of the Alexander Brown of my father's day. Ben Griswold's daughter Carolyn had married McKenny Egerton, who in 1952 was the youngest partner in the Piper firm. Largely as a result of his connection with the Brown family, he became the Baltimore lawyer most experienced in handling the legal aspects of corporate mergers and acquisitions. It had actually gotten to the point that whenever a businessman was seen to be lunching with Kenny, rumors began to fly.

Accordingly, it was natural that Kenny should be consulted when in 1963 conversations began between the officers of the Maryland Casualty Company and the officers of American General Insurance Company, which had its headquarters in Houston, Texas. These conversations struck a snag when it became apparent that the Texans wanted to take control of the Maryland company. This was not at all acceptable to the Maryland management, which felt that such an arrangement would jeopardize the all-important relationship between the company and its seventeen thousand agents, and for this reason the discussions between the two managements were terminated.

At that point the officers of the Texas company announced their intention to make an offer directly to the stockholders of the Maryland company. Thereupon the Maryland management announced its intention to resist this takeover, and for the next several months, under the guidance of Kenny Egerton, the Maryland officers gave a classic illustration of how a hostile takeover could be fought.

I became involved in this fracas when in the latter part of June 1964 a suit was filed in the Superior Court of Baltimore City by American General and several substantial stockholders in the Maryland company to force the management of Maryland Casualty to make its books available so that American General could offer the Maryland stockholders the opportunity to exchange their shares on the basis which the Maryland management had turned down. In the meantime American General filed a registration statement with the Securities and Exchange Commission which was to become effective early in July of 1964. With the help of a young associate in Piper & Marbury named Larry Scriggins, I was successful in defeating this effort to obtain access to the corporate books. It was Larry's first appearance in court, and his quiet and competent presentation of the issues involved was a model of good advocacy. The opinion of Judge Wilson Barnes was a definite setback to the Texans in that it pointed out very clearly the aspects in which the proposed exchange was unfair to the Maryland stockholders and thereby justified the resistance of the Maryland management.

At the same time that Larry and I were working on the suit filed in the Baltimore court, I was exploring the possibility of bringing an action in the District of Columbia to prohibit American General from proceeding with its exchange offer on the ground that the takeover of the Maryland Casualty by American General would involve a violation of the Sherman and Clayton Antitrust acts. In this connection we had to interpret the McCarran Act, which had exempted insurance companies from antitrust laws to the extent that they were adequately regulated by state law. On that point we sought the help of Paul Carrington, a prominent lawyer in Dallas, Texas, who gave us an opinion that nothing in the Texas law would supersede or render inoperable the federal antitrust statutes.

As a result of our studies, we decided to file suit in the District Court of Washington, D.C. At the same time we moved for a temporary restraining order prohibiting American General from proceeding with its exchange offer until a further hearing could be held on our application for a preliminary injunction. On July 8, 1964, I argued this motion before District Judge McGarraghy and succeeded in persuading him to grant the temporary restraining order. At the same time he set the application for a preliminary injunction down for hearing on July 15.

That hearing occupied five days, during which several of the officers of the Maryland and Texas companies testified. Our principal witness was the president of the Maryland Casualty Company, Ellsworth Miller, who seemed to be a bit on the defensive. However, on the all-important question of whether irreparable injury to Maryland Casualty would result if American General were permitted to proceed immediately with the exchange offer, we produced very effective testimony from Charles Peterson, who was the vice-president of the Maryland company in charge of the company's relationship with its agents. After Peterson had testified, during a break in the hearing I was introduced to Mr. Gus Wortham, the president of American General, who congratulated me on Peterson's testimony, saying, "That fellow really knows his business. He is the kind of man that every insurance company needs to have."

This seemed remarkably generous to me, since Peterson's testimony was undoubtedly most damaging to American General's case. I had heard that Gus Wortham was the Texan most likely to step into the shoes of Jesse Jones, and I was much impressed by his objectivity.

On July 27 Judge McGarraghy entered findings of fact and an opinion in which he announced his intention to dissolve the temporary restraining order which he had previously signed and to enter a preliminary injunction which would permit American General to proceed with the exchange offer but would otherwise preserve the status quo until a final hearing on the merits of Maryland Casualty's claim that the exchange would amount to a violation of the antitrust laws. That very same day John Wilson entered an appeal from Judge McGarraghy's order, and the case was docketed by the clerk of the Court of Appeals for the District of Columbia, together with a motion for a temporary restraining order pending a hearing on that appeal. A hearing on the motion was set for July 30 before a three-judge panel of the court.

On July 31 the panel entered an order denying our motion for a temporary restraining order on the ground that Maryland Casualty "has failed to show that it will be irreparably injured within the immediate future." The court further ordered the clerk to set the case for hearing "on as early a date after August 12, 1964, as the business of the court would permit." The court divided two to one, with Judge Miller supporting our application for a temporary restraining order while Judges Bazelon and Wright formed the majority who voted to deny it.

On that same day I left for Northeast Harbor, Maine, where I was scheduled to join what was known as the "doctors' cruise." Every year, on the first of August, Johnny Howard, Dick Shackelford, Oliver Cope, and Oliver's son-in-law, who was then a medical student, sailed out of Northeast Harbor for a ten-day cruise. I had been invited to join them and was immensely flattered by the invitation. As the only sailing I had ever done was at Chester, Nova Scotia, and I had not set foot on a sailboat for nearly twenty years, I was more or less supercargo. We were to sail "down east," headed for the Bay of Fundy, but the night before the cruise was to start a northeaster blew up, and after bucking it for a couple of miserable, cold, wet hours, we unanimously decided to turn around and head south.

While I was allowed to hold the tiller occasionally, I was not a very useful member of the crew. I am no cook and that chore fell largely to Oliver Cope and Johnny Howard. I was relegated to washing the dishes, as Johnny Howard announced in firm tones that he would cook or wash dishes but he would be "damned" if he would do both. That seemed to me to be a very reasonable position for him to take, and I have tried to instruct my children to be scrupulous in observing a similar division of household labor.

On the third day of the cruise we stopped briefly on an island. I went ashore to pick up some supplies and, to my astonishment, was greeted by the storekeeper who called me by name and said that I was to telephone my office in Baltimore immediately. There I was told that on August 2 American General had filed a suit in the federal court in Houston and that a district judge there had signed a temporary restraining order prohibiting the Maryland Casualty Company and its attorneys from "filing any additional suits or taking any action to enjoin, restrain or interfere with the proposed offer of exchange" excepting the pending proceedings in the Superior Court of Baltimore City and in the United States District Court for the District of Columbia.

When I got back to Baltimore on August 7, I learned that on August 4 our Washington counsel had given American General's local counsel, Hugh Cox, a pretty rough time before the panel of the Court of Appeals for the District of Columbia Circuit. The two judges who had voted against our motion for a temporary restraining order were quite indignant at what had happened, particularly as John Wilson made it perfectly clear that we had had no intention of filing additional suits to enjoin or restrain the proposed offer of exchange. Apparently Hugh had apologized to the court and announced that American General would dismiss the Houston suit, which it did on that same day.

On August 19 our case came on once more for argument before the panel of the Court of Appeals of the District of Columbia, where it became quite clear that Judges Bazelon and Wright felt that the shareholders of Maryland Casualty should be given the opportunity to vote on the proposed exchange, and at 4:30 on the afternoon of August 19, with Judge Miller dissenting, they entered an order affirming Judge McGarraghy. The effect of that order was to leave American General free to make its exchange offer while at the same time preserving the status quo as far as the management and operation of Maryland Casualty were concerned until final disposition on the merits of Maryland Casualty's antitrust claims.

When notified of the court's ruling, the president of Maryland Casualty, Ellsworth Miller, announced his intention to "continue fighting," but within two months it became apparent that more than 50 percent of the stockholders of Maryland Casualty had indicated their acceptance of

American General's offer. At the insistence of the Board of Directors of Maryland Casualty Company, negotiations were then reopened and by the middle of October had come to a successful conclusion. Mr. Wortham proved to be reasonable in his approach and agreed to several important proposals which were advanced by the Maryland Casualty negotiators. In particular, he agreed to organize a Delaware corporation of the same name, into which the Texas corporation would be merged. He agreed that the Delaware corporation would have a board of directors equally divided between former members of the Texas and Maryland companies and that the executive committee of that corporation should be similarly constituted. He also agreed that while these changes were taking place the Texas corporation would make no changes in the management or operation of Maryland Casualty. These were and always had been the principal goals of the Maryland Casualty officers, who agreed to deposit their own shares as well as those which were held in the company's treasury. In the end more than 80 percent were deposited and the reorganization was completed. It was and continues to be my belief that as a result of the hearings in Washington which he attended, Gus Wortham had become satisfied with the caliber of the Maryland company's management, and it is my impression that he has scrupulously observed his commitments. True, Ellsworth Miller resigned shortly after the completion of the reorganization of American General, but Charles Peterson took his place as president of the company.

The Advertising Tax Cases

In 1957 the city of Baltimore undertook to require the press and all other media which published advertisements within the city limits to collect a 4 percent tax on all sales of space or time on the air and to pay a 2 percent tax on the gross receipts derived from such sales. These taxes were unique in that nowhere else in the United States was a tax levied on advertising media alone. The attempt of the city to levy these taxes created widespread consternation in the advertising industry and particularly among newspaper publishers, the principal source of whose revenues was money paid by local advertisers. The retail merchants, who were the principal local advertisers in Baltimore, were also very much concerned, as were to a lesser degree the radio and television stations, most of whose advertisements were exempted by reason of their interstate character.

The publishers of all the Baltimore newspapers promptly filed suits challenging the validity of these taxes, and the Retail Merchants Association of Baltimore, as well as two of the radio stations, asked me to file similar suits on their behalf. All together, seventeen suits were filed and heard before Judge Joseph L. Carter in the Circuit Court of Baltimore City, who ruled that the ordinances were unconstitutional.

On appeal, nine lawyers argued the case on behalf of the advertising media. According to my recollection, the principal arguments were made by me and by Dick Cleveland, who represented the publishers of the *Baltimore Sun*. My principal contention was that the ordinances amounted to an unlawful restraint of the freedom of the press guaranteed by the First and Fourteenth amendments of the Federal Constitution and by Article 40 of the Maryland Declaration of Rights. At first some of the judges of the Court of Appeals seemed reluctant to rule that revenues from advertising had any special immunity. During my argument one of the judges pointed out that his salary was not immune from taxation, whereupon I replied that a tax on judicial salaries alone would hardly be compatible with respect for the independence of the judiciary.

In affirming the lower court's ruling, Judge Prescott, speaking for a unanimous court, said:

> The root of the evil in these ordinances lies not merely in the fact that they curtail the dollars received by the newspapers and the stations, but in the fact that being entitled to the advantages granted by the First Amendment, they are singled out and required to pay a special tax that is not required of business in general or some broad portion thereof. The judges are compelled to pay income taxes as other citizens are, but, if the judges' salaries were singled out and they, alone, were required to pay such taxes, there would be few who would try to champion the same as a valid enactment of law.

Thereafter, the news media in mentioning my name identified me as a "constitutional lawyer," which always reminded me of Judge Patterson's low opinion of that ilk.

I Am Called "Warwick"

In one of the early chapters of this book I referred to my father's participation in the "new judges" fight of 1882, when the Reform Movement broke the hold of the politicians on the Baltimore City Courthouse. For a number of years thereafter the political leaders kept their hands off the Baltimore City courts and capable lawyers were elected and reelected to the bench without regard to partisan considerations. However, the time inevitably came when an ambitious politician successfully challenged this idyllic situation, with the result that an able and experienced judge was defeated for reelection by a far less qualified candidate. It looked very much as if Baltimore judges might once again be selected by the political bosses meeting in the back rooms of their clubs.

My father, who had been trying cases in New York City, where the lawyers openly discussed whether a certain judge could be "reached," joined with other leaders of the Baltimore bar in devising what came to be known as "the sitting judge principle," pursuant to which the bar regularly lent its support to a sitting judge who was running for reelection, regardless of the merits of any other candidate for the office. Sometimes the lawyers had to swallow rather hard before they could make up their minds to support a mediocre sitting judge against a better-qualified challenger, but the alternative seemed to them to be so much worse that they always decided to maintain the sitting judge principle.

In the meantime a new method of dealing with this problem was devised in the state of Missouri. It caught the attention of Judge Emory H. Niles, who was president of the Maryland State Bar Association in 1961–62. In his presidential address to the state bar Judge Niles described the Missouri Plan, which thereafter was identified in Maryland as the Niles Plan. In general, the plan called for the establishment of judicial selection committees in each of the judicial districts of the state and of a statewide committee to deal with appointments to courts whose jurisdiction was statewide in scope. The members of these committees were to be selected in such a manner that the organized bar would have representation on the committee along with representatives of the public at large. The duty of these committees was to supply the governor with lists of qualified candidates for each judicial vacancy. Once a candidate had been selected by him and obtained the necessary legislative approval, he would take office and thereafter would never have to stand in a contested election, although provision might be made for periodic referenda to determine whether the judge should continue in office or be retired.

Judge Niles suggested that his successor appoint a committee to explore the feasibility of the adoption by Maryland of the Missouri Plan, and I was named as chairman of that committee. After careful study, the committee decided that the plan was a feasible one and drafted a constitutional amendment which was then presented to the state and local bar associations for study. For several years I attended meetings of these associations, pressing for the adoption of the Niles Plan, and I also persuaded Jenkins Cromwell, a respected Baltimore business leader, to become chairman of a lay committee for the Niles Plan, which conducted a public campaign for the adoption of the amendment. After one of my appearances before the state bar association, a columnist for the *Baltimore Evening Sun* named Bradford Jacobs described me as "a pillar of rectitude," to my intense mortification.

The Niles Plan is still a subject of debate in Maryland, along with the sitting judge principle. It has been adopted in part and applies to vacancies occurring on the appellate courts and the district courts but not in the circuit court, where judges must still undergo the ordeal of contested elections when their terms of office expire. With the mounting cost of an election campaign, the judges in the circuit courts are now faced with the necessity of seeking political and financial aid when they run for reelection, with the all too frequent result that they become indebted to the very people to whom no judge should ever be under obligation.

In 1964 I was advised that I had been nominated as president-elect of the Maryland State Bar Association. Any "hubris" on my part was averted when the chairman of the nominating committee told me that he had had a difficult time persuading the county members to join in that nomination. My term as president-elect began on July 1, 1964, and for the next two years I attended all the meetings of the executive committee of the association.

Shortly after I took office as president of the state bar association a young man named William Murray became involved in a domestic relations controversy which resulted in an order issued by the Circuit Court of Baltimore City (then known as the Supreme Bench of Baltimore City) finding him in contempt of court and directing him to be taken into custody. The Murray youth was the son of Madelyn Murray, the nationally known atheist. Her counsel had recently succeeded in persuading the Supreme Court of the United States that her son could not constitutionally be forced to excuse himself from a public school classroom where the pupils were required to recite a prayer dictated by the authorities of the state government. This was the famous school prayer decision which after two decades is still a political football.

Naturally enough, the press and radio stations had a field day over young Murray's arrest. To add to the fun he had been outraged by the contempt order which had been issued in his absence and without a proper hearing and like a chip off the old block he had resisted arrest. In the Supreme Court Mrs. Murray and her son had been represented by a member of the Baltimore bar, Leonard Kerpelman, and Mrs. Murray turned to him for help in getting her son out of jail. In the aroused state of public opinion Kerpelman despaired of his ability to obtain a fair hearing. He turned to me as president of the state bar association and asked me to assign lawyers to help him.

It seemed to me that Murray was clearly being held in jail illegally, so I asked my law partner Charlie Evans, who had been an assistant state's attorney in Baltimore City, and a young lawyer named Joseph Kaplan (now the chief administrative judge of the Circuit Court of Baltimore City) to enter the case as co-counsel with Kerpelman. This they did and were able to get young Murray quickly released from custody. In the meantime, Kerpelman had managed to get himself charged with contempt of court. When the grand jury was considering whether or not to indict the Murray boy for resisting arrest, Kerpelman had asked to appear before the grand jury, but the state's attorney had refused to allow it. Thereupon Kerpelman, who was characteristically impetuous, had gone to the grand jury room, banged on the door, and demanded admittance, and as a result was himself charged with contempt and was threatened with being indicted for obstructing justice. He came into my office, sat down and said, "I don't know why I bothered to come here because I know you won't want to have anything to do with me." Recognizing this as a symptom of the paranoia for which Kerpelman was well known, I calmed him down and told him that I would personally represent him. I then went to the state's attorney and succeeded in persuading him that this was merely overzealousness on Kerpelman's part, and in the end he agreed to drop the matter.

A few days later I got a letter from Madelyn Murray asserting that Kerpelman had told her she would have to put up five hundred dollars to make a present to me for my services. She wanted to know whether this was true and I immediately wrote her that I had no intention of making any charge and certainly expected no gifts. Kerpelman, who had received a copy of Mrs. Murray's letter to me, apologized profusely, but to my embarrassment a few days later there was delivered to my home a handsome set of copper tableware made in Taiwan.

Perhaps my most significant achievement during that period was the presidential address which I delivered on January 16, 1966. My thesis was that the time had come for the organized bar to provide adequate legal services to persons whose causes were unpopular. I pointed out that "all over the world inequalities between man and man and, I might add, between men and women, which used to be thought inevitable are now considered to be intolerable." I made special mention of the fundamental readjustment in the status of black Americans which had marked the years following the end of World War II. I referred to the fact that a national committee had recently been organized to handle civil rights cases, primarily in southern communities where the bar was unwilling to act, but I argued that what was needed was the organization in each community of committees which would act on behalf of the bar in all such cases.

This address drew more national attention than anything else I have ever done with the exception of my activities in connection with the Hiss libel suit. I got a number of letters from many parts of the country, including a request for copies of the address to be distributed among members of a state bar association committee in California. The address was also reprinted by bar association journals in New York and Pennsylvania and finally, at the request of the president of the American Bar Association, it was published as a lead article in the *American Bar Association Journal.*

For a domestic reason the day I made that speech remains vivid in my memory. My wife, Natalie, had on the day before I was scheduled to speak undergone surgery at the Johns Hopkins Hospital for a malignant breast tumor. In those days conservative surgeons usually performed what was known as a "Halsted radical," which involved the removal of one entire breast and the related glands. Although she happily made a complete recovery and has never had any recurrence, I was, naturally, very much concerned about her condition, although I felt obliged to discharge my function as president of the association in between visits to the hospital.

Even before my election to the presidency of the Maryland State Bar Association, I had occasionally taken a hand in the selection of judges. In 1961 I was named as chairman of a committee of the state bar which passed on the qualifications of candidates for positions on the federal bench. A vacancy had occurred in the United States District Court for the District of Maryland and my committee, after careful consideration, had supplied a list of eligible lawyers to the Department of Justice. Thereafter we were distressed to read in the press that the attorney general had asked a committee of the American Bar Association, headed by Bernie Segal, to report on the qualifications for this appointment of the mayor of Baltimore City, whose name was not on our list.

Mayor Grady had never been admitted to practice in the federal courts, and his trial experience had been almost exclusively as an assistant prosecuting attorney of criminal cases in Baltimore City. His stature as a lawyer simply did not compare with those whose names were on our list. I sent to Attorney General Robert Kennedy a letter describing the situation in our district and spoke to Bernie Segal, who advised me that the attorney general had explained to him that he would have to have very convincing reasons if Mayor Grady was found not to be qualified, since President Kennedy was particularly anxious to make this appointment. He said that President Kennedy had been informed that the president of the Baltimore City Council would automatically become mayor of Baltimore City if Grady went on the bench. Apparently that particular councilman had been the first Baltimore political leader to endorse the president's candidacy for the presidency, and Jack Kennedy felt indebted to him.

So I went to work interviewing key people who were familiar with Grady's work and put together what I felt was a very convincing case against his appointment to the federal bench. At the same time I went to see Archie Cox, who was then solicitor general of the United States, and pointed out that on my committee's list was an exceptionally well qualified candidate named Harrison Winter, who was then the city solicitor of Baltimore by appointment of Mayor Grady. I said that I had been assured that the mayor would be happy to see Winter get the appointment if he himself could not have it. Archie said that while the selection of judges was none of his business, he would talk to the attorney general and his deputy, Byron White, and pass on my suggestion.

I then went to see the attorney general of Maryland and got him to agree to ask the governor of Maryland to promise Mayor Grady the next appointment to the Supreme Bench of Baltimore City. To my great satisfaction it all worked out along those lines. Harrison Winter was appointed and made an excellent district judge and is now the highly respected chief judge of the Court of Appeals for the Fourth Circuit. Grady got the next appointment to the Supreme Bench of Baltimore City and recently retired as chief judge of that court. So everybody was happy, including the city council president, who succeeded Grady as mayor.

My next venture into judicial selection was equally satisfactory. There was a vacancy on the Court of Appeals of Maryland, and I was told that Fred Singley had been prevailed upon to allow his name to be put before Governor Spiro ("Ted") Agnew. When I happened to be at the State House at Annapolis, I dropped into the governor's office and was told by his appointments clerk that the governor would see me for a few minutes between appointments. When I told him my mission, he said, "Mr. Marbury, I don't happen to know Mr. Singley, but in view of what you and Judge Brune tell me about him, I will certainly look into it." Within ten days thereafter the governor appointed Fred Singley to the court, where he served with distinction until he reached retirement age.

Shortly thereafter President Nixon was called upon to fill a vacancy on the Supreme Court of the United States. Nixon's first choice was Clement Haynsworth, a South Carolina judge who was serving on the Court of Appeals for the Fourth Circuit. I had argued a number of cases before him and thought that he was well qualified. Unfortunately, he appeared to be vulnerable on a rather farfetched charge of conflict of interest. When it became apparent that Judge Haynsworth would not be confirmed, Nixon withdrew his name and nominated a Georgia lawyer named Harrold Carswell, who was then serving as a judge on the Court of Appeals for the Fifth Circuit. From all that I could learn, Judge Carswell was conspicuously lacking in the qualifications of a Supreme Court justice, and this time I added my name to a long list of lawyers who published an advertisement in the national press opposing his confirmation.

About that time I received a telephone call from Maryland's senior senator, Charles McC. Mathias, Jr., who told me that he was under very strong pressure from the White House to support Carswell. When I told him what I had done, he groaned and said, "That certainly does not help me very much. Can you suggest somebody else that you and your friends could support?" I asked why Lewis Powell of Richmond had not been thought of. He had been president of the American Bar Association and was highly regarded by lawyers all over the country. Mac replied that the Department of Justice had already sounded Powell out and found that he was not interested. I then said that the only way to get a man like that was to have the president personally talk to him.

A few days later I read an article in the *Baltimore Sun* which reported that the president had sent for Lewis Powell and told him that the country needed him and had obtained his reluctant consent to have his name sent to the Senate. Thereafter I ran into my distant relative Eppa Hunton, who was Lewis Powell's senior partner. He hailed me as "Warwick." When I asked what he meant by that, he said that at my suggestion Mac Mathias had spoken to the president and that this was directly responsible for the president's call to Lewis Powell.

The Constitutional Convention of 1967

The year 1967 was the centennial year of the Maryland Constitution. As it approached, Governor Tawes reported that "many lawyers, judges, legislators and students of political science [have] expressed to me the opinion that our Constitution [is] too lengthy and too detailed to serve satisfactorily as the basic law of our state." Accordingly, in 1965 he appointed a Constitutional Convention Commission to look into the question "whether a Constitutional Convention should be held, the procedures for calling such a Convention and the procedures for the election of the delegates thereto." Vernon Eney, who was named chairman of the commission, took his responsibilities very seriously and held a series of meetings of the commission at which many suggestions were made and debated. At his request I attended those meetings which had to do with the judiciary, and I must confess that I was somewhat concerned with what seemed to me to be the naive quality of some of the discussion.

On August 25, 1967, the commission filed a very comprehensive report which included a complete draft constitution and commentary. In the meantime legislation had been adopted in 1966 calling for the taking of "the sense of the people as to whether there should be a Constitutional Convention and in case of an affirmative answer providing for the calling of a Constitutional Convention to convene on September 12, 1967." The referendum was held on September 13, 1966, and the vote was 160,280 to 31,680 for the convening of a convention. While Vernon referred to this as an "overwhelming endorsement," some knowledgeable politicians were more impressed by the relatively small number of votes cast on so important a question.

I declined to stand for election to the convention on the ground that I was already devoting as much time to public affairs as I could possibly manage. I did, however, agree to act as chairman of a committee whose function was to help guide the electorate in choosing delegates to the convention. We found that many of the people who seemed most anxious to serve as delegates had special axes to grind, and it was no easy task to persuade the right sort of men and women to allow their names to be proposed. When Mayor McKeldin asked me to become the chief counsel to the City Task Force at the convention, I reluctantly agreed, having asked others to serve. At my request, Martin B. Greenfeld of the city solicitor's office and Mrs. Margaret ("Penny") Kostritsky, who had been one of the reporters to the commission, were assigned to assist me.

For nearly three months during the latter part of 1967 I commuted almost every day to Annapolis and watched the delegates at work. They were, indeed, a hard-working group and very serious in their intention to frame a model constitution. Only a minority, however, seemed to me to have much political sagacity, and I became increasingly doubtful whether they were framing a product which the votErs would be willing to accept. Those doubts were strengthened by a report which Senator Joe Tydings made to me after he had toured the state. To his dismay he had found that most of the local politicians were advising their cohorts to line up the voters against the new constitution, primarily because it "threatened their fiefs," as one of them explained to me.

As far as the Baltimore City administration was concerned, the provisions of the proposed constitution were entirely satisfactory, and the mayor congratulated me on the results. As I admitted to him, this was largely due to the work of the city's chief lobbyists, Janet Hoffman and Charlie Benton, both of whom had kept in touch with me throughout the session. In the end all our work went for nothing, as the voters turned the new constitution down.

This was a bitter disappointment to Vernon Eney, who had been the presiding officer at the convention, where he had earned the admiration and respect not only of the political amateurs but of the seasoned politicians as well. On May 16, 1968, I wrote to him, saying:

> You should have no regrets. All that one human being could do you have done, and more than anyone else could possibly have done.
>
> The truth seems to be that no new Constitution can be adopted in any state unless there is a strong public feeling of dissatisfaction with the existing government. That there was no such feeling was sufficiently shown by the extremely light vote by which the calling of the Constitutional Convention was ratified.

Chancellor of the Diocese

Since her childhood my wife, Natalie, has been a steady churchgoer and so far as she is concerned, church is synonymous with Old St. Paul's Episcopal Church, located at Charles and Saratoga streets in the city of Baltimore. So that is where we went regularly on Sundays when we were in the city. During the early years of our marriage the rector was the Reverend Arthur Barksdale Kinsolving, who had baptized Natalie and lived to perform the same office for our children. Dr. Kinsolving was succeeded as rector by Harry Lee Doll, a Virginian who typified all that was best in the graduates of the Virginia Seminary. Dr. Doll read the services in a superb bass voice (which my children identified with the voice of God), and his sermons revealed a spirituality which I found most appealing. On my return to Baltimore after World War II, he asked me to serve on the vestry of Old St. Paul's and I agreed to do so, although I was very conscious of my shortcomings as a churchman.

Sometime in the year 1961 Bishop Powell informed me that Carlyle Barton was going to resign as chancellor of the diocese of Maryland because of ill health and that he himself would retire as bishop of Maryland in 1963. He said that he had consulted Harry Lee Doll, who as coadjutor would automatically succeed him, and they had agreed on me to fill the position of chancellor of the diocese of Maryland. I was told that the duties of the chancellor were not onerous, since the business affairs of the diocese were primarily handled by Paul Holland, a very competent man who had previously been head of the Department of Public Works in Baltimore City. After talking to Paul, I agreed to take on the job.

During the two remaining years of Bishop Powell's incumbency, I found that the demands on my time as chancellor were not great. Bishop Powell was a skillful and experienced executive who handled nearly all the problems which came up without calling on me for help. After Bishop Doll had been installed as diocesan, I found that I was more frequently consulted. The problems presented by conflicts between young activist clergy and conservative laymen, particularly in matters relating to race relations, proved to be increasingly troublesome, and occasionally I sat with Bishop Doll in meetings dealing with such matters.

As chancellor I was called upon to attend meetings of the Diocesan Council as well as the annual diocesan conventions. In 1964 I was elected as a delegate to the General Convention of the National Church, which was held every three years. This gave me an interesting glimpse into the way in which the National Episcopal Church functioned, but I concluded that most of the lay delegates in attendance had very little knowledge of what was going on.

I did not attend the Special Convention which was held at South Bend, Indiana, in 1969, but what took place there had a sensational effect. According to my recollection, the press reported that a group of militants headed by James Forman had interrupted a session of the House of Bishops and had made a demand that the church make a contribution, by way of reparation, to the Black Economic Development Conference, which had previously adopted what was known as the Black Manifesto. That document was full of revolutionary rhetoric, in which the capitalist government of the United States was denounced, and those black leaders who were cooperating with the white moderates in an effort to integrate the social order were vilified as pimps. According to the press report, the convention had yielded to this demand and agreed to make a substantial contribution of church funds to the conference.

This action startled and outraged many faithful Episcopalians and exacerbated the already shaky financial situation of the diocese of Maryland. On October 13, 1969, I wrote to Bishop Doll a letter in which I said:

> I have read with great care all the documents which have been circulated in explanation of the recent action of the South Bend Convention in connection with black community development. So far, I have tried to withhold any comment when asked my opinion of this action. However, it is becoming increasingly impossible for me to keep out of the discussion which is presently taking place wherever two or three Episcopalians gather together, and for this reason I think that I should explain to you just what my position is.
>
> As I am sure you realize, there is a tremendous struggle going on between those Negroes who have for many years been seeking integration into American society on a basis of equality and those who have turned their backs on that objective and are seeking to establish a separate identity as black people. Most of these latter tend to reject the institutions of American society and to seek to identify with black people all over the world. Some of them go to the full length of proposing to establish totally separate communities either within or without the borders of the United States.
>
> The integrationists include people like Martin Jenkins, President of Morgan College, Roy Wilkins, Executive Director of the NAACP, and Andrew Brimmer, member of the Federal Reserve Board and a Harvard Overseer. I think it is fair to say that most of the Maryland Negroes who have spent their lives working for the advancement of people of their race fall into this group. On the other hand, the separatists include most of the younger militants whose names have become familiar in recent years as a result of their participation in demonstrations.
>
> My own sympathies lie strongly with the integrationists. I have tried to work with them in this community, and I believe that they are following the only course which can lead to a full realization of the Negroes' rights as citizens and as members of our society. On the other hand, I am convinced that the separatists are headed down a dead-end street and that if the Negroes of the country follow them, they will end up in even deeper frustration than they are now experiencing.
>
> For this reason it has been a source of great regret to me that the National Church has, perhaps unwittingly, entered this controversy on the side of the separatists. The process began at Seattle when the church committed itself to the principle of "self-determination for minority groups." This ambiguous phrase was followed by the recognition at South Bend of the Black Economic Development Conference as "a movement which is an expression of self-determination for the organizing of the black community in America." The fact is that the Black Economic Development Conference, by endorsing the program outlined in the Black Manifesto, has definitely committed itself to the cause of the separatists. The program outlined in the Manifesto calls for

the establishment of many separate black institutions, even including the establishment of a "black university." By endorsing that program, the Conference has flatly repudiated the integrationists, as has been made crystal clear by the adverse comments of Messrs. Jenkins, Wilkins and Brimmer and other Negro leaders of equal stature.

Whether it would be better for the Negroes to continue along the integrationist road, which has led to such striking advances in the last fifteen years, or to turn off on the untried separatist road does not seem to me to be a religious question. It is a *political* question, on which the National Episcopal Church has, in my judgment, come down on the wrong side. I believe that in doing so it has perpetrated a blunder comparable to the identification of the Methodist Church with the Prohibition Amendment 50 years ago. Thus I find myself unable to defend the recent action of the Special Convention.

If you feel that this position is not consistent with my continuing to act as Chancellor of the Diocese, please do not hesitate to let me know. The last thing I want to do is to add to your troubles.

On October 22, 1969, Bishop Doll replied:

Thank you for writing me as you did on October 13th about the South Bend Convention. I do appreciate your concern and taking the trouble to write me. Your stand is not at all inconsistent with being the Chancellor of the Diocese. I appreciate what you say but I certainly would not muzzle you in any way in expressing your feelings, nor would I consider this a thing that you should not do.

I was somewhat amazed at your premise that the Church had taken its stand on the side of the separatists in the very obvious struggle between the integrationists and the separatists. It was to preserve and strengthen the integrationists that the move was made.

To go back just a little, the first demand on the part of the Negro was for being integrated into our culture and society. Here the Church must hang its head in shame because it did nothing until the Supreme Court decision. Even then we Christians were reluctant and when we brought one Negro family into a parish without losing pledges and blowing the lid off we felt that we had really accomplished integration. We expressed our delight and our satisfaction at what we were doing but unconsciously we were either patronizing or showed that we were really doing this because we had to. It was this attitude that started the separatist movement among the Negroes because they despaired of ever being accepted as equals in a white society. To be sure, there were exceptions to this. A Thurgood Marshall (although he, stung by the rebukes passed upon his people at the St. Louis Convention, got up and left the Convention), a Senator Brooke or a Martin Jenkins, or maybe our own City Solicitor George Russell made the grade although even they will admit to you that they have had to swallow slights and hurts and rebukes because of their color.

The mainstream Negroes, however, had to turn to pride in their blackness.

They realized that until they could stand level with the white man, able as an ordinary citizen to be accepted and dealt with as the ordinary white man, recognized as being able to contribute to the common society that he shared with the white man as an equal, he could never be his own man.

We have been told this over and over and over again but we never did hear it. It was not until James Forman with his revolutionary rhetoric broke through the complacency of white America that we did begin to hear.

The issue at South Bend was whether or not we were willing to trust the men that we so glibly call our black brothers or whether all that we have been saying and all that we have been preaching about the love of Christ and that there was no division in Him was just pious phraseology that had a hollow ring. The black man at South Bend was crying out for this trust because he wanted to be a part of this Church and he wanted to be a part of this society, and I believe that if we had not trusted him, even in the lefthand fashion that we did, the Blacks with their four black bishops would have walked out of the Church and formed a separate Church. This is not what they wanted but they were this desperate, feeling that this was the last chance that the Church had to live by what it was saying. This is why I say we were on the side of the integrationists, not on the side of separatists.

I am sure that you are saying, well, why then didn't they repudiate the Black Manifesto with all of its violent sequential language? It was a very small segment of the Black Economic Development Conference that adopted the Black Manifesto in the first place and already by South Bend much of the leadership had passed out of the hands of the militants. I truly believe that the majority of the members of BEDC have repudiated the Manifesto in their hearts—*but* this was the one thing that they could not do publicly. In the first place, they had to present a united front. In the second place, if they had repudiated the Black Manifesto, they would have been accepting the money on the white man's terms as they have been doing for the last 400 years, and all the ground that they had gained would have been lost in their own eyes— and in ours. All of the things that I have been saying about the need for them to be each one his own man in an actual equality before the law and before God and in the eyes of his white brethren would have been repudiated along with the Black Manifesto.

It is in this sense that the integrationist/separatist struggle is a religious issue. Certainly in any political sense it is not the business of the Church, but what happens to the man, to his soul, to his estimate of himself as a child of God, is very much the business of the Church. Perhaps it depends upon which facet you look into the gem as to whether it is political or whether it is religious. I am afraid that we can only separate the issue to talk about it, it is so intertwined. If this is the case, then the Church must accept the opprobrium of dabbling in politics but it is only in the segment of the brotherhood of man. The Church is committed to and is working for, and I believe in my soul that the action of South Bend furthered the integrationist side rather than the separatist side.

All of the men whom you have mentioned, such as Messrs. Jenkins, Wilkins and Brimmer, are around my age. They are no longer the leaders of the young element among the Blacks. These leaders, so the Blacks that I trust tell me, will come from the moderate element that is in control in the Black Economic Development Conference.

As we have learned from the autobiography of Malcolm X, many of the militant leaders of those days are now conspicuous in their acceptance of the social order which they had previously denounced so vehemently. Whether the white Episcopalians have shown equal flexibility remains a question, although the presence of black leaders high in the councils of the church is surely significant. On one point, however, I can be positive, and that is that my admiration for and friendship with Harry Lee Doll was not in any way affected by the exchange of correspondence which I have just described. When during the following year he took early retirement as diocesan, I submitted my own resignation as chancellor of the diocese and welcomed the appointment as my successor of Arthur W. Machen, Jr., the son and namesake of my father's friend and companion in arms in many legal battles.

Ups and Downs at Peabody

At the Century Association in New York Francis Plimpton introduced me to Benny Goodman with the remark that I was Baltimore's "Music Man." I answered that while music in Baltimore was in some trouble, it was not really quite that bad.

When in 1949 I agreed to succeed Dr. Hall Pleasants as president of the Peabody Institute, I thought the presidency would not take much more time than I had already been giving to that institution, since I had been a member of the board for fourteen years, during nearly all of which I had acted as chairman of the committee on the Conservatory of Music. Since the day when Reginald Stewart had taken over as director of the conservatory, the school had taken on new life and, thanks to the GI Bill, enrollment had reached new heights. While the finances of the Peabody still required careful attention, they appeared to be in better shape than at any time since I had first been elected as trustee in 1935. What I did not fully appreciate was that the stimulus of the GI Bill was wearing off and that the full impact of the postwar inflation was beginning to be felt not only by the conservatory but by the library, as well.

It soon became apparent that something drastic would have to be done if the Peabody was to survive as an independent institution. The obvious first step was to add strength to the board of trustees, and here I turned for help to Howard Bruce. With his advice and that of several other elder statesmen in the business community whose names he suggested to me, I was successful in recruiting a group of young trustees, a number of whom were destined to become leaders in the Baltimore community. Interestingly enough, Morris Schapiro, one of the "elder states-men," indicated that he himself would like to serve on the board.

My next step was to call on a group of eminent librarians headed by Keyes Metcalf, the head of the Harvard University library system, for rec-ommendations as to what should be done about the library. The cost of operating the library was rising rapidly, while at the same time the collec-tions were suffering from lack of proper maintenance and of funds to purchase new items. The Metcalf committee strongly recommended that we explore the possibility of working out a cooperative arrangement, ei-ther with the Johns Hopkins University or with the Pratt Library. With the unanimous approval of the board, I opened negotiations with Hopkins and found that while the Hopkins librarian was eager to acquire the Peabody collections, Hopkins could not afford to leave them at Mt. Vernon Place, where they were (and still are) housed in a building which, with its cast-iron stackroom, has an international reputation as an out-standing example of nineteenth-century library architecture.

When it became apparent that the negotiations with Hopkins were getting nowhere, we turned to the Pratt, where we found a much more flexible attitude on the part of Ed Castagna, who was the chief librarian there. After careful negotiations the trustees of the Peabody entered into a memorandum of understanding with the trustees of the Pratt which called for the maintenance as a part of the Pratt Library of a scholars' library at Mt. Vernon Place, to be known as the Peabody Branch. The memorandum recognized the possibility that some of the Peabody collec-tions might be moved to the main building at the Pratt and that some duplicate items might be selected for sale.

At this point the Hopkins faculty became aroused and passed a reso-lution which, in effect, demanded that the Peabody Library remain intact just where it was. The protestants were apparently quite unaware of the position which Hopkins had taken in the prior negotiations. A re-monstrance was also made public by a group which included John Dos Passos and Walker Lewis. This led to my meeting with Milton Eisenhower, the president of Hopkins, and Charles Garland, who was the chairman of the Hopkins Board of Trustees. In the midst of our negotiations a suit was filed by Douglas H. Gordon, a former trustee of the Peabody Institute who had resigned shortly after my selection as president. Mr. Gordon asked the court to enjoin the transfer of title to any books to the trustees of the Pratt on the ground that such a transfer would be a breach of trust. I testified as a witness in that case and, according to our counsel, Ambler Moss, I argued the case from the witness stand just as if I were at the trial table as counsel for the defendants. In the end the case went to the Court of Appeals, which, in an opinion written by Judge Fred Singley, affirmed an order dismissing Gordon's complaint on the ground that the trustees had exercised proper discretion in entering into the memorandum of understanding with the Pratt.

While the affairs of the Peabody Library were thus commanding the attention of the scholarly community, Baltimore's musicians were equally concerned with developments which were taking place at the conservatory. Reginald Stewart, whose Baltimore career had begun so auspiciously, had found that he had more than he could handle in trying to direct both the Baltimore Symphony Orchestra and the conservatory. He struggled manfully to bring the orchestra up to professional standards but, here again, the lack of funds became so acute that the symphony was tottering on the brink of dissolution.

Immediately after my return from Washington in 1945, Lee Taylor, who was then chairman of the symphony board, asked me to join him in exploring the possibility of working out some sort of cooperative arrangement with the National Symphony Orchestra in Washington, which was faced with similar financial problems. We had several meetings with a committee of the trustees of that organization, as a result of which it became apparent that while the trustees of both orchestras were in agreement as to the desirability of some form of merger of the two organizations, the practical difficulties were insurmountable. Each of the orchestra managers made it perfectly clear that in his opinion the only possible solution was for the other orchestra to be dissolved and to turn over its concert series to the survivor. At this point I insisted upon resigning from the Baltimore Symphony board on the ground that whatever time I could manage to give to musical affairs should be devoted to the Peabody. Not long after that, Lee Taylor resigned as president of the symphony board, and the board's treasurer, Henry Rosenberg, also resigned. Francis Whitman then asked me to serve on a special committee to make recommendations as to the future of the symphony, and I joined in a report which laid it on the line that unless new leadership could be obtained which would be committed to raising a substantial sustaining fund immediately, the orchestra should be disbanded.

The Greater Baltimore Committee then entered the picture, and a retired banker named Robert Bonnell was drafted to take over the management of the orchestra's affairs. Within a very short period it became clear that Bonnell wished to look for a new conductor, and in 1952 Stewart was forced to resign. I was immediately asked to serve on a search committee for a new conductor, but this turned out to be a rubber stamp affair, since the chairman of the search committee was a friend of Arturo Toscanini's, who had a candidate already lined up in Massimo Freccia, then conductor of the orchestra at New Orleans.

Ever since coming to Baltimore, Stewart had insisted that close cooperation between the conservatory and the orchestra was essential to the health of both institutions. He had maintained that position in the face of criticism from both the faculty of the conservatory and the players in the orchestra, and I assumed that he would recognize that he could not abruptly change a position to which he was so publicly committed. In that belief, I arranged a luncheon meeting at which I hoped that he and Freccia would begin to plan for their future cooperation.

This proved to be a serious miscalculation on my part, as Stewart behaved exactly as General de Gaulle is reported to have done when FDR and Winston Churchill arranged a meeting between him and General Giraud at the beginning of the North African campaign in World War II. Shortly after the luncheon meeting which I had arranged, Stewart announced that the Peabody would sponsor a series of candlelight concerts by a chamber orchestra made up in large part of players who held chairs in the Baltimore Symphony. For the next five years Stewart continued to act like a rejected lover, to the amusement—or irritation, as the case might be—of the entire musical community. In the meantime I had come to the conclusion that the Peabody Institute needed a full-time president, and once more at the suggestion of Howard Bruce, I persuaded the Peabody trustees to select a retired business executive named John S. Montgomery, who had recently come to live in Baltimore, where his wife, the former Mary Carroll Frick, had spent her girlhood. For the first time the by-laws of the Peabody Institute were amended so as to provide for a full-time, paid executive president and for a chairman of the board of trustees, to which office I was duly elected. Within a year I found that Jack Montgomery did not get along with Reginald Stewart. What is more, he had found a candidate to succeed him in Peter Mennin, a rising young composer and musical statesman.

The task of asking for Stewart's resignation fell to me and was doubly unpleasant, since our personal relationship had already become somewhat strained. His wife, Ruby Stewart, had taken offense when she discovered that my wife had invited a few of her intimate friends to meet Patty Conant at lunch when she and Jim visited us in Baltimore upon their return to this country from Germany. A few weeks later we were scheduled to give a reception in honor of Jack Montgomery and his wife, and Natalie asked Ruby to stand with her in the receiving line. Ruby sent word through her husband that they would not be able to come to the reception, and Stewart explained to me that she felt unwelcome, since she had not been invited to lunch with Mrs. Conant. I had to explain to him that he and his wife simply could not fail to appear at a reception given for the newly elected president of the Peabody Institute by the chairman of the board of trustees, and in the end they did show up at the reception, but Ruby refused to stand in the same room with Natalie and never spoke to her during the afternoon. Her conduct was so conspicuous that some sharpshooters noticed it, and the whole school was rife with gossip.

Happily for me, my task was made somewhat easier when Stewart, acting as I later learned at his wife's instigation, chose this time to tell me that unless he got a substantial raise, he would have to resign as director of the conservatory. So I simply told him that we could not afford to increase his salary and under the circumstances would accept his resignation. Ruby then sent for me and we had a heart-to-heart talk in which she took the blame for Stewart's failure to succeed in Baltimore. She later wrote me a truly remarkable letter thanking me for having been so candid with her, and I later got a letter from Stewart urging me to be charitable in case inquiries should come from others who were considering him for a position elsewhere.

As a result of all this, I began to feel that with proper leadership I might have been able to inspire the Stewarts to reveal what I now found to be a very appealing side of their characters. Then, however, it was too late, as Jack Montgomery and the board of trustees were quite incensed by what had taken place. So at the end of July 1958, the Reginald Stewarts left Baltimore. Looking back, Baltimore music lovers now realize that Stewart had brought the orchestra for the first time to a point where it could attract a protégé of Arturo Toscanini's. Likewise, the conservatory, which shortly after Stewart's arrival was described to me by Nicholas Nabokov, the Russian composer, as "the kind of school one might expect to find on the lower Volga," during Stewart's regime had attracted, in addition to Nabokov, such outstanding teachers as Nadia Boulanger, Henry Cowell, and Elliott Carter, and such students as Dominic Argento, who later won a Pulitzer Prize in composition.

Some years later Natalie and I spent a few days in Santa Barbara and with some hesitation I determined to call on the Stewarts. I knew that they were living there because my nephew John Marshall Barroll had married one of their daughters and through her we had been kept advised of her parents' movements. So I lifted the telephone and when he answered was astonished to find him apparently thunderstruck at hearing my voice. He insisted that we come to see them and later confided that he had just finished telling Ruby that he had dreamt that I was in Santa Barbara looking for him when the telephone rang and there I was. So we met with much ice already broken, and during the time we were in Santa Barbara they both went out of their way to entertain us and to see that we met their friends and saw the sights of the town.

In the meantime Natalie and I had found Peter Mennin and his wife, Georganne, most congenial. Peter made the Peabody Conservatory the focus of much attention in the world of music education, particularly in the operatic performances, to which he attracted attention from the highest musical circles in New York. As one critic observed to me, "He knows where to put the paint." In addition, he attracted a number of outstanding conductors to inaugurate a course in training aspiring young conductors. George Szell, who had raised the Cleveland Orchestra to the front rank, came to Baltimore, as did other well-known conductors, including Leonard Bernstein and Max Rudolf. When in 1963 Mennin left Baltimore to go to the Juilliard he told me that if the symphony trustees had been willing to accept his suggestion that Stokowski be named as conductor of the symphony in place of Adler, he would gladly have stayed in Baltimore, as he was happy at the Peabody, but with Adler at the symphony he really had no one to talk to.

Shortly thereafter Herbert Watt, who had succeeded Jack Montgomery, resigned as president because the trustees approved a rather ambitious plan for acquiring the entire block bounded by Charles, Monument, St. Paul, and Center streets and erecting a dormitory and cafeteria. Johnny Nelson took over as president of the institute and Charles Kent was chosen to succeed Peter Mennin as director of the conservatory. A campaign was then conducted to raise the funds needed to pay for the building program and to pay off accumulated deficits. The goal of the campaign was set at two million dollars, and at the last moment I succeeded in getting a commitment of half a million dollars from the Ford Foundation on condition that it be matched four to one, so that we had to raise the goal. However, we were successful in raising the full amount, and in 1967 I resigned as chairman of the board of trustees and took emeritus status after serving for thirty-two years as an active trustee of the Peabody Institute.

XXIII ❧ Climbing Down

While the Constitutional Convention was in session I was commuting to Annapolis almost every day, and while doing so I had frequent attacks of what I took to be indigestion which I attributed to the stress of irregular hours and unaccustomed diet. In the winter of 1968 I suffered a mild coronary which put me in the hospital for several weeks. Thereafter I continued to have dull pains whenever I was under stress, and I learned that I had angina pectoris and was told to regard these twinges as warnings to slow down. This proved not very easy to do, as life continued to make demands on my energy. The practice of the firm of Piper & Marbury was growing steadily during this period, as were the numbers of partners and associates, and while I tried to share the responsibilities of firm leadership, this procedure was necessarily gradual. Moreover, my personal practice continued to be quite active.

An outstanding example was my employment in the latter part of October 1970 by the Baltimore Gas & Electric Company to assist its general counsel, James Biddison, who was faced with a very serious problem arising out of the construction of a nuclear power plant at Calvert Cliffs on the shore of the Chesapeake Bay. BG&E had already made binding commitments in the amount of more than one hundred million dollars when the Maryland legislature passed a statute requiring every public utility intending to erect a nuclear power plant to obtain first a certificate of public convenience and necessity from the Public Service Commission of Maryland. The statute contained a proviso exempting plants "under construction" on the effective date of the statute, which was July 1, 1968. In view of the commitments previously made, Biddison had advised BG&E that the Public Service Commission had no jurisdiction over the Calvert Cliffs plant. Spurred on by a group of environmentalists, the People's Counsel had asked the commission to halt construction of the Calvert Cliffs project. The commission dismissed this petition on the ground that the project was indeed "under construction" on July 1, 1968, and on appeal the Circuit Court of Anne Arundel County affirmed that ruling. Thereupon the People's Counsel had appealed to the Court of Appeals of Maryland, which, in October 1970, reversed the lower court and held that

Calvert Cliffs was not "under construction" on July 1, 1968, within the meaning of the statute. By that time the plant was well under way, and to stop all construction would have been financially disastrous and would have resulted in a serious shortage of electricity in the entire region in future years.

At this point I was asked to join in an effort to persuade the commission to permit the work of construction to continue. For the next several weeks I worked with Biddison, preparing for a hearing before the commission which had been set for November 30 at Prince Frederick, the very rural seat of Calvert County. I was assisted by Don McPherson, who had recently become associated with my firm. Don and I had to do a good deal of commuting between Baltimore and Prince Frederick, and on several occasions we traveled by helicopter. To land in Prince Frederick twenty minutes after leaving Baltimore was to experience a time warp which would have done credit to a science fiction movie.

The hearing was a fascinating preview of what has since become the regular routine wherever environmentalists think they have an opportunity to block a nuclear project. We heard expert testimony about the supposed dire injury to aquatic life of the Chesapeake Bay which would result from discharges from the proposed plant as well as predictions that radioactive emanations from the plant would inevitably jeopardize the health of the surrounding community. Some of the most extreme statements came from a witness named Gary Grofman, who insisted that no nuclear reactor could be operated without emitting radiation which would certainly shorten someone's life. He said that the Atomic Energy Commission had been grossly negligent in giving its approval to the plans for the Calvert Cliffs plant. Under cross-examination he conceded that sunbathers at Ocean City and travelers to Denver in high-altitude jets would be subject to just as much if not more radiation.

Another witness, Carleton Ray, who came from the Johns Hopkins School of Hygiene, gave more temperate testimony in which he dwelt upon the possibility that the discharge of warm water from the nuclear plant might have a damaging effect on the aquatic life of the Chesapeake Bay. To counter this testimony, we called as a witness William W. Eaton, who had acted as chairman of Governor Marvin Mandel's Task Force on Nuclear Power Plants, a group of individuals of widely divergent backgrounds who had filed a report in January of 1970 in which they said:

> Based upon careful consideration of available evidence, the Task Force concludes that the Calvert Cliffs Nuclear Power Plant, operating in compliance with Federal and State Laws and Regulations, does not in itself constitute a threat in any significant way to the health, safety, or economy of the State of Maryland or its citizens, nor will the plant seriously impair the quality of the Chesapeake Bay environment.

We also produced James H. Carpenter, an associate professor at the Johns Hopkins University, who flatly contradicted the testimony of his colleague Carleton Ray and said that in his opinion the Calvert Cliffs plant would produce no observable changes in the bay's biology.

The hearings lasted for nearly a week. While they were under way, I lived in a motel which was not too far from Solomon's Island, and on several mornings I walked over there to the bank of the Patuxent River and watched the oyster fleet sail out to the Chesapeake Bay as the sun was rising. The boats glided out in the misty dawn as they had been doing for more than a century, and it was hard to realize that this was a way of life which was rapidly vanishing because of the refusal of the oystermen to listen to the warnings of the scientists. I could not help wondering about the people of Calvert County, who had made it clear that they wanted the Calvert Cliffs plant built as soon as possible so that the county might get the benefit of an increased tax base and increased employment. Might they some day wonder whether they would have been wiser to listen to the environmentalists? On the whole, however, I was pretty well convinced that the risks attached to the use of atomic power under feasible safeguards were no greater than those involved in many industrial activities which are regularly undertaken without public outcry.

One thing which impressed me was the extent to which the top management of BG&E undertook to coach their counsel from Baltimore. Poor Biddison was on the telephone every day for what seemed like hours, and I finally suggested to him that he urge his bosses to get a good night's sleep and let us do the same. I suggested also that he tell them that I felt confident that the commission was going to rule in our favor, which they did. The Calvert Cliffs plant was completed and has now been in operation for more than a decade. So far as I have ever heard, it has not done any damage whatsoever to the aquatic life of the Chesapeake Bay, nor has it proven to be in any way injurious to the health of the people of Calvert County. Furthermore, it has saved the people of the region millions of dollars in what they have had to pay for electrical energy.

During the period from 1968 to 1973, in addition to a law practice which continued to be quite demanding, I found myself involved in other activities which were energy consuming. In 1969, the president of the American Bar Association, Bernard G. Segal, asked me to serve on a special committee of nine judges and lawyers to formulate a comprehensive new code of ethics for the nation's judges. This was to take the place of the Code of Judicial Ethics which had been promulgated by the ABA in 1923 on the recommendation of a distinguished committee headed by Chief Justice Taft. The chairman of the new committee was Roger J. Traynor, then chief justice of the Supreme Court of California, and the membership included Potter Stewart, who was then a justice of the United States

Supreme Court; Irving R. Kaufman of New York, then a member of the Court of Appeals for the Second Circuit; Edward G. Gignoux of Portland, Maine, who was then the only federal judge in a district which included the entire state of Maine; and Ivan Lee Holt of the Circuit Court of the city of St. Louis. In addition to the five judges, there were three practicing lawyers—Whitney North Seymour of New York, E. Dixie Beggs of Pensacola, Florida, and myself—and the ninth member of the committee was a law professor and former dean of the Law School at the University of Arkansas, Robert A. Leflar, who had been at one time a justice of the Arkansas Supreme Court.

Later additions were made to the committee before the final report was made to the bar association at its meeting in San Francisco in 1972. During that period the committee met frequently in New York and elsewhere and conducted hearings at which the bench and bar as well as the general public were invited to express their views on such questions as under what circumstances a judge should disqualify himself from sitting on a case, what nonjudicial activities were permissible, when and from whom a judge could accept compensation for nonjudicial activities, and many other similar questions. While our committee was engaged in its deliberations, several rather spectacular cases of questionable judicial conduct attracted the attention of the news media, and a few politicians engaged in rather crude displays of demagoguery in order to capitalize on these events. At the same time, several members of Congress were sponsoring bills which dealt with the same questions with which our committee was wrestling. As a result the hearings before us were occasionally quite colorful.

It so happened that the ABA was scheduled to meet in England in July of 1971, and through Whitney Seymour, who was himself a "bencher" of one of the British Inns of Court, several members of our committee were invited to meet with a representative group of British judges and administrators, including the Lord Chief Justice John Widgery. The representatives of our committee in addition to Whitney and myself were Irving Kaufman and Walter Armstrong, a practicing lawyer who had been added to our committee after it was originally organized.

I have a very clear recollection of the astonishment with which the British judges regarded the draft of our code. Their reactions were very similar to those of the Maryland judges who were engaged in redrafting a Code of Judicial Ethics on behalf of the Court of Appeals of Maryland. In reporting to Roger Traynor, Irving Kaufman remarked on the fact that the Britons "think nothing of a judge's son appearing before him so long as the judge politely offers to excuse himself should the opposing barrister believe that the judge was incapable of impartiality." In that connection, I well remember the time when the local judge in St. Mary's County, Maryland, had two sons who were lawyers, each of whom appeared constantly in his court, usually on opposite sides. The judge and the two boys would lunch together and then go back to court, and no one ever seemed to think the subject deserving of comment. One of the British judges remarked that he never had any problem where it appeared that he might have a financial stake in the outcome of a case, since he always made a point of bringing this to the attention of counsel on both sides who invariably waived any objection to his sitting on the case. In my own memorandum, written immediately after my return from London, I noted that after our meeting Judge Kaufman had said, "We gave them more to think about than they gave us." As to the political activities of the judges, the Britons were of course horrified at the idea that our judges were required to stand for election while at the same time they saw no reason why a judge should not participate in political activities. After all, the lord chancellor sits in the House of Lords and is a member of the British prime minister's cabinet.

According to my recollection, our Code of Judicial Conduct was adopted by the House of Delegates of the ABA by a unanimous vote and has since been adopted by the Supreme Court of the United States and made applicable to the entire federal system. Most of the states of the Union have also adopted it without substantial change, but so far Maryland is among those which have chosen to go their own way.

Also in the year 1969 I happened, at a meeting of the American Bar Association, to sit at a table with Judge William B. Jones of the United States District Court for the District of Columbia. We found ourselves in agreement as to the need for an agency which would train young lawyers in the art of trial advocacy. Shortly thereafter, I got a message from him telling me that he had been chosen to be chairman of a task force to study this problem and asking me to serve as a member of his group along with a number of other trial lawyers from different parts of the country. I agreed to do this and was called on to attend a number of meetings which led to the creation of NITA, the National Institute for Trial Advocacy. That organization got off to a good start and today is nationally recognized as an important agency in the field of continuing legal education.

In an earlier chapter I described the evolution of the sitting judge principle and explained that it was devised to prevent the political bosses from regaining the control of the judiciary which they had lost as a result of the Reform Movement in the 1880s. Opponents of the sitting judge principle frequently stressed the fact that it made it virtually impossible to get rid of an incompetent judge or of a judge who had otherwise demonstrated his unfitness for office since the only means available under the Maryland Constitution would then be impeachment, which is virtually a dead letter because it is so cumbersome. Moreover, impeachment is obviously inappropriate when the judge's offense requires nothing more than public censure.

The same agitation that led to the appointment of the ABA committee to revise the canons of judicial ethics also led to the creation in many states, including Maryland, of commissions on judicial disabilities. Under a 1970 amendment to the Maryland Constitution the Maryland Commission on Judicial Disabilities was charged with the duty of investigating complaints of judicial misconduct, of holding confidential hearings where the charges appeared to have substance, and of recommending to the Court of Appeals, where appropriate, that disciplinary measures be adopted ranging from public reprimand to removal from office. I had taken a leading part in urging the adoption of the 1970 amendment and no doubt for that reason was one of the persons selected by the governor to serve on the reorganized commission along with four members of the judiciary, another practicing lawyer, and Walter Sondheim, who represented the general public. I accepted the office expressing the hope that it would be a "sinecure."

I could not have been more wrong. Almost immediately the members of the commission found themselves plunged into situations which called for very careful handling. The *Sunpapers* had been for some time engaged in one of their periodic crusades to clean up the Traffic Court of Baltimore City. They had published enough information to stir up the state's attorney's office and the grand jury to conduct an investigation which had resulted in some indictments. As a by-product, there was evidence of violations of judicial ethics on the part of a judge who regularly sat in the Traffic Court, and this was brought to the attention of our commission. After a lot of preliminary skirmishing by resourceful counsel, the commission proceeded to hold confidential hearings occupying eight days which resulted in a recommendation to the Court of Appeals that the offending judge be removed from office. At the conclusion of that hearing I was thoroughly convinced that I was temperamentally unqualified to preside on a tribunal which had to hear criminal cases. I was particularly repelled by the tactics of one of the lawyers; the louder he yelled, the harder it was for me to retain a semblance of judicial calm.

In another equally delicate case, the commission was called on to deal with a judge who had been engaged in a flagrant breach of the canon of judicial ethics which bars judges from participating in partisan political activities. Unfortunately, the offending judge in this case was black, and what he had done was not much more reprehensible than what many of the white county court judges had previously done without incurring any penalty. However, the judge in this case had been so naive as to talk freely to reporters who according to his account violated his confidence by reporting remarks which he claimed to have made "off the record." In this case we established a precedent by handling the matter privately. The constitution required us to maintain confidentiality in all cases except where we decided to recommend action by the Court of Appeals, in which case the entire record of our proceedings would become public. We called the judge's attention to the provisions of the canon, with which he claimed to be unfamiliar, and we obtained his assurances that he would observe them faithfully in the future.

The manner in which we handled this case turned out to set a very salutary precedent, as there were a number of cases where a private word was all that was necessary to prevent recurrence of the offense. In many of these cases, particularly among those arising in rural areas, the judges were simply following the example of their predecessors. As one Southern Maryland judge once said to me, "In my early days the Circuit Judge in this county was always looked up to as the leading citizen of the community. People would consult him informally about their problems and he usually headed most important local committees and sat on the board of the local bank. The politicians consulted him on all sorts of questions and his advice was generally followed." Those were the days!

On April 5, 1972, a riot erupted at the Baltimore City Jail. Everyone knew that the jail was overcrowded, but the mayor appointed a committee to look into not only the conditions in the jail itself but also the procedures by which prisoners were being sent to the jail. Mayor Schaefer asked me to serve as chairman of that committee. After a brief survey I concluded that I needed help and got the permission of the mayor to employ Ben Civiletti, who had been an assistant United States attorney in Baltimore. I was deeply impressed by his character and ability and relied on him heavily in developing the facts which my committee needed to know in making its report.

While Ben was primarily reponsible for conducting the investigations, I personally spent quite a little time at the jail interviewing the warden and some of the members of his staff. I also worked with the administrative staff of the Supreme Bench of Baltimore City and interviewed the judges who were sitting in the criminal courts as well as some of the state district court judges. This was not a very pleasant assignment but I came to respect many of the minor officials who were trying to cope with the nastiest problem that the city's administration had to face. Thanks to their cooperation and to Ben Civiletti's careful preparation of the groundwork, our committee was able to make a convincing case that the resignation of the warden was in order. We were also able for the time being to lessen substantially the time which prisoners awaiting trial had to spend in the jail, thereby lightening the load with which the new warden had to cope. Unhappily, this turned out to afford only temporary relief.

In 1973 I suffered another mild coronary and this time I really did begin to draw in my horns. I was 72 years of age and was beginning to realize that my hearing was becoming impaired. I had been trying a case before Judge Thomsen and found that I frequently had to ask my associate to repeat what the judge had said. Sometimes I found it very hard to hear the testimony of a timid witness. Even after I had sought the assistance of John Bordley, who was then still in private practice and had previously been in charge of the Otolaryngological Clinic at the Johns Hopkins Hospital, I did not feel that I was really fit for courtroom work any longer. I still sat at the trial table in some important cases and acted as an observer and critic, but it was obvious that my days as lead counsel were coming to an end.

However, for a brief period it looked as if I was about to play a prominent role in the trial of a president of the United States. The Watergate scandals were reaching their climax and like all the rest of the country I was fascinated. From time to time I had been receiving telephone calls from the Department of Justice seeking advice on the selection of an independent counsel who would take over the investigation of the rumors that were then being circulated in Washington. To borrow a simile, the media were acting like sharks which had discovered blood on the water. Attorney General Elliot Richardson was looking for someone whose ability and integrity was beyond question and who had had no previous contact whatsoever with the Nixon administration. I suggested that they look into the availability of Judge Erickson of the Supreme Court of Colorado and according to information which I received later, this was done and it was found that he was not available. After the House of Representatives had adopted articles impeaching President Nixon, the leaders of the Senate began preparing for the trial. Early in August I got a telephone call from Senator Mac Mathias, Jr., asking whether I would be available to act as counsel for a staff which he was organizing to conduct the Senate's trial of the president. I wrote to him on August 5 saying that I was much flattered by the suggestion but that I had made certain commitments which would affect my availability from August 9 to September 8. Almost immediately after I had mailed that letter, President Nixon resigned, and on August 16 I got a letter from Mac in which he said, "I'm glad we do not have to impose upon your good nature and public spirit to counsel us during the trial of the President."

After this near-miss I thought I could relax but Mayor Schaefer continued to call on me from time to time to serve on various committees. The most extraordinary assignment was to serve on a committee to save the Orioles. Jerold Hoffberger, who was at that time the spokesman for the family which controlled the corporation which owned the baseball franchise for Baltimore, had announced the family's intention to dispose of their interest in the club, and the mayor and the Greater Baltimore Committee were anxious to prevent a loss of the franchise by the city. To look into this situation the mayor appointed a committee headed by Bart Harvey, then one of the younger partners in Alex. Brown & Sons, which was expected to suggest a means by which this public calamity could be avoided. With the expert aid of Ed Clarke, my partner who was especially familiar with municipal bond law, our committee devised a plan which involved the issue of revenue bonds to be sold in Baltimore City with lead financing by a group of Baltimore business interests. Among those we approached was Henry Knott. Somewhat to our chagrin, Mr. Hoffberger and Mr. Knott did not get along, with the result that our negotiations were suddenly terminated by an announcement from the Hoffbergers that they had decided to sell their interest to a Washington lawyer named Edward Bennett Williams, who promised to keep the franchise in Baltimore for the time being. As of 1987 the Orioles were still in Baltimore.

In February of 1974 Mayor Schaefer asked me to act as special counsel to the Baltimore City School Board. The NAACP had become dissatisfied with the failure of a number of communities to desegregate their school systems following the decision of the Supreme Court in the *Brown* case. They had brought suit in the District of Columbia to compel the secretary of HEW to institute proceedings against a number of named communities, including the city of Baltimore, to cut off federal funding of programs of which those cities were beneficiaries. Although the city of Baltimore was not named as a party in that suit, it suddenly found itself faced with an order which threatened the loss of many millions of dollars in federal funds which the city had been counting on to balance its budget. The mayor summoned the school board and a number of other school officials to a meeting in his office at which he announced that I was to act as special counsel to assist the city solicitor, George Russell, to prevent the loss of these funds.

For some time I had been working with Stephen Derby, who was then a brand-new partner in the firm of Piper & Marbury, in connection with some problems of alleged racial discrimination which had arisen in Charles County. We had tried a case before Judge Thomsen which went to the Fourth Circuit, in which we were successful in convincing the court that Charles County had not been guilty of discrimination against blacks in connection with faculty appointments and assignments, so I turned to Steve for help with Baltimore City's problems. I did not realize that I was giving him an assignment on which he would be working for more than a decade, during which we represented the School Board of Baltimore City in administrative proceedings before HEW and in litigation in the federal courts which required a series of appearances in the United States District Court for the District of Maryland as well as in the Court of Appeals for the Fourth Circuit. While I continued to put in an appearance in most of the court proceedings, the brunt of the work was done by Steve, who became quite expert in what was then a fairly novel field of jurisprudence. Up to the present time, we have been successful in protecting the city from the loss of any federal funds, but in doing so we had to guide the school board through some treacherous waters. Steve has been in touch with lawyers and educational experts all over the country.

At the time of my appointment as special counsel to the Baltimore City School Board, the chairman was Dr. John Walton, who had been a professor of education at the Johns Hopkins University. Prior to John Walton's appointment the school board had been badly split. A new superintendent of public schools, Roland Patterson, and two recently appointed board members turned out to be rather militant black activists and as a result the board meetings had mired down in rancorous debates. While Dr. Patterson seemed to resent the interference of the District of Columbia federal court in the affairs of the School Board of Baltimore City, he was in many other respects uncooperative with the majority of the school board, and it soon became apparent that some steps would have to be taken if a united front was to be presented in connection with the very complex problem of eliminating all vestiges of segregation from the Baltimore City school system. Things reached the point where Dr. Patterson refused to talk to Dr. Walton except at a public meeting where the press was present. Moreover, in his meetings with the mayor, Dr. Patterson was almost contemptuous in his attitude.

Finally the white members of the board decided to initiate proceedings to remove Dr. Patterson as superintendent of public schools, but they proceeded to go about it in an unbelievably clumsy fashion. Without consulting me or Steve they drafted a resolution in which they agreed to give Dr. Patterson a hearing but stated that following the hearing he would be removed from office. They discussed this proposed resolution with Dr. Patterson's supporters on the board and then called a formal meeting to act on it. The meeting was packed with noisy supporters of Dr. Patterson who made such a racket that it was impossible for the board to proceed. Of course, the whole affair was the subject of media scandal, and the *Sunpapers* accused the white members of the board of "shoddy political maneuvering." The actual fact was that they were simply unbelievably naive.

In the end John Walton resigned from the board and the mayor named Norman Ramsey in his place. Norman soon got control of the board and Dr. Patterson was removed from office in a manner which satisfied the requirements of due process. While I had no part in the removal of Dr. Patterson, Steve Derby and I were thereafter able to present a united front in dealing with HEW and with the very complex desegregation plan that was devised in order to avoid the loss of federal funds, and at the same time we kept Mayor Schaefer reasonably happy. The mayor was acutely aware of the dangers to the city's welfare which were likely to result from the exodus of white and black middle-class taxpayers which frequently follows efforts to achieve racial balance in the schools. While the city of Baltimore could scarcely be regarded as a model, we were able to avoid some of the more traumatic experiences which convulsed the greater Boston area.

In 1971 I was named to the Advisory Board of the Institute of Advanced Study at the University of Virginia. That board met twice a year in Charlottesville, where we listened to reports from the president of the university and the director of the institute, Dexter Whitehead. I enjoyed the opportunity to meet the academic leadership at the university, which impressed me as being a great deal more competent and farsighted than it had been during my student days there. Indeed, I got the impression that Virginia was now a dynamic institution and that a number of the departments were gaining national recognition.

One day I saw a crowd of students standing outside of one of the smaller lecture halls. I asked what was going on and was told that Wallace Stevens was giving a poetry reading. I remarked that the place had certainly changed. Some of my friends who are now living in Charlottesville assured me that the intellectual life of the university was alive and well, so I was not surprised when Virginia recently began to be mentioned as a Mecca for undergraduates who were looking for a good education as well as a good time.

In 1976 I was named as chairman of a committee of the Maryland State Bar Association charged with the duty of organizing a statewide agency to coordinate various local groups which were undertaking to give continuing professional education to lawyers. Our committee studied the work of a number of local bar associations and law schools and came to the conclusion that a coordinating agency was essential to avoid duplication and to assure that the courses being offered were of a quality comparable to the quality of courses being offered in other states. With the backing of the state bar and of the law schools of the University of Maryland and the University of Baltimore, a new corporation was organized, called the Maryland Institute of Continuing Professional Education of Lawyers, which has since become widely known as MICPEL. I was named as the first president of the board of trustees, which under the leadership of Larry Katz as executive director (now the dean of the Law School of the University of Baltimore), and subsequently of Bob Dyer, has managed to attain recognition as the most important local contributor in the state of Maryland to this growing industry.

Shepherding this agency through its birth and subsequent growing pains called for a great deal of work on my part, as there were several other groups, particularly in the suburbs of Washington, which stubbornly resisted any form of control by an agency which they regarded as being under the domination of the Baltimore bar. The extent to which MICPEL has been successful in overcoming this initial parochial hostility may, I believe, be ascribed in part at least to my efforts to enlist the leaders of those local groups in planning for the organization and operation of the new agency. Furthermore, after MICPEL had proved to be not only self-supporting but the generator of substantial revenues, I helped its board to fight off an effort on the part of certain other elements in the state bar association to take over this profitable activity.

My responsibilities as leader of the firm of Piper & Marbury eventually disappeared. I had found in Andre Brewster a willing and gifted person to whom I could delegate problems of increasing difficulty, and he gradually took over the leadership of the firm. The business management of the firm became more and more concentrated in the hands of Decatur Miller, who proved to be extraordinarily adept at handling that very demanding aspect of a rapidly growing organization. For a time, I managed to carry a substantial load of work as a consultant to younger members of the firm who were handling cases in appellate courts, but after a while the need for my services in that capacity faded out.

By virtue of my years I began to receive honors that have made life pleasant. At the University of Virginia I was elected to the Raven Society and at the University of Maryland Law School to the Order of Coif. Here in Baltimore I was elected to the Greater Baltimore Committee and have served on a number of its subcommittees. In 1981 I received the Herbert Harley Award of the American Judicature Society, and in 1984 I was chosen for the Fifty Year Award of the American Bar Foundation. This involved a trip to Las Vegas where I was called upon to speak before approximately six hundred lawyers who had gathered from all over the country. Inevitably the Baltimore newspapers began to refer to me as the "Dean" of the Maryland bar, and I was reminded of the story that is told of Nicholas Murray Butler. A would-be benefactor to Columbia University stipulated that his gift be administered by "no one lower than a Dean," to which President Butler replied, "At Columbia there is no one lower than a Dean."

❧ Epilogue

I believe that I have mentioned the highlights of my career as a lawyer and as a private citizen since 1945 when I ended my wartime service. As to other aspects of my life during this period, I suppose I might invoke the constitutional right of privacy which has recently become so well established that those who challenge it are regarded as unfit for high judicial office. However, lest I be accused of "covering up something," I hasten to add that my private life during this period has been so lacking in drama that if I were to attempt to emulate those writers who seek to reveal all their inmost secrets, the result would simply be boring to the reader. Accordingly, I shall not attempt to describe the details of the more than 40 years of happy domesticity I have been privileged to enjoy since September 1945, nor shall I discuss my views on politics or public morals. There were, however, occasions during those years when the Marbury family shared experiences which may be of interest or amusement to the reader, and to these I now turn.

To celebrate my release from the War Department I took a long vacation in the summer of 1946. I had happy memories of the Hackmatack Inn at Chester, Nova Scotia, so we rented a cottage there for a month in midsummer of that year and took all four children with us. We had a very happy time together; the girls learned to swim and the boys to sail. We explored Mahone Bay and the surrounding countryside by car as well as by boat. The children all found friends, including five-year-old Susan, who crashed a party given by a Philadelphia lady who had been among the first summer visitors to Chester, and was universally regarded as a community leader. Susan had escaped from the surveillance of her mother and had joined George Finney whom she saw going to the party.

For several years thereafter we took the children with us on our summer vacations. In 1947 we went to Randolph in the White Mountains of New Hampshire and in 1948 to Alder Creek, where we rented one of the Kernan cottages. In 1949 I arranged through a Denver friend to get Yandes a summer job on a ranch at La Sal, Utah. That same summer we took the other three children to Lake Kanuga near Hendersonville in North Carolina, where the Episcopal diocese of South Carolina had for many years conducted a summer camp much patronized by friends of ours from Macon, Georgia, where my sister Silvine Harrold was living.

At the end of the summer I went out to La Sal to pick up Yandes. When I first arrived at two o'clock in the morning at the nearest point on the railroad to La Sal, I felt as though I were landing in a valley of the moon. The conductor put me off the train and there was literally no one in sight. He pointed to a lighted window about a tenth of a mile away and said that that was the nearest thing to a hotel for many miles. I walked over there and found pinned to the door a note addressed to me saying that I would be met at six-thirty in the morning by a man who would drive me down to the ranch. The drive was through country like that described in the novels of Zane Grey, and by the time I arrived at La Sal I felt that I was in a brand-new world.

The owner of the ranch was Charles Redd, who at that time was the most prominent figure in southeast Utah. He owned the second-largest herd of Hereford cattle in the United States, and in addition to his Utah ranch operated very large ranches in Colorado and Arizona, where he raised sheep and quarter horses. He was one of the largest producers of wool in the United States. The scope of Charlie's activities was truly extraordinary. For example, his wife told me that he once called her on the phone and said that he was bringing two hundred people for lunch the next day. She said that they used to give a party every year for the directors of the Denver and Rio Grande Railroad, of whom he was one, but that they had given this up after the guest list grew to more than one thousand people.

Charlie's views on the balance of world trade were remarkably prophetic. He was the first person I ever heard predict that the productivity of the Japanese workers would undermine the dominance of the United States in both manufacturing and agriculture. At the same time he and his wife were both essentially simple people. When they visited us in Baltimore they wanted to see Ft. McHenry, and when the flag was raised over the ramparts at sunset they both had tears in their eyes.

In the summer of 1951 Natalie and I decided to take Yandes and Luke to Europe. The two little girls were sent to Maine to Camp Four Winds. With the two boys we sailed from New York on the *Media* bound for Liverpool. This was a small, single-class ship where it was easy to get to know all the passengers, and the boys seemed to have a very good time. We were met by a car and driver at Liverpool and for several days we traveled, stopping first at Chester and then touring Cheshire and Shropshire, ending up with a week's stay in Wales. After touring the Welsh castles and climbing Mt. Snowdon, we drove down through the west of England to Oxford and then on to London. Our driver had been born in the Cockney section and made a point of introducing us to some of the most characteristic scenes and people of that area. It was quite a contrast to Brown's

Hotel where we were staying, which at that time was full of country squires and their wives who had come up for a garden party at Buckingham Palace.

In London we did all the usual sights and from there we went to Paris. While I think the boys may have been somewhat bewildered by the extraordinary variety of experiences which crowded our first visit to Paris, they certainly did seem to be interested in what they were seeing and hearing. Perhaps the most remarkable example was a visit which we paid to the Cluny Museum, where some of the finest medieval tapestries still in existence are to be found. The man who undertook to explain the tapestries to us spoke only a few words of English and the boys of course knew no French, yet somehow he managed to get across to them an extraordinary amount of information about these tapestries and about the civilization which they described.

Toward the end of our stay in Paris we made connections with an Italian named Alfredo who was to drive us in his ancient Alfa Romeo for the rest of our trip. We were not long in discovering that Alfredo had his limitations. On the very first day he got lost and we discovered that he had never been to Paris before. As a result we were stranded for two hours while he went back to the hotel to pick up a map and couldn't find his way back to where we were waiting for him. Thereafter I had to become his guide and remained so until we got down to the Italian border. This made him very sulky and when on one occasion I made a mistake in directing him he said in a tone of triumph, "This time, Sor, you have tromped yourself." Altogether travel with Alfredo was a colorful experience which kept the boys entertained, although it put quite a load on my shoulders.

From Paris we drove down to the Touraine, where we visited the Châteaux of the Loire, which were then illuminated at night. Here Alfredo distinguished himself once more by running out of gas at nightfall on a Sunday evening while we were in the village of Chinon, many miles from our night's lodging. He and Yandes went off to look for gas and found that the only gas pump in the entire village was closed for the night. Fortunately, the proprietor lived nearby and although he had gone to bed Alfredo made so eloquent a plea that he put on his trousers and came down to the pump. Such compassionate behavior called for recognition so Alfredo took the half-dressed pump owner and Yandes to a local café for a glass of wine. Meanwhile, Natalie, Luke, and I were sitting on the banks of the river Vienne looking up to the walls of the castle where Joan of Arc first met the Dauphin.

The next day we drove down to the famous caverns of Lascaux, where we were allowed to see the prehistoric paintings on the walls. From there we went to call on Simone Boas's parents, who lived near the charming village of Brantome. After lunching with Simone at the Hotel Modern, which boasted the best restaurant I have ever patronized, we went on down to Cahors, where we spent the night at the Château de Mercues, an old abbey which has been converted into a hostelry perched on the rim of a cliff overlooking the valley of the river Lot.

There followed a succession of fascinating visits to Carcassonne, Nîmes, Arles, Montpellier, Avignon, and the Pont du Gard, ending up with a visit to a villa near Aix en Provence where Natalie's cousin Natalie Dutreil was living. Cousin Natalie was the widow of a retired French army officer, and her villa was in the shadow of Mont Saint Victoire, which has been made world-famous by the paintings of Cézanne. As we entered the villa we were faced by a huge photograph bearing an inscription which ended "With the everlasting gratitude of Charles de Gaulle." We of course asked for an explanation and were told a remarkable story.

It seems that during his days of exile General de Gaulle had used this villa as a meeting place for secret visits which he had paid to France, and thereafter it had become a hiding place for grounded pilots of the Free French Air Force. At one time the commander of a German occupying force in the neighborhood had requisitioned the villa for his headquarters but had permitted the Dutreils to continue to live there. Some grounded pilots had arrived looking for shelter and were taken by the Dutreils into their private rooms, where they were accidentally observed by the German commander, who sent for Colonel Dutreil and said, "I ask no questions but I must have your word of honor as an officer of the French army that hereafter your private rooms will be made available to no one except your own family." Colonel Dutreil gave his word and put out notice through the underground that so long as the Germans were in residence the villa was no longer available as a shelter.

We proceeded to Monte Carlo, which Natalie had visited in her girlhood, and took the boys to the casino, where they were permitted to watch the play for a few minutes. The rest of the time we spent bathing at the beach and driving along the famous Grande Corniche. Once we crossed the border into Italy, Alfredo was in his element. We visited the Italian lakes, spending several days at Sirmione on Lake Garda where the poet Catullus had his villa and where Goethe wrote his famous poem "Kennst du Das Land." For a while we stayed at a hotel at Gardone where I had been in 1945 and where Luke went fishing with some of the local staff of the hotel. One night we all went to the opera at Verona, which was held in an old Roman amphitheater. As we entered the theater we were told by an American that we must buy tapers. Shortly before the opera began everybody in the audience lit their tapers and waved them around in the twilight as the conductor came to the podium. We were told that this custom dated back to Roman times. One of the singers by the name of di Stefano later came to the Metropolitan and for a time was the reigning tenor there.

From Gardone we drove down to Genoa, where we parted company with Alfredo, who by that time was happy to get rid of us. By the beginning of our trip back to New York on the *Constitution* I had come to know the two boys pretty well, and they had had more opportunity to see their father than at any previous time in their lives.

In 1954, I drove Anne and Susan all the way across the continent to pick up Luke, who was working at the La Sal ranch. We went down the valley of Virginia past the Natural Bridge to Sewanee, Tennessee, and from there across the northern borders of Alabama and Mississippi to the river where we crossed into Arkansas. The trip from there to Santa Fe, New Mexico, was remarkable because of the fierce heat. I well remember stopping at a filling station where they said that every cup of water in the town had to be imported by tank truck, as all the local streams had dried up in a drought that had lasted for more than two years. Outside of Oklahoma City we saw a line storm coming up and noticed that a truck which had just passed us had stopped under the canopy of an abandoned filling station. Fortunately, I had sense enough to follow his example, for within fifteen minutes a downpour of rain occurred such as I have never seen before or since. Within half an hour the storm had passed over, and for several miles the road was filled with boulders which had been washed over the road from previously dry arroyos. If I had tried to drive through that storm we would have been swept off the road.

We had another alarming experience driving in New Mexico over the mountain from Los Alamos to a village called Cuba. The road was unpaved, and when a sudden shower caught us the adobe dust became slick as grease. A more terrifying ride I have never had, and when we got down to the floor of the valley we found ourselves blocked by another car which was stuck in the mud. The two girls and I got out and helped the passengers in the front car to rock the car out of the mud, and they in turn helped push us through to firm ground. When we got to Cuba I called our hosts, who were living in Farmington, and explained that we were still in Cuba. They said they would hold dinner, as Cuba was only one hundred miles away and that could be driven easily in an hour and a quarter, so we went ahead and arrived in Farmington covered with adobe mud.

On that trip we visited Mesa Verde, where the cliff dwellers had carved a whole community out of the side of the mountains. After we left La Sal we went down through Monument Valley, which I have been told is the most spectacular example in the world of what wind erosion can do to rocks. We ended up at the Grand Canyon, where all three children went down to the river. I was not allowed to go as I was about ten pounds too heavy for the donkeys to carry. On the way home from the Grand Canyon I found that I could not interest the children in looking at any more scenery. They insisted on passing up the Painted Desert and buried their heads in books rather than look at anything more. When I got home to Baltimore, I told Natalie that I needed a vacation.

In the summer of 1955 Yandes was in Korea in the Marine Corps but the rest of us were in Europe again. This time Natalie went by herself on the *Queen Elizabeth II* and the two girls and I flew to Paris. There we met her and Luke, who had been off on a frolic of his own which included a visit to the Casals Festival in Spain. At Paris we picked up a small Renault and with me as driver headed up to Luxembourg. From there we followed the valley of the Moselle River until we came to the little town of Traben-Trarbach, where a festival was being held to celebrate the arrival of the new vintage. All along the road people were selling samples of the wine to the tourists and at the village there was a miniature carnival. Across the river the Metternich Castle looked down on a very gay and colorful scene. It was from this village that my great-great-great-grandfather Charles Bohn had emigrated to Baltimore in the eighteenth century, bringing his French mother with him.

After a few days in that neighborhood we drove on up to Heidelberg, where we saw the university where my grandfather Slingluff was studying when he met my grandmother. We then drove on to Wiesbaden and went down the Rhine on a car ferry to Bonn. Here we dined with the Conants at the embassy. The following day we left with them for Berlin in their private train, which passed through a part of the Russian Zone of Germany in the middle of the night. We stayed in Berlin at the embassy for several days, during which we saw a great deal of the city, including the Russian sector. I bought some books and sheet music in the Russian sector and attended a lunch at the Free University at which Jim Conant delivered a talk in German which I found easy to understand, perhaps because of his Boston accent. I remember sitting next to a very gracious German lady at dinner. I struggled to express myself in halting German and endeavored to compliment her on her wit, but I could only think of the adjective "komisch." This made her laugh.

Both Jim and Patty Conant had warned me that one subject of conversation was taboo. One should never ask one's dinner companion what he or she had been doing during World War II. Nearly all of them preferred to forget what they had done when the Nazis were in control. One night the Conants took all of us to the theatre where we saw a performance of *The Captain from Kopenick,* a satirical play about militarism in the days of Kaiser Wilhelm. Two things impressed me greatly. First, the respect which everyone seemed to have for the Conants, and second, the gleeful laughter of the audience at the caricature of the military establishment.

Once more we took the private train, this time to Bonn. From there we headed to Karlsruhe, where we visited my cousin Emilie H. von Puttkamer. After dining with her and her daughter Liselotte von Franken-berg, we took Liselotte's two children, Hubertus and Angelika, with us for a visit to Munich and South Bavaria, where we stayed at a hotel on the outskirts of Garmisch-Partenkirchen. We spent about a week in Garmisch climbing mountains, visiting the castles which were built by the mad King Ludwig of Bavaria, and in general having a delightful time together. My children got along very well with the little Frankenbergs. Moreover, we were joined by a young couple from the State Department named Green who also had little children. We took them all to Munich one night to see the opera, which was a little bit over their heads, but a visit to the Nymphenburg Palace where we saw an operetta in the open air was a great success. Then we put the Frankenberg children on the train back to Karlsruhe and Natalie on the train to Paris. She was going by herself as she could not fly and so planned to go first to Paris and then to Cher-bourg, where she would take the *Mauritania* to New York.

These holidays which the family took together between 1946 and 1955 did much to repair the losses in family solidarity that had accrued during the war years. A further step in that direction came in 1956 when I joined the Adirondack League Club. The club was originally organized in the nineteenth century by a group of nature lovers and sportsmen for the purpose of preserving a portion of the Adirondack Forest which was threatened with development by real estate speculators. A number of the members owned so-called camps which had been built in the lavish style of the turn of the century. At the time I became a member, the club still owned nearly seventy thousand acres of forest dotted by scores of lakes and a number of rivers and streams where trout, bass, and landlocked salmon were abundant.

During the next fifteen years we spent nearly all our holidays at Little Moose Lodge or one of the adjacent cottages. During this period the chil-dren were frequently with us. From the time our son Luke entered Exeter in the fall of 1951 until 1962, one or more of our children were always in school or college in the neighborhood of Boston. Our daughter Anne went to Milton Academy for three years, during two of which Luke was at Harvard. Thereafter she went to Radcliffe, where she was followed three years later by Susan. All of them were happy at their New England schools and frequently found the opportunity to join us at the League Club dur-ing winter and summer holidays, as did Yandes when he got out of the Marine Corps. All of us learned to enjoy fishing and the life of the woods and we sometimes camped out for several nights on long hikes to remote lakes. There were tennis courts available for all of us and there were quite a few youngsters there who were the same age as the children. Of course, water sports were also available and I was particularly pleased to find a golf course in the neighborhood where I was not made conspicuous by my amateurish golf.

Of all the friends we made during our years at the club, Sidney Homer and his wife, Marian, were certainly outstanding. Sidney was the only son of Louise Homer, the famous Metropolitan contralto. He had six older sisters and between them they had managed to raise up a remarkable individual. At the time I knew him he was head of the bond department of Salomon Brothers, Inc., which was then one of the leading investment banking houses on Wall Street. He was writing a book on the history of interest rates which was later published. I have a draft which he sent me for my comments which taught me more about the relationship between interest rates and the stability of governments than I ever dreamed of knowing. Sidney was a delightful conversationalist and a confirmed Trollopian, as was I. We discussed the characters and plots of all the novels that we had been able to find. As a matter of fact, I think his collection was probably the most complete of any in this country.

By this time I hope that the reader will have understood my choice of title for this book. As I look back over the years it seems to me that I have been extraordinarily blessed. To have spent my childhood and early youth on the Slingluff farm and at the Marbury home at 159 West Lanvale Street was surely a privilege; to have studied under such gifted teachers as Eleanor Reiley, "Whiskers" White, and Felix Frankfurter was equally so; to have enjoyed the friendship of men like Professor Frankfurter, Judge Patterson, Lucius Clay, Jim Conant, Howard Bruce, and Harry Lee Doll was more than I deserved; to have been the only associate in the firm of Marbury, Gosnell and Williams during its palmy days was unbelievable luck; and to have practiced law for sixty years with partners whom I trusted and with whom I have been on the best of terms was almost too good to be true. Above all, I have had for more than fifty years the loving companionship of a lovely wife and the solace of children whose affectionate care for me has made my old age enjoyable. I have had my share of failures and disappointments but on balance I can honestly say that for nearly all my life I have been in the catbird seat.

❧ Index

IN THE CATBIRD SEAT

❧

Designed by Sheila Stoneham
Composed by Brushwood Graphics, Inc.
in Baskerville and Caslon 540
Printed on Antique 66 Cream
and bound in Holliston Roxite 51507 vellum
by the John D. Lucas Printing Company